The Last Witches of England

The Last Witches of England

A Tragedy of Sorcery and Superstition

John Callow

BLOOMSBURY ACADEMIC
LONDON · NEW YORK · OXFORD · NEW DELHI · SYDNEY

BLOOMSBURY ACADEMIC
Bloomsbury Publishing Plc
50 Bedford Square, London, WC1B 3DP, UK
1385 Broadway, New York, NY 10018, USA
29 Earlsfort Terrace, Dublin 2, Ireland

BLOOMSBURY, BLOOMSBURY ACADEMIC and the Diana logo are trademarks
of Bloomsbury Publishing Plc

First published in Great Britain 2022

Cover design by Dani Leigh
Cover photo by Ann Ronan Pictures/Print Collector/Getty Images)

A catalogue record for this book is available from the British Library.

Library of Congress Cataloging-in-Publication Data
Names: Callow, John, Ph. D., author.
Title: The last witches of England : a tragedy of sorcery and superstition / John Callow.
Description: London ; New York : Bloomsbury Academic, 2021. | Includes bibliographical
references and index. |
Identifiers: LCCN 2021012892 (print) | LCCN 2021012893 (ebook) |
ISBN 9781788314398 (hardback) | ISBN 9781350196148 (epub) |
ISBN 9781350196131 (ebook)
Subjects: LCSH: Trials (Witchcraft)–England–Devon–History–17th century. | Bideford
(England)–History–17th century. | Lloyd, Temperance, –1682–Trials, litigation, etc. | Trembles,
Mary, –1682–Trials, litigation, etc. | Edwards, Susanna, –1682–Trials, litigation, etc.
Classification: LCC KD371.W56 C35 2021 (print) |
LCC KD371.W56 (ebook) | DDC 364.1/88—dc23
LC record available at https://lccn.loc.gov/2021012892
LC ebook record available at https://lccn.loc.gov/2021012893

ISBN:	HB:	978-1-7883-1439-8
	ePDF:	978-1-3501-9613-1
	eBook:	978-1-3501-9614-8

Typeset by RefineCatch Limited, Bungay, Suffolk
Printed and bound in Great Britain

To find out more about our authors and books visit www.bloomsbury.com
and sign up for our newsletters.

'Nobody paid good money to hear reason'

The old Fortune-Teller's advice to Laura (from Gordon Williams'
screenplay, The Duelists, *1977)*

Contents

List of Illustrations ix
Acknowledgements xiv
A Note on Dating and Terminology xvi

Prologue: The magpie at the window 1

1 Fortune my Foe 9

2 England's Golden Bay 35

3 An underground religion 67

4 The cat, the pig and the poppet 83

5 Blood and curses 115

6 A fine gentleman dressed all in black 131

7 The discourse of the sleepy chimney 153

8 The politics of death 183

9 Disenchantment 217

10 At the house of the White Witch 247

Coda: Where are the witches? 261

Notes 277
Bibliography 317
Index 329

Illustrations

1 Temperance Lloyd, an imaginative portrait from the title page of
The Life and Conversation of . . . Three Eminent Witches, published
in London in 1682 (Chris Horsfall).   2

2 The Long Bridge, Bideford (Author's Collection). This Victorian
postcard gives a good idea of Bideford's topography, the wide tidal
span of the River Torridge and the silhouette of a town that had
barely outgrown its seventeenth-century boundaries.   16

3 The Font in St Mary's, Bideford (Author's Collection). This is the one
physical link that we have to the Bideford Witches. Susanna Edwards
was baptized here, in December 1612. By the time that Temperance
Lloyd was married, in October 1648, it had been thrown into the
street and repurposed as a feed trough for the town's swine.   18

4 The Deserving Poor (later engraving after a painting by Gillis van
Tillborch, 1670) (Author's Collection). Although the setting of the
Tichbourne Dole was rural as opposed to urban, and reflected
traditional Catholic rather Calvinist modes of charity, this is one
of the few images from the Restoration showing the poor and needy.
It is a scene that would have been familiar to those, like the Bideford
Witches, who were in receipt of the Andrew Dole.   23

5 Companions in Misfortune: The entries in the Andrew Dole Book
for 1681 show the sixpences given to Susanna Edwards and
Temperance Lloyd as outdoor relief (by kind permission of Chris
Fulford and the Andrew Dole Charity, Bideford). Though they lined
up together to receive the dole, they begged and lived separately.
Temperance begged alone, while Susanna operated within a shifting
group of women.   28

6 Bideford in the mid-seventeenth century (by kind permission
   of the Burton Museum & Art Gallery, Bideford). A detail from
   the portrait of John Strange showing the busy port, with its
   warehouses, town hall and Long Bridge. Curiously, given Strange's
   Puritanism, the parish church does not feature in the panorama.
   However, the former chantry chapel that had been converted into
   the town jail, and where the witches were held in July 1682, can be
   clearly seen.   36

7 Bideford from John Ogilby's *Britannia*, 1675 (Author's Collection).
   The map gives a good impression of the layout of the town as the
   witches would have known it. However, the road network was not
   as important for its prosperity as the sea lanes that connected it to
   North America, South Wales and Ireland.   37

8 John Strange (1590–1646) by an unknown artist c.1640 (Burton
   Museum & Art Gallery, Bideford). His life is told in the form of a
   pictogram recounting the stages of God's providence, from
   garnering mercantile wealth to preservation from accident and
   common assault.   47

9 'Welcome All!': the painted decoration, commissioned in 1686,
   for an alehouse that stood overlooking Bideford's marketplace
   (Author's Photograph).   55

10 The Absentee Landlord: John Grenville, Earl of Bath
   (Wikicommons). This plasterwork from the Earl's house on the
   quayside at Bideford was the work of John Abbot of Frithelstock
   and gives some idea of the vision of taste, wealth and innovation
   that the king's friend intended to project.   62

11 The Conventicle (British Library). This satirical engraving by
   Marcellus Laroon the elder was published in 1686 and formed the
   basis for William Hogarth's later, and better-known, attack on
   witch-belief. A generation earlier, Laroon's original work showed
   that religious dissent and hypocrisy could be made analogous to
   sexual licence, disorder and devilry.   71

12 The King in Waiting? James, Duke of Monmouth, c.1682–5, from
   an engraving produced in Germany and smuggled into England,

through ports like Bideford, for the popular market that celebrated
the 'Protestant Prince' (Author's Collection).   74

13 Memento Mori: the angels looking down from Abraham
   Heiman's monument would have been newly carved and painted
   when Temperance Lloyd was brought to St Mary's Church and
   forced to recite the Lord's Prayer (Author's Photograph, by kind
   permission of the Rector & Parish Council, St Mary's Church,
   Bideford).   84

14 The Witches' Cottage, Bideford, by Charles de Neuville, 1894
   (Author's Collection). By the Victorian age, this range of buildings in
   Old Town had become associated with all three witches and was a
   tourist attraction. However, there is nothing to suggest that the
   women lived together or to associate them with such a substantial
   habitation.   102

15 Gunstone Lane, Bideford (by kind permission of Peter Christie). It
   was here, on this steep street, that Temperance Lloyd struggled to
   carry a bundle of broom and where the Devil, supposedly, offered to
   take the weight of her load. Save for the uniform whitewash of the
   cottages, she would have had little difficulty recognizing the scene
   two centuries later.   132

16 Sir Matthew Hale delivering a judgement during a lightning strike,
   1666 (Author's Collection). The intent of this Victorian print was
   to emphasize the judge's rationality and stoicism. However, his
   treatment of witches was harsh and based upon a willingness to
   accept spectral evidence.   159

17 Sir Francis North (1637–85) is one of the major sources for the trial
   of the Bideford Witches (Author's Collection). However, his account
   is far from impartial and is coloured by cynicism and the calculation
   of political, and personal, gain.   198

18 The Hanging Judge: Sir Thomas Raymond (1626/7–83) (oil on
   canvas, possibly by John Riley, c. early 1670s, by kind permission of
   Gray's Inn). Cultured and conscientious, he was blamed by the North
   brothers for bowing to the will of the mob and permitting the
   execution of the witches at the Exeter Assizes.   199

19 The Devil is in the Detail: the bowdlerized version of John
    Goodfellow used to illustrate the ballad of the Bideford Witches in
    Witchcraft Discovered and Punished (Author's Collection). The faerie
    child has been reconfigured as the embodiment of the Devil, while
    the erect phallus which caused offence on the publication of a 1628
    pamphlet has been erased.   221

20 Sir John Holt from his funerary monument, St Mary's Church,
    Redgrave, Suffolk, 1710 (photograph by Michael Garlick, Creative
    Commons). Flanked by the embodiment of *Justice*, the statue of the
    judge was based upon a portrait by Richard van Bleeck which was
    destroyed in the Blitz of 1940. An opponent of cruelty, political
    absolutism and militarism, Holt was instrumental in ending
    witchcraft prosecutions in England.   232

21 John Abbott of Frithelstock, master craftsman, c.1685–90 (oil on
    canvas by an anonymous artist, by kind permission of Exeter
    Museum). Though separated by a gulf of wealth, social connections
    and personal talent from the Bideford Witches, Abbott would have
    known the women by sight. The worldly celebration of his individual
    artistry stands in contrast to John Strange's stark cosmology. As
    such, it marks a watershed in European thought that, after 1660,
    increasingly separated the Early Modern from the Modern.   243

22 Mary Ann Voaden and the tumbled-down cottage of the 'White
    Witch', Bratton Lane, Devon, c.1890 (Author's Collection). Rural
    poverty was a continuing feature of Victorian society, but the witch
    figure was increasingly being removed from the community and
    consigned to the workhouse.   250

23 Three Poor Women of Bideford: pottery jug by Harry Juniper, 2018
    (Collection of Gill Clayton). One of a series of splendid jugs made
    by the renowned Bideford potter that began with a prize-winning
    entry to a local design competition held at Exeter Museum, in 1966.
    The witches were now firmly established as being persecuted rather
    than persecutor, objects of pity rather than of hatred.   262

24 The Last English Witches: memorial plaque to Temperance Lloyd,
    Susanna Edwards, Mary Trembles and Alice Molland, in Rougemont

Gardens, Exeter, November 2019 (Author's Photograph). There can be few more remarkable changes to historical reputation, and the emphasis on particular societal groups, than that evidenced by this commemoration. 269

25 The Bideford Witches huddle around a cauldron in Andrew Alleyway's mural of 1996, depicting the pageant of Exeter's history (Author's Photograph). Though the depiction of the women as stereotypical, storybook witches divided opinion, this colourful example of figurative public art sits comfortably with the surrounding maze of alleys, characterized by New Age shops selling crystals, Tarot cards and even broomsticks. 270

26 The Last Witches? A mother and daughter at the 'Grand Witches' Tea Party', Rougemont Gardens, August 2014 (photograph by Jim Bachelier-Moore). If the lives of the Bideford Witches were uniformly miserable, degraded and hopeless, then their legacy has been anything but. Their names have been reclaimed through celebration, creativity and activism, entertaining and engaging a new generation for whom witchcraft has positive connotations. 273

Acknowledgements

A wise old owl at the University of Bristol once told me that some books were, by their very nature, 'happy' ones. He did not mean that they necessarily came together more easily or quickly than others, but that the journey taken by the author in writing them was fortuitous in terms of the events, experiences and the new friends made along the way. By such standards, *The Last Witches* has been, and I hope will remain, a 'happy book'.

Though any mistakes or oversights contained within these pages remain very much the preserve and the responsibility of the author, my thanks are due to a large number of institutions and individuals who have given generously of their help and expertise. In spite of the swinging cuts of the last decade, the local records offices and network of county archives remain treasure houses of people's history: and my own especial thanks, in this regard, go to the staff at the Devon Heritage Centre, in Exeter, and the North Devon Records Office, in Barnstaple Public Library. Alison Mills at Barnstaple Museum and Julian Vayne at the Burton Art Gallery and Museum, Bideford, were unfailingly helpful in sourcing images and opening up new avenues of information. Likewise, Simon Costin and Fergus Moffat at the Museum of Witchcraft, Boscastle, combine a passion for – and unfailing interest in – their subject, with a mission to preserve and extend their world-class collections.

In Bideford itself, Harry and Sue Juniper provided – in the form of their magnificent studio on the Ropework – a tangible link with the master potters of the seventeenth century and were unfailingly helpful with my questions, as were Gill Clayton (as the proud owner of one of Harry Juniper's splendid pots) and Peter Christie, who combines true generosity of spirit with an encyclopaedic knowledge of the town's history and development. Lorna Dorrington very kindly took the time and trouble to open up the parish church on a Saturday morning, while Chris Fulford and Judy Bliss, of the Andrew Dole Charity, maintain another extremely important source of continuity with the past and were, in the present, incredibly generous in supplying copies of the materials relating to the operation of poor relief in Bideford.

Though approaching the subject from subtly different angles, Judith Noble, Jackie Juno, and Ben Bradshaw MP were kind enough to share their time, thoughts and expertise in discussing the manner in which three women of Bideford have been commemorated and posthumously recreated over recent years. Likewise, Jim Bachelier-Moore was able to revisit his photographs of the witches' gatherings at Rougemont Gardens, at short notice, and showed great generosity of spirit in making them available to me. Anna Milon took time out from her own researches to seek out a source for me in the Library of the University of Exeter, while Prof. Mark Stoyle, of the University of Southampton, shared his expertise regarding the siting of the Exeter gallows and the execution of the witches.

Books do not, of course, simply happen by themselves and my thanks go out to Emily Drewe, my editor at Bloomsbury, and to Abigail Lane, Editorial Assistant at Bloomsbury, for their help and professional insight in readying *The Last Witches* for publication. My thanks are also due to Jo Godfrey, who was part of the original editorial team, and to Alex Wright, a great friend and support who thought that a tale of West Country witches and rebellion, combining sea-salt, saltpetre, and sulphur, might appeal to a new readership.

On a personal level, we are nothing without our friends and, therefore, I am truly fortunate in having friendships measured in years and counted in constancy with Christina Harrington, Louise Carter, Sean O'Brogain, and Harvey Osborne. To Fred Valetta I owe a debt of thanks for an important set of references and for kindly words, that were much appreciated, on the field by Cropredy Bridge. To Phil and Freddy le Pinnet – companions to myself and Kit on so many of our adventures – let's hope that there are many more in store for us all. Bev and Del Richardson offered the hospitality of their hearth and home, and a vision of what our isle once was and might yet be.

Lastly, this book is for Angus MacLeod (1920–96): a Manxman not by birth but by love and volition, not least because he would have understood the reasons behind it: and in the hopes that his shade and that of 'Ivan', his faithful Labrador, may yet be found chasing the breakers out on the rocks at Scarlett Point.

John Callow, Candlemas 2021

A Note on Dating and Terminology

Although many European nations had adopted the Gregorian Calendar over the course of the seventeenth century, the British and Irish remained stubbornly loyal to the Julian Calendar until 1752. The result was that their calendars lagged some ten days behind that which was generally used on the Continent. By 1700, this difference had further increased to eleven days.

The dating given in this work reflects that of the Julian (Old Style) Calendar acknowledged by the people of Bideford in the 1670s–80s, but with two exceptions. For events that took place after the changeover of 1752, the Gregorian (New Style) Calendar is used, while for the sake of clarity the new year is taken as beginning on 1 January and not on 25 March, as had been the case under the old Julian system.

Prologue: The magpie at the window

On the morning of Thursday 29 June 1682, a magpie came rasping, rapping and tapping at the window of the house of Thomas Eastchurch. The busy quayside, well-stocked shops, and the patchwork of walled gardens and little orchards that backed onto many of the major properties in Bideford usually offered rich pickings for scavengers with a quick beak, a sharp eye and a fast wing. Yet that morning was different.

It was not food that had brought the bird to the family home above their shop. Rather, it was something that lay within the upstairs chamber: something bright, something that sparkled, catching and reflecting the bright summer sun through the glass panes. It was this which had grabbed hold of the magpie's attention, emboldened his spirit and caused him to explore the open window. Fluttering up from the street, he perched on the sill before pushing his head through the opening, intent on securing the wonderful prize that lay within. Like the poor who gleaned the spilled tobacco and foodstuffs from the jetties and alleyways, scavenging was a way of life for the bird, a means to continued existence. However, on this occasion, the choice to abandon necessity in favour of single-minded greed almost became his undoing and threatened to make his latest raid his last. So bright was the prize that the magpie had not stopped to check whether he was being observed, upon his entry, or if the chamber was still occupied. As a result, the presence of humans, the sudden burst of noise and movement, and the swirl of the sheets that threatened to engulf and ensnare him came as a complete surprise.

Figure 1 *Temperance Lloyd, an imaginative portrait from the title page of* The Life and Conversation of … Three Eminent Witches, *published in London in 1682 (Chris Horsfall).*

Anne Wakely and Honor Hooper had been busy airing the chamber, after another long and sleepless night. The house was labouring under a canker of sickness and fear. In February 1681, the master's young and unmarried sister-in-law, Grace Thomas had taken to her bed, muttering of witchcraft, 'with great Pains in her Head and all her Limbs'.[1] Such respite as there was came only in the evenings and was cruelly brief. As the months wore through and the year turned again, the tortured and tormented woman still did not venture far from her bed, the shooting pains returned and her stomach distended. The learned physicians that Thomas Eastchurch had called, and paid for, could offer neither a diagnosis nor a cure 'arising from a natural cause' and ventured that 'Grace could never receive any benefit prescribed by them'.[2] The absence of an explanation for the 'Distemper', the strain that the long-term care of the invalid placed upon his business and household, and what seemed to be no less than the withdrawal of the Almighty's favour left Eastchurch at a loss what to do for the best or how to account for the unexpected misfortune that threatened to turn all that he had built up through graft, industry and acumen to dust. He had been married for barely two years at the time of his sister-in-law's first descent into illness and his household had only been recently established. While he might aspire to the title of 'Gentleman', transcending his origins as a shopkeeper and merchant, his marriage into the Thomas family had brought him far more than he could ever have bargained for.[3] Furthermore, if he had ever envisaged himself as the respectable patriarch, at the head of a seemly and orderly family, then events were rapidly revealing him to be otherwise.

In his distraction, female friends and neighbours of his wife and sister-in-law had rallied around, helping to right and run the stricken household and to nurse the invalid, hoping to alleviate the worst of her ailments and to soothe her thoughts. Alongside Honor Hooper, the family servant, who seems to have increasingly attended to Grace's needs (over and above those of her own mistress and master), Anne Wakely, a friend and neighbour of the Eastchurches, volunteered to care for the sick woman and seems to have enjoyed a wider role in both the community and the management of the Eastchurches' domestic affairs during the time of crisis. A married woman of means and a little older than all the members of the Eastchurch household, it is unclear whether she received any form of remuneration for her services.[4] However, what is clear is that she was the social superior of Honor Hooper, at least the equal of Grace Thomas, and equal in status and wealth to Thomas and Elizabeth Eastchurch. It seems fair to suggest that she represented a form of stability during a period of chaos and a sisterly, or perhaps even a maternal, figure to Grace and Elizabeth. Alongside her, there appear to have been a number of other women, drawn from among friends and neighbours, who also spent days and nights watching over Grace in her chamber. As a consequence, it is reasonable to suggest that the Eastchurches' extended family benefitted from a wide network of personal and professional contacts, and from a well-developed sense of mutuality and sisterhood among its womenfolk that enabled Grace Thomas to be supported and well cared for throughout her long-term illness, which had rendered her incapacitated and, according to her own testimony, on the verge of death on more than one occasion.[5]

However, that very same network that was designed to protect and nurture also served to facilitate the circulation of news, gossip and speculation. After all, time was the one thing that the developing circle had on their hands and it was only natural that the women should seek to discuss, define and attempt to remedy the source of Grace's afflictions. Talk of one misfortune seemed to beget another and accounts of storms at sea, the deaths of infants, the wasting away of the daughter of a local gentleman and the deathbed accusations of a neighbour combined with half-remembered tales of words spoken in anger, of hasty curses, the proffering of poisoned fruit and the exchange of unwelcome, covetous glances. Worse still, the home and the hearth no longer appeared sacrosanct. It felt as though there was always *something* trying to get in: that there was an eavesdropper lurking in the shadows; the taint of the wild, with its animal stench and depredations threatening domestic order and seemliness with scrabbling feet or claws drumming at the wainscoting; the unwelcome visitor soliciting for work or relief at the door. Where there was no privacy, no retreat from the world, there could be no relief. Uncertainty hung in the air and the nights offered no relief, as prying eyes peeked in at the windows, envious hands tried the locks and rattled the shutters, and unseen creatures prowled high up in the rafters or scuttled beneath the floorboards, intent upon harm. So it was that Grace Thomas passed another troubled night that was rent with her cries of pain and torment, peppered with unfamiliar curses and, all the time, with the assertion that Bideford was a town abandoned by God, where familiar spirits chattered and spat filth in the darkness, changing their form at will, and where devils walked abroad tempting mortal souls and hatching murderous plots.

The morning saw Grace rise and wash, while Anne Wakely and Honor Hooper changed the linen and threw open the windows. They were so preoccupied with their own duties and cares that they failed to notice the presence of the magpie until he started up at them, all feathers and fury, still determined to seize his heart's desire. Their shrieks and sudden movement fuelled the bird's own panic. The swirling sheets threatened to become his shroud as he now attempted to fend off their blows and to find an avenue of escape, all thoughts of the valuable trinket abandoned. Fear fed fear, as the women cried out and stampeded towards the door, while the magpie began to flap about the window, croaking in terror and beating his wings in a frenzy against the fine glass panes. Then, in an instant, he was gone. Finally, he had found the open gap and flew out, away over the rooftops the way he had come. Frightened, sweating and flushed, Anne Wakely and Honor Hooper tried to gather themselves together as best they could, straightening the chamber which had become a tangle of chairs, bedding and curtains in the course of the brief struggle, and trying for all their might to work out what manner of ill they had just experienced. A winged creature of some sort had been in the chamber with them, trying to get into the heart of the merchant's home, to breach the safety of its walls and to work its mischief. Later, they recalled its hard, cold gaze, its dark, sleek form and birdlike shape. It was, they considered, 'something in the shape of a Magpie', but they could not be sure what that 'something' was, and whether it was actually a bird or not.[6] In the midst of what they knew to be difficult, emotionally charged and very disturbing times, the whole event profoundly unsettled both women.

Thomas Eastchurch seems to have taken their upset, and the bird's intrusion, to heart. Thundering around the house, he closed all possible points of entry. However, as family and friends moved to secure the front door of the house another form started up from the street: a dark bundle of rags and tatters that Anne Wakely recognized, at once, as Temperance Lloyd, a local beggar woman. Even though it lasted no more than a few seconds, both parties appear to have been startled by this second, unexpected and unwelcome encounter. Wakely shooed Lloyd away from the doorstep and returned, inside, to tell Eastchurch of the figure that she had found poised upon his threshold. It seemed to her to have been more than a chance meeting: the old woman had no reason to be there at that, or at any time, and had seemed to be loitering, in expectation of some act or discovery, when her presence was revealed. The trouble was that in surprising her, in interrupting her activities and in chasing her away before any questions could be asked, there was now no way of knowing what business Temperance Lloyd had been about. That uncertainty grew into something different as the day progressed and, as the events were revisited and retold by Wakely, Hooper and the Eastchurches, the events of that morning assumed a new shape and significance as both disturbances began to be conflated and conjoined as part of the same 'assault'. Now, the appearance of the corvid seemed to manifest the nature of the curse that lay upon Grace Thomas and the house of Thomas Eastchurch, as the bird took on the form of a familiar spirit: an agent of the Devil, intent upon seeking not just the death of their stricken friend but also the destruction of themselves, alongside every other Christian soul in the Devon seaport. However, it did not act alone but, rather, performed the bidding of its mistress, the beggar woman, Temperance Lloyd who directed its attacks, selected the victims and hid her own malefic powers away under the cloak of night and the guise of poverty.

Suddenly, through their discussions, Thomas and Elizabeth Eastchurch, Grace Thomas, Anne Wakely and Honor Hooper felt that they had arrived at the reason that lay behind all their misfortunes. Thomas determined to scour Bideford, at first light, for the beggar woman, to run her to ground, to confront her with the knowledge of her crimes and to force her, whether through persuasion or threat of force, to confess her pact with the Devil and the nature of her career in his service, with all its grim litany of unnatural despoliations and death. On this, all of his household and friends agreed without dissent, and the worsening of Grace Thomas' condition over the night of 29–30 June 1682, and her own express cries linking her increased sufferings to being tormented by a curse, can only have served to harden their resolve. However, to modern eyes, the persistence of belief in harmful magic (or maleficia) in Bideford, during a period more readily associated with the nascent Scientific Revolution, as evidenced through the works of Descartes, Boyle and Newton and the foundation of the Royal Society, appears strangely anomalous. Rather than viewing the Restoration comedies, the growth of commerce and the establishment of coffee shops as symbolizing the spirit of the age, Bideford, during the reign of King Charles II, seems to exude a spirit of disorder and faction, characterized by suspicion, fear and the rule of the lynch mob. This sense is enhanced when we consider that on a number of different levels, the case that was being formed against Temperance Lloyd does not easily fit with many of our contemporary assumptions about the nature of superstition, magic and persecution during the Early Modern period. The charges came remarkably late in the century, defying an increasing pattern towards refusing to prosecute or seeking a legal acquittal; they originated, primarily, in the grievances of one set of women against another, were enacted in an urban as opposed to a rural setting, and were generated and promoted by individuals who (like the extended Eastchurch family) were far from unlettered, ignorant or consumed by worries about failures of the harvest and food supply. Rather, this belief in the efficacy of ill-wishing and harmful magic was rooted in, and sustained by, a community that was increasingly affluent, articulate, mobile and acquisitive, and where individual desires were supplanting the collective.

Thus, the Bideford of the 1670s–80s reflects more closely the values of our own age as opposed to the mythopoeic 'other' of the late Mediaeval or 'burning times'.[7] As a result, the terror of – and rage against – elderly and impoverished women appears all the more inexplicable and unsettling. The simple and often unpalatable fact was that, in deciding that curses, spells and the operation of demonic magic were responsible for sickness and misfortune, the Eastchurch and the Wakely families – operating within the wider context of the belief patterns of the late seventeenth century and the specific religious and political culture of their home town – were expressing ideas that were not extraordinary, delusional or intrinsically irrational.

For Bideford, it was said, had long been a place of witches.

1

Fortune my Foe

The voices of the poor and the dispossessed are rarely listened to in any age. They are too rough, too uncomfortable, too raw and too discordant to sit comfortably within the confines of learned discourse, or to be accommodated within the binary, dog-eat-dog logic of the marketplace. Their day-to-day realities of empty bellies, chilled bones, broken sleep patterns and dependency upon the will and charity of others are hardly the stuff of historical romance, or the reassuring teleology of post-modern theory by which individuals are held to self-create, outside the boundaries of host culture, economics and social circumstance. Over the course of the seventeenth century, we encounter them, more often than not, in court records, when those at the margins of society had broken a law or transgressed an established code of conduct. Even then, their words were often interpreted, filtered and shaped by legal procedures and by the prevailing notions of what constituted suitable evidence, the rules regarding cross-examination and the extraction of a confession. On occasion, the accused might even be unaware that such conventions existed. Within this context, Temperance Lloyd, Susanna Edwards and Mary Trembles – the three poor women who came to be known as the 'Bideford Witches' – were marginal in every sense of the word: in terms of their age, gender, economic and marital status, and even through their lack of physical and geographical mobility. Unsuccessful and unwanted, they not only lacked the sympathy of others but aroused feelings of either fear or condescension among their contemporaries.

As a consequence, the judge's brother soon came to forget their number and their respective fates; the pamphleteers in London conflated their names and gave one of them a face that was not her own; and a Secretary of State brushed aside their case and decided that three women from Bideford were not even worthy of his comment, let alone his consideration.[1] Once the printers and booksellers had made their profits, the last of their stocks in Exeter and London had been sold or pulped, and new strange and exciting stories came along to grip the public imagination, there seemed to be little need to remember their dark tale, or to hum the ballad written about their murderous and diabolical careers to the melody of a purloined, second-hand tune.[2] Only the hatred of their neighbours endured.

Ironically, it was precisely this extraordinary intense level of animosity that permitted something of their stories, characters and words to be preserved through the judicial procedures conducted against them in 1671, 1679 and 1682, and through the pages of the three main popular, printed accounts of their trials produced in the autumn of 1682.[3] Though their long lives are telescoped for us, through the lens of the court proceedings, largely into the space of just two months, when evidence was taken against them first at the makeshift court house at Bideford, and then at the subsequent Exeter Assizes, it is still possible to go in search of the pattern of their lives in the records of the parish, local government and private charities with which they came into contact. While these sources will not necessarily tell us those biographical details that we, now, might wish to know – such as whom they loved, what they valued and truly believed, what shaped them and condemned them to a life of unremitting poverty, and how they attempted to make sense of the two terrible visitations of civil war and of plague that swept over their home town, when they were already approaching middle age – they do reveal something of the contours of their existence that we need to know in order to contextualize them within their own culture and society, within both Devon and Early Modern England.

According to all the contemporary accounts, Temperance Lloyd was the prime focus of attention: the dominant figure in the dramas that unfolded on the streets of Bideford and in the legal proceedings at Exeter Castle and Heavitree.[4] She was a 'grand Witch', 'the most notorious of these Three', 'Audacious' and 'perfectly Resolute' in pursuit of her murderous designs.[5] She was also held to be the oldest, the most lascivious and the cruellest. And it was she who had been 'the Introducer of their Misery' through leading the others into making pacts with the Devil and instructing them for the space of 'Five Years, to learn the Art and Mystery of Hellish, Damnable, Accursed, and most to be Lamented Witch Craft'.[6] Yet, before the troubles that assailed her at the beginning of February 1671, she had left few imprints upon either the records of Bideford or elsewhere in the land. Though Temperance, alongside other such Puritan names as Prudence and Patience, was relatively common in Bideford, the name of Temperance Lloyd does not appear in any of the parish registers. Nor do the ages and marriage records of the other women christened Temperance fit with what we know of her.[7] It is, therefore, reasonable to suggest that she was an immigrant who arrived in the port by sea, as opposed to road.

As a major hub of Atlantic trade, seventeenth-century Bideford was a cosmopolitan place, where many different ethnicities and nationalities rubbed shoulders on the quayside and transacted business. However, while the arrival of trading vessels might greatly increase the port's population for short periods, sailors from further afield than Devon appear to have been there to work, trade and to enjoy their shore leave, rather than necessarily to put down roots. The registered population of migrants, though increased during the 1680s by an influx of Huguenots fleeing religious persecution in France, does not appear to have been particularly large.[8] In this manner, the recording of the death of an unfortunate 'French man being a Traveller', taken sick at the port in January 1650 and buried ashore, and the baptism of John, the son of Edward Carsh, 'a Irishman' on 3 July 1642 were rendered noteworthy for the clerk of the parish on account that they were rare occurrences and, in both cases, reflected events that overtook members of a transitory population rather than the domiciled townsfolk.[9] The exceptions to these patterns lie in the settling in the port of the Anglo-Irish mercantile family of John Strange, who had been made rich by the trade with Ulster, at the beginning of the century, and by the migration of a number of fresh Welsh families to Bideford, concentrated within the period from 1639 to 1653.

Prior to the Civil War, besides the seemingly well-established Thomas family, from whom Grace and Elizabeth descended, there was no clear imprint of Welsh settlement in the parish. However, with the arrival of what seem to be the extended families of the Edwards, Morgans, Joneses, Philipses, Williamses and Lloyds in Bideford, the parish clerks suddenly found themselves having to struggle with the recording of unfamiliar Welsh Christian names and surnames, making best guesses and spelling them phonetically in the registers.[10] In this way, Jones was rendered as 'Joons' or 'Joones', Lloyd became 'Floyd' and Rhys (a common name among these familial groups) became 'Rice'.[11]

John Lloyd, his wife, Cissily, and their young children were settled in Bideford, by the early 1640s, together with Rhys Lloyd who was of roughly the same age as John and was, in all probability, his brother or close kinsman.[12] At roughly the same time, the extended Jones family also settled in the town, comprising a William Jones 'the elder', his son, William 'the younger', and his own growing family, together with Phillemon (or 'Philemon') Jones and his sister, Temperance. It may well be that William 'the elder' was father to all three young adults, but given the partial recordings of Welsh names and familial groupings in the Bideford parish register we have no way of knowing for sure. What does seem evident is that the naming of Phillemon and Temperance stemmed from a Puritan impulse that sought to recall the early days of the Christian church and to celebrate, respectively, the sufferings of one of St Paul's followers and a specific female virtue. It is suggestive not only of a particular set of aspirations on the part of parents for their children but also of a strong engagement with scripture that was fuelled by the written word of God. It is, therefore, possible that the elder generation of Jones were literate or, at the very least, semi-literate, and certain that they considered themselves to be part of the 'godly' people of the nation. Temperance Jones is recorded as having married Rhys Lloyd, in St Mary's Church, on 29 October 1648, while Phillemon Jones married Johan (or Joanna), a young woman whose surname went unrecorded, in the same church, on 8 August 1649.[13] Thus, Temperance Lloyd first appears in the public record not as a harridan or a pauper but as a member of the 'godly' elect, married by the Independent minister, William Bartlett, to a working man. This also raises a question over the traditional assumptions made about her great age and infirmity. Two of the three pamphlet writers agree that she was 'the eldest of the three' women accused of witchcraft in 1682, and one claimed that she was then '70 years old'.[14] However, *if* Temperance Lloyd was the woman married in October 1648, who was of childbearing age, we are looking at someone who was much younger than previously thought and the junior of Susanna Edwards by a considerable margin. If she followed conventional marriage patterns for her gender and class, then it is not unreasonable to suggest that she was somewhere between twenty-six and twenty-eight at the time of her wedding, and that, therefore, she was born somewhere around 1620–2. This places her in her early twenties at the time of her family's crossing of the Bristol Channel and settling in Bideford; she would have been in her late forties or early fifties at the time when the initial allegations of witchcraft were brought against her, and in her early sixties when she was tried before Judge Raymond in Exeter. Her haggard appearance, mental confusion and decrepitude that were noted in the summer of 1682 would, therefore, appear to be the product of her growing poverty, her arduous labours in pursuit of a meagre living and an inadequate diet, rather than being the simple product of the ageing process. Life had dealt her a succession of hard blows with which she was ill-equipped to deal, and which had rendered her prematurely weary and worn. From the first, there is a suggestion of an element of marginality in her family's societal and cultural position in Bideford, inasmuch as her sister-in-law's surname went unrecorded at her wedding. The local authorities did not bother to inquire about people whose ethnicity, gender and lack of resources did not interest them and seemed to be of no great import.

This said, the mid- to late 1640s appear to have been something of a boom time for the new Welsh immigrants to the town and there is no reason to think that the Joneses and Lloyds did not share in an element of this new-found prosperity. Through intermarriage within the fledgling Welsh community in the town, both families had sought to consolidate their position, put down roots and establish networks of mutual support, while still retaining something of their cultural distinctiveness and links to South Wales. Their arrival in Bideford coincided with the employment of Welsh colliers, recruited from the south of the principality, in order to mine the local seam of culm (or anthracite) that fuelled the town's pottery kilns, for firing slipware, and the furnaces, for casting metals associated with munitions and shipbuilding. Consequently, the industries that supported and furthered Bideford's maritime trade required surplus labour and additional expertise to that available in North Devon and looked to the nearest available coalfields in order to supply them both. This accounts for the pattern of short-range migration from the late 1630s to the mid-1650s, and explains the influx of young people, of marriageable age, as young, strong men were ideally suited for such arduous physical work. It also provides valuable evidence that despite the dislocation of trade caused by the Civil War and the rapid militarization of the town, occasioned first by its garrisoning by Parliamentary forces and then through its brief occupation by Royalist troops, local society continued to function and to find new and inventive means by which it could not only survive but prosper. Indeed, it may well be that the spiralling demand for munitions occasioned by the war served as a stimulus for the foundries producing ball, chain and shot which were to be found in Bideford's Gunstone Lane and which, in turn, placed greater demands for productivity and labour upon the town's anthracite pits. The construction of the three great earthwork artillery forts that covered the town and controlled the passage of vessels along the river Torridge necessitated skilled labour of precisely the sort provided by the Welsh miners.[15] If they were not quite an aristocracy of labour during this period, then there is no reason to think that they were drawn to Bideford, and chose to remain for over a decade, by anything other than the promise of ample remuneration.

Yet, the sword of war was double-edged. On the one side, it had generated the spectacular demand for coal that had drawn the Welsh to Bideford but, on the other, following the tramp of armies across the West Country, the plague had descended like a vengeful angel upon a people beleaguered, half-starved and often impoverished by years of war. Most Devonshire towns were infected as, over the summer of 1646, the plague struck right across England.[16] It reached Barnstaple in late April, claiming hundreds of lives and collapsing the normal running of town government. A month later, the plague arrived in Bideford, carried – so it was said – by a ship bearing a cargo of wool from Spain. According to local tradition, three children who had played on the quayside among the wool sacks – the sons of Henry Ravening the town surgeon – were the first to be struck down.[17] Between June 1646 and January 1647 at least 229 townsfolk perished in the visitation. It is likely that the total was somewhat higher than this as the recording of mortality appears to have broken down entirely after October 1646 with 'a blank page and a third' being 'left as though some further entries were to be written' in at a later date when events were not so pressing.[18] The churchyard soon overflowed, unable to accommodate the growing numbers of the dead, while townsfolk occupying the surrounding, tightly packed closes that overlooked St Mary's were fearful of contagion caused by the mounting pile of corpses and the daily reopening of the ground. It was reported that local government shuddered to a halt with many office holders simply fleeing the stricken port. In the midst of the crisis, John Strange, the prominent Bideford merchant and former mayor, filled the vacuum by taking over the duties of magistrate, instituting measures in order to ensure that the plague did not spread further and seeing to it that 'the sick, particularly the poor [were] properly taken care of, [and] the dead decently buried' in a field away from the centre of town at Tynes Lane.[19]

Part acquisitive man of business, part religious visionary, Strange's bravery during the plague was motivated, in part, by his firm Calvinist beliefs and exceptionally strong sense of a providential calling. At every turn in his life, and with every misfortune experienced, Strange discerned the working of the hand of God. Thus, his preservation from a series of accidents and assaults – beginning with a boyhood fall from a cliff while out birds-nesting, and continuing through an attack by a robber, who threw him from the parapet of Bideford bridge, to being struck on the skull by an arrow, in what appears to have been another attempt at murder – appeared not as a dreadful catalogue of violence and sheer bad luck, but as a wondrous testament to his survival through the evidence and operation of divine favour. In accepting his view of God's visitation of the plague upon Bideford as a trial, the townsfolk were encouraged to externalize their losses and their grief as part of a shared teleology, and to work and to suffer together in a common and avowedly godly cause. Unwittingly, this approach – and the moral authority of John Strange, which lay behind it – encouraged a sense of social cohesiveness within this Puritan stronghold, which seems to have dispensed with the need for scapegoating. Even the story of the arrival of the plague with a Spanish ship may have been calculated as a convenient fiction to downplay the various sources of cross-contamination that existed much nearer to home. Barnstaple, not quite ten miles further north along the River Torridge had been afflicted by the plague for almost a month before the outbreak in Bideford, and provided both a source of infection that was much closer to home and an example of how a different interpretation of divine will, within a similar bastion of Puritanism, could serve to split a community apart.

Figure 2 *The Long Bridge, Bideford (Author's Collection). This Victorian postcard gives a good idea of Bideford's topography, the wide tidal span of the River Torridge and the silhouette of a town that had barely outgrown its seventeenth-century boundaries.*

Unlike Bideford, where Strange's hold on town governance was backed by the radical religious impulse of its preaching minister, William Bartlett, Barnstaple's victorious Parliamentarians were now bitterly divided between the Presbyterian and the Independent factions. The former wanted a more centralized, Calvinist form of worship, while the latter believed in a more decentralized, personal and non-prescriptive relationship with a Protestant god. As a consequence, both sides sought to attribute the coming of the plague as the result of the sins and derelictions of the other. The Presbyterians raised a mob against the Independents, stoned them and their houses, and attempted to drive them forcibly from the town, claiming that once they were gone, the plague would vanish. However, a letter sent from one of Barnstaple's Independents to a sympathetic Parliamentarian officer, who had recently been stationed nearby with the Exeter garrison, argued that God's will was being made manifest in very different ways. It was claimed that upon returning home, those who had joined the mob:

> immediately fell sick of the Plague, and they and all their families dyed of the Plague within one weeke, which causeth most of the people of the Towne, to speake well of the honest [ie. Independent] partie, and to take notice of the hand of God on the other . . . which is to be observed, [as] not one family of those railed against had not, neither hath as yet, had any

sicknesse amongst them, though it hath been on each hand next dore to them.[20]

Just like a biblical plague, appearing as a punishment upon an erring or unjust people, those who were preserved seemed to be sifted by God like the winnow from the chaff.

In an age dominated by religious belief, where signs, providences and portents were eagerly sought and interpreted, Bideford – even amidst its misfortune – was lucky in possessing both John Strange and William Bartlett, who emphasized collective action and refrained from apportioning blame. Within the context of what happened in Bideford a generation later, this was extremely significant. A cohesive town government, led by two charismatic individuals, was confident enough in itself and its citizens to preserve public order and to pursue policies that did not descend to populism, factionalism or the need to scapegoat. Presbyterian and Independent were united in the struggle for survival, and no one looked twice at Temperance Lloyd, or felt the need to seek the presence of devils or to cry: 'Witch!'

Yet, the plague in Bideford was no respecter of persons. It cut through rich and poor, and the ranks of the garrison and townsfolk, alike, slaying whole families and wiping out a whole generation of the town's children.[21] John Strange died at the end of July, while Temperance Lloyd's family was also hit hard, with William Jones 'the younger' and his wife (whose name is not recorded) being buried on 12 and 14 October 1646, respectively.[22] Her future husband's family was also ripped apart with John Lloyd 'the elder', Cissily, his wife, and John, his son, all succumbing to the plague within days of each other and being buried between 7 and 11 August 1646.[23] Unlike the other branch of their family, Temperance and Phillemon Jones escaped the ravages of the visitation and possessed sufficient means to marry and to think of raising families of their own in its wake. Temperance Lloyd, as she had now become, bore her husband three children between 1649 and 1655. A daughter, Johan or Johanna (who was presumably named in honour of Temperance's sister-in-law) was baptized at St Marys' Church on 14 October 1649, with a son, William (who might have been named after her father or brother), following, who was baptized on 4 June 1651. A second son, Thomas, was born on 13 May

1655 and baptized a little more than a month later.[24] The unusual delay in Thomas' baptism is intriguing, as the interval of a fortnight was the maximum upper limit noted for the parish during the period and, conceivably, might point towards an unsettled or shifting family. This creeping sense of marginality had been reinforced, in November 1652, by the death of William Jones 'the elder' and by the fact that, post-war, the little Welsh community appeared to have far fewer economic opportunities within the town.[25] Put simply, the achievement of peace had reduced the demand for the production of munitions while, at the same time, the town's reserves of anthracite were being worked out and increasingly replaced by imports of coal from elsewhere in North Devon.

The cluster of Welsh names, including those of the extended Lloyd and Jones families, vanish from the records after the early 1650s just as quickly as they

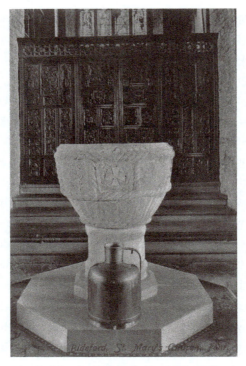

Figure 3 *The Font in St Mary's, Bideford (Author's Collection). This is the one physical link that we have to the Bideford Witches. Susanna Edwards was baptized here, in December 1612. By the time that Temperance Lloyd was married, in October 1648, it had been thrown into the street and repurposed as a feed trough for the town's swine.*

arrived. This would seem to fit with what we know of the peaks and troughs of anthracite mining in Bideford. The seam was opened up in 1629 and inaugurated a boom time which reached its height in the late 1640s and early 1650s, when William Bartlett was taking an annual profit of around £100 from the workings on parsonage land. However, the main mine (which had given its name to the town's Pitt Lane) was exhausted by 1655, and the few remaining stocks in Bideford produced only diminishing returns during the years of the Restoration, as imports from South Wales increasingly replaced the shortfall. By the 1670s, the local industry had completely collapsed and the 'coalpit', or 'culme work', was abandoned as little more than a water-logged hole ten years later.[26]

As a result, it seems fair to suggest that the families who had migrated to Bideford from the South Wales coalfield specifically in order to mine the anthracite seam moved on, once again, in search of fresh work as soon as the last high-grade deposits of coal had been exhausted. There are no records for the deaths of Phillemon Jones, his wife, or their children in the Bideford parish records. It would, therefore, seem likely that at some point after May 1655 (when the main pit had closed) they left the busy port town as quickly and as quietly as they had come. Rhys Lloyd seems to have lingered for a little longer, was well-known in the town and was easily recognizable, in a way that his wife was not. By the autumn of 1660, he too had left Bideford together with any of his surviving children. In what appears to be a case of abandonment and familial breakdown, his wife was left behind and, for the first time, fell back upon the parish and private charity for poor relief. She appears in the accounts of the John Andrew Charity, audited on 7 September 1660, as simply 'Ryce Floyd's wife' who was awarded a tuppence dole together with two other paupers, Elizabeth George and Phillip Gamond, who received the same sum.[27] She appears, again, as 'Rice Floyd's wife' (this time receiving the increased sum of threepence in relief from the trustees of the charity) in the accounts audited on 16 July 1661. Though she missed further payments in February and August 1662, she was well enough known by them to be registered as 'Temperance Flood' in January 1663 and to be thought in need of a further increment of her dole, bringing her to fourpence.[28] This mirrors the treatment of another Welsh woman, Mary Morgan – who may have been the wife of Evens (or Evans) Morgan – who came before the trustees for assistance at the same time.[29]

Likewise, she was not initially accorded a Christian name – being recorded as simply the 'Widdow Morgan' – in July 1661 and February 1662, but by January 1663 she was sufficiently well-known to be entered into the Dole Book as 'Mary Morgan', as she thereafter appeared. This suggests that both John Wadland and George Middleton, the trustees of the charity, were initially unfamiliar with the town's Welsh community and that they sought to differentiate between widowed and married, or otherwise unattached, women.[30] Indeed, widows are consistently distinguished from other recipients of aid, in the same way as those who had suddenly fallen sick and were incapable of work, throughout the book.

The pamphlet accounts of Temperance Lloyd's trial are at variance upon the matter of her marital status, preferring to comment upon what they considered to be her general licentiousness, rather than supplying any hard biographical fact. We may choose to accept or reject the anonymous slurs as we think fit. One guess is as good as another. However, they do suggest what her contemporaries thought of, or projected onto, her personality and lifestyle. There is certainly the suggestion that she prostituted herself, which given Bideford's status as a port town and her lack of other methods of earning a living, is not beyond the bounds of possibility for a highly vulnerable woman in her late thirties and early forties. Significantly, unlike Mary Morgan, or for that matter Susanna Edwards, Temperance Lloyd was never referred to as a widow, which further reinforces the sense of her abandonment around the time of the Restoration of the Monarchy in May 1660. She was left as the remaining member of her family, quite literally stranded upon the shores of Devon, without resources or a visible means of support. Thereafter, she appears in the account book as being in receipt of the dole payment for each year – excepting 1662 and 1678 when no doles were paid – until 1682.

Unfortunately, the decayed state of the Bideford Hearth Tax Returns for 1674, with a lost page and many names obscured or unreadable, makes it difficult to assess the nature of poverty in the town and to reconstruct the identities of all those whose maintenance was held chargeable to the parish.[31] Temperance Lloyd's name is not among those whose names have survived in the records. However, the survival of the John Andrew Dole Book does permit a reconstruction of Bideford's underclass and the variations in the numbers seeking charitable assistance. It notes the rates at which they were paid and gives some idea of the fluctuating levels of poverty in the town. The year 1667–8 seems to have been a particularly hard one with the numbers of the poor in Bideford swollen far beyond their normal numbers. Although poverty appears to have been concentrated among a few familial groups – the Kingsland, Davy, Coaden and Galsworthy families stand out – the majority of those seeking assistance were single women and men, without familial support or kinship networks, and the elderly. Thus, we find: 'The old woman Dyre, Widow', who was in periodic receipt of relief from the late 1650s onwards and was granted a total of ninepence in two separate payments spanning late 1663 and early 1664, or 'old lady Row' who was granted sixpence at Christmas 1676, and 'Old [Robert] Webber' an elderly man granted a shilling – at a time when other doles were being slashed – in the financial year ending February 1679.[32] There was a kernel of poor, in receipt of charity, year in, year out, that was hardly altered – save by death, as in the case of Mary Umbles – over the decades that stretched from the 1660s to the 1680s.[33] Alongside Temperance Lloyd, Mary and Jane Kingsland, Justinian Prance, Mary Umbles and Susan Winslade were all long-term recipients of the dole. Mary Bartlett, perhaps a less fortunate relative of the family of dissenting clergymen, was a staple recipient of the dole over the period and when, in the winter of 1679–80, she became increasingly frail, the trustees chose to alter her entry to 'Old Bartlett'.[34] At times, the poor from outside the parish – shifting and unknown – were also helped, with 'two people whom we Conceive needy' being awarded two shillings in September 1660, 'severall poor people' given a shilling and sixpence between them in February 1662, 'three poor people' given sixpence between them in the January 1671 accounts, and two lots of 'Two poor women' awarded threepence each in January 1676.[35] A doorkeeper was employed in order to marshal the queues of the poor appealing for relief and he doubled as a 'crier' about the town, calling out when the awards – which seem to have made a real difference in alleviating absolute poverty and starvation in the town – were to be made.[36]

From 1664–5 onwards, Temperance Lloyd received an annual payment of sixpence, which often coincided with the Yule festivities, and which appears as the standard dole afforded to a single person, known to the trustees, and without dependants. However, in 1678 the dole went unpaid and when the charity's accounts were signed off on 27 February 1679, for the previous financial year, the numbers of poor in receipt of the dole were drastically reduced and the sums that they received were – almost uniformly – halved, with Temperance Lloyd receiving just threepence's worth of cheer.[37] It seems that there was difficulty in collecting the expected rents upon which the charity depended and though the levels of payment returned to their previous amounts, in January 1680, there were far fewer poor being paid.[38] As it seems unlikely that rising living standards could have so suddenly lifted approximately a third to a half of recipients out of poverty, in the period after 1680, it is fair to suggest that restricted funds and a change in trustees, in 1682–3, accounted for a more proscriptive approach to the granting of the dole, with only those well-known to the trustees or considered 'deserving' increasingly winnowing away the numbers of successful applicants for financial relief.[39] It is tempting to speculate that changing attitudes towards poverty and the absence or reducing of payments in the period 1678–82 – which might have been mirrored in the parish poor rate – could have added a desperate edge to the begging of Temperance Lloyd, Susanna Edwards and Mary Trembles in the months immediately prior to their arrests. It was certainly the case that, with the exception of Jane Kingsland who had worked her way back onto the list of recipients by January 1684, the identities and numbers of those in receipt of the John Andrew Dole in Bideford were remarkably different after the watershed years of 1678–83 than they had been over the previous twenty-five years.[40] In part, this might have been through natural wastage through death, but the clear break that occurred after the non-payment of the dole in 1678 does suggest a reordering of personnel and priorities that boded Temperance Lloyd and her sisters no good at all.

If Temperance Lloyd was in perennial need of poor relief, then this was not the case with Susanna Edwards, whose early life – though no more fortunate – is far clearer and easier to reconstruct. Due to her lifelong residence in Bideford, we know somewhat more about her than we do about the other women involved in the case. Susanna was baptized, at St Mary's Church, Bideford, as Susan, the illegitimate daughter of Rachel Winslade, on 2 December 1612.[41] Her uncle, John Winslade, had two legitimate daughters, Mary and Ellinor, born in 1613 and 1618, respectively, but there was something that struck contemporaries as being unseemly, disorderly and far from respectable in his household.[42] It was observed that 'A strange woman's childe that came

Figure 4 *The Deserving Poor (later engraving after a painting by Gillis van Tillborch, 1670) (Author's Collection). Although the setting of the Tichbourne Dole was rural as opposed to urban, and reflected traditional Catholic rather Calvinist modes of charity, this is one of the few images from the Restoration showing the poor and needy. It is a scene that would have been familiar to those, like the Bideford Witches, who were in receipt of the Andrew Dole.*

hither [to Bideford] and had [a] childe at John Wynslads house was baptized the last of November 1630'.[43] The suspicion was either that the child was his, or that the unknown woman, fleeing from a neighbouring locality, had come to his own to hide out during the latter stages of her pregnancy and access the unofficial services of someone attached to John Winslade's household skilled in midwifery. Another possible interpretation, given Bideford's constantly shifting population of mariners, paid off after voyages, with no ties to the place, but with money to spare and urges to satisfy, was that the Winslades were in the business of keeping a brothel. Whatever the case, they were unusual figures within local society. Despite Bideford being a port town there are relatively few illegitimate births highlighted in its parish registers. Of these, we find Christopher 'son of a walkinge woman', who had taken to the highway to avoid the opprobrium of her own parish, who was baptized on 10 January 1625, the baptism on 12 May 1633 of Ferdinando, the son of Ferdinando Squier, 'a base' or bastard child, and the baptisms of a Peter and a Margaret baptized on 29 and 30 September 1652, respectively, without any parents' name being given.[44] Thus, the association of illegitimate births around the Winslade household – with tales of mysterious young women arriving at the door during the late stages of their pregnancy, and the disgrace of Rachel known to all in the town – must have marked the family out within a close-knit and cohesive society, dominated by Puritan values, as disorderly and dangerous.

The stigma of illegitimacy impacted upon both mother and child on a number of different levels. The unmarried mother might have conceived through consensual sex or through rape. She might have embarked upon a sexual relationship on the promise of marriage or have enjoyed sex for its own sake. Whatever the case, the preoccupation of Early Modern society was to circumvent the need for formal intervention by the Justices of the Peace, and the responsibility of the parish to pick up the maintenance costs of an illegitimate child, by urging the marriage of the respective parents. Indeed, it has been estimated that as many as a third of marriages during the first half of the seventeenth century were contracted, or fast-tracked, as the result of an unplanned pregnancy. Only when this option failed were increasingly draconian public measures used in order to either persuade the mother-to-be to name the father (thus permitting the levying of a maintenance grant upon him that would relieve the parish of its financial obligations to the child) or to shame and punish her as a deterrent to others. In theory, an unmarried mother might face being stripped to the waist, tethered to the back of a cart and flogged through the town, or village, in which she lived. She might also face the humiliation of the pillory or, in the case of a second offence, be sentenced to hard labour in a house of correction. This said, cases of corporal punishment were far rarer in the south west of England than in the north and, as the seventeenth century progressed, the concern of local government focused more heavily upon avoiding paying child maintenance out of the public purse than upon enforcing particular moral codes or exacting a form of revenge upon transgressors.[45] In the case of Rachel Winslade, it is notable that she was unwilling or unable to marry the father of her child and then, despite undoubted pressure from the authorities – including perhaps even from the midwives, who were often employed by Justices of the Peace to gather information – to disclose his identity. Consequently, Susanna was born with the odds stacked against her: with the stigma of illegitimacy and without property rights.[46] She did, however, have some form of familial support, possibly due to the presence of her uncle, John Winslade, and there is no evidence to suggest that her upbringing was regulated and financed through the parish.

What is clear is that in spite of her disadvantaged background, and the taint of her birth, she was able to contract a conventional, respectable and seemingly advantageous marriage with David, or Davy, Edwards. The couple were married in Bideford on 9 October 1639.[47] Davy was the eldest of three brothers, again of Welsh extraction, and his younger siblings, William and Rhys, also settled in the town, took local wives and raised large families. With trades to pursue and skills to practise, they had means and do not seem to have been accustomed to want or to have troubled the authorities. Susanna and Davy had three sons and, possibly, three daughters born to them between 1645 and 1657.[48] In contrast to the Lloyds, they appear to have been a settled family group tied by choice, sentiment and their livings to Bideford. There were no delays in the christening of their children.[49]

Yet, something was not quite right. Another Susan, Winslade appears as an individual charged to the parish and in constant need of the support of the John Andrew Dole between August 1658 and January 1680. Initially, she was awarded threepence, but this rose to sixpence in the 1660s before increasing to a shilling – the highest monetary award granted by the charity – from 1672 to 1677. Her dole was halved in the lean year of 1679 but rose back to its previous level in 1680 before she disappears completely from the records.[50] From 1665 to 1680, she appears at – or very near – the top of the lists detailing parish relief and the payments of the discretionary dole, indicating that she was judged to be particularly needy.[51] Furthermore, the granting of a shilling as a dole payment was almost invariably only given to those with dependants to support. The trouble is that neither *this* Susan Winslade, nor any of her possible children – including Sarah Winslade who received a small dole in 1668–9 – appear in the parish register.[52] While it is entirely possible that she might have come from a collateral branch of the family, the naming of Susanna, her approximate age as a woman capable of childbearing in the early 1670s and her unmarried status all suggest that she might have been the illegitimate daughter of Susanna Edwards (nèe Winslade) and that she, too, had a series of illegitimate children by unnamed fathers. Her sudden disappearance from the records, in 1680, whether through death or migration, would again reinforce what we know about Susanna Edwards' own sense of increasing abandonment.

There is no doubt that fortune's wheel began to turn back against Susanna Edwards, picking up speed and severity as age withered her and her misfortunes mounted. The plague struck at her family, too, and she lost a young or newborn child to the visitation as the burial of 'Susan Edwards childe' was registered by the parish clerk on 1 October 1646.[53] Yet it was not until her late forties and early fifties that she began her inexorable slide down the social scale as death prised her closest family members from her. She lost Elizabeth Winslade (possibly an unmarried aunt or even another natural daughter) in June 1661, while her youngest child, Richard, died in September 1661 at just four years old.[54] Worse was to come as she was widowed in September 1662 and lost her uncle, John Winslade, in May 1668, who may well have been her last and surest means of support.[55] We do not know what became of her other children, though it is possible that John Edwards, the child buried on 1 March 1679, was the illegitimate child of her daughter Katheryn, who would then have been twenty-five years old.[56] If this is so, then Katheryn would seem to have been following in an unenviable family tradition that reached back three generations. With 50 per cent of the recorded illegitimate births recorded in Bideford during our period being located within the extended Winslade-Edwards family, it is more than likely that the idea that the Bideford Witches 'had been lewd Livers many a day' – bawdy, sluttenly and lascivious – as well as slovenly and cruel had its roots in the stories surrounding this group.[57] As we have already seen, it might have been reinforced by the reputed behaviour of Temperance Lloyd. Again, it is possible that the Winslade-Edwards women practised prostitution or that they were part of that sub-strata of Early Modern society that Lawrence Stone memorably described as being part of that 'small segment of the population, at the lowest social level, which failed to conform to the prevalent norms from generation to generation: a bastardy prone minority group'.[58]

Furthermore, it appears that Susanna Edwards' household was in dire financial straits even before the death of her husband. She was granted the Andrew Dole at a rate of fourpence in August 1658, was given sixpence in August 1662, and took threepence from a halved share together with Alice Web in the payment that covered the last part of 1662 and January 1663.[59] She does not appear again in the Dole Book until February 1679, when as the 'Widow Edwards' she shared a shilling with two other bereaved women.[60] In the accounts that were settled on 2 January 1680, she is listed as having been given sixpence, while in those listed on 2 January 1682, she is recorded as sharing sixpence with another poor woman, Joan Conden.[61] This last entry is particularly tantalizing, as her name and that of her friend are immediately above that of Temperance Lloyd. It does not take much in the way of historical imagination to picture the women queuing up in a line next to one another and with Temperance Lloyd being ushered into the trustees' room immediately after Susanna Edwards had left it, with the three pennies clasped tight in her hand.[62] There is nothing else in the administrative records – as opposed to the pamphlet literature – to connect the lives of the two women before the summer of 1682. Furthermore, while Temperance Lloyd always begged and petitioned alone, both Susanna Edwards and Susan tended to act as part of a group of women. Susanna Edwards was given charity, as we have already noted, in conjunction with other women on three out of the five known occasions; she was also accustomed to begging together with Mary Trembles. Similarly, until her money was increased to a shilling (presumably to cover her dependent children) Susanna Winslade frequently received a shared dole with one or more women. She shared the gift of a sixpence with Mary Willis in July 1661, and seems to have been on good terms with the impoverished Kingsland family, having shared a sixpence with Mary Kingsland in November 1659, and taken a threepence share of a shilling along with Mary and Jane Kingsland, and

Grace Rowlands in September 1660.[63] In 1664 and 1665, she shared eight and ten pence, respectively, with Meg Rork, an Irishwoman who was another unfortunate who intermittently relied upon the dole from the early 1660s until the late 1670s.[64] The picture seems to have been one of rough and ready alliances formed in the face of want and adversity, that pitched small groups of women together in mutual support that promised a greater chance of survival. Susanna Edwards and Susan appear to have been social beings, capable of forming alliances; by way of contrast, Temperance Lloyd was certainly not and seems to have been entirely dependent upon her own meagre resources and counsel. Moreover, Susanna Edward's widowhood also served to lend her an identity and a protective status that Temperance Lloyd had lacked. She appears as the 'Widow Edwards' in the Dole Book accounts at midsummer 1663 and again from 1679 to 1681, and with it held the potential for being

Figure 5 *Companions in Misfortune: The entries in the Andrew Dole Book for 1681 show the sixpences given to Susanna Edwards and Temperance Lloyd as outdoor relief (by kind permission of Chris Fulford and the Andrew Dole Charity, Bideford). Though they lined up together to receive the dole, they begged and lived separately. Temperance begged alone, while Susanna operated within a shifting group of women.*

viewed as one of the 'deserving' poor, alongside the likes of 'Symon Jeffrey's Widdow' and the 'Widow Dyer'.[65]

Yet, mud sticks and the sense that the Winslade women and Temperance Lloyd were not objects of pity on account of their poverty, but figures of contempt on account of their promiscuity gained ground among Bideford's gossips, primarily due to the long memories in the town of the behaviour of Rachel Winslade, Susanna Edwards and Katheryn Edwards that stretched across seven decades. Worse still, by the early 1680s, Katheryn Edwards together with Susanna's other surviving children had quietly faded out of the historical records and they were neither willing nor able to speak up for Susanna Edwards when she needed them, and were in no position to offer her any manner of financial support. It is possible that Katheryn had left the town and its scandals behind her and taken passage from the port in the hopes of beginning a new life, somewhere she would not have been known. There is nothing to suggest that Susanna's other children, Roger, Robert and Elizabeth, who would have been in their thirties, had predeceased her and it is more likely that they, too, had taken advantage of the high levels of mobility offered by the maritime trade that operated out of Bideford and had chosen to seek their fortunes elsewhere. Susan remains something of an enigma but her own disappearance from the records in 1680 – whatever her relationship to Susanna Edwards – would seem to be further evidence of the increasing isolation of the latter woman. Of the Bideford Witches, Susanna Edwards was, therefore, the one who seems to have fallen the furthest and to have lost the most. By the time she was in her late sixties, she was alone in the world, thrown back upon her own meagre resources and forced, through the irregularity and partiality of parish poor relief and charity, to scratch a living on the streets through begging and striking up chance acquaintances.

This brings us to Mary Trembles. Both at the time and ever since, she is the least known and regarded of the three women and often appears almost as an accessory to events, sidelined, overlooked or entirely forgotten. Roger North, who had sat through her trial at Exeter Castle, was able to forget about her identity entirely, so transient and ineffectual was her presence in the court room.[66] She left no imprint upon the records – other than in the allotments of the John Andrew Dole – until her arrest, and (in contrast to what we know about Susanna Edwards and Temperance Lloyd) she is unequivocally described as being a 'single woman' in the accounts of her trial, as opposed to a widow or an abandoned woman.[67] A 'Trudging Trembles' appears for the first time in the John Andrew Dole Book accounts for 1667–8, when he received sixpence from John Wadland and George Middleton, the trustees.[68] It would seem that Trudging (or 'Trojan') Trembles was the husband of Honora Trembles, and the father of Mary. It is conceivable that the family were Anglo-Irish Protestant immigrants, recently arrived from Ireland, and worth noting that among the indigent poor, scraping a life at subsistence levels, it was not uncommon for parents to specifically choose grand-sounding names for their offspring in the hopes that they might seem more considerable in a harsh and class-conscious world. Thus, Trojan Trembles would not have seemed out of place in appealing for the dole and poor law relief in Bideford alongside Justinian Prance, one of the town's long-term recipients of charity.[69] A further sixpence was awarded to Trojan in 1667–8, but his dole was raised in the accounts audited on 6 January 1669 to a shilling and this sum was maintained in the awards for the following year.[70] As we have already noted, this was the maximum amount awarded for a dole in our period and, with the possible exception of the case of 'Old Webber', it was only granted to those with dependants. This suggests that the condition of the Trembles family was worsening as age gripped Trojan, reducing his ability to toil and even debasing his identity, in the eyes of the charity trustees, to the descriptive epithet 'Trudging'.

By 1669, the whole family were thrown back upon the support of the parish and, when Trojan died in May 1671, his widow received the customary shilling, in his place, for the upkeep of herself and her daughter.[71] However, this rate was not maintained for the last year of Honora's life, with her share of the dole falling to fourpence in 1672.[72] It might have been the case that she was expecting another award, to help carry her through the winter of 1672–3, but her death in November 1672 prevented that from being made. Once again, her identity is wrapped in her widowhood and she is described as the 'Widow Trembles' in all the extant documents, including the note of her burial in St Mary's churchyard on 21 November 1672.[73] Her daughter, Mary, incapable of either work or finding a marriage partner, was accorded no such recourse to respectability. She appears in the accounts of the Dole Book for 1673–4 as a dependant: the 'daughter' of

Trudging Trembles. The sense of her vulnerability, and of her mental and physical dependency upon others, not the least of whom being Susanna Edwards, is the only sure sense we have of her in both official records and the trial literature.[74] Then and thereafter, until the year of the dole's temporary stoppage in 1678, she received the standard gift of sixpence for an adult woman but was never accorded her own identity: she was always the daughter of 'Trudging' or 'Trojan' Trembles.[75] She was missed off the list of reduced payments for 1679 but reappears – for the first and only time – as 'Mary Trembles' in 1680, when she took a tuppence dole as her part of a shared allocation with two other women.[76] Again, there is a sense that some poor women were banding together for mutual support in Bideford and that if she was to be found begging alongside Susanna Edwards in 1682, then she was also begging with the 'Widdow Germmin' two years earlier. Whatever the case, she – unlike Temperance Lloyd, Susanna Edwards and Joan Conden – missed the allocation of the dole for 1681–2 or was judged as being unworthy of receiving it.[77] On these grounds, it is possible to suggest that by 1682, Mary Trembles was an unmarried woman, whose family had predeceased her, and who had settled within the confines of Bideford at some point not later than 1667, when she was already a grown woman. We have no way of gauging her exact age, though it is reasonable to guess that she was a middle-aged dependant of elderly parents by 1669. As in the case of Temperance Lloyd, her age therefore appears to have been exaggerated in the trial pamphlets, and by the North brothers. She could have been no more than seventy at the time of her arrest in the summer of 1682. Quite probably, she was in her early sixties and misfortune, want and uncertainty had worked to undermine her health, wits and appearance. If this decay united her with Temperance Lloyd, then there is nothing else to draw the lives of these two women together in advance of their joint trial. They neither lived nor begged together, and even their names on the lists of the dole allocations are separated by a distance, with Lloyd appearing increasingly towards the top of the pages and Trembles appearing at the bottom. In terms of her utter lack of agency, or separate identity, hers is a somewhat different biography to those of her fellow accused and Mary Trembles is, in some respects, the 'odd woman out' among the three.

At this point, from what we have been able to reconstruct of their various backgrounds, one common thread that runs through the women's lives is their early link to people and places outside Bideford, and what seems to be a shared familial connection to the Celtic peripheries, whether Wales – in the case of Lloyd by both blood and marriage, and by marriage as in the case of Edwards – or Ireland, as in the possible case of Trembles. Therefore, it is reasonable to ask whether an element of xenophobia was responsible for actuating the charges of witchcraft against all three women and whether differences of language, dialect and culture were the decisive factors in setting them apart from their neighbours and in turning all hands against them. It is certainly the case that the women, individually and collectively, suffered from the adverse – and frequently savage – judgements of their neighbours on the grounds of a range of issues including their pursuit of sensuality, their gender, age, lack of wealth and resources, infirmity and helplessness that, today, we might think of as being profoundly discriminatory. Differences were certainly noted, as we have already seen, through the careful recording of the origins of travellers who died, or mothers who gave birth, while in transit through the port. However, Bideford society in the late seventeenth century was far from parochial and its people do not seem to have been unreceptive to, or unduly critical of, settlers from different lands and other parts of the British and Irish archipelagos. As a major Atlantic port, the importance of Bideford's position on the sea lanes brought trade and people from Ireland, South Wales and Northern England into far more regular proximity and contact than with the folk of the remoter Devon parishes, who remained isolated from them despite their geographical proximity by the poor state of the road network. Anglo-Irish, Welsh and a number of Huguenots (even before the Revocation of the Edict of Nantes in 1685) were, by the middle of the seventeenth century, no strangers to one another, or to the people of North Devon, as they worked and traded together in Bideford.[78]

While it is conceivable that a different accent or dialect may have set Temperance Lloyd, and possibly Mary Trembles, further apart from mainstream society, there is nothing in the records, or the pamphlet literature, to suggest that this was the crucial factor in their literal demonization by their fellow townsfolk. Though they were accused of many things – from licentiousness and violence to filth, theft and greed – no pamphleteer or ballad-writer attempted to mention the strangeness of their speech patterns, or to claim that a Welsh or an Irish background had served to ally them more closely to preternatural forces, made them more susceptible to the advances and flattery of the Devil, or caused their neighbours to suspect and to shun them. In this – had ethnicity been a major issue – then the pamphleteers who sought to excoriate the memories of Temperance Lloyd and Mary Trembles were certainly missing a trick. The Irish and Welsh women scratched, savaged and murdered when the Royalist baggage train was overrun at the battle of Naseby had been traduced as screeching witches and harridans by London pamphleteers in an attempt to excuse the blood lust and frenzy of Parliament's victorious soldiers.[79] Had Mary Trembles been an Irish Catholic and a Gaelic speaker, as opposed to an Anglo-Irish Protestant, who knew no language save English, she, again, might have been easy prey for such slander. Yet, in this one area – just like the young Temperance Lloyd – she had some form of protection and fitted at least some of the paradigms associated with good and godly citizenship by the host society. Furthermore, one might advance a contrary – though equally unprovable – proposition, in that as several of their accusers, such as Grace Thomas, Elizabeth Eastchurch, Joane Jones, William Herbert and William Edwards had some form of Welsh ancestry, the ill-feeling that assailed Susanna Edwards and Temperance Lloyd may well have come about not as the result of English prejudice but as the result of a simmering internal feud within Bideford's expatriate Welsh community. Given that nothing was ever said, either by their accusers or their judges, it seems safe to suggest that the fault lines that lay between Celtic and English cultures were not the primary factors that isolated Temperance Lloyd, Susanna Edwards and Mary Trembles from their neighbours. What really did set them apart from others and drew them together – both then and in the eyes of posterity – was quite simply their poverty in the midst of plenty.

2

England's Golden Bay

Bideford seems an unlikely setting for the last great outbreak of English witchcraft prosecutions. It defies all our preconceptions about the subject. Instead of being poor, rural and backward, it was prosperous, urban and cosmopolitan: a major Atlantic port and entrepôt, basking in the steadily increasing profits to be had from foreign trade and fishing, localized industry and global commerce. Moulded by its position at the major crossing point over the fast-flowing, wide tidal waters of the River Torridge, barely three miles from the sea, the town possessed plentiful natural resources (wood, coal and clay), and enjoyed a mild climate and warm winters, thanks to the Gulf Stream. Yet it was its magnificent fifteenth-century toll bridge that served to define Bideford's civic and commercial character.[1] Writing in 1674, James Yonge – a naval surgeon who made his fortune in part from the Newfoundland trade that centred upon the port – commented upon 'the good strong Bridge' that stretched for approximately 670 feet and noted the rapid waters that swirled under it and bore Bideford's 'great trade' to its 'great marketts':

> mostly to Newfoundland, thence to Portugall and the Streights, they send a few to Virginia, New england, W. India, Ireland [and] many to Wales and Bristoll.[2]

A generation later, Daniel Defoe's praise of the architecture of the 'very fine Stone Bridge' was bound up with a Mercantilist critique of the town's rapid development. This recognized the divisive nature of the toll system that had funded new building projects along the quay but also obliged the drivers of many carts and wagons to wait until the tide had gone out in order to cross the sands, in order to

Figure 6 *Bideford in the mid-seventeenth century (by kind permission of the Burton Museum & Art Gallery, Bideford). A detail from the portrait of John Strange showing the busy port, with its warehouses, town hall and Long Bridge. Curiously, given Strange's Puritanism, the parish church does not feature in the panorama. However, the former chantry chapel that had been converted into the town jail, and where the witches were held in July 1682, can be clearly seen.*

avoid paying the fee.[3] Defoe stressed the inconvenience that the monopoly caused to the middling sort, and the brakes it put on their ability to trade freely.

However, the levying of tolls and the funnelling of traffic had also impacted upon the poor. In the 1670s–80s, the bridge had ensured the rapid flow of business traffic and pack trains through the town, and offered Temperance Lloyd, Susanna Edwards and Mary Trembles ample opportunity for begging from the passers-by at the chokepoint at its western end. They might have sought to glean the mussels from the base of its pillars to supplement and vary their meagre diets. Yet, even at the best of times they would not have been capable of wading too far across the foreshore in order to gather this river-borne harvest on the ebb tide. If the bridge effectively channelled travellers towards their outstretched hands, and increased the opportunity of one-off charitable gifts, then the combination of tolls and tidal waters also worked against them. They further restricted the beggars' mobility and effectively confined them to the western shore of the Torridge. The way to the opposite bank, with its thin suburb (known as East-the-Water) extending like a ribbon along the riverside, carried a fee that they could hardly afford. Its shipyards and kilns offered no obvious advantage to them as either beggars or scavengers over the neighbouring and far more prosperous town.[4] If Temperance Lloyd could not afford to take ship from Bideford alongside the rest of her family, then the roads that terminated abruptly after Appledore's ford or stretched

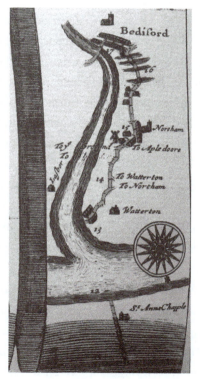

Figure 7 *Bideford from John Ogilby's* Britannia, *1675 (Author's Collection). The map gives a good impression of the layout of the town as the witches would have known it. However, the road network was not as important for its prosperity as the sea lanes that connected it to North America, South Wales and Ireland.*

away out of sight, through broken and hilly ground, to Barnstaple and Ilfracombe seemed as difficult and daunting, to both cross and comprehend, as the sea lanes that led to Waterford, Swansea, Chester and Liverpool.[5] Poverty eats away at the soul within not just because it denies the body nourishment, but because it also starves the mind, narrowing horizons and collapsing the imagination. In this respect, Temperance Lloyd, Susanna Edward and Mary Trembles were truly impoverished and rendered powerless because they were denied choice and autonomy at every turn. Bideford would, through the force of circumstance, become their whole world. It encompassed all that they knew.

By way of cruel contrast, from the mid-sixteenth century until the early years of the eighteenth, the discovery of Newfoundland and its fisheries transformed the economic fortunes of the port town, and opened enormous vistas of enterprise, discovery and imagination. The Grand Banks swarmed with codfish, swimming in vast shoals that, on occasion, even impeded the progress of the fleets of fishing vessels that set out from the quayside of Bideford in increasing numbers throughout the first half of the seventeenth century. Returning with the cod already cut and cleaned, ready for drying and making into stock fish, vast quantities of this valuable foodstuff were then re-exported to the Mediterranean, Holland, France and Spain. Thus, in 1675, the *Willing Mind*, the *Nightingale* and the *Consent* 'all of Bideford' sailed from the port to the Newfoundland fisheries, farmed there for the season – 'the ships all unrigged, and in the snow and cold' – and returned via St Sebastian, where they sold their catch at market.[6] So important was this trade that, during the First Dutch War (1652–4), Bideford's merchants had successfully argued against the impressment of their sailors who worked these fisheries, on the grounds that it would prove extremely detrimental to the wealth of the nation. Despite this war fought over the possession of resources and control of trade routes, and two further – far more debilitating – conflicts waged against the Dutch in 1665–7 and 1672–4, the trade pursued by Bideford fishermen continued to grow.[7]

Passes were issued by the mayor of Bideford licensing vessels to fish and trade in the waters around Newfoundland, which served as an additional and highly lucrative source of income for local government, creating a monopoly which successive mayors fought tooth-and-nail in order to preserve.[8] Consequently, the plans advanced in 1675–6 by Charles II's central government to regularize the trade, through the establishment of a formal colony in the region, complete with an aristocratic governor and an attendant bureaucracy, struck at the heart of the autonomy of Bideford's merchants and threatened to levy a fresh burden of taxation upon their voyages. Agents were employed to lobby for their cause at Whitehall, while Thomas Gearing, as mayor of Bideford, made common cause with Richard Hooper, the mayor of Barnstaple, in order to petition the Council for Trade and the Plantations, in March 1675, to preserve the monopolies and privileges of West Country merchants across the Gulf of St Lawrence and the Great Banks.[9] What happened in Newfoundland impacted directly upon Bideford and the laying-off of crews from the trade, in the autumn and winter months, contributed to seasonal peaks in under- or unemployment, as sailors and their families were threatened with being thrown back upon parish relief. Furthermore, the size and regularity of the Newfoundland catch could not be estimated accurately or relied upon, leaving many of Bideford's townsfolk entirely dependent upon the luck and judgement of the mariners, the vagaries of the Gulf Stream and the Arctic current, the raising of storms and the passage through the ice flows. Therefore, it is hardly surprising that dissenting religion, with its rugged individualism and Calvinist concern with providence and the direct favour of God, fitted the life experiences of many of those whose lives and well-being depended upon the maritime trade.[10]

By the mid-1670s, there was a palpable sense among West Country fishermen and shipping owners that the best days were behind them. Costs and competition were rising while the numbers of both vessels and sailors engaged in the Newfoundland run were on the decline. Indeed, in February 1675, there were mournful reports that amid French encroachment and the dislocation of the recent Dutch War, many Devon fishing boats and ships 'lay by the wall'.[11] However, the effects of relative (as opposed to absolute) decline and the tendency of Bideford owners to accentuate the obstacles they faced when lobbying central government for concessions can lead to an overstatement of Bideford's plight. If the Newfoundland trade for dried cod was slackening after 1670, then the demand for tobacco was more than taking its place. By the end of the seventeenth century, there were twenty-eight merchant vessels, ranging between 60 and 220 tonnes, operating out of the port, together with a number of privateers, fitted out by the wealthier shipowners in order to protect the sea lanes and safeguard their cargoes from the depredations of the French and Spanish raiders, who had come to describe Bideford as England's 'Golden Bay'.[12] This was largely on account of the burgeoning tobacco trade with the newly established North American colonies of Virginia and Maryland. Importation of the crop peaked in 1700–1705 when a greater volume of tobacco from those colonies was imported into Bideford than into any other port in the kingdom, excepting London, which had originally held the sole monopoly.[13] John Strange shouldered his way into membership of the Virginia Company, while in 1676 a single vessel – the *Bideford Merchant* – brought 135 lbs of tobacco out of Maryland.[14] In 1683, Bideford merchants imported 566,718 lbs of tobacco, easily eclipsing Barnstaple's share of the trade, establishing vast fortunes and creating an elite whose property, interests and aspirations now stretched across the Atlantic Ocean, from Newfoundland in the north, to Virginia and the Carolinas in the south.[15] The majority of the members of the Town Council were also shipowners and some of them, and in particular the Buck and Strange families enjoyed extensive holdings in Maryland and Virginia, while William Titherley's family owned both land and a major shipyard in Maine.[16]

News from the Americas was quickly transmitted by crews docking at the port to anxious townsfolk who came, increasingly, to have friends, family and commercial interests in the colonies. Thus, in 1676 it was reported at Falmouth that 'the *Jacob* of Bideford' had docked, having come from 'Miller River, Maryland, laden with Tobacco ... [and bound] for Holland'. On their arrival, the sailors dolefully explained to the authorities 'that the Indians have done much mischief to several families' in the colony.[17] Bideford's sailors and settlers had long been familiar with native Americans, their customs and culture. Through the patronage of Richard Grenville (1542–91) and his family, the town's merchants had been closely involved with the foundation and early development of Virginia, and the failed Roanoke colony, off the coast of North Carolina. Indeed, an unfortunate Native American, an Algonquin warrior taken as a hostage after a raid, in 1586, was brought to the town aboard one of Grenville's ships and celebrated as a 'Wynganditoian' (a mistranslation of a chance comment on the Englishmen's fine clothes). He was baptized in St Mary's church, in March 1588, as 'Raleigh' in honour of Richard Grenville's celebrated cousin, Sir Walter. However, he was dead within the year, a victim of the same influenza outbreak that claimed the life of other members of Grenville's household, including his daughter, Rebecca.[18] If his mournful fate stood as an individual testament to the wider existential threat posed by Europeans to the indigenous peoples of the Americas, then it also demonstrates that Bideford was at the forefront of engagement with, and the destruction of, these tribal societies.

When the overproduction of the tobacco crop threatened many of the colonial planters with ruin in the 1670s–80s, then Bideford's merchants led by Abraham Heiman found innovative ways in which to secure their fortunes, re-exporting cargoes to the Baltic where there were comparatively untapped and highly receptive markets among the Hanseatic towns.[19] The trade impacted upon Bideford in two other respects, stimulating consumer demand for clay pipes from the local potteries – which constitute a large share of Bideford's industrial archaeology – and creating a demand for labour to work the plantations along the Chesapeake Bay. Bideford's merchants were only too glad to advertise for, and to ship, the poor, the hopeful and the needy out to the colonies as indentured servants, laying the groundwork for the later slave trade. It was not until 1698, when the Royal African Company lost its monopoly on the slave trade, that the trade in human cargoes sailing from North Devon to the Chesapeake shifted decisively from the transportation of indentured white labourers to black slaves. Therefore, when the citizens of Bideford thought about slavery, in the 1670s–80s, it was primarily in terms of the depredations of the Barbary Corsairs who raided the sea lanes and, within living memory, the Devon coast, for captives to row their galleries, to be sold in North African markets, or to be worked to death in Morocco on Mulay Ismail's vast building projects. This explains why they gave so readily to the collections raised to buy the freedom of Englishmen and women, who might well have been their friends and families, from the bagnios in Algiers and Tripoli, and why the dereliction of the Rev. Ogilby in collecting for their relief and ransom was so keenly felt in the town. In 1680, Samuel Showers, Thomas Mills and David Mighill of Bideford, and Jeffery Ward, James Hilman and Thomas Mitchell from Barnstaple were among the names of 392 – predominantly Devonian – mariners listed as being redeemed from slavery in Algiers upon a ransom paid by William Bowtell, a London merchant.[20] If the Bideford men

returned home, shortly before the arrest of the alleged witches, with tales of
their sufferings in the slave pens and the cruelty of the Corsairs, then there was
also evidence in Bideford of other crosscurrents, suggestive of more peaceful,
tolerant and inclusive experiences.

The town appears to have had its own, modest African presence as the
Blackamoore family appear well-established and well-integrated in Bideford
by the 1660s. John Blackamoore was in receipt of the John Andrew Dole from
1660 to 1669, while Philip Blackamoore, who was possibly his son or brother,
was awarded charity from 1669 to 1675.[21] If these men were forced to seek the
dole and to access parish relief to provide for themselves and their children,
then there is evidence to suggest that their condition was not entirely hopeless
as, within a generation, their family appears to have risen to hold property, to
have been literate, and to have taken a stake in the politics of the town. If you
possessed talent or guile, and the 'right' sort of politics and religion – as by the
1680s the Blackamoores did – then Bideford appears to have been an open
elite.[22] For those excluded by ability or belief, it was a different story. One of the
many ironies about the Bideford Witches is that they were not, on account of
their age, intelligence, and physical frailty, considered fit even for transportation
to Virginia or Maryland as bonded labour.

Maritime trade ushered in a new age of prosperity and conspicuous
consumption to the town which served to transform its appearance, with the
construction of large new warehouses in East-the-Water and the unloading of
great hogsheads of tobacco along the quayside. While profits were easily
diverted into the building of substantial new dwellings for the merchants and
their families, funds were less forthcoming from the collective purse in order
to improve the existing infrastructure of the port. The sudden upsurge in the
volume of imports swamped the quayside, while the quay, itself, proved wholly
inadequate to accommodate the large numbers of merchantmen attempting to
berth. Cargoes piled up on the docks and the riverfront became, at times,
intolerably overcrowded, while the hogsheads – filled beyond their capacity to
avoid additional customs duties – often split open and spilled their goods.[23]
Yet, if Bideford's would-be witches were forced to scavenge among the
towering barrels and the remains of spoiled and rotting goods, scraps of leather
and strands of tobacco, then the town's new elites had not yet been able to seek

ways of removing themselves from the unwelcome sights and stenches that their pursuit of the Atlantic trade had created. The major redevelopment of the Bridgeland area – that would so impress Daniel Defoe – had not yet been undertaken and so the vast majority of the town's mercantile elite (such as John Davie) and shopkeepers (such as Thomas Eastchurch) were to be found living cheek-by-jowl with their workmen, servants, customers, clients and the town poor. Even if some of Abraham Heiman's family owned a number of properties in nearby Frithelstock and the surrounding countryside, then he – as patriarch and the head of a vast commercial empire – still felt the need to keep for himself one of the largest houses in Bideford, which boasted no fewer than ten hearthplaces in the tax returns for 1674. Similarly, John Davie – who looms large in committal process of the witches – invested his profits from the trade with New England in building a mansion for himself at the eastern end of the Long Bridge, that survives in part to this day.[24] Private and public spheres were far from clearly delineated and this sense of the dividing lines between class, commerce, leisure and individual privacy being blurred seems to have contributed substantially to the allegations of witchcraft in 1682.

If the quayside represented a hive of commerce, then the town it nurtured and enriched was no less industrious and entrepreneurial in its activity. Bideford stood on the slopes of two long hills, which faced each other east and west, backed by a large stretch of woodland, and ran down to the edge of the water. A 'difficult and dangerous hilly road known as Old Town' threaded its way across the tops of these hills, like a bony spine, and it was here – in all probability – that Temperance Lloyd lived. With the exception of the High Street, the houses were crowded together in narrow streets, the rich and poor packed tightly together, until the late 1680s, with 'yards, backsides or Courtage's' bordering a honeycomb of lanes that ran down the hillside. A network of tanneries and potteries, located around North Street, provided centres of additional employment for the townsfolk, and fashioned a town dominated by smoking kilns and tall chimneys, where according to one contemporary 'divers ... Potters, Bakers [and] Brewers' practised their trades, kept their fires stoked around the clock and erected 'great piles and ricks of Furze' outside their properties to be used as fuel. Wood was expensive and seems to have been one of the few natural resources that Bideford lacked.[25] Consequently, brambles, brackens and furze were gathered from far and wide, largely by the urban poor foraging the hinterlands, and stockpiled in the teetering, unsightly and highly flammable ricks that so enraged the authorities. Fearing the spread of fire 'to the greate danger of ... houses and goods', the mayor and town council soon attempted to set limits upon the height of the stacks of furze and ordered all householders to 'place hogsheads or Tubbs filled with water' outside their properties 'from the first day of May until the tenth day of September' each year.[26] We have a glimpse of Temperance Lloyd bowed down under the weight of a great bundle of sticks, as she struggled up Gunstone Lane, and it is likely that the gathering of gorse for the furnaces was one way she found to make an income.[27] It would certainly have helped to establish her as a regular visitor to the lane, where part of the tragedy of her life turned.

Given that Bideford's people prided themselves upon their industry and endeavour, it is not surprising that the street names of the town bore testament to their lives and labours. Thus, Buttgarden Street had been the stretch of lawn where archery targets had been hung for practice; Conduit Lane was where an open drain spilled down a steep incline into the River Torridge; Cooper Street was where barrels and casks were manufactured; Gunstone Lane was where cannon balls were cast; Potter's Lane was the scene of both cottage industries and significant workshops where the Beale family employed considerable numbers of men to work upon their latest designs; Pitt Lane was the site of the anthracite mine, worked by men such as Thomas Williams the 'collier' and, in all probability, John and Rhys Lloyd; while at the Rope Walk ships' cables were plaited by John Garrett, his brothers and son.[28] The potteries were located at the north end of the town, where – as Alison Grant pointed out – access to a tidal stream (known as the Pill) permitted barges to bring in raw clay and take out the finished fired goods (utilitarian earthernware, decorative slipware and innovative fire-backs).[29] With little competition, Bideford pottery – cheap, durable and attractively produced – managed to corner markets across the Atlantic rim and made fortunes. At the height of the industry, in the 1680s, 290,000 'parcels' of pottery were produced annually to be shipped out of the port, often for market in Ireland or the North American colonies.[30]

In 1664, Thomas Beale 'the second' – one of a dynasty of gifted Bideford potters – was paying tax for eight hearths in his home on the Washcombe Road.

This evidence, together with the creation of elaborate plaster ceilings entwining his initials and those of his wife with sprays of flowers, suggests levels of disposable wealth and the enjoyment of comfort by the artisanate that was barely matched by the Earl of Bath's townhouse on the quayside.[31] By the 1670s, the extended Beale family were employing a dozen men in their potteries across town and had begun to buy properties not just for additional warehouse space but for rent to tenants. Disposable income could be used, as we shall see, to buck the law and signal the family's strident religious and political radicalism, but it could also be used to forge a durable society of financially independent men (and, on occasion, women) within Bideford, who were convivial, literate and conscious of fashion and prevailing taste. Money offered them the opportunity for greater leisure and to experience new tastes – of tea, coffee and chocolate – to pursue their interests – whether circulating religious texts, in defiance of the censor, or collecting rare manuscripts and china – or to signal their preferences in dress and display. Late in the century, London agents had been retained in order to purchase luxuries: rare books that had originated in Muscovy and the Italian states, fine leather saddles and flaxen periwigs, that could not easily be sourced closer to home.[32] As early as the 1630s, John Strange had been importing porcelain from Japan for his own collection, while the father and son team of master plasterers, both named John Abbott family (from nearby Frithelstock), steadily rose up the social ladder, from building tradesmen to artisans with the status and buying power of gentlemen. If their fortunes had been made through the redecoration of the homes of Bideford's mercantile and landowning elites, over more than a sixty-year period that ran from the late 1640s on into the early 1700s, then, they, in turn contributed to the growing consumer society, through the commissioning of portraits, and purchase of everything from specialized working tools, to fine glass, furs and leather-bound prayer and design books.[33] Their stucco work mermaids, sea serpents, angels and wild men and wild women that looked down from the ceilings of the dining rooms of Bideford's merchants and self-made craftsmen spoke of imagination, creativity and adventurous enterprise, but they also reflected the mythology and superstitions attached to the hazardous waters upon which Bideford's wealth had been built.

Goods might miscarry, plague and smallpox ravage, and sudden storms wreck ships and drown mariners. For the most part, the wealth of Bideford's merchants and artisans was recently created and hard-won: and they knew it. As a consequence, their self-confidence had the aspect of a thin veneer. If they could rise by luck, art and the workings of providence, they could fall by the same. If Thomas Beale and his sons enjoyed their successes and the good things in life, then little separated them, culturally or geographically, from John Berryman and Thomas Smith, listed as poor potters in the returns of 1672 who could not afford the upkeep of even a single hearth.[34] On 2 January 1674, Joseph Chope, 'mariner of Bideford' made and signed his will: 'Being about to take a voyage at sea, and knowing the certainty of death and the dangerous accidents at sea leading thereunto, he commends his soul to his Maker, and devises all the property that he bought of his brother [in law] Samuel Leach to his dear and loving wife Elizabeth.'[35] The waters claimed Peter Nelso, a cavalry trooper, who drowned on 5 August 1645; John Sherman, one of Bideford's aldermen, who drowned on 5 July and was buried at St Mary's on the same day; Edward Pollard, who drowned on 19 July 1655; and Thomas Umble, who drowned in the Torridge on 7 March 1657 and was fished out and buried two days later.[36] The death of Richard Burdon, who was struck by lightning in the town on 6 July 1682, thoroughly unnerved the borough council who thought fit to record the event in the sessions book and attempted to make sense of his sudden and dramatic demise.[37]

Amid such uncertainty, others consulted almanacs and looked to discern the will of God in the operation of chance. If John Strange had chosen to view life, in its entirety, as a single spiritual 'pilgrimage' as his funerary monument made clear, then the town's Whigs were, even in the 1680s, gladdened to hear of the workings of divinely providential forms of judgement upon earth. Thus, it was reported in April 1688 that 'one Mr. Rous a Middlesex Gent. of reasonable quality, comely personage, about 62 years of age' had been 'with some company and taking a pipe of Tobacco and very merry and in seeming good health' when suddenly 'his pipe dropt out of his mouth and hee instantly dyed without speaking a word.'[38] Whether or not his love of tobacco helped to further engender God's disfavour, his untimely end was not attributed to a sudden stroke but to divine providence and revenge for his role as a Tory juryman during the trial that sent the radical Whig and popular hero, Lord William Russell to a martyr's death upon the scaffold at Lincoln's Inn Fields, five years earlier. Such valedictory news seemed all the more heartening when, as we shall see, Bideford's own Whigs – including many of the leading commercial families, and the majority of artisans concentrated in the pottery and rope-making industries – had found themselves excluded from public office and political power in the town for more than a generation, and could only watch from the sidelines as their Tory opponents appeared unwilling, and largely unable, to comprehend and tackle the mounting problems caused by the impact of Bideford's rapid growth and pursuit of new patterns of trade.

Figure 8 *John Strange (1590–1646) by an unknown artist c.1640 (Burton Museum & Art Gallery, Bideford). His life is told in the form of a pictogram recounting the stages of God's providence, from garnering mercantile wealth to preservation from accident and common assault.*

In viewing the scorched remains of Richard Burdon, John Davie, John Hill and their Tory colleagues had refrained from making an explicit link to providence, but their palpable disquiet is evident in their recording of the manner of his death. The lack of an obvious motive for Burdon having drawn down the Almighty's wrath and the absence of scapegoats – given that the Bideford Witches were already imprisoned in Exeter Castle – probably accounts for their quandary and certainly did nothing to ease their anxiety about the town's governance.[39] Wealthy merchants like the Davie family, as well as poor labourers like the Lloyds, had been attracted into Bideford, placing fresh demands upon living space in an already crowded and heavily built-up area, limited in its further growth by the river to the east and the range of hills hemming in the town to the west. In the decade that ran from 1660 to 1669, the population had been estimated by Frank Gent (who used data from the parish registers) at 1,767. By the 1670s, this had risen modestly to 1,920 while at the close of the 1680s the population has been estimated to have spiked at 2,610 immediately before the impact of the last smallpox epidemic. However, it should be noted that the figures for Bideford's population only reflect its settled residents, rather than the volatile, shifting surplus of discharged and visiting sailors, short-term migrants and hopeful vagrants drawn to the 'Golden Bay'. This might explain conflicting figures given for Bideford's inhabitants and the far larger estimation of 4,327 people being resident in the town in the 1670s given in the Ecclesiastical Census of 1676.[40] This latter vision of dramatic increase in population placing a considerable burden on resources that were already overstretched, at the time of the witch trials, is hampered by the incomplete Hearth Tax Returns for Bideford in 1674.[41] With one or more folios missing, any statistical attempt to calculate the town's inhabitants based upon the number of households taxed is bound to fail. This said, the knowledge that Bideford was a boom town experiencing heavy volumes of cargo landed at its quayside, with no adequate provision for clearing away enormous amounts of industrial and commercial refuse, and with a surplus population of mariners that could not easily be gauged or controlled, does indeed seem to have had immediate implications for public health and order.

Having made his fortune through re-exporting tobacco to Limerick, John Davie became mayor in 1673 and urged rich and poor, alike, to repair their properties, threatening those who 'shall throw or cast or suffer to lye in any of the streets or lanes or the Key of this Towne any filth, dung, coale ashes or rubbish' with imprisonment. He clearly recognized 'the great danger that the inhabitants of this Towne may be in as to their bodily health by noisome and stinking Dung hills and other filth which too frequently hath been cast out in heaps in severall streets and on the Keys of this Towne and suffered to lye long there, whereby the ayre (especially in the summer time) is apt to be corrupted'. Ironically, one of the most persistent offenders was the lord of the manor – John, 1st Earl of Bath – who had neglected his properties and was censured by Bideford's Justices of the Peace for having:

allowed the roadway and pavement belonging to and in front of his house ...
on the East side of the river Torridge to become in a pestilent and ruinous state
and in particular has allowed a pool of filth to remain in front of the aforesaid
house to the danger of the King's pople [i.e. subjects] passing that way.

He was ordered to repair the road within two months, and to remove the 'pool of filth' within a month, or face fines of twenty and ten shillings respectively.[42]

If Bideford's elites, in the form of John Davie and the Tory-dominated common council, aspired towards the clear demarcation of public and private spaces, railed against pollution and sought to sweep clean the streets, the problem was that they, themselves, were not prepared to pay for it through the parish rates and preferred to throw the costs back upon the individual, rather than the community. When this failed, as it invariably did, they showed few scruples about turning to coercion when it came to dealing with those least able to afford the costs. In this way, Justinian Prance – who seems to have fought his way out of his poverty-stricken origins – was fined for working a 'dangerous' lime pit and the industrious Thomas Beale 'the second' was charged with permitting piles of dung to accumulate outside his home 'near the Markett House' and for bundling together great piles of furze to fuel his pottery kilns. George Burdon – a relative of the unfortunate, Richard – Sarah Dennis and John Luxton were all presented before the town's magistrates for permitting 'nasty places [ie. middens]' to exist 'at their back doors and garden walls'. Orders to better regulate – or at least to mitigate – 'the dunghills & filth' that built up on the streets and wharves were a staple of town's governance, with prosecutions and prohibitions regularly made during the 1670s–80s.[43]

Despite its use in the wool industry, water supply and, in particular, the provision of clean drinking water remained a serious problem for the people of Bideford throughout the period. The ornate metal water pipes excavated in the town, dated 1691 and 1693, serviced wealthy households with a private supply and testified to rising living standards among those most closely associated with mercantile trade, town governance and manufacture. However, public provision was variable, at best, and often became contaminated with the rubbish that had built up along the quayside. Pumps were installed in order to carry streams of liquid sewerage and slurry out of the town and, indeed, were not finally abandoned by the townsfolk until the nineteenth century. Dorothy Kinge was charged with 'stopping a water course at the piggs pound' creating a build-up of manure and a 'very noysome' smell that sickened the townsfolk and prompted the magistrates to act against her.[44] There is every reason to think of the Bideford of the 1680s as a cramped, claustrophobic and often unsanitary place, pockmarked with middens and open sewers, and strewn with split barrels and the detritus of manufactures. As the same injunctions given by John Davie were reissued, word-for-word, by the town council in 1685, there are few grounds for the belief that the edicts had been particularly well conceived or that they had ever been capable of effective enforcement.[45] There is certainly no evidence that the recalcitrant Earl of Bath ever heeded the written warnings and carried out the repair works to his properties, or that the threatened fines were ever actually levied let alone paid.

However, if the town council was unable to drive thoroughgoing change, then the trustees of the Long Bridge – a formidable interest group within the town – were not slow to hit upon an entrepreneurial solution to the problem by redeveloping, and opening up, the previously waste and unprofitable plots of land that they owned in order for the building of substantial new houses.[46] Though the sale and purchase of property was regulated by the civic authorities, with the town clerk supervising the transference of deeds in October 1674 and again in January 1677, there were scant objections to the sweeping, if somewhat ad hoc, developments forced through by the bridge trustees. The personnel of the Bridge Trust and the various arms of local government effectively dovetailed, while successive mayors and magistrates had no desire to cross the most effective source of patronage and charitable provision in the town. Thus, speculative building completely transformed the appearance of Bideford, following the Restoration, refashioning the central closes that nestled by the western end of the bridge and creating whole new neighbourhoods at the town's northern boundaries, as far as the Pill stream and marshes. From the leases, given and renewed, we have a sense of the trades and professions of Bideford's 'middling sort': shipowners, like Thomas Gist, mariners such as Joseph Chope and John Tracey, merchants of the stamp of John Shurt and his son, blacksmiths like John Lambert, clockmaker's such as Ephraim Dyer, cordwainers like Samuel Perrin, 'soapboylers' such as Bartholemew Shapton and ironmongers, like Josias Elliot.[47] In addition, Bideford possessed a not inconsiderable number of independent and propertied widows and spinsters, like Mary Holman and Grace Wills, respectively, who also renewed and granted leases to the Bridge Trust.[48] As early as 1670, the Earl of Bath had bought a house and garden from a certain Mr Willett, in order to demolish them so that a more substantial thoroughfare (which became known as Buttgarden Street) might connect Maiden Street with the High Street. Furthermore, his gift in 1673 of 'a plott of the garden of the old place house' adjoining the north side of St Mary's Church permitted the extension of the town's burial ground which, since the time of the plague, had reached its full capacity. The Buttgarden now became a centre for new development, with the market relocating there in 1675 – and necessitating the shifting of its great bell – together with many other businesses, including pottery shops.[49] Although the Free Grammar School had been rebuilt in 1657 and was extensively repaired in 1680, a new town hall would not be built until 1698. Thus, the 'flourishing', 'pleasant, clean, well-built town' surveyed by Daniel Defoe, in the 1720s, with its 'very noble quay ... new spacious [Bridgeland] street' and 'very large, well-built and well-finished meeting-house', where a 'multitude' of non-conformists worshipped, did not yet exist and was the product of the post-1688 settlement and commercial revolution, as opposed to the Restoration.[50] The Bideford that had been familiar to the Bideford Witches fifty years before had been a very different place. In the 1670s–80s, it had been a town experiencing a state of flux, whereby a spate of unregulated building gobbled-up a substantial portion of what had previously been common ground and had served to concentrate the town's poor together in the neighbourhood of Cold Harbour Street. Moreover, the northern limits of the town that were cleared after 1685 to form the Bridgeland development of high-status housing were, up until that time, occupied by a few ruinous houses, old warehouses, and rambling gardens, where the women might well have hidden, sheltered and foraged.[51]

According to local tradition and later novelists, Temperance Lloyd, Susanna Edwards and Mary Trembles shared a cottage together that once stood on Old Town Street opposite what, in the Victorian age, had become the new church cemetery.[52] Situated on a steep rise, on the western fringe of town, it might have appeared as something of a 'crow's nest' offering commanding views over the streets, potteries and quayside. *If* they had lived there – and it is a big *if* – then there was little that could have escaped their attention and this might help to account for their unerring ability to pinpoint trouble, and seek out individuals, in the town, seemingly appearing and disappearing at will. Though the cottage burned down in 1894, a photograph of it survives together with a romanticized, if not quite 'chocolate box', drawing by Claude de Neuville. The photograph was presumably taken in the late 1880s or early 1890s, while the drawing is helpfully dated by the artist, after his signature, to the year that saw the destruction of the cottage.[53] The immediate difficulty is that both images show us not one, but two – and quite possibly three – distinct cottages. The one to the left of the frame is a lower, ramshackle, structure with a steeply sloping tiled roof and narrow gables. Though fallen into a picturesque state of decay by the nineteenth century, there is nothing to suggest that this was a particularly poor habitation by the standards of the seventeenth century. Indeed, its two stories and brick-built chimney suggest otherwise. The central range of thatched buildings, together with an ancillary wing that juts out onto the street corner, are substantial and may represent two separate dwellings divided between what had once been one large farmhouse. With two stories, three solid brick chimneys and wide window frames this would, in the 1670s–80s, have been a considerable property suitable for a yeoman rather than the indigent poor. At best, it would seem possible that the unknown photographer and de Neuville, who seems to have based his picture closely upon the photographic print and may never have even visited the site, were unclear about which building was of significance. The lower, though later, cottage to the left seems to be the likely candidate for the traditional designation. However, there is nothing at all in the contemporary records to suggest that the three women ever lived together, or to provide a clue as to where their habitations were in Bideford. Indeed, as we saw in the course of the previous chapter, there is nothing to link Temperance Lloyd with

either Susanna Edwards or Mary Trembles before 1682. All we know for sure –
and even that may be no more than a rhetorical flourish – is that the anonymous
author of *The Life and Conversations of . . . Three Notorious Witches*, thought that
Temperance Lloyd lived in a 'poor Habitation' in the town.[54] She frequented
Gunstone Lane, where she is said to have met with the Devil and there is a much
later story that a grocer's wife thought that her pigs had been 'overlooked by the
Cock-street witches'.[55] Cock Street (later renamed as Hart Street by bowdlerizing
Victorians) led off Cold Harbour Lane and, in the 1670s–80s, was certainly in the
poorest area of town. Though folk memory is notoriously unreliable, it is at least
possible that the oral tradition that associated one or more of the Bideford Witches
with Cock Lane might have had some veracity. At present, we know no more and
might conclude that given the lack of concrete evidence, one guess is as good as
another. Yet, even if there is no reason to identify the traditional 'Witches' Cottage'
with the three women, its general location at the outer edge of the seventeenth-
century town, on the very margins of the available waste ground, where a lean-to
or shack might be surreptitiously constructed with access to gleanings of broom,
berries, nuts and rushes from the neighbouring commons and hedgerows, would
fit with what we can piece together of Temperance Lloyd's life and movements.
Similarly, Cock Street, near Cold Harbour where the town's poor were concentrated,
seems another possible fit with Susanna Edwards, Mary Trembles and, perhaps,
even Temperance Lloyd, all living independently in its vicinity.

Both then and now the witches would seem to be hidden from the face of
Bideford. It is, therefore, no wonder that in attempting to recover them historians
have gone in search of other traces of disorder or perceived difference in order
that the lives of the three women might be better understood and contextualized.
Conjoining spheres of women's autonomy and self-assertion, met by official
criticism and legal repression, would appear fertile and original areas for
exploration. The pioneering work of Janet A. Thompson on Bideford's alehouse
keepers sought to chart the limits of patriarchal and social control upon what
appeared to be an exceptional sphere of female economic independence, that
was held capable of forging a distinct matriarchal subculture within the town.[56]
Alehouses were firmly equated in the mind of the authorities with loose living,
drunkenness and prostitution: vices which could only be exacerbated in a busy
port town, where the population was continually shifting and therefore much

more difficult to control. Of the five borough towns of North Devon, Bideford appears – according to Thompson's thesis – to have been the most violent and lawless in its character. The number of women charged with drunkenness in the town was also far higher than elsewhere in Devon, indicating that women not only provided the ale but also consumed it.[57]

For those of sufficient means, the keeping of an alehouse offered, for a minimum capital investment, a measure of independence and a reasonable level of income, since the granting of a licence permitted an individual to sell beer, cider, and ale from the comfort of their own home. The number of female alehouse keepers in Bideford rose dramatically after 1635, due initially to the dislocations of the Civil War and plague during the following decade, but levels continued to rise, even after the Restoration, as the result of the increased demand for alcohol in the flourishing port town where visiting or resident sailors, after voyages to Newfoundland, Spain or the American colonies enjoyed comparatively high levels of disposable income and a limited amount of leisure time in which to spend it in seeking entertainments. During the periods for which figures for Bideford exist, from 1660 to 1662 and again from 1671 to 1687, some seventy women are recorded as being licensed to sell ale in the town. Of these, one was jointly licensed together with her husband, while all the others existed as independent operators, constituting roughly 50 per cent of the total number of licensees in Bideford.[58] By 1672, women had come to outnumber the men in the trade and some of them clearly succeeded in building businesses that were both profitable and extremely durable.[59] The great majority of the women who kept alehouses were widows and a large proportion of them had inherited the businesses after the deaths of their husbands. This said, many widows and single women set up alehouses themselves. It was recognized that if many of these women had not been permitted to continue in business, then their financial support – and that of their children and aged dependants – would have had to fall back upon the parish. This harsh economic reality, and the question of female poverty and dependency, served to concentrate the minds of those who sat upon the town council, and in large measure ameliorated the hostility of the civic authorities towards this particular group of self-sufficient, property holding women. It was very much a case of financial expediency overcoming moral considerations, or patriarchal rhetoric. Of those women engaged in the trade in Bideford, whose status can clearly be defined, forty-nine were widows, two were married, and two were spinsters. Of the male licensees the majority practised another profession, with a third of their number described as 'mariners' who, it might be reasoned, would have been absent for some months of the year, leaving the day-to-day running of their businesses to their wives, mothers or children.[60]

There was money to be made in the licensed trade and there is every reason to think of the town's alehouses as a riot of colour, with richly painted interiors and gaudily painted advertising signs hanging outside their doors. The surviving evidence from a 1680s alehouse, which had been located close to Bideford's market place, is part of a colourful fresco painted onto the plaster walls of a substantial property, with swirling scrolls, foliate trails and the face of an angel framing the owners' initials, suggesting that this was another business run by a husband and wife team (see Figure 9). However, it is worth

Figure 9 *'Welcome All!': the painted decoration, commissioned in 1686, for an alehouse that stood overlooking Bideford's marketplace (Author's Photograph).*

noting that the dedicatory inscription reflects, in its verse, the preoccupations of the owners with commerce as well as conviviality. The guests to the home are 'lovely' and 'welcome all' but criticism over the size of the drinks served, and their cost, is pre-empted by the promise that 'When there is no excise, I'll pay for all'. In railing against Bideford's vigilant and, it seems, often heavy-handed customs men, the owners were seeking to celebrate an idealized view of free trade that had much in common with the mores and preoccupations of the town's disenfranchised, godly, community of artisans, craftsmen and mariners, and little to say – or appeal – to the indigent poor.

Over the course of the 1660s it has been estimated that there was one licensed alehouse for every fifty-five inhabitants of Bideford, although this figure ignores the influx of large numbers of sailors into the port every time a large vessel, or fishing fleet put in.[61] Confronted by the proliferation of drinking holes, instances of drunkenness, disorderly conduct and prostitution, Bideford's Tory governing council attempted, in the early 1680s, to institute its own thoroughgoing reform of manners and to link its two greatest concerns – namely public disorder and religious nonconformity – together. By sleight of hand, the Grand Jury of Devonshire very cleverly – if disingenuously – combined its assault upon both areas of resistance and appropriated the language, and critiques, of its Whig opponents, turning their arguments back upon them and attempting to prohibit anyone who did not attend Anglican church services (regardless of their gender) from retaining their liquor licenses. In an order issued on 25 April 1682 aimed at punishing 'all profane cursers and swearers', 'profaneness and debauchery . . . in every part of this county' religious dissent and alcoholism were taken as being synonymous:

> Because disorderly alehouses are most commonly the rendezvous of profane, debauched and lewd persons, we order all alehouse keepers suffering any such persons to sit tippling in their houses to be carefully suppressed . . . and we further order that no persons be permitted to keep alehouses that do not repair every Sunday to their parish church to abide there orderly during the whole service and shall not likewise produce a certificate that they have at least twice in the last year received the sacrament according to the use of the Church of England.[62]

All constables, churchwardens and tithe collectors were required to bring before the authorities 'all drunkards and such as remain tippling in alehouses at unreasonable times' in what amounted to an attempt to stamp out late night drinking and drunkenness in towns such as Bideford but more remarkable – beyond the granting of sweeping powers to the parish officers in order to implement social policy – was the lengthy justification for why it was held necessary, couched along not just moral but political grounds. The dissenters and Whigs, thrown onto the back foot since the proroguing of the Oxford Parliament and the breaking of Shaftesbury's party the year before, were held as an integral part of the problem. The worm nestling away in the Royalist bud had been sliced away at the national level, now it was the job of local government to finish the job by skewering its constituent segments in the regions, as:

> We would have those schismatical, factious people, who upbraid us with countenancing debauchery and lewdness, look back and they will find it was their schism and rebellion (which was prologued with such an outcry as this) which first weakened and at last broke down the banks of government and let in on us a deluge of profaneness and irreligion and, though they now call themselves the sober party, it is evident that they take the same methods again and would, if possible, bring us into the same confusion.[63]

The trouble was that the rhetoric did not, necessarily, fit the facts. From the records contained within the sessions book of the Bideford Justices of the Peace, there is no sense that drunkenness was the preserve of any one political persuasion. Indeed, the most habitual offender – as licensee of an alehouse, a brawler and drunkard – was a Tory, Peter Bagelhose. He had first been censured for his conduct in 1670, he was jailed for being drunk and disorderly in 1676, fined five shillings for the same charge in 1680, and was fined for selling ale without a licence and presented as 'a common drunkard' in 1681.[64] On 25 July 1681, he was the subject of a complaint to the magistrates by Grace Barnes, who a year later would bring charges of witchcraft against Susanna Edwards and Mary Trembles.[65] Unfortunately, we do not know what the source of the altercation was, or the precise nature of the charge. However, the case does reinforce the sense that Bagelhose was a bully – given to violence once he was in his cups – and that Grace Barnes was opinionated and litigious. On

3 February 1682, an argument with Elizabeth Gard quickly spiralled out of control and led to him being charged with using 'very Abusive language' towards Thomas Gist, the mayor of Bideford, and John Hill, the town clerk.[66] A succession of further charges followed throughout the early 1680s, establishing Bagelhose as the most persistent, troublesome and thoroughly unpleasant figure that the town's magistrates had to deal with over a twenty-year period. However, his wealth, his Anglicanism and his Tory politics combined to ameliorate the routine fines handed down to him.[67] Indeed, his ability to pay – together with his display of political and religious conformity – made him largely untouchable, as he seems to have minded neither the odd night spent in the town gaol or the damage done to his reputation through his bad temper and alcoholism.

Periodic attempts were made to punish 'Tipplers', drunkards and 'Transgressors of the Lord's Day'. In 1677, Margaret Davies was 'suppressed . . . from selling ale' and was forced to 'pull Down her [inn] sign'. A major clampdown on unlicensed alehouses followed in 1680 that continued unabated until 1682, and saw Bagelhose convicted and fined, together with Evans Poole and David Davies for keeping unlicensed premises.[68] Though the efficacy of the measures is in doubt, not least as the Davies family simply seemed to have swopped the ownership of their business each time they were prosecuted, between husband and wife, it is tempting to see the authorities' push against drunkenness as the other arm of their offensive against religious and political dissent that aimed to bring about both the reform of manners and the unquestioning acceptance of Crown and established church in Bideford. Alongside drunkenness, prostitution was the other sizeable problem for a borough council intent upon moral reform and one which could, equally, land the owners of alehouses in trouble. In this way, Rebecca Lang was charged in 1677 – just as Margaret Davies would be a year later – for keeping 'ill rule' in her house and for permitting prostitution to flourish.[69]

However, there is nothing in the town records to directly link Susanna Edwards, her daughter Katheryn and her mother, Rachel, to the burgeoning alehouse culture with its allure of illicit, transactional sex and the financial benefits that the commodification of both drinking and carnality might bestow. Despite the sale of beer, bread and ale, it is notable that the witches do not seem to have begged from any of the numerous alehouses, and it was never alleged – even by the worst of their detractors – that they were drunks. Once again, the sense of their testimony is that they were so marginalized and isolated from the mainstream experiences of Bideford's townsfolk that their experiences did not even impinge upon the dominant, if less respectable, subcultures that flourished along the dockside. They could neither afford to buy the alcohol sold within the establishments, nor – on account of their advanced aged and haggard looks – hope to sell their favours towards that end from within the drinking dens. Consequently, the alehouses were as forbidden, and forbidding, to them as were the doors of the rich.

However, the stigma of illegitimacy that served as a by-product of the alehouses, and which had hallmarked Susanna Edwards' life, certainly did interest the town's government as part of its administration of the poor law concerned the maintenance of fatherless children and the signing of bastardy orders. Thus, John Davie, as mayor, signed an order for 'Samuel Shapmans Bastard' in 1671, and Robert Boole, in the same capacity, for the 'maintenance of Margaret Nobells Bastard' in 1676.[70] Questions of paternity led the town's magistrates to examine Margaret Willis, described as a 'singlewoman begotten with child', on 7 October 1683, in order to establish whether or not Samuel Rosser was the father; while fears of an abortion or secret birth led to 'severall Examinations' of the householder and his neighbours after 'some Blood was found in the Garden of Robert Hill', on 12 February 1684. It seems likely that a caul, the placenta or the remains of a foetus was found amid the bare bushes 'which was supposed to be a child'.[71] On 20 April 1685, Mary Brown was questioned by William Titherley and John Hill about: 'A Male Child born of her body in her Lodging at Magdalen Conarks house', while, on 19 October 1685, Hill together with the new mayor, John Darracott, cross questioned Susanna Lamb, a 'Singlewomen begotten with child', the father of whom they believed to be one of the town's apothecaries.[72] There appears to have been a particular drive by the authorities to enforce stricter moral codes in the early 1680s, as the presentments of unmarried mothers cluster around 1683–5 and the mayoralties of Thomas Gearing, William Titherley and John Darracott. This came in the wake of attempts to exert greater control over the town's youth, with the institution of new regulations intended to regulate apprentices and the committal of 'An idle Boy . . . to the house of correction'.[73]

These were troubles – and troubling individuals – which stood outside those primary misfortunes, common to all English men and women during the seventeenth century: namely, war, want, food shortages, disability and the ravages of contagious disease. They could easily be laid at the door of the 'dangerous' or 'vicious' poor who operated as a distinct substratum within the hierarchy of need, distanced from both their fellow paupers and wider civil society.[74] The primary trouble, for the authorities – in the shape of the parish poor law overseers – lay in the determining of who was genuinely in need of assistance and who, through vice or stupidity, was largely responsible for their predicament. The poor represented a very significant section of the population. Almost a third of all households were completely exempted from taxation and beneath this level were, of course, the homeless and the vagrants, the nature of whose existence was hard to gauge and whose numbers defied any easy computation by the authorities.[75] Failed harvests and fears of complete social breakdown had led a faltering Queen Elizabeth I to give her assent to legislation aimed at alleviating and containing the worst cases of suffering in 1598. These measures were confirmed and extended by the Poor Law Act of 1601, which sought to provide outdoor relief on a parish level and divided the needy into three distinct groups. The first of these, the 'impotent poor' were those too young, too old, or too physically or too mentally disabled to be expected to work. Secondly, there were those who were working but for such low rates of income that they could not hope to support either themselves or their families. They, together with men and women who sought work but could not – despite their best efforts – find any to hand, were considered to be deserving of a level of income that would enable their survival and provide for their most basic needs, in terms of food, shelter and clothing. This much was agreed upon and enshrined in the poor law.[76] However, it was the third group of paupers, those who simply had no intention of working and preferred a life of idleness, that unsurprisingly attracted the most comment and concern. Such idleness, it was held – then as now – could only be funded through crime or prostitution, while the individuals themselves were remorselessly characterized as being shifty, feckless and promiscuous. There were few taxpayers who exhibited much desire to support this grouping and such handouts as were administered to them were designed to be punitive in nature. Yet, the creation of abstract groupings is one thing – and, as Paul Slack has memorably pointed out, the category of 'pauper' was created by this raft of legislation – while the categorization of living, breathing, needy individuals is entirely another.[77]

There were clearly those within Restoration Bideford who qualified as being particularly 'deserving' of help and relief. Symon Jeffrey had been born and raised in the town. Before the outbreak of the Civil Wars he had been a mariner but, in a rare act for a Bideford man, he had chosen to join the Royalist, as opposed to the Parliamentarian, army in the West. He had served for 'the space of seaven yeares & upwards' under the commands of Major Richard Pomeroy and Captain John Gealard and had been commended for his bravery and diligence in the field by both Prince Maurice and John Grenville, the Earl of Bath. Seriously wounded in a number of engagements, captured and suffering 'long imprisonments' on account of his fidelity to the Royalist cause, his health by April 1663 had irretrievably broken down. 'Scarcely able to stirre in his bed, and become miserably poore & an Object of all peoples pitty & compassion', but backed by Bideford's mayor and new governors, he successfully petitioned the Devon Sessions for relief and was granted an annual pension of £2, with ten shillings paid out to him as an immediate advance in order to alleviate his sufferings.[78] However, his plight continued to worsen and, by the spring of 1664, he was reported to have 'growne into a more deplorable state than formerly' with Bideford's Royalist elites vouching that he was 'so decreeped in all his body not able to help himself, but is now in a very low & sad condicon'.[79] Once again, the authorities chose to look favourably upon his case advancing a further five shillings to him, through the Treasurer for Maimed Soldiers, and raising his pension by a further ten shillings a year.[80] The wheel of fortune had, in 1660, turned to his advantage and he was now viewed, rather than as a desperate malignant and man of violence, as a loyal and valiant subject who had suffered disproportionately 'in the late unhappie warre' and 'under the late usurped power'.[81] His was an exceptional case made all the starker by Bideford's otherwise solid allegiance to the Parliamentary cause and through the uniting of the provision of welfare with a desire to publicly reward loyalty to the Crown. Few other cases that came before the Devon Quarter Sessions or the poor law overseers in Bideford were quite so cut-and-dried. The settlement laws that tied the provision of welfare to places of birth and long-term residence

Figure 10 *The Absentee Landlord: John Grenville, Earl of Bath (Wikicommons). This plasterwork from the Earl's house on the quayside at Bideford was the work of John Abbot of Frithelstock and gives some idea of the vision of taste, wealth and innovation that the king's friend intended to project.*

had the potential to create administrative nightmares but, on the whole, the overseers at Bideford appear to have behaved in a way that was reasonably equitable, accepting financial responsibility for two families, and their dependants, who had settled at St Stephen's, near Launceston, in Cornwall.[82] All the evidence suggests that Temperance Lloyd, Susanna Edwards and Mary Trembles were judged eligible and received a modest form of parish relief but that this was not enough to keep body and soul together, with the result that they took to begging and sought out other forms of charity in the town.

Although Bideford was far less well endowed with charitable trusts as its neighbour, Barnstaple, it did possess a number of different, and differing, charities and almshouses.[83] The Bridge Trust, reinvigorated in 1608, had set aside £20 out of its profits from river fees and fines 'which should be employed in a continual stock, for setting the poor inhabitants of the said town and parish on work'; while a further 13s 4d was to be provided 'annually, for ever' to the poor of the town from the estate of Alexander Arundell, who died in Bideford in October 1627.[84] John Strange, under the terms of his will dated 15 March 1642, left 'five houses and gardens in Maiden Street with a close of land adjoining ... for the benefit of such poor people as the Trustees [of the Long Bridge] with the consent of the Mayor should think fit', while his funerary monument in St

Mary's Church stressed 'his liberality of hand to the needy' as being among his chief virtues.[85] The will of Henry Amory, who died in March 1663, left 'six small dwellings ... each of which has a garden attached' to be converted into almshouses for the poor and the elderly, while in 1681, George Baron – who had made his fortune as a merchant in London – gifted an annuity drawn upon the rents and profits from a number of farms, orchards and houses in the neighbouring parish of Northam, 'for the perpetual relief of poor seamen and their widows, in the town of Bideford'.[86] Yet, the most significant of these – in terms of its continuity and the light that shines upon the lives of the alleged witches and the seventeenth-century poor of the town – was the John Andrew Dole. This gift derived from a charitable trust established by John Andrew who, in October 1605, bequeathed the annual rent on 'a close of land called the Three Acres' in Bideford, to be used in perpetuity 'to be bestowed and distributed for the relief of the poor of the town and parish ... according to the discretion of the lessors'. However, a legal challenge made by the mayor, aldermen and burgesses to the rights of the surviving executors of Andrew's will and trust, in 1637, effectively brought the operation of the lease and the gift of the charity into the hands of the town government. As an expedient, 'all the rents ... should be paid to the mayor, and the mayor, in turn, would pay 20s per annum to the poor of the said town'. However, by 1664, the business of administering the leases appears to have become onerous to the mayor and the administration of the land and established premises was made over to a new set of trustees upon the proviso that the annual dole of twenty shillings should continue to be paid to each of Bideford's poor, an arrangement which remained unchanged until the financial troubles of 1678 and the administrative reorganization of 1682–3.[87]

We are left to fall back upon the inferences drawn from the John Andrew Dole Book, where the other sources – the records of the poor law overseers and the other charities – do not survive. As we have already seen, the impression that emerges is that Temperance Lloyd, Susanna Edwards and Mary Trembles were all long-term recipients of the dole and that there seems to have been little or no hesitation on the parts of John Wadland and George Middleton in allotting them the customary dues. If they initially stumbled over Temperance Lloyd's Christian name, then they did not think of her as a recent arrival in Bideford or someone to be intrinsically denied charity. Yet, if the 'Golden Bay' had winners, these women were certainly ranked among the losers in a town where money permitted agency and everything had its price. One individual they would have encountered was Thomas Michelson, a well-to-do linen draper, who served as one of the overseers of the poor. It would have been from his hand that the women would have received their payments of parish relief, usually in the churchyard after the conclusion of a Sunday service. Yet, in Bideford in the 1670s–80s, no one was quite what they seemed. Michelson was – just like Temperance Lloyd and Mary Trembles – an immigrant to the town, though he hailed from Lowland Scotland as opposed to Wales or Ireland. He held what appeared to be an outwardly respectable position within the town but he was the only individual whose behaviour – and that of his household – came close to rivalling Peter Bagelhose's unenviable reputation for disturbing the peace. However, unlike Bagelhose, he was not a drunk. His simmering disputes with the mayor and town council were rooted not only in his rumbustious personality but also more importantly in his position as a Whig and a religious dissenter within a Tory polity. In 1680, he had refused to answer a summons and administered a sound beating to the constables sent out by John Davie to arrest him.[88] In August 1682, just as the witches were facing trial at Exeter, testimony was taken against him from a constable and two citizens, saying that they had overheard Michelson using 'abusive words' against Thomas Gist, who was then the mayor. Michelson seems to have intervened in a case that was brought against two other men, Robert Knolman and Edward James, and snapped out his words to the sergeant-at-arms, who he felt was ill-using them at the mayor's behest.[89] Michelson had been fined for attending an illegal Conventicle – or religious meeting of the town's nonconformists – and it may be that his words were honed by principle as well as pure anger. However, stranger things were in store. Less than a year later, he and his servant got themselves into an altercation with a woman by the name of Elizabeth Angell as she was crossing the Long Bridge, on 13 June 1683. They shouted out abusive words at her before Michelson's servant grabbed her hat from her head and threw it 'out over into the river'.[90] Then, he seems to have lost all control of his own household and dismissed his servants, Samuel Bryant and Mary Webb, who then appear to have gone on a mini-crime spree in the town. It is unclear whether Michelson, himself, was the target of their actions but the implication is that they ranged far wider and, on 15 February 1685, a 'Hue and Cry' was raised against them by the town council.[91] Now, while it is debatable as to whether or not Thomas Michelson's tussles with the law were the products of his religious and political activism or of simple thuggery, he certainly despised Thomas Gist – as many others in the town had cause to – and paid scant attention to summonses emanating from the town hall. Just as significant is the sense that Temperance Lloyd, with her Puritan background, was in regular contact with a religious dissenter who controlled her access to welfare but, like all of the town's leading nonconformists, took no part in the circulating of allegations of witchcraft against her.

It seems fair to conclude that, when attempting to locate triggers for the witch-hunt of 1682, it is safest to avoid functional and monocausal explanations – whether based around trade depression, sexual licence or the prevalence of alehouses – and to suggest, instead, that while every society experiences at any given time elements of upheaval and change, the desire to activate the persecution of witches as a control mechanism in the face of internal or external challenge is a very specific – and thankfully comparatively rare – response to economic and social pressures.

Moreover, while the sale of alcohol and sex have been highlighted as establishing female independence in Bideford and seen as creating a patriarchal backlash in the midst of which allegations of sorcery might flourish, the impact of religious nonconformity proved far more challenging for the likes of Thomas Gist and John Hill, who sat at the heart of local government. It threatened to undo all their work, destroy public order and give fire to rebellion in the West. Thus, there was, indeed, a radical underground religion pulsing through the veins of many of the townsfolk in Bideford, which was largely sustained, forwarded and articulated through the commitment, bravery and faithfulness of women. However, it was not the survival of witchcraft but a form of Protestant dissent that had once been normative, and binding, in the affairs of Bideford but which, since 1662, had been proscribed by law, rooted out by the town's constables, and judged with exceptional severity by both the town's court and the county assizes, that provided the port with a potentially revolutionary culture. It was this fear that increasingly held Bideford's ruling council in dread.

3

An underground religion

The Restoration of the monarchy, in May 1660, had left Bideford bitterly and increasingly divided along cleavages of religious and political principle.[1] The enforcement of oaths of allegiance to the Stuart monarchy and the episcopacy, the imposition of a new prayer book, and the passing of the Act of Uniformity and the Five Mile Act by a vengeful 'Cavalier Parliament' served to disenfranchise a significant tranche of the town's ruling elite, who had thrived throughout the rules of the Long Parliament, Commonwealth and Protectorate.[2] The Strange family were toppled from their pre-eminent position in the town's government, with George Strange – though he was still classed as a 'Gentleman' – being far more likely, by the 1670s, to find himself fined or imprisoned for his politics and religious beliefs than to serve as mayor or pass town ordinances. Thomas Beale, a one-time mayor of Bideford refused to take the new oaths in 1661, while the effective barring of religious dissenters from public office denied his youngest son, Gabriel, the role in civic affairs that his ability and wealth would otherwise have easily secured.[3] However, the biggest losers were the Bartlett family, who went from being the lynchpins of the community to hunted fugitives in less than a decade.

William Bartlett had been the lecturer, or preacher, at Bideford since at least 1641 and had acted as balance in the parish to the Laudian rector, Arthur Gifford. As a 'very solid and useful preacher ... whose labours were attended with very signal success', he was active in rallying the support of the town for Parliament during the Civil War and was regarded by other nonconformists, such as Edward Calamy as an independent and radical, and as 'a man of great courage in the cause of God'.[4] From 1648, he had the sole charge of the parish of Bideford, while his son, John, held the living of the parish of Fremington, near Barnstaple, during the Republic. However, both father and son were removed from their offices at the Restoration and refused to subscribe to the 1662 Act of Uniformity, pledging in a letter sent to a minister in New England that they would choose 'rather to dye in prison than take it.'[5] After a failed attempt to escape to Chesapeake Bay, where among other migrants from Bideford a branch of the Strange family had settled, father and son prepared to weather the storm of Anglican reaction, setting themselves the task of preaching, illegally, in the houses of members of their former congregations. They were joined in their endeavours by the Rev. Lewis Stucley, who had once preached before Oliver Cromwell and served as his chaplain, but who had similarly lost his living, in Exeter, at the Restoration, and returned to Bideford, in 1670, in order to preach covertly.[6] These three charismatic, capable and highly experienced ministers – who appeared to possess complimentary traits and facets of personality – provided a focused leadership for the large dissenting community in Bideford that the established church was increasingly unable to answer with anything but the application of repression and force. As the parish fell back under the control of the Grenville family, successive Anglican appointees to the parish proved to be far less adept preachers and far more divisive figures in respect of local politics and sensitivities.

As a result, religious nonconformity remained a significant presence in Bideford throughout our period and on into the eighteenth century, with about a quarter of the adult population of the town, at any one point during the 1670s–80s, being prepared to shun the services and rituals of the established church and to run the risk of fines or imprisonment for attending, or aiding, the home churches or conventicles. Indeed, participation in these more intimate, shared meetings – where the Bible was read and an exegesis provided and preached that often related directly to contemporary affairs – may well have appeared as a uniquely inspiring experience when other forms of political expression and collective action were being denied to Bideford's 'middling sort'. Certainly, it provided women with an otherwise unprecedented agency, as the conventicles brought together cross-sections of Bideford's society that – on account of gender, age and differentiations of station and wealth – would not, otherwise, have met and mixed under the same roof, and permitted them with a voice in both the organizing of these illicit prayer meetings and in extemporizing upon certain aspects of the sermons and teachings. As such, within the constraints of the times, the holding of conventicles provided women with a heady combination of danger, excitement, self-realization and ecstatic religious vision. Unsurprisingly, women and spinsters, in particular, seem to have been well-represented at these meetings, often equalling or outnumbering the menfolk, and on occasion hosting and choreographing proceedings.[7] Alongside significant numbers of potters, shipwrights, rope-makers and mariners, and individual barbers and tailors, there were many prominent, independent, women of means who attended the conventicles: widows and spinsters who owned considerable property in the town, such as Susan Davy listed as a 'widow'; Sarah Dennis described as a 'single woman' but possibly also a widow; Mary Greening 'spinster'; Frances Buike 'spinster'; Joanne Wadland 'spinster'; Joanne Hartnell 'spinster'; and Susanna Williams, whose marital status was not set down.[8] Mary Greening had, as the family gravestone in the churchyard at St Mary's made plain, already had to flee from her original home in Gloucestershire 'for conscience's sake' following the passing of the Five Mile Act in 1665. Each suffering, arrest and fine that did not break their spirit or ruin their finances seems to have drawn them closer together in a common cause of millenarian hopes, shared experiences and steely resistance to temporal power.

Furthermore, it was not lost on contemporaries that, in his defence of witch trials published in 1716 – which served to popularize the Bideford case – Richard Boulton, an Anglican and Tory, sought to claim that the witches acted in imitation of 'the Manner of Congregational Churches, and that they have a Baptism and a Supper, and Officers amongst them, ostensibly resembling those of our Lord'.[9] When Marcellus Laroon the elder, a French artist who travelled extensively through England and settled in London in 1674, chose to draw the meeting of a Conventicle he angled his vision towards the market for Tory propaganda and, in his portrayal of women worshippers, reworked several themes that we, today, might more readily associate with witchcraft rather than the Congregational Churches (see Figure 11).[10] The scene is set in a barn that echoes Gabriel Beale's refitting of 'a great barn' or cowshed, in the summer of 1672, so that the Bartletts might preach to the hundreds of townsfolk who wished to hear their sermons.[11] Children play and lounge amid bundles of hay and sheaves of corn, while the faithful – drawn from among all age groups and walks of society – gather to listen to a youthful preacher, who may remind us of the youthful John Bartlett. Some are fixed upon the words of his sermon and a wealthy young woman looks chastely down at her folded hands, lost in contemplation. However, all is not quite what it seems and here is the rub of Laroon's satire; for underneath the veneer of 'godliness' we are given to understand that these are a carnal and hypocritical group intent on inverting social and sexual norms. Thus, the men depicted are either much older, or of a lower social status than the women they accompany: the meek paragon is seated beside a seemingly disinterested elderly yeoman, whose practical homespun clothes contrast starkly with the finery of her tapering bodice and gauze skirt. Elsewhere, a youth who is possibly even a servant uses the pretext of helping another wealthy young lady down onto her stool as an opportunity to lift up her skirts and pat her arse. To the right of the group, yet another young woman squats down upon her launches; her right hand traces out a verse in the Bible even as her skirts are drawn back to reveal a shapely, gartered leg and a pair of pointed shoes set off with ostentatious ribbons. She regards the viewer with a direct, unflinching, shameless gaze, even as the fingers of her left hand slip underneath petticoats and play about her thigh, alleviating her boredom with a casual, if practised, auto-eroticism. Peeking out of the press above her are the features of Titus Oates, the arch-perjurer, copied from another print and clumsily inserted between the other figures. At the time that Laroon was working upon his own illustration, Oates had been sentenced to life imprisonment by Judge Jeffries for his part in fabricating the Popish Plot. In addition, he was to be whipped through the streets of London in order to stand in the pillory for five days each year as an additional punishment, clearly in the hopes that such treatment would kill him.[12] Degraded and thoroughly discredited, his appearance in Laroon's print was an attempt to spread guilt by association and to suggest that all religious dissenters were similarly perjured. Appearances, as we are shown, can deceive – with the mask of virtue hiding nothing but vice.

At the back of the meeting, an older countrywoman wears a tall sugarloaf hat, of the type that we, today, might associate with witches but that, in the 1670s–80s, more accurately denoted a rustic or someone who, through age or poverty, had fallen behind fashion. She fixes the preacher with rapt attention while all around her inappropriate and demeaning behaviour – of the types often associated with

Figure 11 *The Conventicle (British Library). This satirical engraving by Marcellus Laroon the elder was published in 1686 and formed the basis for William Hogarth's later, and better-known, attack on witch-belief. A generation earlier, Laroon's original work showed that religious dissent and hypocrisy could be made analogous to sexual licence, disorder and devilry.*

witches – makes a mock of her own piety and dangerous charlatans out of her fellows.[13] The reactionary charge that 'these zealots' that he had portrayed were as guilty of 'profaneness, debauchery and irreligion' as others but chose to 'hide it under the vizor of hypocrisy' was certainly gaining ground after the collapse of the Oxford Parliament.[14] In the case of Laroon's print, it seemed to matter little that this strong political message was served up alongside exactly the same pornographic content that he was supposedly attempting to critique. Sex sold far beyond any attempt at reasoned argument, as Laroon's printer acknowledged when he sent the 'bawdy' scene to be engraved.[15] A generation later, the composition of the engraving provided William Hogarth with his inspiration for his better-known tilt at the Anglican Church's continued preaching of witch-belief, that was published as *Credulity, Superstition and Fanaticism*. It would appear significant that the form and the polemical edge of Laroon's satire could be so easily switched from religious nonconformists to witches. In this manner, one form of dissonant behaviour was made analogous with another, and both might seem to be a part of a single demonically inspired plot against the realm. What is notable, however, is that none of the group of women who came to be known as the Bideford Witches, nor any of the other women in the town who fell under suspicion of witchcraft in 1682 but were not prosecuted, had anything to do with the conventicles. Rather, even though none of their numerous accusers had been prime movers in the Bartletts' preaching circles, Elizabeth Eastchurch and Dorcas Coleman had been fined for their participation in the mass meeting of May 1674, while William Edwards was a repeat offender, being brought to court and fined twice in the May and June of that year.[16] As a consequence, it is possible that the flurry of accusations of witchcraft in 1671, 1679 and 1682 were the products of one persecuted minority turning, in the midst of a protracted existential crisis, to vent its rage upon another.

It was certainly the case that Bideford's new, Tory, governing class were similarly unsure of themselves and their power to govern. For a start, they were in a numerical minority and cut off from the other section of propertied society that might have provided additional support and expertise through their partisan and religious differences. They were hamstrung by the fact that Bideford, despite its growing size and disproportionate creation of wealth within the county, lacked a parliamentary representative to speak upon its behalf. Furthermore, the Grenville family who had been the lords of the manor since the Middle Ages and founded its maritime trade with the Americas during Queen Elizabeth's reign, had – under John, 1st Earl of Bath (1628–1701) – physically removed themselves from the town, preferring their mansion at Stowe to their town house in Bideford. In taking on the aspect of an absentee landlord, the Earl of Bath created a power vacuum at the apex of Bideford's society which successive Tory mayors, of the stamp of John Davie, Thomas Gist and John Darracott, as the result of their lack of support, talent, tact and social status were entirely ill-equipped to fill. The lack of the Earl's direct input to the town's affairs was particularly unfortunate for Bideford's nascent 'Church and King' party, as John Granville (as he had now began to style himself in point of difference to his ancestors) was uniquely placed to be an effective source of authority on both the county and national stage. The son of a Royalist war hero and martyr, and the close friend from youth of Charles II, Granville had followed his king into exile and been a prominent figure in engineering his Restoration to the throne, through his kinship with General Monck. Every inch the assured courtier, he had shown bravery during the Civil War, being knighted after the bloody storming of Bristol and wounded at the Second Battle of Newbury, but he projected into adulthood the diplomacy of the council chamber rather than the forcefulness of the camp.[17] He knew when to ask for favours from his monarch, and when to hold his peace. In that respect, he was a rare companion at a Whitehall that had become savage and rapacious, and was one of only a few who – over the span of a friendship that lasted for forty years – never managed to lose Charles II's affection and favour. As a result, honours, titles and sinecures regularly flowed towards him. He was ennobled as Baron Grenville of Kilkhampton and Bideford, Viscount Grenville of Landsdowne and the 1st Earl of Bath. Bishop Burnet, who like the Earl of Clarendon thought little of his character and abilities, pithily dismissed him as but 'a mean minded man, who thought of nothing but getting and spending money'. However, this disguises the fact that he was for over four decades the 'crown's most important servant in the West' and, though a distant and disinterested figure as far as Bideford was concerned, represented the primary conduit of the king's will in the battles against republicans, dissenters and Exclusionists who had sought to bar the Duke of York from the throne.[18]

If national and wider county affairs removed him from the day-to-day governance of Bideford, then his quayside home was redecorated – possibly by the elder John Abbott – in the late 1660s with his family's coat of arms and his own, large figurative portrait, resplendent in the modish 'Turkish' waistcoat and long-skirted coat made fashionable by the king. If he was not present, in person, in the town, then at least his image was there to look down from the fireplace on the visitors to his town house. Whereas his ancestors appeared to the people of Bideford primarily as warriors, through the mailed effigies of knights in the parish church or the oil paintings of his father and grandfather as armoured soldiers, John Granville preferred to present a spectacle of wealth and fashionable taste that sat well with Bideford's acquisitive and status conscious civil society. In a similar manner, the Abbotts were put to work fashioning plaster copies of the royal arms for display in county churches as a visible demonstration of the return of the monarchical power, while the Earl showed his own favour towards the new vicar – his friend and client, the Rev. Michael Ogilby – upon his appointment

IACOBUS D.G. MONUME THENSIUM DUX *etc.*

Figure 12 *The King in Waiting? James, Duke of Monmouth, c.1682–5, from an engraving produced in Germany and smuggled into England, through ports like Bideford, for the popular market that celebrated the 'Protestant Prince' (Author's Collection).*

to the parish, in 1674, through bestowing gifts that visibly altered the practice of the giving of communion and sought to physically remove the appearance of the church from its Puritan past. The Norman trough that had been thrown out into the street during the Civil War, and put to use as a pig trough in a backyard, had already been recovered and reinstalled at the Restoration but the Earl of Bath now signalled the triumph of the 1662 model of Anglican church government through the installation of a 'new cedar Communion table', damask tablecloths and napkins, satin and plush cushions, and 'a large Carpett of sky-coloured sattin, with a deep fringe of gold and silk'.[19] His presents to Ogilby included the new chalice, communion dish and flagons, that were hallmarked as being manufactured in London, in 1675, at the Earl's request.[20]

With the church back within the patronage of his family, the Earl was also effective in ensuring that the secular wing of county government was similarly returned to the control of individuals who owed him their advancement and could be counted upon to faithfully implement the policies of the king and the fledgling Tory party.[21] The passing of the Conventicle Act, in 1670, struck at the freedom of worship enjoyed by Protestant Dissenters and handed the mayor and common council of Bideford sweeping new powers to stamp out the congregational churches that thrived within their midst. The act specifically linked religious and political radicalism and aimed to curtail 'the growing and dangerous practices of seditious sectaries and other disloyal persons, who under pretence of tender consciences have or may at their meetings contrive insurrections'. Henceforth, the 'meeting under any colour or pretence of any exercise of religion in other manner than according to the liturgy and practice of the Church of England' was to be banned, while the gathering together of five or more people 'in a house, field or place where there is no family inhabiting' or in an 'outhouse, barn, yard or backside' was also to be strictly prohibited.[22] The legislation had a savagely unpleasant genius to it, in that while local government could not hope to accommodate the large number of people criminalized by its terms in prison, it could aim to break the financial power of the dissenting communities and drive the most active participants in the conventicles to ruin and poverty through the levying of large fines. In this respect, it not only saved the government of Charles II prison costs but actually acted as a revenue generator for it, through the fines levied on the highly productive 'middling sort' who formed the backbone of the nonconformist movement. Thus, John Hill – the town clerk, who would later note down the evidences lodged against the Bideford Witches – wrote that he was 'preparing a scorpion according to the statute' and wished 'the coercive power' well in the hopes that it would smart and sting the 'obstinate'.[23] It did not take much pressure from above, or the promptings of the Rev. Eaton, to prompt the borough council of Bideford to swing into action against its resident dissenter community, with the mayor, Robert Boole, repeatedly deploying the town constables in order to raid and break up prayer meetings. On 19 June 1670, Robert Wren and two other constables, together with a churchwarden, obtained a search warrant for the home of Sarah Dennis after they presented evidence to the mayor of what they had heard while 'standing & listening' outside the front door of her house. Upon returning and gaining entry they saw:

> Mr. John Bartlett a young Minister sittinge at the higher end of the table with a little Booke [presumably the Bible or an edition of the psalms] in his hand. Assembled together Besides the said Mr. Bartlett [and] the said Sarah Dennis, [were] Susanna Dennis, her sister and some of there family in Bideford & alsoe one Samuel Johns of Bideford ... yeoman, Agnes Duillam, the wife of Edward Duillam of the same towne, mariner, Elizabeth Matthews of Bideford ... spinster, and one John Shorte of the Parish of Littleham in the County of Devon.[24]

Though, in the event, the front door of the house had been readily opened up to them, Wren had been anxious that 'None within the same house might Escape' and had sent two more constables to watch the back of the house. Unable to hear anything within they forced an entry which later in the day, before the mayor, they appear to have been overly anxious to explain away.[25] Each of those attending was, on 8 July 1670, fined by the mayor the sum of five shillings – as set out in the act – with John Bartlett fined an additional £20 for preaching and Sarah Dennis fined a further £20 'for willingly and wittingly suffer[ing] the said preaching and meeting to be in her ... house [and] shee being present thereat'.[26] Now, £20 was the equivalent in the late seventeenth century to the average yearly wage – if we think of it representing some £25,000 in today's money, we would not be far off – and this clearly threatened Sarah Dennis with ruin. Finding herself 'agreed by the Conviction ... and the levying of the Penalty ...

upon my goods and chattels', she lodged an appeal at the next quarter sessions and unlike almost all of her fellow accused does not appear to have reoffended.[27] In her case, the act appears to have been effective as either a deterrent towards her continued dissent or a deadly blow that pauperized her and precluded further religious and political activism. That her co-accused, and the large numbers that followed them into the Bideford courtroom over the next fifteen years, do not seem to have registered similar appeals may reflect upon the outright rejections of such claims by the governing authorities; the extreme recalcitrance of those convicted; or their wealth and ability to pay. What is remarkable is the resolve of Bideford's dissenters over this period to risk arrest, imprisonment and bankruptcy for the sake of their religious beliefs.

Despite the frequency of these raids and convictions that, at times, almost seemed routine occurrences in the governance of the town, the dissenting community refused to bow to the pressure and continued to gather together, often in considerable numbers, in order to hold the illegal prayer meetings in their homes. Indeed, some of those arraigned were serial offenders who were prepared – and clearly able – to pay these fines time and time again. Foremost among these were Samuel Johns, a yeoman, Susan Davy, a 'widow', and Gabriel Beale, a master potter, who seem to have provided the leadership for the underground movement that was soon looking towards political remedies, through the Earl of Shaftesbury's Whigs, the Green Ribbon Clubs and even the Dutch and the Duke of Monmouth's partisans, to religious problems. Defiance of the existing order, after being first taken, can often become a habit driving forward through its own form of radicalism and political realization; and having set aside the respectable cloak of their past lives (Beale's father had, after all, been mayor in 1658; Johns seems very conscious of his social status; and Davy risked being branded as a virago), these two men and one woman appear to have devoted themselves, and their considerable personal fortunes, to the service of the town's nonconformist community.[28]

Not every attempt at persecution worked or had the effects that the authorities had expected. John Budd a London upholsterer, described as being 'a dangerous Quaker refusing to take the oath of Allegiance' to the king, had already been prosecuted at the Dorchester Assizes in 1673, when he was apprehended in Bideford and sent under guard to 'the Common Gaol' at Exeter Castle. However, on the way he managed to slip away from his escort and effected a successful escape to the palpable anger of the town council, who attempted to prosecute one of his guards for aiding and abetting his flight.[29] Though his family appears to have hailed from Martock, near Yeovil, and his kinsman Thomas Budd, a former Baptist minister who left his settled parish at the calling of an inner light and was frequently prosecuted for his Quaker beliefs in the West Country; the Society of Friends appears to have made few inroads in Bideford, itself.[30] The dominant force of the Bartletts appeared to have effectively united nonconformity in the town around their own Congregational Church, satisfying those religious impulses that sat outside an engagement with the 1662 Prayer and Anglican ritual, and leaving little room or reason for Protestant dissenters to look elsewhere for sustenance.[31] If John Budd was the only Quaker positively identified in Bideford during this period, then he was functioning within a much wider movement that sought to resist the encroachment of Stuart power and his flight suggests that the policing powers of the authorities in Bideford and across the wider county were not as extensive, or as infallible, as they had believed.

As early as May 1674, the mayor and common council had felt themselves to be in danger of losing control of the governance of the town, as the Bartletts citing their licenses to preach under a recent dispensation, had held a prayer meeting openly at the house of Gabriel Beale, which was attended by a great crowd of people and brought the constables running. However, what they found there shattered their illusions about their ability to coerce the townspeople through force. Six constables, two sergeants at mace and one of the churchwardens had been despatched by the mayor, the old Royalist, Abraham Heiman, to take the names of everyone present but they soon lost count as they estimated there were around 400 men and women present, 'most of them of this Towne, and divers of severall parishes adjacent'.[32] Father and son brandished their licenses to preach, dated two years earlier, in the faces of the sergeants, as the crowds jostled and catcalled them, and William Bartlett:

> told the said officers, that he preacht there by the same authority that constituted the Mayor to be Mayor of this Towne, or words to this purpose, and soe proceeded on his sermon, and very few (if any) of his auditors did leave the place, untill Mr. Bartlett had ended his sermon.[33]

Dumbfounded, the little posse beat a retreat to the town hall and proceeded to work on a list for the mayor setting down the names of around 200 inhabitants of Bideford that they had positively identified at the meeting. Heiman, too, was at a loss as to how to proceed, as the local authorities appeared caught between two differing sets of licence and legislation issued by central government; the former to grant dispensations to particular preachers and the latter to continue breaking up prayer circles wherever they were found. After some deliberation, Heiman had the town recorder take down a letter dictated by himself and other members of the common council begging the Earl of Bath to provide them with clear advice and direction. The answer, when it finally arrived in June 1674, seems to have been a sanction for further persecution with 129 individuals being fined for attending the mass meeting and a decision being taken to target, in particular, the leaders of the movement: namely, William and John Bartlett, as subversive ministers, and Gabriel Beale and Samuel Johns as the pillars of their support. The disturbances of 19 May 1674 had demonstrated the popular appeal of the Bartletts as preachers and also the resolve of Gabriel Beale to convert his own house 'into a meeting place' for dissenters where they might worship openly. This was a blatant challenge to the local authorities, in the form of Abraham Heiman, and also to the terms of the Conventicle Act, framed by Charles II's Cabal of Ministers who, in the spring of 1674, were in the process of tearing themselves apart. The house, itself, was likely to have been the large property on the Washcombe Road left by Gabriel's father, in the terms of his will, the year before, though he owned and rented other houses across the northern, potter's quarter of town. Whatever the case, the fact that it was thought capable of accommodating even a portion of the hundreds of townsfolk who flocked to hear the Bartletts preach is a further indication of Gabriel Beale's success and standing within the town. Without such resources he could not have survived, yet alone seemingly flourished, against the wall of court summons and fines that assailed him over the course of some fifteen years. In July 1674, he was once more fined, together with Samuel Johns and William and John Bartlett, and while the elder Bartlett successfully evaded another attempt at capture, his son was not so fortunate.[34] Seized by the parish constables and dragged off under guard to prison in Exeter, John Bartlett described the conditions of his imprisonment and the attentions of a Tory mob to his wife in an, unfortunately, undated, letter:

We came into Exeter, yesterday, in the afternoon, and were carried up
Northgate Street and down along High Street, through Westgate, multitudes
of rude people gathering about us and flouting us at their pleasure. I bless
the Lord I was as cheerful as ever. Oh, how small a matter is to be reproached
by worms, when respected by the Lord! We were carried out to Saint
Thomas's parish, and at last brought to the prison and carried in, but stayed
there not long, till Mr. Greenhill Weeks ordered our removal to an inn near
by, where we were, having a sentinel to our chamber door.[35]

His imprisonment, combined with spending much of his adult life on the run
from the authorities, and a spell standing in the pillories in Stoke Cannon and
Exeter, broke John Bartlett's health and he died in September 1679. His
heartbroken father gave an emotional eulogy over his grave and did not long
outlive him, dying in 1682.[36] Their passing deprived Bideford's underground
community of dissenters of their natural leaders at a crucial point in the run-up
to the witch trials, denying them the secure sense of authority and purpose that
had seen them through the plague of 1646 – when temporal and spiritual power
had acted as one – and leaving them effectively rudderless in the face of increasing
assaults by the town's judiciary. By the spring of 1682, Shaftesbury and Monmouth
had been stripped of office and driven into exile, Parliament dissolved, and the
boroughs that had served as the bastions of opposition to the Crown were falling
like ninepins, due to the recall of their charters, thanks to the skill of established
county governors – like the Earl of Bath – and a new generation of shrewd,
ambitious and highly politicized lawyers – such as Sir George Jeffreys, Sir Thomas
Raymond and Sir Francis North – who were there to do Charles II's bidding and
reap the rewards. It was the high-water mark of Tory fortune, unthinkable a
decade earlier in terms of its scope and sweeping success in the crushing of
dissent, the accruing of power to the monarchy and the acceptance that the next
king, in all probability, would be a proselytizing Roman Catholic. In April 1682,
the Grand Jury of Devonshire, now packed with the Earl of Bath's chosen men,
had sent an order to the Justices of the Peace and 'chief magistrates' in the
borough towns, including Bideford, that signalling its resolve 'to proceed in the
method we have begun' in order to destroy the conventicles and to ensure that no
one, in a freshly purged local government, would think to:

shelter from justice any of those people who are professed enemies of the King and his government, but more particularly we desire them to deliver up to us those ungrateful monsters (Nonconformist ministers we mean), who in the late rebellion preached up sedition-treason, and who, we have reason to believe, endeavour to debauch the people with the same doctrines still.[37]

Thomas Lamplugh, the High Tory Bishop of Exeter, had already written with glowing pride to the Secretary of State at Whitehall about the purge of the Justices of the Peace in Devon and of the efficacy of legislation in the 'suppressing of seditious meetings, [that] will check the insolency of Fanatics and reduce the people, who are misled to order and conformity'.[38] The continual attrition of the fines for attending illegal religious meetings certainly had the effect of tipping some of Bideford's radicals over into poverty and want but, in the case of Gabriel Beale and Samuel Johns, it also seems to have reinforced a sense of pride in separateness and the ability to demonstrate the economic power of the 'Middling Sort' through the repeated flouting of the law and the paying of fines. It was certainly the case that Bideford's dissenting community remained unbroken and unbowed in spite of everything that was thrown against it in the 1670s–80s and that it seems to have increasingly acted as an umbrella group for a number of interlocking movements and causes, including the radical political underground and the Duke of Monmouth's partisans. Indeed, in the summer of 1683, we find Robert Davy bound over for using 'seditious language' while his house was being ransacked by the parish constables on the hunt for evidence that he was linked to a potential rising, while Margaret Johnson was similarly charged for her own sedition against the Crown.[39] Both the swearing of the oath of allegiance to the Crown and the established church, enforced by the town council on 15 June 1682 – at precisely the time that Hill and Gist were forwarding the prosecution of the suspected witches – and a further clampdown against 'the seditious practices of certaine phanatikes', pushed by Hill and Gearing in October 1682, seem to be indices of Tory concern about the strength of opposition within the town.[40] Even then, John Hill was grudgingly forced to admit that the oath of allegiance was 'generally' but not wholeheartedly taken in Bideford.[41]

After two decades, Bideford's religious dissenters and political radicals seem to have been able to bear the weight of external persecution with fortitude, grit and – on occasion – even insouciance. What did damage their self-confidence and cohesion were the twin hammer blows of the deaths of the Bartletts, which created a moral, political and theocratic vacuum at the centre of the town's nonconformist politics that lasted from 1682 to 1698.[42] William Bartlett was succeeded by John Bowden, who had been ejected from his living in the nearby parish of Littleham by the Clarendon Codes. It seems that he had been active in the underground preaching community in Bideford for some time but, in 1682, he invited James Wood – a minister and author of a book of spiritual allegories who had held the rectory at Mintown, Tipperary – to join him as his assistant, in the town. This seems to have been a disastrous appointment, as Wood brought with him an Irish serving girl whom he kept as his mistress.[43] When he refused to marry her, she revealed their affair to Bideford's 'godly', provoking a storm of fury and consternation that resulted in a schism among the Congregationalists. Though the scandal broke in 1694, when it was the subject of public debate of the Exeter Assembly, the allegations had circulated for some time and Wood seems to have been a divisive figure, while Bowden never enjoyed the complete confidence of Bideford's dissenters.[44] Thus, at the moment when the charges erupted against the witches, the 'godly' party within the town was experiencing, at best, a period of introspection and uncertainty and, at worst, was actively turning in upon itself. Neither John Bowden nor James Wood was capable of providing any kind of effective leadership and, in their stead, the activists who organized the meetings of the conventicles took over and drew in other preachers, whom they trusted, from outside the town.[45] Unattuned to the cries of the poor, yet similarly marginalized, Bideford's dissenters understood relative but not absolute poverty, wished to impose a strict reformation of manners and morality upon a dissolute town but lacked even a toehold upon its government, and were compromised by scandals brewing in their own midst. Through their millenarian language and knowledge of the Old Testament they looked for evidence of an imminent God struggling in a daily battle with the Devil to temper and try his people in order that they might know and experience His will upon earth, and experience His glory in the everlasting life thereafter. However, in the spring of 1682, there were few providences to be discerned and many troubles to be weathered. It was no longer clear just who in their midst should be punished and who they should seek to preserve.

4

The cat, the pig and the poppet

Thomas Eastchurch had lost control of his own household. It was a hard, and even shameful, thing to admit but that was the rub of it. The marriage that should have enhanced his status within the town was, within a matter of months, threatening him with disgrace and ruin. Elizabeth, his wife, had come from a well-connected family and her father, Christopher Thomas, styled himself as a 'gentleman' of the parish. Thomas Eastchurch had made his money through trade and was unduly sensitive about his background and the perceived imbalance in their social positioning. Consequently, following his marriage, Thomas Eastchurch made sure that he signed himself as a 'gentleman', too.[1] Yet, respectability always seemed to be eluding him, slipping through his grasp and paining him through its absence and the consequences of its pursuit. Rather than the bounty of children and stability, marriage had given him the care of an invalid sister-in-law and a surprisingly independent wife. No one appears to have been particularly happy about the arrangement, not least the sickly, troubled and troubling Grace Thomas. If her sister, outwardly at least, had conformed to the expectations of a patriarchal society, then – under its terms – Grace was a singular failure. Despite the promise of an adequate dowry, whether on account of her looks, her illnesses, or her temperament, she had been unable to succeed in the pursuit of a husband that, in the Early Modern period, did so much to define a woman's life, function and social class. Denied the material comfort and enhanced status that a good – or indeed any – marriage might have brought her, Grace Thomas resigned herself to the life of a dependant:

first in her parents' home, and then in that of her married sister. Though it seems that she was close to both her sister and her brother-in-law, who provided and cared for her as best they could, there is evidence that she did not submit to this role as a meek subordinate, quietly or with any particular relish.

When the Anglican Church attempted to enforce a narrow and highly proscriptive brand of religious conformity through the law courts, she and her sister attended prayer meetings held in private houses and listened to banned preachers. They were observed by the parish constables among the crowds that thronged Gabriel Beale's house to hear the Bartletts speak, in May 1674. Their names were taken, they were brought before the magistrates and fined. In terms of their youth, their gender and their marital status (at that time), they appeared representative of the Bideford women who through their defiant participation sustained the conventicle movement through more than twenty years of

Figure 13 *Memento Mori: the angels looking down from Abraham Heiman's monument would have been newly carved and painted when Temperance Lloyd was brought to St Mary's Church and forced to recite the Lord's Prayer (Author's Photograph, by kind permission of the Rector & Parish Council, St Mary's Church, Bideford).*

repression. This brush with the law seems to have done nothing to dampen their religious principles, and it appears that Grace Thomas, thereafter, fell within the social and preaching circle of Francis Hann (who was also known as 'Hanne' or 'Hamme'), a low church minister unofficially attached to St Mary's as curate.

Yet all was not seemly, or as it seemed. There was something not quite right about Hann, in terms of his ministry, his conduct and his biography. His identity – both then and now – is frequently muddled, despite his holding the living of St Michael and All Angels, in Loxbeare, from 1663 to 1691.[2] Though he had been an independent preacher during the Commonwealth and Protectorate, and benefitted considerably from the patronage of the local Puritan gentry (including Alexander Popham and Daniel Cudmore) and the popular support of local nonconformists (such as Grace Thomas and Elizabeth Eastchurch), he did not figure in the wealth of celebratory literature written, after the passing of the Toleration Act in 1689, in order to commemorate the sufferings of the faithful. He was also absent from the accounts of the Bartletts and the histories of the Congregational Church in Bideford. Why, then, did Hann leave such a superficial imprint on the records? Why did he choose to devote his attention to ministering at Bideford rather than at his own parish, more than thirty miles (or two days' journey) away? And what he was doing there? These silences suggest concealment or duplicity and we are left with the sense that he, just like Grace Thomas and the three Bideford Witches, occupied a marginal and less than comfortable role within the life of the town. Bishop Thomas Lamplugh clearly wanted him removed not just from Bideford but his entire diocese and described him as 'a taylor by trade, a preacher under Cromwell and one who scarce understands common sense'.[3] It seems that Francis Hann was ordained in the relatively short window between 1660 and 1662, before the penal codes began to bite, and that he was prepared to reach an accommodation with Royalism in both its political and religious forms in order to accept ordination by a prelate. He did not fall foul of the Test or Conventicle Acts, although Bishop Lamplugh suspected him on other grounds, as he attempted to clamp down on the behaviour of his own clergy in the late 1670s and early 1680s.[4] He was, thought the bishop, marked by a 'lewdness of life, [and] is guilty of marrying several persons clandestinely'.[5] This latter charge resurfaced throughout his career alongside charges brought against him by his own parishioners, in

Loxbeare, for drunken and bawdy conduct. In 1677, he had been brought before ecclesiastical courts for a range of derelictions of duty, including not using, or altering, the *Book of Common Prayer*, and for his neglect of services and festivals. As a consequence, he was suspended from his post as the rector of Loxbeare.[6] By the summer of 1682, fresh accusations – over his beliefs rather than his behaviour – threatened to strip him of his preaching licence, while the enduring hostility of Loxbeare towards him made Bideford seem like a welcome sanctuary. He had found a kindred spirit in its parson for, after the death of the harsh and vindictive Rev. Eaton in 1674, the living had passed, through the Earl of Bath's patronage to Michael Ogilby, a man of an altogether different stamp.[7]

Ogilby, a Scotsman used to the extremes of confessional conflict, was in many respects emblematic of generational change during the Restoration period. He was the young son of an aristocratic family and the Earl of Bath enjoyed his company and conversation, over and above any consideration of his piety. Upon taking up his residency in Bideford, Ogilby used the last of the parish's profits from the anthracite mines to rebuild and beautify the parsonage, adding 'new made gardens' to his evident pride and delight.[8] He seems to have been something of a free-thinker, a Cartesian and possessed a wry cynicism that expressed itself when he unexpectedly met with one of his parishioners in the street. Ogilby, knowing full well that the man was a dissenter and friend to the Bartletts, tackled him with his failure to attend Anglican services:

> 'Faith,' said the man, 'I can read the prayers at home, and as the sermons, I have much better ones to read than you ever preach.' 'You are right,' replied the parson, 'and I wish all my parishioners were of the same opinion, for then I should have little or nothing to do.'[9]

Unfortunately, having little to do seems to have been one of Ogilby's aims in life. Though cultured, he was relaxed in his attitude towards doctrine and ritual, and was both rapacious and phenomenally lazy. Within the context of Bideford in the 1670s–80s, this was an especially disastrous combination of personality traits. His friendship with Francis Hann was founded on two pillars: the first was their shared love of the bottle and the second was Ogilby's need for someone to take on all the onerous aspects of running the parish that he did not want. Indeed, the criticisms of the two men by their respective parishioners, at Bideford and Loxbeare, were remarkably similar. It was alleged that Ogilby was 'a very great drinker, and immoderate lover of wine and strong drink' who 'has been very many times guilty of profane and dreadful swearing'. Moreover, townsfolk felt that he had broken custom 'by demanding, extorting and receiving ... from several of the inhabitants and parishioners, unreasonable, immoderate, and unjust fees or sums of money for marrying, baptising and burials'.[10] The contrast with the temperate, commanding and studious presence of William and John Bartlett could not have been starker; and there was little chance that when faced by such a strong Presbyterian challenge to his authority he would ever be capable of showing either the example or the dedication needed to win back hearts and minds. In the event, he managed to alienate and enrage both dissenting Whigs and Anglican Tories. He was certainly not trusted by the town council and, in particular, by John Hill who made sure that the provisions of the Test Acts and oaths of allegiance were publicly applied to him.[11] His authority appears to have been frequently challenged by his own congregation, who registered their disapproval of Anglican rites and their forced attendance at services by refusing to doff their hats and heckling the rector during his sermons.[12]

On the opposite side of the religious and political divide, he also clashed violently with the town clerk, the High Anglican and Tory, John Hill who had been the chief persecutor of the town's dissenters. After morning prayers, on Sunday 8 October 1679, Rev. Ogilby caught up with Hill as he was leaving St Mary's and 'did rail and bestow very much ... unchristian language upon the said John Hill, holding out his staff, threatening and assaulting him therewith'.[13] The two men loathed one another on a personal level but there was also the sense that Hill disapproved of both the rector's friendship with Hann and his continuing reticence in informing upon dissenters within the parish.[14] He certainly intended to ruin him, and his hand was behind the lengthy charge sheet that detailed eight separate accusations brought before the Bishop of Exeter. These ranged from the failure to make a collection for the English captives held as slaves in Turkey, to charging for marrying, baptizing and burying his parishioners, being 'a lover of wine and strong drinks', and the common assault upon the town clerk. He was said to have permitted excommunicated clergymen (presumably Francis Hann and the other excluded preachers at large in the town) to administer the sacraments; and to have 'for the space of three or fower years past hath been much given to raylings and vilifying the Clergy in the County of Devon and Magistrates of Bideford.'[15] Clearly, Ogibly possessed both an impulse towards toleration and an explicit critique of the town's Tory elite. In order to hammer home the point and help secure a conviction from the bishop's court in Exeter, Hill added that:

> the said Mr. Ogilby did say and utter many unbecoming words against the Revd. Father in God Thomas [Lamplugh] Lord Bishopp of Exon his Surrogate and Revd. Clergy belonging to the Cathedral Church saying they should not order him to putt any Curate into his Church, and swearing oftimes in a very profane manner that they were knaves or words to this purpose or effect.[16]

While Hill attempted to pursue Ogilby through the ecclesiastical courts, the carnival-like atmosphere continued at the parsonage with only one serious check. In September 1680, Ogilby's wife, Letitia died, casting a pall over the rectory and further removing his thoughts from the everyday concerns of his parishioners. His ministry had always been characterized by leeway and licence, and this had suited Hann well, permitting him to expand his role as curate, taking services and continuing with his profitable trade in the sale of semi-official marriage licences.[17] Nature, after all, abhors a vacuum. And, as a result of the yawning gap that Ogilby's lack of leadership left in the spiritual fabric of Bideford it was possible for Francis Hann to grow his own profile and authority in the parish. Thus, he was there to first support Grace Thomas, and then subsequently Thomas and Elizabeth Eastchurch, during a time of protracted crisis in a way that Michael Ogilby simply could not.

Quite what Thomas Eastchurch made of the potentially dangerous religious beliefs held by his wife and sister-in-law is hard to gauge. From the available evidence he seems to have held Tory, or at least strongly monarchist, sympathies. He would sign Bideford's 'Loyal Address' to Charles II in 1683, expressing his horror at the republican Rye House Plot which had allegedly sought the king's life, and would be one of the first in the town to rush to proclaim his loyalty to James II on his accession to the throne in 1685. Such behaviour does not appear consistent with an individual who was simply trying to provide a veneer of respectability to his household, or to throw up a smokescreen to hide his own true feelings alongside the activities of his wife and her sister. Rather, this status conscious businessman, happy with the concept of a Divine Right monarchy, found himself destined to spend his life in the company of two women who held religious and political opinions that were diametrically opposed to his own.[18] We cannot now hope to know if this made for interesting debates over the dinner table, or if it had a steadily worsening effect upon the state of his marriage. What we do know, however, is that it ensured that his household was far from at ease with itself. Furthermore, like most of those who played a part in formulating the charges against the Bideford Witches, he, too, was no stranger to brushes with the law. Indeed, at the very time his sister-in-law was taken ill, in October 1681, he found himself charged with committing a series of – sadly for us – unspecified offences outside the home of one Maria Adverts, on Bideford High Street. No action ever appears to have been taken against him, but the intriguing possibilities as to what these 'offences' actually consisted of serves to open up all kinds of avenues of unprovable conjecture. Were they political? Was he really, despite it all, no friend to the House of Stuart? Were they sexual? Could Maria have been his mistress, or simply a woman he bothered and pestered for favours? Or, was he just a plain, troublesome and angry man, given to drink, swearing, and brawling in the gutter, proving a plain nuisance to honest householders trying to get a night's sleep? In the light of this evidence, we can suggest that in a particularly litigious town, rife with political, religious and commercial enmity, he and his immediate family were all too well aware that, despite all their social climbing, they were not trusted and certainly, in some quarters, were far from being liked.[19]

Ailing, unmarried and representing a strain upon her sister's own marriage, Grace Thomas could not fail to have been anxious about her own position and her eventual fate. Moreover, the shifting sands of religious conformity had ensured that her own low church brand of Protestantism, which had been successfully accommodated within the Elizabethan settlement and had emerged triumphant from the Civil Wars, had since the return of the monarchy come to be seen as being the preserve of the lower orders and political radicals. Presbyterianism, as Charles II is once held to have sniffed to the Earl of Lauderdale, was 'not a religion for gentleman'.[20] This sense of being somewhat outside the mainstream of Bideford society, on account of her marital status, economic dependency and religious convictions, can have done little to imbibe Grace with a sense of self-worth and well-being.[21] Indeed, it is one of the many ironies bound up in this case that, in some respects, Grace Thomas was just as marginal a woman in the eyes of many of the townsfolk as the Bideford Witches, whom she came to fear, to despise, and to equate with the root of all her own misfortunes and ailments. What did separate them, driving an insurmountable gulf between them, were their respective positions as – on one side – a deserving, morally upright woman, with friends and family to take care of her; set against the notion of the undeserving poor, who were entirely without morals, friends and kindred, upon the other. It was this difference in perception of women who were suffering from many of the same problems caused by their age, gender, and dependency upon the goodwill and charity of others, that gave rise to the mutual recriminations and suspicions that would eventually coalesce around the notion that witchcraft was at play in the town.

For the time being, however, Grace Thomas knew only that she was sick and unlikely to any get better. She had first been afflicted at the beginning of February 1681, when she was 'taken with great Pains in her Head and all her Limbs'.[22] These pains continued unabated until the beginning of August, when she began to feel strong enough to leave her brother-in-law's house and go for walks in the neighbourhood 'to take the Air'. However, with the onset of evening – or the 'Night-Season' as she termed it – her symptoms returned, she found herself 'in much pain' and could not sleep.[23] The 'Country Physicians' called in to help by her family could offer neither diagnosis nor remedy, further adding to her unease about the seemingly inexplicable condition that had, effectively, ruined her life. At least her summertime walks through the town provided her with an interest, some colour and a measure of exercise, away from the confinements of her chamber and the well-meaning attentions of the Eastchurches' servant girl, and her few friends. Yet, even this small joy was soon taken from her in a manner that was as unexpected as it was unsettling.

On Thursday, 30 September 1681, she had been going for her usual walk when, turning to go into the High Street, she was accosted by Temperance Lloyd, the old beggar woman. Despite having no previous relationship with one another and probably no more than a nodding acquaintance based upon a vague knowledge of each other's identity and reputation in the town,

Temperance now showed a great familiarity towards the recovering invalid that seemed far from appropriate, or becoming, in the eyes of all who witnessed it. She fell down upon her knees and prostrated herself at Grace's feet, weeping and crying out to her: 'I am glad to see you so strong again.' Taken aback and confused as to why a virtual stranger – Lloyd could have known little about her personal circumstances as she referred to her as 'Mrs. Grace' throughout their conversation – Miss Thomas asked her: 'Why dost thou weep for me?' At this, the widow woman looked up and said that it was because 'I am so glad to see you again'. Still startled and not knowing what to think, Grace hastened to end the conversation, stepped round her and hurried off on her way down the High Street, anxious that she should not be followed or opportuned again.[24] Nothing more was said, Temperance Lloyd had not threatened her, nor even asked her for charity. It seems probable that the old woman had thought to ingratiate herself with a woman of higher social status who, as the whole of Bideford knew, had suffered a misfortune with the breakdown in her health. She may have hoped to offer words of comfort, as best she could, in order to strike up an acquaintance and to be rewarded, in time, for her consideration and solicitude with a little food or the odd coin. In this she fatally miscalculated. The sudden manner of her approach, her coarseness of manner, and her tear-stained and dirty face, suddenly thrust into that of a nervous and delicate woman, produced entirely the opposite results from those that she had intended. Instead of comfort, she had created a sense of fear and a fear that grew worse, and was magnified, with every step Grace Thomas took away from her along the cobbles of the High Street.

This brings us to the framing of the request for the charity of strangers. As the academics brought together by Hartley Dean, in a volume detailing the conditions and perceptions of modern beggars, suggest that the poverty of the petitioner can be expressed actively or passively, through aggressive words and actions, or by mute gesture and abasement. This significance of the direct, face-to-face encounter upon which successful begging relies is, therefore, extremely subjective and the encounters engendered by street level economic activity 'exemplifies in extremis certain processes by which any one of us may fuel the creation of another's self-identity'.[25] Temperance Lloyd seems to have attempted to show kindness, concern and meekness towards her social superior.

Unfortunately, Grace Thomas read into her behaviour premeditated malice, intrusion and over-familiarity.[26] Her attempt at over-wrought deference failed in its object as it appeared as a sudden attack, emphasizing the gulf that separated the lives and perceptions of the two women, and thereby 'unbalancing everyone'.[27] It was to be the last time Grace Thomas would walk freely about the town for many months to come.

That evening, she fell sick 'with sticking pricking pains, as though Pins and Awls [slender needle-like implements used by bodice makers] had been thrust into her Body, from the Crown of her Head to the Soles of her Feet' and lay awake all night 'as though [she] had been upon a Rack'.[28] The coming of the dawn brought only partial relief, as the 'pricking Pains' continued and she was confined to her bed.[29] As first the days passed by, and then weeks lengthened into months, without relief from – or explanation for – her sufferings, the invalid had plenty of time to wonder if there was not some unnatural ill afflicting her and, by extension, her brother-in-law's household. The brief conversation with Temperance Lloyd stuck in her mind and was constantly replayed with, each time a more sinister interpretation placed upon the old woman's manner and words. Grace's room became her whole world, and any change in its order or appearance now seemed strange and unsettling. On Thursday, 1 June 1682, her symptoms worsened again as the light began to fade and Honor Hooper lit candles about the house. Fearing for her life, her extended family gathered about her and prepared themselves for another sleepless night at her side. However, there was little that they, the serving girl or Anne Wakely could do when the shooting, stabbing pains came again and her cries rent the night air. For close on two hours, she was paralysed:

> bound and seemingly chain'd up, with all of her sticking Pains gathered together in her Belly; so that [all of] a sudden her Belly was swol[e]n as big as two Bellies, which caused her to cry out, *I shall die, I shall die*.[30]

Her sister and her brother-in-law prepared themselves for the worst, and the physician pronounced himself at a loss to explain or to cure. All they could do was wait for the end. Yet, death did not come to the Eastchurch house that night. As daylight stole into the chamber, Grace rallied somewhat but with every dusk and dawn that came after, the pattern repeated itself with the respective waxing and waning of the stabbing pains that set her skin on fire. The household attempted to adjust to her needs, and began to evolve a routine whereby Anne Wakely and Honor Hooper would watch over her during her nightly torments.

Then, on Friday, 23 June 1682, a child's doll was discovered perched on Grace's bed. It would not normally have seemed such a sinister discovery but the introduction of a toy associated with joy, children and motherhood into a private space marked by pain, a barren womb and a single life seemed uncomfortable and almost cruel in its pathos. Initially, no one knew how it came to be there until someone – perhaps Thomas Eastchurch, himself – remembered that a tabby (or 'Braget') cat had scampered into his shop, snatched up a doll and darted away up the stairs with the poppet hanging limply from out of its mouth.[31] Whether the doll was one of the items for sale in Eastchurch's shop, or if it had been abandoned by a forgetful little girl, is unclear from our sources. What is certain, however, is that the incident was now connected, in the minds of the extended family, with the appearance of the same cat on the day that Grace Thomas had met with Temperance Lloyd and taken sick. The worsening of her condition appeared linked, in some manner, to the animal's comings and goings, and its ability to leap in and out of Thomas Eastchurch's shop. Moreover, in depositing the image of a human female on the sick woman's bed, the cat had seemed to be threatening her life and enacting a sinister ritual that appeared to be at the root cause of her sufferings. The image and the reality now became linked: with the doll appearing as the mummet on which a harmful magic could be worked upon Grace's body. Where no explanation for her illness had existed before, now one did. And it was witchcraft.

Grace's symptoms grew in their intensity once again but, on the morning of Thursday 29 June, she was evidently strong enough, though badly bruised and still bloated, to wash and to venture downstairs for breakfast. The suspicion of witchcraft was now preying on the minds of all those in the Eastchurch house and they dreaded the coming again of the 'Braget' cat and the unpredictable evil that it seemed to bring in its wake. If the doll had been associated with Grace as the victim, then the cat – which prowled the same derelict properties, back alleys and waste grounds as the scavenging poor – had become associated with the appearance and behaviour of the beggar woman. Yet, even in the midst of their fears, there were still domestic chores to be done. Rubbing the sleep from their eyes, Grace's friend, Anne, and the serving girl, Honor, roused themselves and used the few minutes available to them to try to air the invalid's musty chamber and to freshen her rumpled and soiled bedding. Consequently, it was at precisely this moment – when taut nerves had just started to relax, equilibrium seemed to have been restored to the household and tiredness was about to take a welcome hold upon them – that the magpie chose to make his unexpected appearance and to throw everything into fresh turmoil.[32]

The sudden commotion caused by the startled bird flapping wildly around the chamber, and by the screams and shouts of the two women above, ended Grace Thomas's brief respite from pain. The stabbing and needling jabs returned, shooting through her nerve endings and shattering all that was left of her fragile peace of mind. Since her unpleasant encounter, the previous September, the beggar woman's words, and her contorted, tear-stained face had increasingly sat uneasy within her waking thoughts. With the intrusions of the cat, the doll and the magpie heralding the sudden uncanny appearance of Temperance Lloyd, in the street and at her door, it was no short leap of the imagination for Grace Thomas to conclude that she was suffering not from a normal illness, but from a savage enchantment and that this had been effected through the use of a witch's familiar spirit (a demon in animal form) and the use of the poppet to direct the stabbing pains and pricks onto particular parts of her body. Her fevered speculations might have ended there and been waved away by Thomas Eastchurch, like the smoke from the last night's candles, had it not been for one thing: Temperance Lloyd had been infamous, for more than ten years, in Bideford, as a malignant, and possibly even murderous, witch.

Such a reputation took many years to develop, but once it had attached itself and began to grow, like a moth trapped and beating upon the inner ear, it took hold in the minds of the townspeople of Bideford and proved impossible to dislodge. Tale built upon tale, and inference upon inference, before fear of the strange old woman began to mingle with the general contempt. Yet, for Temperance Lloyd, the changing attitude of her neighbours was perhaps not without its advantages. Having spent all of her life without any sense of power at all – whether physical, sexual, political or even domestic – she was gradually invested by those around her with a reputation for being able to harm with a look, and to curse with a mere word that was, undoubtedly, perversely empowering. That her social superiors who had previously ignored, or looked down upon her, were now compelled to fear her and to avoid her gaze in the street could not but have struck her as an unexpected, grimly pleasing and potentially profitable development. It is clear from her testimony at Bideford and last confession at Heavitree that her poverty was such and her resources so meagre that she was almost invariably at a disadvantage when trying to sell her own labour or her few goods.[33] Aware of her desperation, those with money could afford to take or leave her, bargaining her down to the lowest price or, as happened on one occasion that we know about, just simply taking what they wanted from her with a laugh and a shrug.[34] She had no recourse to the law, or to any kind of formal restorative justice. The working of magic did, however, offer the prospect of another kind of redress.

Violent words have their own particular power, and a permanence, that all but the most serious physical blows lack. They sting and cut, boring their way into the memory and the psyche of the victim. They are intangible and difficult to expunge from one's consciousness even after the passage of many months or years. At this remove, it is impossible to know if Temperance Lloyd really believed that she enjoyed preternatural powers and the ability to curse and to inflict suffering at will. In her old age, she certainly confessed as much to her accusers and carried on professing a belief in her abilities right up to the moment of her death.[35] It may well be that her mind was infirm by the summer of 1682 or that the shock of her arrest had unbalanced her and made her suggestible. Much more likely is the sense that the continual identification, and reinforcement, by her neighbours of her possession of particular, destructive gifts and powers gradually began to influence her own behaviour and self-conception. How often have people been told the most improbable things about themselves, and others, only to accept them as veracity rather than to take a stand against popular opinion and authority? Yet, for Temperance Lloyd this was also a two-way process. The suspicion – and increasingly the hatred – of others was fastened onto her, but in owning her supposed powers she developed and manipulated those self-same fears.

In this way, begging became a less hazardous occupation. Where once she could be simply dismissed by all, chased down the street by gangs of children, slapped or abused: the townsfolk of Bideford now had to be more careful in their handling of her. She had a means of retaliation, which offered her not only a measure of personal protection but also the prospect of increased rewards. It was easier for the young wife or tradesman to get rid of her quickly, through the granting of their charity, and to return to the normal course of their lives without a worry, than to provoke a scene by the rejection of her begging and to go to bed troubled by the uncertainty of just how and when the old woman might seek her revenge. However, this strategy was also not without its risks. It depended for its success on the power of the curse as a deterrent. No one would think to cross a reputed witch, in case she took offence and decided to hurt them. However, once a quarrel had begun and curses had started to fly, there was no telling where the incident might escalate, or how it might end. In a worst-case scenario, it might result in a beating at the hands of an angry mob or an arrest under the formidable powers of the Witchcraft Statutes. The prudent wise woman, or man, would take care not to be too objectionable, to threaten selectively and not to rack up too many enemies, if at all possible, within their locality.[36] Unfortunately, Temperance Lloyd, the simple beggar woman, was unwilling or unable to do any of these things. While she could certainly threaten, she was incapable of charm.

Temperance Lloyd was the product of a society dominated by questions of salvation and damnation, to a degree to which we, today, find very difficult to understand. The eternal life of the soul was of far greater concern to the men and women of the seventeenth century than a purely fleeting existence upon earth.[37] Indeed, all human life was seen as being the prelude to, and a preparation for, an everlasting one. The nature that this eternity would take depended entirely upon the manner in which the individual had spent their earthly life. Their actions would be weighed and judged before the Almighty, and the reward of heaven or the condemnation to hell would be rigorously apportioned. Such concerns acted as forcefully upon Temperance Lloyd, as they did upon her neighbours and accusers. She was well aware of the opprobrium in which she was held, and the nagging doubt that she was behaving in a manner likely to endanger her immortal soul appears to have grown within her.[38] She traded on the reputation fastened upon her by others as a witch, in order to secure a level of charity to which she would otherwise have been denied but needed to own that identity – as the possessor of forbidden knowledge, and the worker of sinister and blood-stained spells – in order to make her threats believable and herself to be feared in the town. Yet the gradual assumption of her identity as a witch, or cunning woman, came at the price of guilt and, probably, even shame at her actions and at what she had been forced to become. Her neighbours believed her to be a witch: so witch she was. This made it harder for them to ignore her begging for alms and ensured that she gained steadily increasing – though still very modest – rewards from them, mainly foodstuffs but on occasion also money. The trouble was that if, and when, trouble came it would be very difficult for her to defend herself with any great sense of conviction. She had consciously played upon the suspicions and fears of others for many years and so would increasingly come to feel that she was far from innocent in the matter of transgressing against God's laws in the manner of her magical practices. This sense of guilt, combined with the steadily rising number of her enemies within the local community, who felt themselves hurt and damaged by her actions, would soon come to cost her dear.

At the beginning of 1671, William Herbert, a husbandman (a farmer of modest status below that of a yeoman) of Fremington a village approximately six and a half miles north of Bideford, took sick. This was not the first visitation that the family had suffered in recent months. Between 29 July and 4 August 1670 a clutch of children – five boys and a girl – had all died, the possible victims of smallpox or some other unrecorded epidemic. Among them was John Herbert, William's grandson.[39] Misfortune, as so often happens, followed misfortune and the boy's father (another William Herbert, who plied his trade as a blacksmith in Bideford) could only watch, powerless, as an unknown ailment gripped the head of the household. As the condition of William Herbert the elder grew steadily worse, his anxious family gathered around his bedside and kept vigil over the stricken man. To add to their worries, there seemed to be neither obvious cause, nor an effective remedy, for his sufferings. The local physicians could offer no explanation and the younger William became concerned about the appearance of blotches, small scars, and wounds that resembled pinpricks all over his father's body. On 2 February, the patient – now in considerable distress – resigned himself to his death, settled his affairs as best he could, and made a last shocking allegation to his son and heir. He had, he thought, been 'bewitched . . . unto death' by Temperance Lloyd, and laid all of his misfortunes upon her malice and murderous intent. He died, it seems, with her name upon his lips, crying out that he 'did lay his bloud to the charge of the said Temperance Lloyd', imploring his son to seek justice for him and urging him 'to see her apprehended' for her crime.[40] He was buried in St Mary's churchyard on 16 March 1671, with the Rev. Ogilby officiating.[41] In a state of grief and anger, the younger William – still grieving over the loss of his son – determined to avenge his father's death and held a viewing of the wasted body for all his relations in order that they 'should see what Prints and Marks . . . Temperance Lloyd had made upon' his flesh.[42] However, more than a month passed between Herbert's death and any official action being taken against the suspected witch. There may have been some initial hesitancy on behalf of the local authorities to countenance the charges. It had, after all been thirteen years since a woman from Bideford – Grace Ellyott – had last been brought before the courts in Exeter and, on that occasion, she had eventually been discharged.[43] Therefore, it seems likely that the dead man's family spent a month of intense lobbying, calling in all the favours and mustering all the support they could, before Temperance Lloyd was finally apprehended and taken into custody, on 14 March 1671.

The Herberts were people of modest property, at arm's distance – both physically and socially – from the bustling commercial hub of the port of Bideford and unlike the Eastchurches they were engaged in agriculture as opposed to commerce. The younger William Herbert was plying his trade as a blacksmith in Bideford by the spring of 1671 and this – or the simple fact that his father brought farm goods to sell at the weekly market held in the town – may have occasioned a meeting with Temperance Lloyd. It is highly unfortunate that we do not know how, or why, she and the husbandman originally quarrelled. He might have denied her charity, refused her milk or suspected that she was interfering in some way with his livestock: causing them to sicken or die through the use of magic. Whatever the cause, there was certainly a confrontation between the two, and one of sufficient power and unpleasantness to cause William Herbert the elder to go to his grave in the belief that the encounter had occasioned the onset of his terminal illness through her ill-wishing. As such, it indicates the level of fear engendered by Temperance Lloyd in her local community and suggests a temerity and a recourse to temper in her dealings with her social superiors. Whether she was purely malicious, or simply acting out of a sense of self-defence, is now – as then – a matter of opinion. However, it is undeniable that she was able to play upon her reputation as a skilled and deadly practitioner of magic in order to get her way in the midst of a society which if not yet openly hostile towards her was at least, by the spring of 1671, deeply troubled by her presence within it and anxious that she be gone, speedily and by whatever means came readily to hand.

However, it is worth noting the relatively long gestation between the first accusation and official intervention in the case of 1671, with the extremely swift response of the local authorities to the similar claims of witchcraft made in 1679 and 1682. This may be accounted for by the cumulative snowballing of evidence against, and suspicion of, Lloyd and by the deteriorating position of the town's governing elite. In 1671, the Tories had been confident of their power, eleven years later, with the religious and political dissent reaching a crescendo in the attempt to exclude James, Duke of York from succeeding to the throne, they were far from sure that they would be able to hold onto their offices and felt that they could not afford to overlook the claims of witchcraft. Conversely, the delays that beset the original case may simply have been the product of the Herbert family's lack of direct influence in the town, or the result of the difficulty of evidence gathering from people who lived half a day's journey away on foot. Whatever the case, the younger Herbert's testimony – together with that of Lydia Burman, a single mother and servant in the household of Humphrey Ackland, who had once been town clerk – was finally held sufficient to ensure that Temperance Lloyd was brought before the borough magistrates, charged for witchcraft and sent under guard to Exeter to await judgement at the Spring Assizes.

We cannot know quite what an impression the journey to Exeter made upon the consciousness of a woman, already entering her seventh decade, who was entirely without support and stood accused of a crime which might, if judged guilty, result in the loss of her life. It was doubtless a disorientating, thoroughly dispiriting and – at times – terrifying experience, though the impression made on her by the county town cannot have been totally overwhelming or out of all kilter with her previous conceptions of the world. Bideford was, after all, a commercial hub where information was readily exchanged between seafarers, travellers and merchants. Thus, while Exeter was much larger and more populous than Bideford, it was in precisely these terms of scale, rather than the nature of its architecture or wealth, that would have struck her as being dramatic and different. Far more influential and damaging to her well-being were the seven long weeks she was forced to spend amid the darkness and the damp of the dungeons of Exeter's Rougemont Castle. The poor diet would not have troubled her as much as wealthier prisoners, accustomed to regular mealtimes, but close confinement and a lack of both sunlight and exercise cannot have had anything other than a debilitating effect. If she had not already recognized it, authority was harsh and unchallengeable. However, on this occasion, Temperance Lloyd does not seem to have been broken by her experiences or overawed by the situation in which she found herself. She had the presence of mind to deny every allegation brought against her and enough wit to keep her mouth firmly shut when it came to implicating herself, or others, in the charges brought by the Herbert family. Infuriatingly, detailed records of her trial, held on 5 May 1671, do not survive.[44] We do know, though, that the younger William Herbert and, presumably, several of his relatives, gave evidence against her and that the charges of demonic magic presented against her centred upon her method of 'pricking' her victim to death. The driving of a needle, or other sharp object, into the surface of material or a waxen image, was held to have been responsible for the scars that appeared on the body of the elder Herbert and his sudden, shooting, pains.[45]

The indictment against her had expanded to include other allegations about her practice of witchcraft. Lydia Burman testified that while she had been at work in the Ackland house in Bideford, brewing ale for the family, Temperance Lloyd had appeared 'unto her in the shape of a red Pig'.[46] Burman was convinced of Lloyd's employment of familiar spirits and of her ability to shape-change. In many respects her testimony echoes that given by Anne Wakely and Honor Hooper more than a decade later, concerning the visitation of the magpie, and it is conceivable that the encroachment of nature upon an increasingly enclosed, ordered and urbanized environment was of significant concern to the women of Bideford. There seemed to be something wild, alien and foreboding about the presence of animals in the home and the loss of domestic control that their unwelcome appearance brought. Just two years after the trial, John Davie, during his term as mayor, had railed against the 'hoggs and swine have been permitted to run up an down in the towne which doth so greatly conduce to breed diseases'.[47] With spilled cargoes littering the quayside, together with domestic rubbish, and the 'noysome and stinking dung hills and other filth which too frequently hath been cast out in heaps in severall streets ... of this Towne', there were rich pickings to be had by the large numbers of scavenging animals attracted by the overturned barrels and rotting foodstuffs. It is, therefore, not too surprising that magpies and cats were drawn to the area, or that pigs ran riot through the narrow streets and along the quayside. The keeping of livestock in the gardens and yards that honeycombed the town, and ran down to the riverside, seems to have been a commonplace means of supplementing diet and income, and after the Civil War the church font had been pressed in to service as a feed trough for swine. Consequently, it seems probable that a pig did root its way into the Acklands' kitchen, attracted by the smell of malt, hops, and rich foodstuffs, and that it had surprised Lydia Burman at her labours. What we are compelled to ask ourselves is why she should have been frightened by the animal, and why she should then choose to associate its presence with both witchcraft and the person of Temperance Lloyd? When faced by a large, slavering semi-wild animal – preparing to charge – a slight, nervous woman might have felt herself threatened or compromised. Certainly, her personal space and domestic surroundings were invaded, if not explicitly violated. Whether she associated the appearance of the animal with the death of William Herbert in a neighbouring village, or with some other act of maleficia, is unclear. One possible conclusion, however, is that she associated the disagreeable activities of the pig with those of Temperance Lloyd. Just like the later cases of the magpie and the 'Bragget cat'; both lived on the fringes of Bideford society, both appeared as unwelcome visitors at the threshold of respectable houses, and both scavenged through the town's refuse piles in order to survive. In this manner, the actions of both wild animal and witch are analogous: they feast upon carrion and human waste that no one else would touch. Moreover, if this

Figure 14 *The Witches' Cottage, Bideford, by Charles de Neuville, 1894 (Author's Collection). By the Victorian age, this range of buildings in Old Town had become associated with all three witches and was a tourist attraction. However, there is nothing to suggest that the women lived together or to associate them with such a substantial habitation.*

was the case, then Temperance Lloyd as an unwanted beggar and witch was already well on the way to being dehumanized by those who lived alongside her.

Despite Lydia Burman's memorable evidence, the victim's dying testimony, and a storm of protest from the younger Herbert – which would lose nothing of its ferocity over the next decade – the judge brought in a verdict of 'Not Guilty' and Temperance Lloyd was acquitted, on 5 May 1671, and sent back to Bideford.[48] What is striking from the court records – other than their lack of corroborative detail – is the sheer volume of cases brought to the spring assizes. It appears that many of the cases were tried in batches, with Temperance Lloyd's case being the fourteenth of 85 to be tried. The impression is of limited time and of the pressure of bodies processed through the court. The finer points of the law may have been lost along the way as this was very much the practice of 'machine' justice.[49] On this occasion, it may well have served Temperance Lloyd well. Her blanket denial of the charges brought against her, and the unwillingness and inability of the legal apparatus to devote precious time and energy in unpicking the nature of the allegations of witchcraft, spurred her acquittal. The simple refutation threw the onus of proof back upon her accusers, which made their case – of stitching together haphazard instances of misfortune and personal tragedy – into a grander, coherent narrative of demonic plots and the workings of harmful magics, extremely difficult if not impossible to prove. It was certainly above the ability of the younger William Herbert and his family in the spring of 1671. Everything, therefore, turned upon the suspect's giving – or withholding – of a confession. This was a bitter lesson that Temperance Lloyd should have taken to heart but had neither the intellect nor the reserves of strength to recall a decade later. This utter helplessness was compounded by both her isolation and alienation from those around her. Significantly, in the later testimony of the younger William Herbert he styled her as the 'Widow [who] had bewitched his . . . Father unto death'.[50] This is the only time that she is designated as such and it might, just, suggest that if Temperance Lloyd had been thrown back upon the charity of the parish by her husband's desertion in the late 1650s then, by either 1671 or 1682, news had trickled back to Bideford of Rhys Lloyd's death.

For Temperance, hers was anything but a happy homecoming. Although she may have been found innocent in the eyes of the law, in the eyes of many of her neighbours and fellow townsfolk she had the blood of William Herbert indelibly stained upon her hands. Each time she crossed the path of the younger William Herbert and his family, or that of Lydia Burman, her continued presence reopened their old wounds, created by unresolved grief, fear and a profound sense of injustice. There was a murderess and a witch at large among them, and the authorities had proved unwilling – or simply unable – to act to protect both one particular family and the wider Bideford community. Moreover, in destroying William Herbert the elder, Lloyd had struck at the roots of patriarchy – killing the head of the family – and being seen, in the eyes of the Herbert household and Ackland's servants – to get away with it. Certainly, Lydia Burman seems to have been terrified by the thought of Temperance Lloyd's approach. Long after the trial was over, the bitterness and fear remained. Worse still, this hurt could not be easily expressed, or acted upon, without running the risk of enflaming the rage of the witch. She had used magic to kill once, so she could easily do so again.

Consequently, when Lydia Burman took sick and died at the end of May 1672, there were many who recalled that she had given testimony against Temperance Lloyd's witchcraft almost exactly a year before. A hand, possibly guided by the Rev. Francis Hann, noted down her burial in the parish register on 6 June 1672 but noted beside it that she had died 'bewitched'.[51] It is uncommon for the cause of death to be noted in the Bideford register and it usually occurs through violent, accidental or uncommon circumstances such as drownings, the deaths of garrison soldiers during the Civil War or the outbreak of plague. Therefore, in attributing the death of Lydia (or 'Lyddia' as she is referred to in the document) specifically to witchcraft, Rev. Ogilby and Rev. Hann were making a strong and pointed statement: namely, that they believed in the power and reality of witches in their midst. If they were prepared to express this officially as part of the parish records then, one wonders, what was said in their sermons that week or over Lydia Burman's shroud. The town must have been buzzing with the thought that the woman whom they had consigned to the earth had been killed by unnatural, diabolical means and, if there was a victim in the case, there had to be a perpetrator.

These thoughts certainly played upon the mind of William Herbert the younger. If the main witness against Temperance Lloyd had been struck down by witchcraft, might not he – or other members of his family – be next? Something had to be done and three possible remedies presented themselves. The first was a recourse to counter-magic in attempt to break the power of the witch's spells through the employment of beneficent charms, the burying of 'witch bottles' (also known as Bellarmines). In this manner, the power of the bond forged between afflicter and afflicted could be tapped and then turned, inflicting back upon the witch the very pain she sought to inflict upon others and, hopefully, convincing her to give up her attacks upon her victim and to turn her malevolent attentions elsewhere. Certainly, there is evidence that counter-magic was known about and actively practised in Bideford by those who felt themselves afflicted by the witches. But such measures required knowledge, skill and a willingness to dabble at the edges of magical practice, which was not without its attendant risks and carried with it the disapproval of the authorities, not least of these being the clergymen who had been the firmest in believing and advancing the claims of Herbert and Burman. Secondly, address could be sought through private violence. The witch could be assailed in the street, beaten and, on occasion, 'swum' or ducked in a millpond, in order to determine her guilt. A spell could be broken through the drawing of the witch's blood, through 'scratching' her face, which was thought effective in breaking a witch's power and in restoring a victim to health.[52] Thus, in Wiltshire in 1661, Andrew Camp pinned an elderly woman suspected of harming his children to the ground while his wife 'came and clawed her by the face and said she would claw the eyes out of her head, and the tongue out of her mouth, and called her a damned ... old witch'.[53] These extra-judicial methods continued into the eighteenth century but risked killing the object of the mobs' hatred – especially if she were frail and old – and leaving those responsible liable to prosecution, in turn, for murder or manslaughter.[54] There is no evidence in Bideford to suggest such recourses to rough justice, though it does not in any way preclude the possibility that Temperance Lloyd and her companions were accustomed to beatings, as well as the scoldings of their neighbours. The third possible means of redress was through the law, as laid down in the Witchcraft Statutes of 1563 and 1604. For the individual who believed themselves to be aggrieved, this offered several advantages. It offered little personal risk, placed the ultimate matter of judgement in the hands of the Crown and acted to physically remove the suspected witch from her surroundings. This might enable a community to regain its sense of equilibrium, while waiting for the convening of the Quarterly Assizes, and also reinforced the popular notion that a witch lost all of her powers – and most importantly her ability to inflict pain – at the moment that she was locked up in jail.

It was this third option which seems to have been the most favoured by those who sought the destruction of Temperance Lloyd. On 15 May 1679, she found herself accused of bewitching Anne Fellow, the daughter of Bideford's gauger of excise, and within forty-eight hours was brought before the borough magistrates for questioning. This time she had a different, but in some ways more formidable set of accusers, comprising the girl's mother, a local apothecary – Oliver Ball – and three women – Elizabeth Coleman, Dorcas Lidston and Elizabeth Davie – who were well-connected, wealthy and respected in the town. Dorcas Lidston, would, within a little more than twelve months, marry Elizabeth Coleman's brother, John, while Davie was the wife of a Justice of the Peace and Alderman, who had been the Mayor of Bideford in 1671, when Lloyd had first stood trial. They were a tight-knit group, whose friendship cut across the obvious divides of politics and faith, through conviviality and personal affection as well as by commercial and kinship networks. All would figure again, playing roughly the same parts, during the arraignments for witchcraft in 1682. On this occasion, however, they were not successful.

On 17 May 1679, Temperance Lloyd was taken the few yards from the dilapidated lock-up, located at the west end of the Long Bridge (which prior to the Reformation had been the Chapel of Allhallows), to the town hall. There she was stripped naked by Sisy Galsworthy and 'other' respected matrons of Bideford and searched for the 'Witch's mark' or supernumerary teat by which the Devil, or a familiar spirit might suckle her milk or menstrual blood.[55] It was a humiliating experience, with the women prodding and poking at her body and examining in every painful detail the curvatures and form of her vagina, clitoris and colon. Perhaps the only mercy was that, unlike Continental practice, the hair of the suspected witch – on both the head and body – was not shaved off prior to an examination. Still, the spectacle of an aged, naked, dishevelled, and very dirty woman being pushed about and pinched by her juniors, after two nights spent lying on the floor of the town lock-up, cannot have been particularly edifying in the eyes of anyone concerned. Yet, these women had volunteered themselves for the task and, furthermore, Sisy Galsworthy appeared to relish the task: undertaking the same intimate examination of Lloyd some three years later. This raises the question of what these women thought they were doing by violating the bodies of other women and undermines the notion that witchcraft was simply a device used by men to humiliate and destroy all those of the opposite sex. This is not to suggest that matron Galsworthy and her friends had not been brutalized in their own turn, and might have accepted and acted out roles defined for them by men that cut across, and acted in direct opposition to, their true natures. However, it does signify that notions of witchcraft were more subtle, more pernicious and far more disturbing than often thought by some Feminist scholars in the 1970s and early 1980s.[56] There is no clear sense in which the allegations against Temperance Lloyd and her companions, in Bideford, were motivated or driven by men alone. Rather, in the case of Temperance Lloyd, the majority of her accusers were women and issues centring around age, motherhood, and the menopause were as, if not perhaps more, important than a simple question of gender. In a savage twist, some – like Grace Thomas and Lydia Burman – were also on the margins of the community, but due to their differing expressions of sexuality rather than on account of poverty. Grace Thomas was disadvantaged through her chasteness and spinsterhood, while Lydia Burman had been through her pursuit of sex outside wedlock and her pregnancy resulting in an illegitimate child.[57] Furthermore, three of Temperance Lloyd's alleged victims – Grace Thomas, Lydia Burman and Ann Fellow – were female, while only one, William Herbert the elder, was male. This did not appear to contemporaries as a binary struggle between propertied and professional men and dispossessed women on the other: but as the deployment of a particular – feminized and demonized – form of violence that struck at all the productive and normative pillars of society (whether the working father, the godly spinster, the serving maid or the child) alike.

In addition to be being a troubling, difficult and potentially dangerous force in the locality, Lloyd may also have been targeted – and become an object of hatred for other women – because she was something of a rarity in an Early Modern town. She had borne children, survived into old age and had gone through the menopause, yet had failed to perform any of the normative and defining duties of a mature woman. Her children had died or deserted her, and her husband had vanished first from the town and then into an unknown grave. Most damaging of all, she had no tangible stake in the life of her own community. Instead of being a worthy matron, like Sisy Galsworthy, she was unbiddable and perceived to be a rootless, skulking harridan. The physical ungainliness commented on by many of her contemporaries and wrought no doubt by poverty and by advancing age, further served to distance her from the other women of the town. Young women, in particular, feared the reflection of their own inevitable fate, through the aging process, in the haggard face and wizened body of Lloyd, while those with children and infants could wonder if she was not touched by some foul distemper, which seemed to cause her to be preserved while all about her sickened, withered and died. Anne Wakely's discovery of 'two Teats hanging nigh together like a piece of flesh had suckt', 'in her Secret Parts', 'each ... about an Inch in length' was confirmed by Honor Hooper and appeared to be confirmatory medical evidence pointing towards the sealing of a demonic pact. In effect, the act of committing oneself to the service of the Devil was thought to distort not only one's soul but also one's physiognomy. If today we would associate cervical polyps with growths not uncommon in post-menopausal women who have had children, then the presence of these long fibrous, stalk-like tissues – sometimes greyish white, sometimes a livid red – came as a shock to the women who examined Temperance Lloyd. They seemed unnatural and to have been triggered by something – allegedly intercourse with a demonic entity – since her previous examination in 1671. There is nothing to suggest the presence of doctors or apothecaries at these examinations and, so far as the search for 'Witch Marks' was regularized and practised in Bideford, the manner, definition and detection of the 'teats' fell entirely within a female sphere of governance.[58]

Again, we are hampered by a lack of crucial evidence for the underlying tensions that generated such intense hatred towards Temperance Lloyd from a substantial cross-section of women in the town. While the Bideford Court Sessions book survives and records the charge and process, 'the papers' containing the sworn testimonies of Anne Fellow, Oliver Ball, Elizabeth Coleman, Dorcas Lidston and Elizabeth Davie that were lodged against her, have not been preserved.[59] As a result, we are in large measure forced back upon the subsequent testimonies of those involved in the 1682 arraignments and trial in order to reconstruct the events of three years earlier. We know that Ann Fellow, the daughter of Edward and Anne Fellow, had fallen ill with a lingering and unidentifiable complaint in the spring of 1679, and that it is possible to locate the kernel of the original disagreement between her mother and Temperance Lloyd in the events alluded to by the Rev. Hann during the very last minutes of the old beggar woman's life. Hann thought to revisit the previous charges of witchcraft brought against her, and asked if Temperance or her companion, Susanna Edwards, had ever bewitched children. Significantly, Lloyd answered in the singular rather than in the plural. She was thinking of one particular case and was ignoring, with some skill, an open-ended accusation. We know of only the one occasion when Temperance Lloyd was held to have bewitched a child and this was the one that was under consideration in May 1679. Thus, we can proceed with some certainty in reconstructing the events that resulted in the second round of allegations against her.

Temperance Lloyd had been selling apples in the town when Ann Fellow passed by with her mother. Whether intrigued, or simply hungry, the child took an apple from the old woman and wandered back to her mother. Temperance pursued her, wanting payment. However, the mother just took the apple from the little girl and walked away, ignoring the beggar entirely. For her, the incident was funny: a childish foible acted out at the expense of a foolish old woman. The apple – a thing of no value in the eyes of the mother – was assumed to be a gift and had made her happy. The trouble was that an object that had no worth to the wife of an exciseman was everything to a beggar woman. It constituted a significant portion of Temperance Lloyd's marketable goods – probably having been gleaned from the orchards above the town – and its sale constituted a major contribution to her meagre income, signifying the difference between her going hungry and cold that night, or being fed and warm. She had, for once, tried to sell the only goods available to her openly and honestly: as did the 'respectable' townsfolk. Yet her reward seemed to be that she was scorned and stolen from. Worse still, she had been robbed by an infant from whom she could not even hope to seek redress and scorned through the attitude of indifference to her plight by a social superior, who Temperance thought, should have behaved better towards her. The incident seemed to sum up the injustice and utter powerlessness of her personal situation: if she could not even stand up to a child, then who could she ever hope to stand up to? Yet it also underlined the enormity of the gulf that had opened up between the 'haves' and the 'have-nots' in Bideford. The young mother could not conceive of hunger and want, finding the old woman's predicament a source of amusement, while Temperance Lloyd knew of nothing but poverty, and considered that the child's actions were of a criminal, rather than comical, nature.

Understandably, the reaction of the beggar woman was one of fury. She made no attempt to claim otherwise when called to account, long after the event. 'I was very angry,' she told the Rev. Hann in August 1682.[60] Though she did not seek to elaborate on quite how this anger manifested itself, but it seems likely that she followed the mother and child up the High Street abusing them, calling them names and threatening retribution against the thieving child. It was a terrible scene, which turned a mother's amusement to shock and to fear as she was confronted by a wild and shrieking old hag, who berated her and threatened her precious baby with violence. Though she spirited her child away, the conflict went unresolved. The apple was never paid for, leaving Temperance Lloyd out of pocket and nursing a grudge, while Anne Fellow would be left to dwell in the weeks and months that lay ahead upon the fact that an old woman – popularly believed to have the ability to kill through the utterance of a curse – had never taken back her words. When the child fell ill, the quarrel was instantly recalled and the affliction was attributed to the efficacy of the old woman's words and the operation of witchcraft. Oliver Ball, the apothecary called in by the parents to help, whether on account of plain ignorance or an inability to diagnose or cure the little girl's ailments, preferred to concur with the parents' belief in the workings of witchcraft rather than to admit to his own lack of knowledge.

With the depositions taken, and Temperance Lloyd still denying her guilt, the magistrates contented themselves with putting the case on hold. They received no official sanction to proceed further and there was little appetite among the governing elites at county level, to countenance a new witchcraft prosecution where one had singularly failed against the same suspect almost exactly two years before. The decisive factor was the failure of Sisy Galsworthy and her companions to find evidence of the defining 'Witch's mark' upon Temperance Lloyd's body. These 'four Women of the Town of Biddiford' were forced to conclude that the 'proofs then against her [were] not so clear and conspicuous' and, confused and disappointed, Edward Fellow decided not to press the charges against her any further.[61] For the moment, she had emerged vindicated from her ordeal, and the borough magistrates who clearly believed the examination to be the definitive test for a witch were compelled by their own logic to recognize that she was untainted by guilt.

Then, the child died. She was laid to rest in St Mary's churchyard on 5 October 1680 but, this time, there was no record of bewitchment in the parish register, or of laudatory sermons, only of a rancorous, undignified brawl at the graveside and a spiral of recrimination.[62] The bereaved parents struggled in the midst of their sorrow to make any sense of their little girl's death, and it seems that they were actively seeking for someone – perhaps even anyone – to blame for the tragedy. The child's funeral provided a further scene of controversy with her father, Edward Fellow, railing against the Minister of the parish, Michael Ogilby, for charging a shilling (apparently the clergyman's 'going rate') for performing the rite. He attached his complaint to the growing charge sheet that was being collected against Ogilby by John Hill and was joined by John Coleman who was enraged by the 'extortion' of 'unjust fees' for marrying him to Dorcas Lidston.[63] We can see the same group of friends (comprising Edward and Ann Fellow, John and Dorcas Coleman, and Elizabeth Coleman) turning against Ogilby, in October 1680, just as they had against Temperance Lloyd in May 1679, and were to do again against all three suspected witches in August 1682. Furthermore, this time, the Rev. Ogilby was less minded to countenance witchcraft as the cause of death. A smallpox epidemic had swept through the town in the autumn and winter of 1680, carrying off his own wife, Letitia, together with many others including Mary, the daughter of William Herbert the younger.[64] The appearance of pockmarks on the infant's skin did not speak to him so much of witchcraft but of the telltale symptoms of a virus with which he and all of those that had survived, and suffered it, in Bideford were all too familiar. If he countenanced the existence of witches, as evidenced through the scriptures and legal statutes, then he was neither credulous nor stupid.

The graveside argument was a rare piece of luck for Temperance Lloyd. Though she had already been identified by the grieving parents and their friends, as the cause of the little girl's sufferings and faced cross-questioning on that account by the local magistrates, she seems to have been forgotten in the midst of the allegations levelled at Rev. Ogilby. Further charges of witchcraft were not sparked by the death of the child. However, what is significant in terms of the resurfacing of allegations of witchcraft in 1682 is that the controversy surrounding Rev. Ogilby ensured that the Anglican Church, in Bideford, just as surely as the dissenting community had lost faith in its natural leader at precisely the point when societal tensions were once again coming to a head. There is no doubt that Michael Ogilby was a disappointment to the High Tories in the parish, both in terms of his lack of attention to church administration and willingness to act as a break upon their passions and their drive to ensure religious conformity. The combination of a loss of leadership and control among both Anglican and dissenting communities, absentee gentry; a disinterested and disillusioned rector, and a town council that was barely able to maintain itself or public order was nothing short of a recipe for disaster.

However unwittingly, Temperance Lloyd stepped into the midst of that power vacuum. Her career as a beggar had been anything but successful. She had relied upon fear, intimidation and insinuation to eke out a living and had stored up a mountain of trouble for herself on each account. Ranged against her were an increasing number of foes, who were united by grief, deep personal tragedy and a sense of mounting indignation at the fact that they had twice been unable to secure the conviction of a 'known' witch and that their own evidence had been held wanting in the eyes of the law. Such a combination of circumstances was extremely dangerous for a woman like Temperance Lloyd. All that was required to spark a fresh outburst of allegations against her was another row in the street followed by unexplained sickness, or a sudden death. It was her particular misfortune that just such a spark was provided to set the whole town on fire against her by the chance actions, and natural curiosity, of a magpie and by the sudden glint of sunlight upon glass.

On the night of Friday 30 June 1682, Grace Thomas found that she could not sleep and was assailed once again by wave after wave of pain, feeling that she was being 'pinch'd and prick'd to the Heart, with such cruel thrusting pains in her Head, Shoulders, Arms, Hands, Thighs, and Legs, as though the Flesh would have been then immediately torn from the Bones with a mans Fingers and Thumbs'.[65] So intense were these sensations of being pulled and pushed by unseen external forces, that she 'was even pluck'd out over her Bed' and dashed against the floor like a rag doll.[66] As Anne Wakely and Honor Hooper attempted to alleviate her sufferings, and the Eastchurches watched over her, 'she lay in this condition for the space of three hours', crying out, insensible, and unable to find any sort of relief.[67] When, next morning, the sun rose above Bideford, tiredness and terror were beginning to give way to feelings of anger. It was, after all, exactly a week since the discovery of the ominous doll and there now seemed to be no doubt that the beggar woman was intent upon taking the life of Grace Thomas, and would stop at nothing in order to achieve her ends. Rheumy, red-eyed and seething with rage, Thomas Eastchurch came to the decision that something had to be done quickly to release his household from the dreadful pall that had settled upon it. With Wakely and Hooper in tow, he gathered his friends together and escorted his invalid sister-in-law to the town hall to request an interview with the borough magistrates and to demand that action was taken against the depredations of Temperance Lloyd.

He found a receptive audience. The new mayor, Thomas Gist, and the aldermen, led by John Davie, knew only too well of Temperance Lloyd's malign reputation and were ready to believe that the bane that had gripped the Eastchurches' household was her doing. An arrest warrant was quickly sworn, on Saturday 1 July 1682, and the parish constables despatched to apprehend the old woman.[68] They had little trouble in finding her, or in dragging her, bewildered, garrulous and uncomprehending to the town lock-up. There she spent the rest of the day while the town raged and rejoiced at the news of her latest crimes and the swift manner of her apprehension. As lists of the names of the witnesses against her were taken, Sisy Galsworthy was asked if she would conduct another body search and Grace Thomas slept well for the first night in months, Temperance Lloyd curled up on the floor of the dilapidated old chapel, watched by a jailer and well aware, from the threats and curses of all those gathered outside, that she now had the whole town at her heels. Sitting high above the rooftops of Bideford, the magpie could not possibly have known quite what he had done, or what forces he had unleashed on one unfortunate old woman, her few friends and the seething mass of the people who lived down below.

5

Blood and curses

Easter Week, 1682, brought no great comfort to Susanna Edwards. Her timing was bad. The doors that were usually open to her were slammed in her face by sneering servants and their angry mistresses, and she went hungry once again. Like Temperance Lloyd, she eked out a meagre existence along Bideford's quayside, gleaning scraps of food and finding a measure of comfort in smoking the tobacco that she begged from passing mariners or found scattered among the overturned and split hogsheads. At seventy years of age, with the stem of a long clay pipe clamped between her few remaining teeth and swirls of grey smoke rising from beneath the brim of her hat, it is scarce to be wondered that many of the townsfolk considered her to be a witch or that a nobleman who saw her, some three months later, thought that an artist might have chosen her to represent the archetype of the fearful, hunched and wizened figure.[1] With few options open to her, it was perhaps not too surprising that she made friendships, alliances and acquaintances where, and with whom, she could or that she should band together with other, similarly marginal, women. She certainly grew to know Temperance Lloyd by sight and seems to have enjoyed a rough sort of friendship with Mary Trembles, with Susanna assuming the role of the stronger – and at times dominant – partner. Yet this friendship – or at the very least their convenient alliance – was destined to unravel amid dramatic and disastrous recriminations in the summer of 1682. To suggest, as some recent historians have done, that there is nothing to link the women seems to be taking the point too far. After all, the circumstances that fuelled the accusations grew out of a sense that everyone knew everyone else, and their business, in a somewhat claustrophobic town. As has been said, there is no evidence that the three women lived or begged together, and it is reasonable to associate Temperance Lloyd with other members of the indigent poor, such as Joan Conden and Widow Germinn, as it is with Susanna Edwards or Mary Trembles. Rather than Temperance Lloyd, it was Mary Trembles who partnered Susanna Edwards on her frequent forays to search out food in the town and who accompanied her, on 18 May 1682, to the house of John Barnes, a well-to-do yeoman who had previously served as a constable in Bideford.

We can reconstruct something of what happened that day. Mary Trembles had woken hungry and went out 'about the Town of Biddiford to beg some Bread'.[2] Finding no success, she continued from door to door until she happened to meet with Susanna Edwards in the street. It is possible that she recognized in her friend a more accomplished, and certainly a wilier, operator: for, when asked by Susanna where she had been, she significantly upped her game. Replying that 'she had been about the Town, and had begged [for] some Meat, but could get none', she was subtly shifting the purpose of her little expedition in the hopes that Susanna might permit her to join in the search for tastier morsels that were usually far beyond her reach.[3] In this she was not to be disappointed, though later she might well have wished that she had been. Susanna brightened at the idea and suggested that they go to the home of John Barnes, who had often treated her kindly and permitted her to take the leftover scraps from his table. Falling in to step together, the two women made the short journey from the riverfront to his door. Unfortunately, on this occasion, they mistimed their arrival. John Barnes was not at home and they were confronted on the threshold by his wife, Grace, and her maidservant. An altercation ensued, in which the beggar women were denied first meat and then bread, before being sent away from the premises empty-handed. Susanna Edwards spent the afternoon brooding upon their treatment and refusing to be thwarted, chose a different tactic. Believing that John Barnes would, in the meantime, have returned home, she dispatched Mary Trembles back to his house to ask, this time, if she might have 'a Farthing's worth of Tobacco'.[4] Once again disappointment awaited her. Barnes was still not at home – or at least he would not venture to the door – and it was his angry wife who, for a second time that day, confronted Mary Trembles on the step. Driven off and beating a hasty retreat up the street, the old woman rejoined Susanna Edwards and told her tale of woe. In deciding not to go back to Barnes' home, herself, and sending the pliable Mary Trembles in her stead, Susanna Edwards had more than half-expected a poor outcome. However, she still took the refusal of the tobacco as a personal insult and raged 'that it should be better for her, the said Grace, if she had let ... [her friend] to have had some Tobacco.'[5] The vehemence of her speech and anger of her intent was such that these words lodged in Mary Trembles' mind, to be repeated guilelessly before the magistrates of Bideford exactly two months later. They would do much to help propel both women down the path to their ruin.

Like Grace Thomas, before her, Grace Barnes had endured a long history of ill-health. She explained to the Justices of the Peace that 'she hath been very much pain'd and tormented in her Body these many years last past' and that she had 'sought out for Remedy far and neer'. However, according to her own deposition before the court she had 'never had any suspicion that she had had any Magical Art or Witchcraft used upon her Body, until it was about a year and a half ago [about late January or early February 1681, when], ... she was informed by some Physicians that it was so'.[6] This diagnosis, coming as it did from men of apparent learning and expertise in the field, proved decisive and, henceforth, it seems that she increasingly came to accept that she was, indeed, the victim of a malevolent enchantment. This raises some interesting questions about the medical profession in Bideford. In each of the cases involving Grace Thomas, Ann Fellow and Grace Barnes it was the suggestion by a doctor, or an apothecary, that witchcraft was the cause of their unexplained ailments that proved decisive in framing charges against the women as witches. Unfortunately, with the exceptions of Oliver Ball and Dr George Beare, we do not know their identities or anything more about them, though it does appear that Bideford was especially well served by individuals practising the trade of apothecaries. On the face of things, this might be thought to suggest that conflict between the burgeoning, male-dominated medical profession and the 'traditional' female healers, herbalists and midwives was the trigger for the prosecutions.[7]

This would certainly fit with the popular explanation given for the European witch-hunts by many academics and writers influenced by the second wave of Feminism, in the 1970s and early 1980s, namely that in an attempt to destroy a woman's autonomy over her body and reproductive cycle, a monetarized and professionalized group of male physicians was prepared to help launch an all-out assault upon traditional methods of healing that were the preserve of women herbalists and midwives. The intuition and skill of these folk-healers, according to this thesis, won them the support and trust of their communities in a manner that was impossible for the empirical and impersonal medical establishment to challenge.[8] Moreover, doctors demanded fees for their services, while the cunning women and midwives helped alleviate their neighbours' sufferings as part of a wider vocation, attuned to the natural cycles of the Earth, and operating without thought to personal profit. Thus, their success proved a barrier to the attempts both to commodify medical care and to assert male control over the female body and psyche. Charges of witchcraft were, therefore, manufactured in order to discredit and destroy those midwives and herbalists who had enabled women to regulate their own bodies, through birth control, abortion, and knowledge of sex and its pleasures. Unfortunately, the thesis – however plausible and liberating it might have been – falls apart due to an almost total lack of historical evidence. It reflected the widespread disaffection with traditional medicine, and its disregard for female needs, widely felt by members of the counter-culture of the late 1960s and early 1970s, and reflected that generation's fascination with alternative medicines and treatments as practised by other – and, in particular, Eastern – cultures. Its strength derived from the premise that these societies, which had experienced uneven or limited industrialization, maintained an a priori intuitive wisdom that had been lost in the West due to its embrace of capitalism and scientific method. Unfortunately, while this made for interesting politics and superb polemic, it made for bad history. Though the Dominican authors of the *Malleus Maleficarum* were quick to single out midwives for bitter and violent censure it is doubtful just how far this single text was known, and acted upon, in England. By way of contrast, the overwhelming majority of other demonological writers made no particular mention of midwives as being particularly susceptible to witchcraft, while the extant court records fail to reveal any correlation between the practice of either healing or midwifery and convictions for the crime of bewitchment. Furthermore, midwives were actually far more likely to be employed by the court in order to search for witchmarks on the genitals of suspects, than to appear as the innocent victims of persecution.[9]

Their vocation, rather than existing outside the limits and direction of patriarchy, was actually employed in its service.

If that is the macrocosm of the argument, then in the microcosm that was Bideford it was certainly the case that the belief in the efficacy of witches legitimized and touted by Bideford's medical men targeted the accusations in directions that they would, probably, not otherwise have taken. However, the difficulty lies in the fact that, once again, there is no evidence that any of the women promised or sold cures, or that they knew anything at all about the properties of herbs. If they had, or if they had possessed any sort of skill at all, then it is likely that their lives would have developed along markedly different trajectories and led to much happier results. Furthermore, the three – both individually and collectively – were about as far from the image of intuitive and altruistic matriarchs, beloved and trusted by the other women in their community, as it is possible to get. As we have already seen, they were marginalized at every level: devoid of skills, prospects and charm. They were objects of hatred and scorn in the eyes of the other women in the town and were desperately needy individuals who were incapable of giving any form of assistance or insight to others. Temperance Lloyd was, after all, accused of killing a child with a curse, rather than of helping to bring one into the world with love.

Moreover, the 'knowing women' of Bideford, called upon for gynaecological advice, were not drawn from among the ranks of the Bideford Witches or their associates but rather from those of their accusers.[10] Yet, if we can dispense with the thesis that a struggle over the control of women's bodies, and their access to and practice of medicine, was the decisive factor in fuelling a witch-hunt in Bideford, the sense remains of the authority figures, in the form of both the doctors and Anglican clergy, in the town being prepared to articulate and, thereby, validate beliefs in witchcraft for at least a decade before Grace Thomas and Grace Barnes fell ill. As a consequence, the populace could be forgiven in seeking out witches in their midst. Every source of intellectual and political authority in Bideford – whether vested in the pulpit of the church or in the pages of the Bible, the diagnoses of the physicians and doctors, or the legal statutes enacted by the councilmen and burgesses – reinforced the belief in malefic witchcraft, which was not an abstract but a palpable reality. Moreover, given the complete disarray of the dissenting community and the defeat of the town's radical Whigs, by the spring of 1682, there seems to have been no one capable, or interested enough, to advance a sceptical counter-position. The Bartletts were dead and Gabriel Beale, labouring under the eyes of informants and the weight of successive fines, was fully preoccupied with his own business and with the sustaining of the underground Conventicle movement.

Having decided upon medical advice that witchcraft lay behind her symptoms, Grace Barnes looked around for a likely suspect, or suspects, who bore her ill-will. Initially, it seems that no one sprang to mind but gradually she came to see the visits of Susanna Edwards to her door as being strange and threatening. While in court, though she chose to skate over the nature of her row with Edwards and Trembles on 18 May 1682, she chose to describe in detail their visits to her home. Susanna Edwards, she said, 'would oftentimes repair unto [her] Husband's house upon frivolous or no occasions at all'.[11] Thus, an activity which for a poor woman was viewed as a necessity, in order to supplement a subsistence level diet, and which may have even been viewed as a right, was seen by a woman of means, who had no need to worry about just where her next meal was coming from, as a meaningless and capricious act. A yawning gap had opened up between the rich and the poor in Bideford, which fractured traditional ideas about the dispensing of charity and ensured that women, on either side of that divide, could no longer find an acceptable common form of language with which to air their grievances, or a manner of custom and behaviour that was commonly understood. However unfashionable it may now appear, when reduced to their most basic element, the charges against Susanna Edwards did not stem from differences in gender but, rather, from growing antagonisms between competing classes. There had been winners and losers in Bideford's rapid mercantile expansion as a major Atlantic port and the winners, among the town's artisanate and nascent bourgeoisie, had little interest in continuing to subsidize the losers, among the shifting ranks of a pauperized underclass, with anything more than their direct – and always grudging – contributions to the poor rate and to a handful of well-run, respectable, charitable institutions within their community. The direct giving of charity on an individual basis was becoming a much rarer event and, as the old consensus broke down, it was possible for affluent young women, like

Grace Barnes, to view beggars as no more than a pack of greedy freeloaders, seeking to take advantage of the industry and labour of others.

It is inconceivable to think that, in a small town like Bideford, Grace Barnes could have been unaware of Grace Thomas' symptoms and that she would not have drawn some form of conclusion from the similarity of their illnesses. It is even possible to go as far as to suggest that their fears cross-fertilized, reinforcing a sense of persecution and combining, on a psychosomatic level to exacerbate their nervous attacks. It was certainly the case that within hours of her altercation with Susanna Edwards and Mary Trembles, Grace Barnes had taken to her bed 'with very great pains of sticking and pricking in her Arms, Breast, and Heart, as though divers Awls had been pricked or stuck into her Body, and was in great tormenting pain for many days and nights together, with a very little intermission'.[12] Her husband believed that she was about to die and gathered around him his friends and neighbours, in the hope that they might offer some comfort to the stricken woman.[13] At this point, any assistance, or ray of hope, would have been welcomed by a tired and very frightened man who by now had firmly come to believe that his wife had been bewitched. Therefore, the news that Grace Thomas had begun to recover her spirits from the moment that Temperance Lloyd had been removed from the community and thrown into the town lock-up offered John Barnes a solution to his problems and called for immediate action.

The narrow, winding streets that led up to the marketplace from the quayside seemed friendless and benighted, and every squall blowing in stinging salt from the Bristol Channel suddenly appeared threatening and hell sent. Neighbours eyed one another with suspicion, for now Bideford had become known as a place of witches. Through the lengthy questioning of Temperance Lloyd at the town hall, several days previously, everyone now believed that they knew how they worked and how they stalked their victims in their homes, coming with smiles and good wishes, but intent upon the basest of murders: casting themselves with a pall of invisibility in order that they might pinch and prick their quarry to death.[14] These thoughts were running through John Barnes' mind when his wife suffered a fresh attack, on Sunday 16 July 1680. At 10 in the morning, she was overcome with such violent spasms that 'Four Men and Women could hardly hold her' down.[15] Her symptoms were far worse than before and John feared that she would soon die. Yet amid the sounds of struggle and cries of pain, one of Grace's friends – Agnes Whitefield, the wife of cordwainer and a relative of the mayor – heard the sound of somebody outside the front door. She was disturbed enough by the unknown presence upon the step to leave the side of her crying, twitching and convulsing friend and to hurry down the hallway in order to investigate. She shot the bolt on the door and, thrusting her head outside into the street, came face-to-face with Mary Trembles, 'standing with a White-pot in her hands, as though she had been going to the common Bakehouse'.[16] Both parties had barely time to recover from their surprise, when Grace was heard calling out, asking who was there. Agnes replied at once, confirming Grace's worst fears that:

> Mary Trembles together with . . . Susanna Edwards, were the very persons that had tormented her, by using some Magical Art or Witchcraft upon her . . . Body [and that the witch] was come now to put her . . . out of her life.[17]

What Mary Trembles made of this unexpected confrontation is not recorded, though it would seem likely that she had spent the morning making her habitual rounds, going from door to door in search of scraps of food, wheat, salt and yeast, before heading back up the hill to the communal bakehouse, where for a small fee the poor without hearth or oven could bake their bread. The possibility remains that she was attempting, by playing on the Barnes' fear of witchcraft, to extort foodstuffs or even a little money from them. What is certain is that from the moment that the door flew open and Grace Barnes called out against her, Mary Trembles must have known that the game was up and the town was turned against her. It is likely that, uncertain what to do, she fled back up the street and rushed to find Susanna Edwards, who had now effectively been cast as her partner in crime. We know that they were observed talking together about their deeds and their hatred for Grace Barnes by William Edwards, another of the town's blacksmiths, the very next day, and that they were in a considerable state of agitation.[18] With no avenues of escape left open to them, all they could do was to continue wandering the streets until they were arrested by the parish constables. Unsurprisingly, with no one else to turn to for help or advice, they began to blame each other for their predicament. Mary was overheard, just minutes before their arrest on Tuesday 18 July 1682, railing against her friend and blaming her for all her woes.[19] If anything, things were about to get very much worse for the two hapless and shuffling figures. They had not only been positively identified as being witches, working magic in manner already exposed through the evidence taken against Temperance Lloyd, but also other townsfolk began to put two and two together and to recall past suspicions and fears about the activities of the two beggar women, which could now be thrown into a far clearer and altogether more damaging light.

Soon after their arrest, Dorcas Coleman, the wife of a sailor operating out the port of Bideford, came forward to the authorities with her own tale of bewitchment. In both its outline and particulars, it provided the justices with an uncanny echo of the earlier testimonies made against the witches by Grace Thomas and Grace Barnes. There may even be some reason to think that, given the lateness of her testimony, she embroidered some aspects of the original statements to give added credence to her own sad story. However, it seems clear that her own sufferings were genuine enough. In August 1680, she had been struck down by a mysterious affliction, which confined her to her home and rendered her an invalid. As in the cases of Grace Thomas and Grace Barnes, 'she was taken in tormenting Pains, by pricking in her Arms, Stomach, and Heart, in such a manner, as she was never taken so before'.[20] With her newlywed husband presumably away at sea on a voyage, Dorcas turned to his uncle, Thomas Bremincombe, for assistance. He was a man of some considerable standing in the local community, he was wealthy enough to be described as a 'Gentleman' but unlike her husband – who seems to have oscillated between religious conformity and dissent – he was a firm Tory who would be quick to sign the town's declaration of loyalty to the new king, James II, in February 1685.[21] He found the necessary money for a doctor's fee and rode to Barnstaple in order to hire Dr George Beare so that they might discover 'some Remedy for these Pains'. The doctor visited the patient in Bideford, examined her body and quickly concluded 'that it was past his skill to ease her, by reason that she was bewitched'.[22] His diagnosis, coupled with the speed and certainty with which it was delivered, suggests that he was also numbered among the 'physicians' called in a few months later to see Grace Barnes and Grace Thomas. They too were very keen to diagnose witchcraft and it is not beyond the realms of possibility that, armed with a study of demonology and a firm personal belief in the efficacy of witchcraft, that it was Dr Beare who drove the process of accusation forward from behind the scenes. If this were the case, then elusive personality and practice of Dr Beare were the crucial components in forming the matching pattern of accusations – with their common elements of invisible assailants, meetings with the Devil, and the employment of familiar spirits – as Dorcas Coleman, Grace Barnes, Grace Thomas and Elizabeth and Thomas Eastchurch did not arrive at the conclusion that they were experiencing bewitchment on their own account. Furthermore, Dorcas Coleman recalled the death of Ann Fellow, her friend's little girl, and would have known of the pronouncements of the apothecary, Oliver Ball, determining witchcraft as the cause of death.

Dr George Beare had enjoyed a successful career after studying at the universities Padua and Oxford during the years of the Republic, and became a member of the London College of Physicians, practising medicine at Exeter and Barnstaple.[23] Middle-aged by the 1680s, he was hardly a parochial or unintelligent man: yet he seems to have wholeheartedly believed in the deadly efficiency of witchcraft to harm and to kill. This being the case, we might well ask ourselves why Dr Beare, together with the other local physicians and the apothecary, were so ready to jump to the conclusion that these women were the victims of witchcraft? Thomas Ady, a doctor who was extremely sceptical about witch-beliefs, had written that such diagnoses provided nothing more than 'a cloak for a physician's ignorance. When he cannot find the nature of the disease, he saith the party is bewitched.'[24] A generation later, those professional practitioners of medicine called in to examine Dorcas Coleman, Grace Barnes and Grace Thomas were unanimous in their opinion that witchcraft was the cause of their sufferings. Yet there is nothing to indicate that either they in general, or Dr Beare in particular, were negligent or incompetent. They charged high fees for their service and were well respected in their local communities, enjoying the confidence of members of the local elites, such as Thomas Bremincombe and Edward Fellow. If we can dismiss the idea that Dr Beare was motivated solely by a sense of murderous professional jealousy towards women healers, then it is still not so easy to ignore the sense of misogyny that was embedded within the assumptions of Early Modern people from every strata of society. It is entirely conceivable that George Beare was a woman-hater but, as he left no writings – and his words are only those reported by others – it is impossible to speculate with any sense of certainty. However, the fact that he treated the women of Bideford suggests that he was not too averse to taking their coin. What does remain is the possibility that he was acting within a framework of rational thought about the nature of illness and demonology that was widely disseminated throughout the Early Modern scientific community. As witches were thought to act in opposition to the natural order, demonologists generally held that it was impossible for them to inflict naturally occurring diseases upon their victims. A witch could not inflict the plague, smallpox or even a common cold upon those whom she hated. It was beyond her power. However, she might seek to inflict unnatural, or previously unknown, diseases of her own – and by extension, the Devil's – creation, that defied classification and conventional treatment. Therefore, at a time when diagnosis remained a difficult and inexact art, the spread of illnesses of a nervous or psychological type that conformed to no known pattern but which exhibited frightening symptoms, could readily lend themselves to the suspicion of witchcraft. Sudden bouts of vomiting – especially where strange items, pins, nails or congealed bile were disgorged – paralysis, or fits, might be held to be the results of bewitchment and the stabbing pains that confined Grace Thomas, Grace Barnes and Dorcas Coleman to their beds appeared particularly suspicious. Dr Beare and his colleagues were, thus, no mavericks or charlatans but were attempting to apply what knowledge they had to the situation at hand. This was located in biblical and classical authorities for the existence of witchcraft, and in the prolific trial accounts of localized outbreaks in Essex, Suffolk, Norfolk and Lancashire, that had been published in the period between 1641 and 1678.[25] However, their readiness to ascribe the women's ailments to witchcraft was unusual, even by the standards of the time. Stemming from neither credulity nor fanaticism, it may be thought that the speed and certainty of diagnosis may have grown out of a genuine attempt to alleviate the sufferings of their patients and that the resulting tragedies originated not as the result of any sense of cruelty but on account of a misplaced, and misinformed, desire to 'do good' within a society characterized by concerns about the maintenance of order, confessional strife, and the 'reform' of morals and manners.

By giving a previously inexplicable ailment a name, and a cause, Dr Beare had transformed Dorcas Coleman's predicament and given her the hope of a cure – provided that the witch responsible for her condition was tracked down and her spells combated, either through judicial punishment or by magical counter-measures. Thus, Dorcas began searching her mind for a likely suspect who bore her ill-will. One readily presented herself when, on one of her regular calls from door to door in search of charity, Susanna Edwards had come to beg for assistance. In her eyes, the event was probably of no consequence, part of her daily drudge in search of food and a little comfort, but to Dorcas Coleman, confined for weeks at a time within her chamber, and with little else to focus upon, it was – just as in the case of Grace Thomas – a threatening and unwarranted intrusion into her private space. In a similar fashion, whereas the quality of Susanna's existence depended entirely upon the success, or failure, of such forays, her neighbour's wealthy husband saw her visit as, at best, a pointless imposition. Consequently, when, at the end of April 1682, Susanna Edwards came to beg at John Coleman's door and to ask if she could see his wife, he regarded it as merely being 'a pretence to visit her' and that her true purpose was of a far more sinister nature. It is significant, however, that she was granted admission, this time, and was led upstairs, by Coleman and his uncle, to the room where Dorcas Coleman was resting in an armchair. As soon as she spied Susanna, the invalid was overtaken by rage and 'did strive to fly in the face' of the supposed witch.[26]

This assault did, however, have a purpose behind it. It was not a simple outpouring of frenzy but a practical attempt at counter-magic in order to break the power of the spell that Dorcas Coleman believed had been cast upon her by Susanna Edwards. This could be done by scratching – effectively drawing blood – from the witch who had cast it. Though the uttering of the witch's curse was deadly and demanded the lifeblood of the victim, it was also thought that this left the witch vulnerable to reprisals. The casting of a spell was believed to establish a sympathetic magical link between the witch and her victim, which permitted two-way traffic between the hunter and the hunted. Thus, under certain circumstances, the victim might seek redress from her oppressor by restoring the balance in their relationship and, effectively, nullifying the witch's power. If the witch had desired the shedding of her victim's blood, then the drawing of the witch's own blood by the victim would cancel out the evil of the action and break the enchantment. Clawing the witch's face or forehead –

usually with fingernails, but also with thorns, needles or knives – was held to be the most effective method, especially if she could be lured back to the scene of her crime. As late as 1717, a witness at a Leicester witch trial affirmed that drawing the blood of a witch was 'the most infallible cure' for ailments brought about by witchcraft.[27] Consequently, in flailing out at Susanna Edwards, Dorcas Coleman was attempting to effect both restorative justice and a cure for her lingering illness. Moreover, it is possible to place a different interpretation on the confrontation than that given by the Colemans and Thomas Bremincombe before the Justices of the Peace, some three months later. It seems probable that having been convinced that she was suffering from witchcraft by the learned arguments of Dr Beare, she and her family sought a solution to their problems through a recourse to popular beliefs in counter-magic. This was quite a different route than that pursued by Thomas Eastchurch and one that was neither straightforward nor respectable when it came to explaining events before justices, judges and jury. The supposed witch was brought – we may even go so far as to suggest that she was lured, under promises of charity – back to the Coleman household, the scene of the her crime, and ushered into Dorcas Coleman's room by two men who, under normal circumstances, might not be expected to give her the time of day, still less grant her free access to their private apartments. Unfortunately for all concerned, at this point, the plan went wrong.

Dorcas Coleman was simply too sick to strike out effectively at Susanna as she drew close. Her arms struck wildly about her but she was too weak to rise out of her chair and, as her husband and his uncle struggled to help Dorcas up onto her feet, a now very frightened and confused Susanna Edwards retreated out of the range of her blows, backing out towards the door of the room. As Susanna 'was almost gone out of the Chamber', Dorcas Coleman slid out of her chair and began to crawl her way across the floor, on her back, in an attempt to reach Susanna and claw at her legs. Her menfolk intervened, once again, in order to help her onto her feet. However, they failed to lift her up – whether on account of her violent thrashing or her sudden dead weight – until 'Susanna was gone down over the Stairs'.[28] While the terrified old woman fled out of the house and away down the street, Dorcas Coleman began to recover from her fit and was lifted back onto her chair. Though both of the men present now chose to link Dorcas' sudden improvement and return to strength to the flight of the witch from the room – with the magical link between the two women appearing to be so strong that it increased in direct proportion to the proximity of the witch and her victim – the fact remained that their attempt at counter-magic had failed dismally. The witch had escaped unharmed and was unlikely to let herself become trapped within the house for a second time. Worse still, the witch had once again been angered and a further form of retribution could be expected as 'pay back' for the botched assault. Thus, when Dorcas Coleman's condition deteriorated over the following days no one was left in any doubt that this stemmed from the witch's revenge. John Coleman recalled the intensity of his wife's 'tormenting Pains', while his uncle testified that 'Dorcas hath continued in such a strange and unusual manner of Sickness ever since unto this day, with some intermissions'. Chillingly, each time the illness came hard upon her 'when she could neither see nor speak, by reason that her pains were so violent' she would raise her hand and point at the spot on which Susanna Edwards had stood in her room and indicate 'which way [she] was gone'.[29] For John Coleman and Thomas Bremincombe this was a further terrifying development, signalling that their house had been violated and providing proof positive – if any more were required – of the identity of the witch who was the source of all their ills.

Had Susanna Edwards been cornered in the house and successfully scratched, then the Colemans might have believed themselves released from the shadow of her witchcraft and she, at the price of being bloodied and bruised, might well have been permitted to slip back into that quiet anonymity she had formerly enjoyed. However, as matters stood, the attempt by the Coleman family to take the law into their own hands and to dispense a form of rough justice, out of sight and mind of the courts and the authorities, had been an abject failure and appeared to have confirmed, rather than to have destroyed the witch's hold over them. If private counter-magic had failed, then the only course that now remained available to them was a public, judicial one. This suddenly, and perhaps even unexpectedly, became open to them once a hue and cry was raised against Susanna Edwards by Grace Barnes and her kin. The arrest of Temperance Lloyd had given credence to the idea that witchcraft was being practised in the town and, by the time the Colemans came to level their own charges, temperatures had risen to such a level that the veracity of the crime seems to have been hardly doubted by the majority of the populace. Indeed, by the time they belatedly came forward, on 26 July 1682, to give their evidence against Susanna Edwards' past crimes, four other women had already been arrested for witchcraft and questioned, alongside her, about working far more recent spells on other inhabitants of Bideford.[30] With the town ranged against her, Susanna's every conversation appears to have been observed and noted as her tone increasingly began to oscillate between the desperate and the boastfully fanciful. After a lifetime of being ignored, her utterances and movements were suddenly held to be of great account by her neighbours, who saw in her a servant of the Devil. Yet it was a poor master who failed to reward his followers and who could not even provide Susanna Edwards with the sweepings from the giant hogsheads of tobacco which littered the quayside or even the scraps of meat that had fallen from Grace Barnes' table. As she turned this way and that, to avoid the hostile gazes of the townsfolk during her last hours of freedom, Susanna could probably appreciate that her fate had come to hinge upon a farthing's worth of tobacco just as surely as Temperance Lloyd's had hung upon a child's desire for a shiny, fresh apple. Yet, as she was pushed and pulled through the door of the town jail, Susanna could not even hope for solace from her friend: for a tumbrel had long since carried Temperance Lloyd far away from Bideford, and back along the road to Exeter and the assizes.

6

A fine gentleman dressed all in black

The Devil had walked beside her in Gunstone Lane. That was what Temperance Lloyd had told the Justices of the Peace, on the morning of 3 July 1682. John Hill, the town clerk, took down her words just as he had done countless times before when dealing with other forms of religious dissent. Thomas Gist, the mayor, and John Davie, one of Bideford's aldermen, did the questioning in their capacity as justices. Anne Wakely, Grace Thomas, Thomas and Elizabeth Eastchurch and their serving maid, Honor Hooper, were also in the room. We have no way of knowing who testified first – though, on balance of probability, it is likely that it was the Eastchurches – if voices were raised, threats were issued, or if the questioning was especially leading. However, given the events of the seventy-two hours that followed the arrest of the beggar woman, it seems as if the two Justices of the Peace were prepared to hand over the entire running of the inquiry to the hands of Thomas Eastchurch. He suggested particular courses of action and they followed his recommendations, admitting new statements and evidences on his appeal, and that of his wife.[1] This was a remarkable development, which placed the accusers firmly in control of the prosecution and the gathering of evidence of witchcraft in Bideford.

It blurred the dividing lines between the official and private pursuit of justice, as the initial questioning of the suspect, while she was still in jail on 2 July, was left entirely to Thomas and Elizabeth Eastchurch without the supervision of the authorities. Thus, Elizabeth Eastchurch took the old woman to task, and:

Figure 15 *Gunstone Lane, Bideford (by kind permission of Peter Christie). It was here, on this steep street, that Temperance Lloyd struggled to carry a bundle of broom and where the Devil, supposedly, offered to take the weight of her load. Save for the uniform whitewash of the cottages, she would have had little difficulty recognizing the scene two centuries later.*

did demand of the said Temperance Lloyd whether she had any Wax or Clay in the form of a Picture whereby she had pricked and tormented the said Grace Thomas?[2]

Though this was denied, Thomas Eastchurch appears to have been more successful in wringing a full confession out of Temperance Lloyd, in which she admitted to having met with the Devil and undertaken to destroy Grace Thomas through witchcraft.[3] Whether before or after this was done, the old woman was brought before the Justices of the Peace and strip-searched for the Devil's mark by Anne Wakely 'in the presence of Honor Hooper, and several other women'.[4] Anne Wakely was at pains to point out that she conducted the search 'by the order of the said Mr. Mayor [i.e. Thomas Gist]', in giving her the responsibility for determining Temperance Lloyd's guilt. Yet, as friend and nursemaid to Grace Thomas, she was one of those bringing charges against the accused – the authorities were again abandoning any sense of objectivity and were facilitating the prosecution according to the wishes, and preoccupations, of the extended Eastchurch family.

Searches of this kind were not uncommon in witchcraft cases. In 1613, Frances, Countess of Essex had been examined by six women, including two midwives, who were held to be 'expert in matter of marriage', before a commission ostensibly formed at Lambeth Palace to nullify her marriage.[5] At the other end of the social scale, John Cotta's medical discussion of the properties of the witch's mark had been employed and amplified by Matthew Hopkins and John Stearne, during the East Anglian trials of 1645–7, to subject suspects to brutally degrading bodily searches. The discovery of supernumerary teats or lesions now became central to proving the identity and practices of a witch and were taken to be empirical proof of the crime.[6] As Stearne wrote in his account of *A Confirmation and Discovery of Witchcraft*, that was published in London in 1648, these blemishes marked the Devil's own, just as surely as baptism signified the people of God, and was 'that which maketh a Witch'.[7] They might appear, internally or externally, as 'a little red spot . . . little differing from a flea bite', as 'a blue spot' insensible to pain, as indents, sunk or hollow flesh, or as dangling strips of gristle.[8] Crucially, 'where this mark is, there is a league [with the Devil] and Familiar spirits'.[9] The manner of evidence gathering, garnered from Stearne and Hopkins, clearly informed and drove the prosecution of the Bideford women and, though the trial literature was more than a generation old, it honed a conception of witchcraft – and its detection – that emphasized the importance of suckling, familiar spirits, and the presence of the witch's mark.

We cannot know how roughly Temperance Lloyd was handled, on 2 July 1682, or how public was her humiliation. However, the presence of 'several' women does suggest that it was hardly done in camera. It can hardly be disputed that such an invasive examination of an elderly woman's genitals was both unedifying and shaming. If the examination was not as savage and brutish as the exorcists' assaults upon the nuns of Loudun – which Aldous Huxley once famously equated to 'rape in a public toilet' – it certainly carried with it all the overtones of abuse.[10] In its aftermath, Anne Wakely swore before the justices that:

> upon search of her said Body, she this Informant did find in her Secret Parts two Teats hanging nigh together like unto a piece of Flesh that a Child had suckt. And that each of the said Teats was about an Inch in length.[11]

Today, we might see these growths as no more than cervical polyps, reasonably common in post-menopausal women and, while unsightly, think of them as no more than benign tumours that might be removed through a cosmetic operation or in the course of a biopsy. Yet, to Anne Wakely, these cherry-red or light grey strands of long – and it was Temperance Lloyd's misfortune that they were, indeed, so lengthy – stalk-like gristle, appeared as additional, secreted, teats on which a devil or familiar spirit might suckle. Immediately upon their discovery, she:

> did demand of her the said Temperance whether she had been suckt at that place by the black Man? (meaning the Devil).[12]

That Anne Wakely, like Elizabeth Eastchurch, made 'demands' for information from the suspect would seem to be significant and to indicate close, forceful, or angry, questioning. Furthermore, it is suggestive of female-on-female violence (as with the attempt of Dorcas Coleman to scratch Susanna Edwards) rather than the popular modern view that witch-hunts were solely motivated through a murderous brand of misogyny.[13] After the discovery of the 'teats', Temperance Lloyd bowed to Anne Wakely's line of questioning and confessed to everything put before her. She had known the Devil carnally, 'been suck'd there [at the teats] often times by the black Man' and that the magpie that had 'come at the Chamber-window where . . . Grace Thomas did lodge . . . Temperance did then say, that it was the black Man in the shape of the Bird'.[14]

How much Temperance Lloyd understood of her predicament, or how she was bearing up after her arrest by the town's constables, is unclear. By the morning of 3 July 1682, when John Hill prepared to take down the first written evidence, she had already spent two nights in jail, been forced to submit to questioning by her social superiors, and endured the scrutiny of officials and the jeers of those who had come to accuse and show their hate for her. In contrast, Grace Thomas was in fine form. She had slept for the first time in weeks and attributed her return to health to the breaking of the witch's power upon her imprisonment. A witch without a spell or the ability to curse was no threat – just a worn-out old woman – and this knowledge served to embolden all those who came to testify against her. Indeed, what they said – and all that John Hill sealed – seemed to validate Lyndal Roper's maxim that 'witchcraft trials are one context in which women', in the course of the tumultuous sixteenth and seventeenth centuries, '"speak" at greater length and attract more attention than perhaps any other'.[15] If no one had thought to listen to Temperance Lloyd before, then they certainly listened now. And that was precisely the problem. It is not uncommon for individuals to wish to please those whom they identify as their 'betters', or those who have power over them, in providing what are suggested to be the 'right' answers. Though torture was forbidden by English common law, and there is no record of the old woman suffering sleep deprivation in the manner employed by Matthew Hopkins against his suspects, a combination of fear and flattery may well have proved decisive in the extraction of the 'right' sort of confession from Temperance Lloyd.[16] Certainly, the local authorities had been prepared to leave her in the hands of her accusers for the first day of questioning.

It is hardly surprising, therefore, that her testimony neatly dovetailed with that of her accusers and made explicable all of Grace Thomas' sufferings. She told them that on, or about, 30 September 1681:

> she met with the Devil in the shape or likeness of a black Man, about the middle of the Afternoon of that day, in a certain street or Lane in the Town of Biddiford ... called Higher Gunstone Lane: And then and there he did tempt and sollicite her to go with him to the house of Thomas Eastchurch to torment the Body of the said Grace Thomas.[17]

At first, she said that she had refused. However, the Devil was persistent. He promised 'that no one should discover her', came and went at will, was able to shift his size and shape, and caused both of them to become invisible to those they sought to harm. At times he worked through an imp, or familiar spirit, in the form of the 'Grey or Braget' cat; at others he, himself, appeared before Temperance as the 'black Man' or as a diminutive creature 'about the length of her Arm', with very big eyes, who capered about her, hopping or leaping 'in the way before her' as she walked up the street.[18] Thomas Eastchurch added other details that she had supposedly told him, that the Devil 'had blackish Clothes . . . and a Mouth like a Toad'.[19] Thus, already, in her testimony, one can see the fusing of several separate strands of thought. Lloyd was unclear, at times, as to whether it was the Devil or the familiar that appeared before her. The stray cat might have been him, forcing a way into the Eastchurches' home, but it might as easily be one of his servants. The magpie, however, was the Devil. Unlike many other trial testimonies, the familiars that she encountered did not do her bidding and she had no relationship with them; neither seeking to feed nor to name them as other reputed witches had done. In fact, the familiars seem to have had control over her rather than the other way around. She waited upon them and was led by their actions which she seemed, in most cases, barely able to understand.[20]

Furthermore, the Devil – with his large eyes, shrunken body and gambolling gait – appears to have taken on the form and function of the familiar spirit, or even a faerie, seeming more comical in its behaviour and appearance than terrifying. Her stories appear jumbled, even halting. Consequently, John Hill attempted to set them down in such a way as to provide them with a coherence and a form of chronology. When it came to the formal signing of a pact, or covenant, with the Devil, Temperance Lloyd suggested that a deal had been struck but that in her eyes, it took the form of a sexual, rather than written, compact. She made no mark with her blood and, it seems, on account of her illiteracy, the idea of signing away her soul with words, as opposed to actions, appeared entirely alien to her. Thus, the Devil again fulfilled the functions and behaviours more normally associated with a witch's familiar spirit, when:

> the said black Man (or rather the Devil, as aforesaid) did suck her Teats which she now hath in her Secret Parts: And that she did keel down to him in the Street, as she was returning to her own house . . . and afterwards did suck her again as she was lying down; and that his sucking was with a great pain unto her, and afterwards vanish'd clear away out of sight.[21]

Temperance Lloyd's devil was, therefore, not just degrading but degraded. Moreover, her association with him was guided by no promises of wealth or advantage. Oral sex with the Devil was reported as being unpleasant, humiliating and painful, and there was no offer of gain beyond the savour of revenge. The promise that she would not be detected won her over to his side for, otherwise, there is little to suggest a motivation either for her to serve him or for her grudge against Grace Thomas. Indeed, she attempted to suggest that it was the Devil, not she, who wanted to harm the victim.[22] The trouble was that Temperance Lloyd had now admitted to having made a demonic pact and to having been given a witch's marks. On top of this, she had already told the Justices of the Peace of her desire to harm Grace Thomas and the manner in which she had inflicted pain upon her over the past months.

In looking at Temperance Lloyd's confession it is striking that its contours mirror, remarkably closely, the concerns and evidence of her accusers: Thomas and Elizabeth Eastchurch, and Anne Wakely. Hence, the disturbing appearance and disappearance of the 'Braget Cat' was referenced and accounted for through Thomas Eastchurch's questioning, and the similarly threatening intrusion of the magpie was addressed directly by Anne Wakely. If the thieving magpie, rather than the stray cat, loomed large in the subsequent examinations and the framing of evidence, then it was because Thomas Eastchurch – as opposed to Anne Wakely – drove the proceedings. Between them, however, they had already been permitted, between 2 and 3 July, to shape Temperance Lloyd's confession and we may wonder how many of her recorded words, before her terse exchange with the Rev. Hann at Heavitree, were actually her own. Thus, she described the manner in which, after being rendered invisible by the Devil:

> she did then and there pinch with the Nails of her Fingers the said Grace Thomas in her Shoulders, Arms, Thighs and Legs.

in a way that accurately reflected the descriptions of pain given by Elizabeth and Thomas Eastchurch, and by the victim, herself.[23] Worse still, on cornering Temperance Lloyd as she was leaving the communal bakehouse on 30 June 1682, Thomas Eastchurch had apparently forced her to demonstrate to him how she worked her spell 'with both of her Hands'.[24] What we do not know is what level of force, or persuasion, was used against her and whether or not the old woman had decided, at this point, that there might be financial gain to be had in owning the identity of a witch. After all, she might have expected an inducement, in coin or kind, to lift the spell and break her curse. If this was her calculation, then once again she disastrously misinterpreted the gravity of the situation facing her. For Thomas Eastchurch had no intention of bargaining with a witch.

Threatened or not, her revelations became ever more chilling as she revealed that she had slipped into Grace Thomas' chamber, with the Devil, 'and that there they found one Anne Wakely the wife of William Wakely of Biddiford, rubbing and stroaking one of the Arms of the said Grace Thomas'.[25] This appeared as proof that Temperance Lloyd had, indeed, possessed preternatural powers and had witnessed a scene that she could not have done otherwise than by magical means. Here lies the nub of the problem that surrounds the character of Temperance Lloyd: she unnerved people and appeared to know things about them, their lives and behaviour that she should not. This was what had originally brought her into contact, and conflict, with Grace Thomas. Now, there are other explanations for her ability to acquire this knowledge. Not least of these is the evidence of her habit of lurking about the eaves and on the doorsteps of houses, listening for gossip, on the off chance that it might benefit her. Even if Thomas and Elizabeth Eastchurch did not put the words into her mouth, there is a straightforward explanation for Temperance Lloyd's knowledge of the bedside scene. She might have overheard the servants' conversations or simply looked up from the street into the upstairs window, or found a vantage point in the steeply sloping town from which to spy down upon them.

Questions of the nature and extent of her powers aside, the immediate problem for Temperance Lloyd was that the testimonies provided by her accusers were coherent and fitted the substance of her confession. Many Early Modern cases concerning property, assault or theft had proceeded on far shakier grounds of 'evidence'. She had been accused of a crime and she had confessed to it. However, neither the justices nor Thomas and Elizabeth Eastchurch were satisfied. Thomas Gist and John Davie were determined to clear up, once and for all, the earlier accusations of witchcraft in their town and, again, Temperance Lloyd obligingly confessed to all that was placed before her, without even the need for supplementary witnesses. If the Eastchurches had driven the initial proceedings, then Gist and Davie (in their roles as Justices of the Peace) now sought to widen them. Old cases were reopened and Lloyd confessed that though 'acquitted by the Judge and Jury' at Exeter Castle, in 1671, she was guilty of having pricked William Herbert to death 'by the perswasion of the black Man' and the art of witchcraft.[26] Furthermore, she also admitted that despite being searched for witch's marks, in May 1679, she had as had been alleged all along sought to kill the child of Edward and Anne Fellow, and that 'thereupon the said [child] did shortly die and depart this life' following the dropping of the charges against her. Yet, she was once again vague over whether or not it was 'the said black Man or Devil, (or some other black Man or Devil)' who helped her to do the hurt.[27] While there may be many demons, there is only one devil and, here, Temperance Lloyd was thoroughly conflating the idea of familiar spirits with Satan himself. The back-projection of the Devil into her confessions of the killing of William Herbert and Ann Fellow was necessarily muddled because her account of striking a demonic pact appears in her initial admission of guilt and is tied, very specifically, to a date around the close of September 1681. She felt that *something* had happened to her in Gunstone Lane, when she was hurrying home from the bakehouse with a loaf tucked under her arm, and that this encounter was the one that changed and subverted her life. Her subsequent admissions appear to be blanket confessions of guilt with her modus operandi and experiences of the Devil simply carried over from her initial statement. No one felt the need to examine the inconsistencies or to tease out the fine detail once her guilt was admitted.

As in the case of Grace Thomas, the justices were prepared to permit the other families of those believed to be afflicted by her witchcraft to conduct their own interrogations of the suspect. That Edward Fellow did not, further underscores his refusal to believe that his little girl died from anything other than the smallpox. However, William Herbert the younger remained convinced that his father had, as he claimed upon his deathbed, been murdered by Temperance Lloyd's witchcraft. Therefore, he was permitted access to the prisoner in the town gaol, on Tuesday 4 July. It must have been an extremely fraught and unpleasant meeting for both parties. Herbert later testified that he:

demanded of her whether she had done any bodily harm or hurt unto the said William Herbert deceased . . . [his] late Father; unto which she answered, Surely William I did kill thy Father.[28]

It was a stark admission and one that, within the pamphlet literature, has a ring of veracity to its words. The reported speech is less florid and far more direct: we are actually hearing Temperance Lloyd speak to us down the centuries. However, the words affected Herbert at the time, he claimed that he had pressed on with his questioning and:

> did demand of her further, whether she had done any hurt or harm to one Lydia Burman late of Biddiford Spinster. Unto which the said Temperance Lloyd answered and said, that she was the cause of her death.[29]

She then also confessed to having killed Ann Fellow and that she had also been the cause 'of the bewitching out one of the Eyes' of Jane Dallyn.[30] This was an entirely new twist and an admission of guilt which had not been pressed upon her. It may be that Temperance Lloyd had decided that if she had already been branded as a witch, she might as well behave as though she were one and act out her own revenge fantasies on all of those who had ever wronged her. Alternately, she may just have been so battered, frightened, frail, tired and cold that she would have agreed to absolutely anything and everything that was suggested to her. However, William Herbert the younger was not entirely credulous and wanted to know why she had not confessed to his father's murder at the time of her trial at Exeter Castle, in May 1671. Her answer not only confirmed his worst suspicions but also appeared entirely coherent within a framework of witch-belief, for:

> her time was not expired; For the Devil had given her greater power, and a longer time.[31]

This idea of the demonic pact having a set duration – rather like the contract struck by Dr Faustus with Mephistopheles – was well-established in the consciousness of Western Europeans by the 1680s, and provided a rationale behind Temperance Lloyd's changed behaviour when brought before the law. Her power was at its end, her master had forsaken her and her course was run.

As a consequence, with nothing else to lose, she might as well confess all and, from the mounting papers on Thomas Gist's desk at the town hall, it seemed that she had a long history of murderous crime. By the morning of 4 July, she had admitted to responsibility for no less than five murders, over the course of more than a decade, in the town.

Gist and Davie would satisfy themselves with clearing up their casebook. However, even then Thomas and Elizabeth Eastchurch wanted to go further in order to establish the guilt of the suspected witch. They wasted little time, petitioning Gist and Davie for further means of redress:

> because we were dissatisfied in some particulars concerning a piece of Leather which the said Temperance had confessed of unto the said Elizabeth Eastchurch ... and we conceiving that there might be some inchantment used in or about the said Leather.[32]

Clearly Elizabeth was looking for the evidence of sympathetic magic to tie Temperance Lloyd to the crime. On the previous day, Temperance had denied all knowledge of clay or wax figures, 'but confessed that she had only a piece of Leather which she had pricked nine times'.[33] This admission, probably no more than a chance comment evidencing one of the few possessions of any kind that the old woman had, preyed on Elizabeth Eastchurch's mind and she immediately associated it with 'the nine places in [Grace Thomas'] Knee which had been prickt ... as though it had been the prick of a Thorn'.[34] Consequently, she and her husband pressed for clarification on the means by which the old woman worked her magic and argued that a further examination should be held to determine the enchantments that lay behind the leather strip.

Once again, the two justices acquiesced in their demands, abrogating all responsibility for the conduct of the investigation. On Tuesday 4 July, they authorized the temporary removal of Temperance Lloyd from the jail so that she could undergo further questioning at the direction of Thomas Eastchurch. He had the constables march her up the road to St Mary's where she was brought before the Rev. Ogilby.[35] What Michael Ogilby made of the mob of 'divers other persons' which flooded into his church in the wake of the suspected witch and her escorts, we do not know.[36] There is a sense from Thomas Eastchurch's testimony, given later in the day – and the fact that

Ogilby made no attempt to involve himself further or swear his own evidence in the case – that he wished the matter to be resolved, and the frightened woman removed from St Mary's, as quickly as possible. According to Thomas Eastchurch, he wanted to know 'how long since the Devil did tempt her to do evil'.[37] This time, she said that it had been 'about twelve years ago [ie. in 1670/71, that] she was tempted by the Devil to be instrumental in the death of William Herbert', and added a more conventional rationale for her agreeing to do his bidding, in that 'the Devil did promise her that she should live well and do well'.[38] No one, least of all Temperance herself, appears to have noted or dwelt upon the irony of that promise, given the witch's continuing poverty and misery. The Devil was held to be deceitful in all his dealings, a bad, cruel and ruinous master. But there still might have been space for Temperance Lloyd to reflect over more than a decade that her circumstances had never once shown even the slightest measure of improvement. Neither during her freedom, nor under the duress of her captivity, does she appear to have had the capacity for reflexivity. Uneducated and unaware, she permitted others to completely control her fate and to read their own meanings into her life and actions.

So, she once again confessed all, this time embroidering the story a little for the benefit of the reverend. This time she tied the mysterious appearance of the child's doll upon Grace Thomas' bed to her own shape-shifting actions, rather than those of the Devil or a familiar spirit. She, herself, had changed form into the 'shape of a Cat' and fetched the doll into the shop run upstairs into the sick woman's chamber. The Rev. Ogilby then asked her 'particularly' – or so Thomas Eastchurch thought – if 'she had prickt any Pins in the said Puppit' but this she categorically denied.[39] If she had shown sense in this, then she confessed again to the murder of Ann Fellow and also to the new charge:

> that she was the cause of death of one Jane Dallyn late wife of Symon Dallyn of Biddiford Marriner, by pricking of her in one of her Eyes, which she did so secretly perform that she was never discovered or punished for the same.[40]

Unfortunately, we know little about the Dallyns save that Symon gave little trouble to the established order, signing the Oath of Allegiance to Charles II in

1661, and Bideford's *Loyal Declaration* to James II in 1685. Jane Dallyn was married in 1656 at St Mary's church, and sickened and died in Bideford in 1674.[41] All that we can say for certainty is that Temperance Lloyd was willing to admit that she had employed sympathetic magic to maim and murder Jane but that her family were unwilling to bring a prosecution against her. It may have been that Symon Dallyn was away in the Newfoundland fisheries, in the summer of 1682, or that he simply did not believe in the efficacy of witchcraft and its role in his wife's death. It seems probable that William Herbert the younger was among those crowded into the nave of St Mary's and that it was he, acting upon the confession that Temperance Lloyd had made to him the day before, who raised the matter again. Whatever the case, this potential for a fifth capital charge to be levelled against Temperance Lloyd was never acted upon. It also appears significant that Temperance Lloyd again dwelt upon her success in going undetected in her crimes. The idea that she could 'get away with things' appears to have been a source of consolation and pride that appears as a genuine character trait, unfiltered by Thomas Eastchurch's shaping and recording of her testimony.[42]

She was then set a test. She was asked to recite the Lord's Prayer – something that a servant of the Devil was incapable of uttering – together with the Anglican creed from the 1662 prayer book. She stumbled badly over both, 'imperfectly performing' the task.[43] However, Eastchurch did not elaborate upon this point before the Justices of the Peace when he testified later in the day. He seems to suggest that she managed to garble both forms but did manage to get some of the words out. This is not quite the same as a complete inability to utter her prayers because the words of God were literally choking her. Furthermore, the possibility remains that given her Puritan background, the 1662 prayer book was largely unfamiliar to her. She would not have been able to say the credo because she had never uttered it. The Rev. Ogilby did not wish to labour the point and seems to have wanted to draw the interview to a close as quickly as he could, giving her 'many good Exhortations, and so departed from her.'[44] This suggests that he left the crowd of townsfolk in possession of the church and, again, we do not know what happened next or if the Rev. Hann sought to fill the void left by Ogilby's departure. Certainly, Michael Ogilby never sought to trouble himself with the case and after having coerced him into interrogating the suspected witch neither the mob, nor the local authorities, sought to trouble him again. Indeed, the 'many good Exhortations' he gave to Temperance Lloyd seem to have been little more than platitudes to, henceforth, avoid the Devil and to lead a better life. It does not sound as if Ogilby was concerned with threatening her life, or with damning her soul. If he had, it seems more than likely that Thomas Eastchurch would have included his words in his evidence. Instead, it was Francis Hann who took his place within the later pamphlet literature as the prime target for the witch's hatred and the agent of her detection and destruction.[45] This is a sleight of hand by the authors of two of the three trial pamphlets, which has acted to fundamentally distort our knowledge of the mechanics of the prosecution.

The unknown author of *The Life and Conversation of . . . Three Eminent Witches* purposely conflates the identities of Ogilby and Hann, alluding to the 'Minister of the Parish' without naming him.[46] In addition, though he seems to have had access to the earlier committal documents, he projects the failure of Temperance Lloyd to correctly say the Lord's Prayer forward in time, from July to August 1682, and changes the setting, moving it from Bideford church to the dungeons of Exeter Castle. Thus, we are told that the Minister desired all three women:

> to say the Lords Prayer; of which the last could not repeat one word, but Temperance Floyd [sic] said all, with these alterations; when she should have said Lead us not into Temptation, she said Lead us into Temptation, and instead of Deliver us from evil, said deliver us to evil; and protested she could say no otherwise.[47]

It is conceivable that the Rev. Hann, who was in Exeter for the trial in August 1682, repeated Ogilby's test but it seems that the earlier account was reworked in order to provide a clearer and more coherent, demonological, explanation for the prosecution and conviction of all three suspected witches. As a consequence, it sought to make the trial appear as a single witchcraft case as opposed to two, or possibly even three, with the inconsistencies and elements drawn from folk belief downplayed and the role of the Devil accentuated. Thus, the women's crimes and their powers became uniform and enjoyed a far grander scope. Furthermore, the writer confuses the identity of the initial victim, muddling Elizabeth Eastchurch and Grace Thomas, in order to create 'Madam Thomas, the Wife of a worthy Gentleman of Biddiford', whose sufferings over 'Thirteen Years' seem to further conflate the case with that of William Herbert.[48] There was little space within an eight-page pamphlet so the action was compressed, and the character list shortened. Thomas Eastchurch vanished from the account and was replaced by the 'Minister of the Parish' who swiftly moved to centre stage. It is entirely reasonable to adopt a reductionist argument and to dismiss the text entirely as the product of a London bookseller's creative imagination. Conversely, it is also possible to see through the flaws and knowing omissions, an attempt to make both a defence of witch theory and a hero out of the Rev. Hann. Strictly speaking, he was not the Minister at St Mary's but because of Rev. Ogilby's dereliction and disinterest, he fulfilled that role in an 'acting' capacity. He was not where – or what – he was supposed to be. However, this is in keeping with the entire set of circumstances that permitted charges of witchcraft to arise in Bideford. No one from the lord of the manor down was fulfilling the roles that had been assigned to them within Early Modern society. It was not so much as a glamour that had settled over the busy port, but a distorting lens.

By this token, the Rev. Hann became the central figure. He was the one who detected witchcraft as the root cause of all her sufferings:

> which was hidden from Physician, nor could she obtain from them any remedy; sometimes she would be seized with Fitts or raveing, sometimes of laughing, but alwaies of pain. The Minister of the Parish, observing her Fitts of laughter and by his Reading, knowing something more than those Countrey Physicians, had a strong presumption that they must be the Effects of Sorcery, and therefore desired that in those Fitts, the bottoms of her Feet might be held, and covered with Hands, which Project had good successe for it always stayd her laughter, and proved consequently more effectual then the magical charme by which she was inchanted.[49]

This passage suggests something of the background to the case. It references the failure of the 'Countrey Physicians' hired by Thomas Eastchurch, as already discussed, but adds something new: the idea that it was through the studying of demonological texts – 'by his Reading' – that Francis Hann sought to define the problem and provide a solution. Thomas and Elizabeth Eastchurch had to have been getting their obsession with the 'science' of demonology and the workings of image magic from somewhere: and, from this account, it seems likely that it was the Rev. Hann who was instrumental in guiding their thoughts towards witchcraft. He was, however, an intellectual and from his travels in Italy would seem to have been well versed in Continental witch theory. Thus, he attempted to make the 'facts' fit the ideology. This is at its most obvious in the rewriting of Temperance Lloyd's meeting with the Devil, which shifts the location from Gunstone Lane to a broom field outside the town. Again, he comes to her 'in the Shape of a comly Black Man: With (as it were) a civil offer of Friendly assistance'.[50] However:

> she viewing him discerned his Feet to resemble those of an Oxe, and thereupon returning him an answer in which she used the Name of GOD ... the Tempter immediately transformed himself into a Flame, so disappeared.[51]

None of this fits with the testimony given by Temperance Lloyd on 3 July 1682, or that reported by Thomas Eastchurch on 3–4 July 1682. It strikes out the image of the capering little devil with its wide, toad-like eyes, and substitutes the more usual idea of the Devil appearing as a good looking, wealthy man, who proffers to help the woman – bent double under the weight of a load of broom – with her load; but who cannot disguise his cloven hooves. In this account, the Devil makes a second appearance, in animal form, as Temperance Lloyd went down the alleyway that led to 'her own poor Habitation', where:

> she saw (in appearance) a Black Dogg, which as she thought grew still bigger, and bigger, but that Vanishing she presently saw the same Black Gentleman, who but a little before met her in the Broome Field, who being now grown a little wiser then he was before, proceeded with those Suttile Insinuations that he prevailed with her to consent to his compact.[52]

In the initial court testimony at Bideford, the emphasis on the conclusion of the pact between the witch and the Devil was verbal and sealed through non-consensual sex. In this version, it was a far more formal, even legalistic affair, with the drawing-up of a contract that would be familiar to anyone who had read the leading learned writers of demonology, such as Remy, Bodin, de Lancre or King James VI and I, or who had read the popular literature written by John Stearne or Matthew Hopkins in the wake of the outbreaks of 1645–7.[53] Temperance Lloyd's contract with the Devil is now recast as having been:

> (Drawn up in writing, wherein he bound himself for a time, and her his forever) which she Signed with her own Blood, which the Devil (as an ingenious Chyrugion) drew from her with little or no pain.[54]

The sealing of the contract fundamentally altered Temperance Lloyd's being. It stripped her of both her gender and her basic humanity, and renders her as a 'Devilized creature' without a soul.[55] Seen from this perspective, her humiliating treatment at the hands of Anne Wakely and Bideford's 'knowing women' and midwives becomes more understandable. If she was not held to be fully human, and had willingly abandoned her womanhood, then her gynaecological examination was akin to that of a beast rather than a person. Of course, as soon as 'this poor wretch Struck Hands with the Devil' and the pact was concluded, she became his bond slave and the Devil revealed his true nature, for:

> where the Devil once becomes a familiar there he always makes himself an insulting Master; for no sooner was the Instrument Signed, but he immediately issues out his commands ... to make them [ie. the witches] further and greater Instruments of Hell.[56]

Therefore, what is significant in this account is the conclusion of the demonic pact rather than the operation of familiar spirits – such as the magpie and the cat – which are more particular to English witchcraft cases than those found on the continent, where the Devil himself tends to preside. Such a skewing of the evidence to make it fit with academic theory might, again, be more likely to sit well with someone like Francis Hann rather than with Thomas and Elizabeth Eastchurch. Where the interests of both parties conjoin is in the belief in image magic and the efficacy of protective counter-magic and it might be suggested that the Rev. Hann was behind the preoccupation of the Eastchurches throughout the process of evidence gathering in order to establish a link between the pricking of clay, wax or leather with a thorn in order to induce the corresponding pain in Grace Thomas and Jane Dallyn. Indeed, a major purpose of the pamphlet is to restate, in blunt terms, the reality of both image magic and measures to counteract it for an educated, urban readership. Thus, the unknown author offers:

> the Learned, (for this is certain Truth) whether or no it may not be thought, that Witches do torment in Effigie, (as surely this did by Tickling) and if they do whether there may not be infallible countercharmes, successfully and laudably applied, as we find this was, and it so whether or no it will not be highly beneficial to the Publick (especially to those of Scotland) to publish something to that end effectual.[57]

The author and publisher were, therefore, calculating that their new account would stimulate a fresh witch-hunt in Scotland and had an eye upon plentiful sales north of the border. This places a particularly sinister motive upon both the activities of the Rev. Hann and 'J.W.' – the publisher who may just have been John Weld – as they were not just attempting to garner money and fame from the Bideford case but to use it as a blueprint for an ongoing persecution.[58] Memories of the great Scottish hunt of 1662 and the outbreak in East Lothian in 1678 would have still been fresh in mind and though the 1680s turned out to be a relatively fallow period for witch trials north of the border, the potential was still there as was to be evidenced in 1697–1700 with the kirk driving a last major cycle of prosecutions that centred upon the town of Paisley and the Covenanter heartlands of the Lowland west.[59] The demonic pact was central to the conception of witchcraft in these cases and the fresh evidence from Bideford suggests that the publication of the pamphlet was consciously intended to be an incendiary act in order to stimulate further prosecutions and convictions, providing legal 'proof' of what was, in effect, a theological proposition.[60] It was certainly the case that the anonymous author, couching his account in language that was appropriate and acceptable to members of the Scots kirk left no doubt that it was 'The Minister abovesaid [who] caused this Witch to be apprehended, and committed to Exeter Goale.'[61]

If the pamphlet fought shy of directly naming Francis Hann, then the *The Tryal, Condemnation, and Execution of Three Witches* did not. In fact, by this time 'Mr. Haan' had become the main protagonist in the struggle against the witches, while Grace Thomas' fate and identity have become hopelessly garbled. She appears upon the title page and then only once in the text, as 'Hannah Thomas' who was 'Squeezed' to death 'by pretence of Love' in Temperance Lloyd's arms 'till the blood gushed out of her mouth'.[62] The deaths of 'Two more', presumably meaning William Herbert and Ann Fellow are glossed over. It was the Rev. Hann and his struggle with the Devil that mattered here.[63] In this account the three witches act in concert throughout, 'being all of one mind', in order to begin:

> to exercise their Divelish Arts, and upon Mr. Haan a Minister in those parts; a person of good Repute and honest Conversation, who sought his souls eternal happiness, while they design'd their everlasting Ruine.[64]

Fortunately, Francis Hann as opposed, one supposes, to 'Hannah Thomas', is held to be one of the godly elect and is, therefore, protected by divine providence from the Devil's assaults. Though:

> These Hellish Agents intended mischief and misery to the person of Mr. Haan: but the Over-ruling Power prevented the; but because they could not be suffered to exercise their Diabolicalism upon his body, they thought they would be some other way Reveng'd; so Witch like, they laid their Diabolical Charms upon his Cattle, so that those Cows that used to give Milk, when they came to be Milked they gave Blood, to the great astonishment of the Milkers.[65]

The bewitchment of livestock, as opposed to humans, is never alleged in the evidences taken against Temperance Lloyd. Furthermore, Francis Hann never sought to press any sort of charge against her, whether relating to himself or his livestock at Loxbeare. However, the passage does enable the accusations to appear to conform to the accepted notions embedded within the demonological textbooks about the limitations placed by God upon the Devil's power and the predilection for witches to strike at cattle in the fields, as well as other sources of wealth and happiness surrounding the hearth and home.[66] The Bideford outbreak did not fit the paradigm, as those afflicted were urban rather than rural dwellers, whose industry did not revolve around domestic production or the struggle for subsistence. Thomas Eastchurch was a merchant and shopkeeper; Edward Fellow was an exciseman; John Coleman and Symon Dallyn were sailors. None of them owned livestock, and for their wives and families whether or not the milk and butter, bought or manufactured by their servants, happened to churn was of very little significance. However, this did not stop the anonymous author of *The Tryal, Condemnation, and Execution of Three Witches* from attempting to shoehorn the facts of the case into a state of theoretical conformity. Thus, while the evidence of the worrying depredations of the familiars is largely ignored, the Devil – 'Man's Enemy, [the] Souls destroyer' – and the consequences of forging a pact with him loom large, as all three witches:

> made an Interchange, accepting a Hell for a Heaven, rather willing to please the Devil then the great Creator, whose smiles are more precious then refined Gold, the loss of whose love is no less then Everlasting Destruction ... these poor soul (aiming at nothing but ruine) imbrace Folly instead of Wisdom, present pleasure for eternal pain; take Flames for Crowns, misery for happiness, change God for a Devil, and a Soul for Hell. It is much to be lamented, that these persons should take delight in nothing more then to converse with Divils, who reason tells, seeks nothing but Destruction, Gods dishonour, Mans overthrow (to, if it were possible) empty Heaven and fill Hell.[67]

Here the witches 'wickedly, presumptuously, and prophanely, [made] use of the Devil to statisfie their Impious wills' and evidence of their contract is found in the alteration that he had wrought upon Temperance Lloyd's body causing her to grow 'Paps about her about an Inch long, which the Devil us'd to suck to Provoke her to Letchery'.[68] Thus, she consented and confessed 'that the Devil lay Carnally with her for Nine Nights together'.[69] Within this account, the original testimony of Temperance Lloyd – and, for that matter, Thomas Eastchurch – became twisted into something other than was intended. The teats that were held to suckle the witch's familiars are now held to stimulate her unnatural desire, while the pain they provoked is substituted for pleasure. With each remove, what the original actors in the case thought and felt was reworked, possibly by Francis Hann, himself, in order to convey a different and more readily appreciable meaning for those schooled in demonology. This is understandable, and all the more significant, if he was hoping to make a name for himself as an expert upon witchcraft who hoped to rise to national, and even international prominence, through the defence of witch theory and its validation through a wave of convictions at fresh trials. As a consequence, Temperance Lloyd's experience of 'the black Man', rooted in West Country folklore and a belief in familiar, animal spirits was comprehensively refashioned in order to remove from it the elements of improbability and potential humour in order that it conformed to a much more threatening of demonism, and she – by association – assumed the form of a fully demonized, soulless, witch. When faced with the apparent evidence of her multiple confessions, to no less than four murders over the space of eleven years, Bideford's Justices of the Peace forwarded the documentation to the authorities in Exeter and made arrangements to commit Temperance Lloyd for trial at the next county assizes. They moved with speed, hoping no doubt to remove the problem from their midst, and to provide a space in which the anger and fear aroused by the arrest of the witch might be permitted to subside. Within three days of her questioning at the church, she was on the move to Exeter under the guard of the town's constables. However, if Thomas Gist and John Davie thought that they had put an end to the accusations of witchcraft in Bideford, they were much mistaken. It seemed, that two fine gentlemen clad in black trod the cobbles of their town: one was thought to have been the Devil, the other was the Rev. Francis Hann. It is for the reader to decide upon which truly smelled of sulphur.

7

The discourse of the sleepy chimney

Witchcraft no longer sat at the margins: it was the talk of the town. It made people stop, think and reconsider the rules that governed life and death, and that separated those who were to be saved from those who were already damned. As the Devil's murderous intent was revealed through the multiple confessions of the imprisoned witch, and the impassioned evidence of her victims, something of the reach and overwhelming majesty of God's design became apparent through the discovery of the plot and the providential release of Grace Thomas from her afflictions.

It was understandable that others now sought answers to ailments that defied medical explanation or sought to resolve grievances against those who had troubled or 'ill-wished' them months, or even years before. Few were as direct, and perhaps so honest, as Grace Barnes who owned that she 'never had any suspicion that she had any Magical Art or Witchcraft used upon her Body, until it was about a year and a half ago, that she was informed by some Physicians that it was so'.[1] Oliver Ball and George Beare had clearly laid the groundwork but if their expertise might hope to diagnose the effects of witchcraft it required other specialists to cure it: namely, professional demonologists, or as they were popularly known witch-hunters. From what we have already seen, Rev. Francis Hann seems to have been more than willing to assume this mantle in order to make a name for himself. However, it appears that some of those who believed themselves to be afflicted by witchcraft were prepared to hire in the services of a professional witch-hunter from outside the locality. This is what the families of Dorcas Coleman, Grace Barnes and Anthony Jones appear to have done in the third week of July 1682, when John Dunning 'of Great Torrington' travelled the seven miles north in order to conduct an interrogation of Susanna Edwards while she was incarcerated in the town jail.[2] As in the case of Temperance Lloyd, what defines the behaviour of the authorities was the almost total abrogation of their authority – in marked contrast to the manner in which they dealt firmly and directly with nonconformist religious dissent – the absence of sworn evidence from the parish constables, and the willingness of Thomas Gist and John Davie to devolve (or perhaps even privatize) the gathering of pre-trial evidence to the accusers or those whom they had employed.

John Dunning was another of those individuals, attracted like moths to the smoke and flame of witchcraft allegations, who was not quite what he seemed. Indeed, in most subsequent accounts of the trials he goes largely unnoticed or unremarked.[3] His name does not appear in the 1674 Hearth Tax assessments for Great Torrington, though a 'John Duning' was taxed on the possession of two houses – one with a single hearth and one with two hearths – at Aveton Giffard in March that year, while a 'Jonathan Duninge' designated as a 'gentleman' owned a considerable property with fireplaces at Whitchurch, as well as a house at Buckland Monachorum that had two hearths.[4] It seems that the extended Dunning family owned a range of properties in Buckland Monachorum, Walkhampton and Meavy.[5] The problem with John Dunning's presence in the pre-trial records is that he appears and disappears without comment or explanation. He visited Susanna Edwards in prison, on Tuesday 18 June 1682, subjected her to a long barrage of questions – centring about her relationship to the Devil and the signing of a demonic pact – and is assumed to have been acting under authority and to be informed by a particular insight, or expertise. However, he did not give a sworn testimony before Bideford's Justices of the Peace, and he vanished from the scene just as swiftly as he arrived. The pattern of his questioning is reported, second hand, by Joane Jones, the wife of a husbandman (or small farmer), who had accompanied Dunning to the jail and had sat in on – or eavesdropped – the resulting interview with Susanna Edwards.

It is reasonable to ask why he sought to interrogate one of the imprisoned witches but not the other? Given the timing of his arrival in Bideford and Mary

Trembles' confession before the Justices of the Peace at Bideford town hall, on the same day, it is perhaps reasonable to suggest that John Dunning had been permitted access to Susanna Edwards while Mary Trembles had been taken out of prison for questioning by Thomas Gist and John Davie. He had attempted to speak to both women but had found one of them already gone. Moreover, given that he was intruding on the powers more normally exercised by the justices of the town, as a witch-finder, he might have wished to cause as little noise as possible in collecting his 'evidence' and securing his fee. In this way his interrogation of Susanna Edwards seems almost covert and was certainly opportunistic.

As a consequence, he was able to coax or threaten – we have that word 'demand' used in relation to the questioning – a confession out of Susanna Edwards in which she explained to him 'how and by what means she became a Witch'.[6] It was the proof of the demonic compact that interested him, as opposed to any particular desire to understand – in the way that Thomas and Elizabeth Eastchurch had – the manner in which the use of images transmitted pain to the witch's victim. As a result, it was left to Joane Jones to attempt to establish a link between demonological theory and the magical practice of Susanna Edwards.[7] John Dunning, by way of contrast, homed in on the matter of her dealing directly with the Devil, rather than operating through the agency of any manner of familiar spirits. Thus, Susanna Edwards provided him – and by extension, later her judges – with an account of her meeting with the Devil that, given both Temperance Lloyd's earlier testimony and the popular pamphlet literature surrounding English witchcraft, might readily appear as a 'textbook' example of how the Devil sought to prey upon the poor and the disaffected in order to damn a soul and fashion a witch. For:

the said Susanna did answer, that she did never confess afore now [how she had become a witch] but now she would ... that she was on a time out gathering of Wood, at which time the said Susanna Edwards did see a Gentleman to draw nigh unto her; whereupon she was in good hopes to have a piece of Mony of him ... [then] the said John Dunning did demand of the said Susanna, where she did meet with the said Gentleman; she the said Susanna did answer, that it was in Parsonage Close.[8]

This exchange established, at least for John Dunning, the core evidence for identifying a witch: namely, the meeting with the Devil and the sealing of a pact. However, his conversation with Susanna Edwards appears to have been somewhat brief and, having achieved what he set out to do, in securing a confession of guilt, he was quickly 'gone'. However, Joane Jones lingered and claimed to have heard further confessions tumble from the mouths of both Susanna Edwards and Mary Trembles. Later in the day, she testified before the Justices of the Peace that she had heard the women admit to pricking and tormenting Grace Barnes and Dorcas Coleman, and to bewitching both her own husband, Antony Jones, and one of the town constables.[9] She also overheard the two suspects fall out with each other, amid a flurry of mutual recriminations:

> the said Mary Trembles [did] say unto the said Susanna Edwards; O thou Rogue, I will now confess all: For 'tis thou that hast made me a Witch, and thou art one thy self, and my conscience must swear it. Unto which the said Susanna replied unto the said Mary Trembles, I did not think that thou wouldest have been such a Rogue to discover it.[10]

This bitter little exchange does carry with it a sense of veracity, and of accurately reported speech. One frightened woman attempted to shift the blame onto the other, in the hopes of saving herself, while the other remonstrated over her attempted betrayal. It certainly sheds some light upon Mary Trembles' subsequent confession before the justices.[11] Yet, Joane Jones wanted more. She must have hung about the town jail for several hours, listening out for snippets of information and attempting to memorize or write down what she had overheard. Once again, either Mary Trembles was absent for most of the time or else she said nothing that was either incriminating, or worth reporting. Susanna Edwards, on the other hand, had too much to say for herself. For, she was overheard to say that 'the Devil did oftentimes carry about her Spirit' and that:

> she was suckt in her Breast several times by the Devil in the shape of a Boy lying by her in her Bed; and that it was very cold unto her. And further saith, that after she was suckt by him, the said Boy or Devil had the carnal knowledge of her Body Four [sic] several times.[12]

These were far more explicit developments upon Temperance Lloyd's confession, together with something akin to the idea of 'night flight' that was well-known from the readings of continental witch trials or to the out-of-body experiences recently recounted in Joseph Glanvill's monumental best-seller, of 1681, *Saducismus Triumphatus*. Like any solipsism, academic witch theory fed itself through constant reinforcement and recapitulation. It seems clear, in the case of the Bideford Witches, that Temperance Lloyd's attempts to articulate some sort of folk belief, about the presence of toad-like familiar spirits and dark, imp-like or faerie creatures, was rapidly conjoined to elite notions of the striking of the diabolical pact by her accusers. Seventeenth-century England was characterized by rising literacy rates, generated in part by the relatively free press that had existed between 1640 and 1660, and fuelled by a public desire for news, views and gossip that was provided by a range of cheap broadsides, chapbooks and pamphlets.[13] Consequently, Bideford's apothecaries and doctors, its clergy, justices, and merchants had access to the official newsletters issued by Charles II's government and to a print market that, through long experience, knew that accounts of the discovery of witchcraft sold in large quantities. There was a popular appetite and interest in the subject, plentiful manuals on the detection and prosecution of the crime, and the recent example – which seems to have fascinated both the Rev. Francis Hann and Joseph Glanvill – of a witch-hunt, in Pollok outside Glasgow in 1678. On that occasion, six women went to the scaffold upon the evidence of Annabel Stuart, a fourteen-year-old girl, who informed against her mother and her mother's friends, and Jannet Douglas, 'a Dumb Girl', who gave her testimony through a form of sign language indicating the manner in which wax images had been stowed away by the suspects in a chimney piece.[14]

This case, as related by Glanvill, bore certain similarities to the outbreak of witchcraft at Bideford. Annabel Stuart testified at the Paisley assizes:

That on Harvest last, the Devil in the shape of a black Man, came to her Mother's house, and required the Declarant to give herself up to him; and that the Devil promised her she should not want any thing that was good.[15]

The Devil then 'took her by the hand and nipp'd her arm' bestowing the witch's mark upon her, and then 'in the shape of a black Man lay with her in the bed under the cloaths, and . . . she found him cold'.[16] Subsequently, the Devil would appear to her, in the company of her mother and her friends, as 'a Man with black Cloaths' whose feet were cloven, and whose voice was rough.[17] In his company, the coven then fashioned wax effigies made to resemble the local laird, Sir George Maxwell, which they bound upon a spit and turned over a fire, repeating Maxwell's name as they did so in order to bind the image to the man. Several figures in wax and clay, struck through with pins, were found in the houses of suspects, one being discovered among the bed-straw of one of the male witches seized, and another was 'found in a little hole in the Wall at the back of the fire' in Jannet Mathie's house. Testimony was given that as soon as the discovery was made of Jannet Mathie's poppet, that:

> Sir George's sickness did abate and relent after the finding of the said Picture of Wax, and taking out the Pins that were in the Effigies.[18]

In terms of the appearance of the Devil, his desire to strike a pact with the witches, his conferring of a witch's mark, and the employment of image magic to destroy an individual at the Devil's behest: the exposures of witchcraft at Pollok and Bideford have much in common. However, the Scottish witches appear to have been far more sophisticated in terms of their understanding of their art. They worked together in a coven, were firmer in their rejection of baptism and in the partaking of a counter-ritual in which they accepted the Devil's service, and each took a particular familiar spirit unto themselves, which they named, variously, as 'Landlady', 'Sopha', 'Rigerum' and 'Locas'.[19] By way of contrast, the inability of the Bideford Witches to provide coherent testimony, even when confessions were forced out of them, seems to have placed a greater emphasis upon the attempts of their accusers to fit fragmentary evidence (such as the scrap of leather and the child's doll) into a wider schema that they gleaned from their own partial readings of witchcraft texts. In this way, the accounts produced at the Paisley trials in 1678 may have provided a framework for the accusations at Bideford, not least as Glanvill's book was one of three literary sources, aside from the Bible, that was cited in the pamphlet literature as supporting the convictions of Temperance Lloyd, Susanna Edwards and Mary Trembles.[20]

The anonymous author of *A True and Impartial Relation of the Confessions of Three Witches* emphasized that the case against witches was built upon three pillars: namely, scripture, the law, and the study of demonology, itself. As a result, he cited King James VI & I's 'Learned' book *Daemonologie*, first published in Edinburgh in 1597; the widely reported cases of witchcraft judged by Sir Matthew Hale at Bury St Edmunds, in March 1664; and the text of Glanvill's *Saducismus Triumphatus*, which he attributes to the pen of Henry More (who edited Glanvill's notes on witchcraft in the south west for their posthumous publication a year before the trial of the Bideford Witches). It was a skilful combination of sources that permitted the arguments for continuing witch-belief, and prosecution, to be made briefly and authoritatively for a popular audience. Furthermore, it is reasonable to suggest that these same sources underpinned the intellectual and legal rationale behind the prosecutions at Bideford. We shall, therefore, look at each in turn.

King James VI and I's theorization of witchcraft, published as *Daemonologie* (literally the 'science of Demons') was intended as a manual to aid the detection of witches, as a codification of demonological practices, and as an attack upon

Figure 16 *Sir Matthew Hale delivering a judgement during a lightning strike, 1666 (Author's Collection). The intent of this Victorian print was to emphasize the judge's rationality and stoicism. However, his treatment of witches was harsh and based upon a willingness to accept spectral evidence.*

sceptical writers who had sought to deny the reality of witchcraft. Written against the background of major outbreaks of witchcraft in Scotland in 1590–1 and 1596–7, James sought to theorize demonology not only because he had a special interest in the subject, but because he felt it was his Christian duty to do so. Witchcraft was a religious and a political crime, striking at the order of the heavens and the governance of the earth. Thus, the king as 'a godly magistrate' was impelled to act upon it, and any serious intellectual seeking to express a consistent philosophy of nature could not afford to exclude what was a necessary and logical, if perhaps not a particularly edifying, extension of it. Therefore, when viewed from this perspective, the study of witchcraft could be regarded as being an entirely legitimate branch of theology, political theory, and basic statecraft. James wrote on witches because he felt he had to, in order to confirm the totality of his learning and the centrality of his concern for good, and 'godly', governance.

Significantly, he chose to write his treatise in the vernacular, in order that it should be as widely read as possible, not just by scholars and the judiciary, but by the people over whom he ruled. Moreover, it was popular in tone, unencumbered by the lengthy digressions and copious references to biblical and classical sources, that were so beloved of demonologists, and concise with the 80 pages, of the slim, quarto volume, split into three separate books. These covered a description of Magic; Sorcery and Witchcraft; and, lastly, the world of Spirits. *Daemonologie* took the form of an imagined dialogue between two friends, Philomanthes (literally, a 'lover of learning') and Epistemon (the 'man who knows'); who, in the exchange of a series of questions and answers, attempt to impart an understanding of the power and practices of witches. This type of didactic conversation, with one person (in this case, Philomanthes) feeding questions to another (Epistemon), who would provide an authoritative answer, was a familiar device in the religious and educational primers of the age. Both Protestants and Roman Catholics memorized their catechisms in this manner; and the authors of the *Malleus Maleficarum* had first adopted this approach when dealing with witchcraft. As the question and answer format lent itself particularly well to the business of the inquisitor, it is unsurprising that the formula caught on among demonologists, with two dialogues – Lambert Daneau's *Les Sorciers*, translated as *A Dialogue of Witches*, and Henry Holland's

Treatise Against Witchcraft – being published in England, just prior to *Daemonologie*, and possibly serving as models for the king's own work.[21]

However, the most important influence upon James was Jean Bodin's *On the Demon Mania of Witches*, a landmark text, published in 1580 and running through no less than ten editions before 1604. Although Bodin was a French Catholic, his work was acceptable to Protestants, on account of his consistent advocacy of toleration for the Huguenots, Jews and other minorities.[22] Indeed, his theories were particularly seductive for a centralizing monarch, concerned with the divine authority and majesty of kingship, as they projected an ideal of sovereignty and governance located within a single person or ruling group.[23] Within the context of witchcraft, Bodin was significant for urging the brutal treatment of suspects and for his polemical assault upon those who denied the reality of witchcraft. Thus, he delighted in providing examples of sceptics who had, later, been unmasked by the courts as being witches, themselves. However, he also wrote with economy and with a concern to record empirical 'facts' as he perceived them. Unlike the king's book, Bodin's was not, as was once thought, based upon his personal experiences as a judge in witch trials. Rather it served as a compilation of evidence, often drawn from cases in, or around, Bodin's home town of Laon, and was written, specifically, as a reference work in order to help magistrates weed out witchcraft from their communities. In this lay its particular, deadly, appeal.[24] Against the backdrop of the Reformation, both the church courts and the power of the Inquisition were on the wane, and new secular judiciaries were in need of the kind of fresh synthesis of the type that Bodin's *On the Demon Mania of Witches*, provided. It filled a gap in the market, which ensured its author spectacular sales, and created a whole new genre of works examining the phenomena of witchcraft and offering aids to its detection.

King James VI and I was, thus, part of a new, reactionary group of writers upon witchcraft, who – influenced by Bodin – sought to restate the imminence of both God and the Devil in human affairs, and to codify a disparate set of ideas (from trial records to folk beliefs) into a coherent theorization of malefic magic. Had James been a private individual or a lawyer, then his work would still have represented a significant attempt to introduce Continental witch theory – with its primacy of the demonic pact – into Scottish and, later, English intellectual life and legal practice. However, given that he was a reigning monarch, who sought a role as the political and intellectual arbiter of Europe, his pronouncements carried with them an immediate authority and a set of political imperatives, that enabled theory to jump into immediate practice in the governance of the state. He did not write *Daemonologie* upon scholastic whim and intellectual conceit. He wrote it in order to further the impact of his own conception of statecraft, as both a practical and a deadly tool in the art of state building in Scotland. Moreover, he lavished considerable time and attention upon the work.[25]

Scepticism is not a phenomenon unique to the modern age and James began his own treatise with an assault upon the intellectual foundations of disbelief to be found located within the works of Johann Weyer (1515–88), a physician to the Duke of Cleves – whose *De Praestigiis Daemonum* ('On Demonic Magic'), published in 1563, had already been the target of Bodin's devastating pen – and Reginald Scot (1538–99), an English gentleman, Presbyterian and Member of Parliament for New Romney, who had published *The Discoverie of Witchcraft*, in 1584.[26] The king, therefore, assumed the role of religious radical, following Bodin in overturning the consensus among an older generation of writers (Weyer had been writing a full generation before him) about the psychological and delusional, as opposed to the demonic and efficacious, nature of magic.[27] Weyer and Scot appeared so dangerous to the king because they seemed to be engaged in an attempt to diminish the threat posed by the Devil to humanity, thereby subverting the divine will and retarding the accomplishment of all God's plans. Viewed in this light, belief – or disbelief – in the reality of witchcraft could be seen as the ultimate test of Christian faith.[28] This was, in effect, the nub of the argument that spurred Joseph Glanvill to write in the 1660s and which motivated both the 'Countrey Physicians' and the Rev. Hann to accept the efficacy of the powers wielded by the Witches of Bideford, in the 1680s.

For them, as for King James VI and I, witchcraft was common to all ages and to all lands. Its existence 'is clearly provided by the Scriptures', while the activities of the witches, themselves, were revealed through 'daily experience and confessions'.[29] Above all else, they were in the king's words desirous of 'revenge, or of worldly riches, their whole practises are either to hurt men and their goods, or what they possess, for satisfying of their cruel minds in the former ... [and] to satisfy their greedy desire in the last point'.[30] It is worth noting the gendered language, for James's misogyny ran deep and while private prejudices may be unpleasant or hurtful, public ones when expressed by those in positions of authority may be deadly. Witches, wrote the king, were more likely to be women as:

> there are twenty women to that craft, where there is one man ... for as that sex is frailer than man is, so is it easier to be intrapped in those gross snares of the Devil, as was over well proved to be true, by the Serpent's deceiving of Eve at the beginning, which makes him the homelier with that sex since.[31]

Moreover, they could work their destruction in particular, well-defined ways. This could take the form of love magic in order 'to make men or women to love or hate'; maleficia, by which 'They can lay the sickness of one upon an other', as had the Devil upon Job; the practice of image magic, so that 'They can be-witch and take the life of men or women, by roasting of the Pictures' of wax or clay, so that 'the persons that they bear the name of, may be continually melted or dried away by continual sickness'; and through harnessing weather magic in order that 'They can raise storms and tempests in the air, either upon sea or land' and direct the flight of meteors through the agency of spirits of the air. They could fall victim to possession by demons or seek to obtain the ingredients for the casting of their spells through digging up graves, in the same manner as swine, and disjointing the exposed corpses.[32] Within this list of operations, and types of magical practice, it is possible to discern the kernel of the charges formed against the Bideford Witches, and forcefully articulated by Thomas and Elizabeth Eastchurch, Joane Jones and the Rev. Francis Hann.

For James, therefore, as for Judge Hale and Joseph Glanvill who followed him: the Devil was not a true rival to God but a perverse and degraded instrument of His will. He was permitted only as much room and power as God would permit him. As a result, he was 'the father of all lies' and 'the author of all deceit' who makes himself 'so as to be trusted in ... little things, that he may have the better commodity thereafter' and who is 'that old and crafty enemy of ours'.[33] On account of his powers being stolen, or loaned, from God; the Devil is forced to trick the gullible, the vicious and the greedy, as he 'may delude our senses, since we see by common proof, that simple jugglers will make a hundred things seem both to our eyes and ears other-ways than they are'.[34] Thus, the false miracles wrought by Pharaoh's magicians, in the *Book of Exodus*, were mere delusions. 'For that', wrote James, 'is the difference betwixt God's miracles and the Devil's, God is creator, what he makes appear in miracle, is so in effect. As Moses' rod being casten down, was no doubt turned in a natural Serpent: where as the Devil (as God's Ape) counterfeiting that by his Magicians, made their wands to appear so, only to men's outward senses: as kythed in effect by their being devoured by the other'.[35] Similarly, acting in imitation of God, with a stolen magic and a stolen power, the Devil could trick witches into thoughts of night-flight: 'For he being a spirit, may he not so ravish their thoughts, and dull their senses, that their body lying as dead, he may object to their spirits as it were in a dream, & (as the Poets write of Morpheus) represent such forms of persons, of places, as he pleases'.[36] Here, James neatly subverts the arguments of Weyer and Scot. The improbability of flying by broomstick, or the transformation of the witch into animal form, are no longer the issue: as they are accepted as being illusory. However, the agency of the Devil, in inducing these visions, is sustained and held as proof positive of the witch's guilt. In similar fashion, James appropriated Weyer's idea of the witch as an isolated melancholic but shifted the nature of the delusionary experience in order to condemn, rather than to exonerate, the suspect. Depression is, according to this new schema, only the outward symptom of the greater malaise, rooted in a demonically inspired delusion. However, the Devil prepares his ground carefully, alluring the would-be witches 'to follow him, by promising unto them great riches, and worldly commodity. Such as though rich, yet burns in a desperate desire of revenge, he allures them by promises, to get their turn satisfied to their heart's contentment'.[37] Thus:

> Finding them in an utter despair ... he prepares the way by feeding them craftily in their humour, and filling them further and further with despair, while he find[s] time, either upon their walking solitary in the fields, or else lying pansing in their bed; but always without the company of any other, he either by a voice, or in likeness of a man, inquires of them, what troubles them: and promiseth them, a sudden and certain way of remedy, upon

condition on the other part, that they will follow his advice; and do such things as he will require of them.[38]

Such a view dismisses the impact of depression upon the old, the poor, and the vulnerable and renders it as being but 'a cloak to cover their knavery with: For as the humour of Melancholy in the self is black, heavy and terrene, so are the symptoms thereof' of the greater distemper of witchcraft.[39] Therefore, the dispossessed and needy, perversely, become the aggressors. Nowhere, perhaps, was this to be seen more clearly than in the case of the Bideford Witches. For, once ensnared, the Devil would press upon them to conclude a demonic pact and would set upon them a witch's mark. As King James explained:

> he first persuades them to addict themselves to his service: which being easily obtained, he then discovers what he is unto them: makes them to renounce their God and Baptism directly, and gives them his mark upon some secret place of their body, which remains sore unhealed, while [ie. until] his next meeting with them, and thereafter ever insensible, how soever it be nipped or pricked by any, as is daily proved, to give them proof thereby, that as in that doing, he could hurt and heal them; so all their ill and well doing thereafter, must depend upon him ... At their third meeting, he makes a show to be careful to perform his promises, either by teaching them ways how to get themselves revenged ... Or else by teaching them lessons, how by most wild and unlawful means, they may obtain gain, and worldly commodity.[40]

The contract, or pact, was for James administered differently depending upon whether or not it was struck between the Devil and a learned male magician, of the type of figure made popular by Johann Faustus and John Dee, or the often illiterate – and, for James, always female – village witch, to be found in the Lowlands of Scotland or upon the slopes of Pendle Hill. In the former case, it 'is either written with the Magician's own blood: or else being agreed upon (in terms his school-master) touches him in some part', while in the latter, the witch often takes to her familiar spirits 'either in likeness of a dog, a Cat, an Ape, or such-like beast'.[41] Here, as elsewhere, James breaks from a strict adherence to Continental demonology in order to weld features drawn from

Lowland Scottish and English conceptions of magical practice, surrounding familiar spirits, onto his own projection of witchcraft. Universal principles take on local characters, as the demonically inspired witch rubs shoulders, in the pages of the king's book with all manner of spirits, faeries and wraiths.

It was unsurprising that 'the king's book' began to be employed by many officials in both national and local government, in Scotland and in England, as a textbook upon the subject. Significantly, in 1602, before James came to the English throne, *Daemonologie* was already being quoted as providing evidence in a Dorset witch trial and was quoted by name during the famous trial of the Lancashire Witches in 1612, helping to shape both the substance of their confessions and the framework for the manner in which their stories were subsequently told.[42] It was frequently referred to in Scotland in the course of indictments for witchcraft and in governmental exhortations to implement the laws against witchcraft with greater severity, and would appear to have influenced the attitude of the Earl of Mar and the Council of State to major outbreaks of witchcraft, in 1608 and 1610, which were swiftly and brutally suppressed through torture and the flames of the bonfire, by both central government and purely local authorities.[43]

In England, the new Witchcraft Act of 1604 may well have been formulated with *Daemonologie's* conclusions, and especially its emphasis on the demonic pact in mind, and was almost certainly aimed at flattering the king's intellectual vanity while addressing one of his major fears. The passing of the statute into law demonstrated that witchcraft was not merely the base prejudice of the uneducated multitudes but was also the pressing concern of society's elites. The Bill was framed by some of the highest and most learned men in the land, including the Earl of Northumberland, the Bishop of Lincoln, the Attorney General and the Chief Justice of the Court of Common Pleas. This statute of King James's repealed a similar act of 1563 passed under Queen Elizabeth, and although it retained most of the phraseology of the earlier legislation it codified aspects of the English attitude to the crime, bringing it into line with Continental doctrines of the diabolical pact with the Devil, making it a capital offence to 'exercise any invocation or conjuration of any evil and wicked spirit, or [to] consult, covenant with, entertain, employ, feed, or reward any evil and wicked spirit to, or for, any intent or purpose.'[44] The Act also made hanging a mandatory punishment for a first offence of maleficia, even when the victim did not die; whereas under the Elizabethan law the penalty had been far lighter, only a year's imprisonment. However, for divination of stolen property, the making of love potions or the damaging of property, the penalty remained unchanged: for a first offence, one year's imprisonment and an appearance in the pillory.

On a popular level, King James's two 'good helps' in the trying of witches struck a particular resonance. In *Daemonologie*, he had described 'the one is the finding of their mark, and the trying the insensibleness thereof', and the other as trial by water, on account that 'the water shall refuse to receive them in her bosom, that have shaken off them the sacred Water of Baptism, and wilfully refused the benefit thereof'.[45] Ironically, for a king who had been so concerned to monopolize the business of witch-hunting, and its attendant terror, on behalf of the state; these two 'helps' or 'tests' became the staple techniques of village vigilantes and the independent witch-finders, like John Dunning, who plied their trade for pay, over the course of the next century or more. If witch-pricking predated the king's book, then this form of torturous detection was certainly popularized by James's approval, while the 'swimming' of witches was effectively introduced into England through the pages of the *Daemonologie*.[46]

It might reasonably be presumed that the passage of a more severe Witchcraft Act under James VI & I, replacing the Elizabethan statute of 1563, would necessarily have ensured an increase in the tempo of witch-hunting and far more savage proceedings against suspects. However, the statistical evidence, pioneered by L'Estrange Ewen, in the 1920s, and continued by Alan Macfarlane and Jim Sharpe, in the final decades of the twentieth century, has shown that the actual numbers of persecutions following James's accession to the English throne (at least in the well documented and strongly affected counties of the Home Circuit) actually dropped from Elizabethan levels. Furthermore, a closer examination of the 1604 legislation has revealed that it was only marginally more severe than its Elizabethan predecessor and, far from being the individual statement of the king's position, was actually a fairly accurate representation of the state of contemporary elite opinion on the subject.[47] The actual day-to-day proceedings of the courts changed very little after its enactment. Indeed, the strongest clause in the 1604 Act, which had demanded capital punishment for a first offence of harmful magic, was not in fact enforced during King James's rule at all, and was only activated much later, during the East Anglian outbreak, fuelled by Hopkins and Stearne, in 1645. The argument remained after 1604, just as it had after 1563, as to whether or not witches could actually do harm. There was little, or no, reference to Sabbats or other rites common to Continental witchcraft trials; and there was no enaction of the use of torture into English law.[48] Even after accounting for the disparity in the lengths of their respective reigns, there were no more, and possibly even fewer, executions in James's reign than in Elizabeth's.

A marked dip in prosecutions characterized the reign of Charles I and, after the county elites reined in the surge of extra-judicial witch-hunting that had broken out in the eastern counties at the close of the First Civil War, the trend towards acquittal at the assizes continued through the latter years of the Republic and on into the Restoration. However, in the course of a landmark judgement, delivered at the assizes held in Bury St Edmunds in March 1664, Sir Matthew Hale (1609–76), the leading jurist of his day, sent two widow women to the gallows and provided a powerful legal restatement of witch-belief. The case not only resembled that at Bideford but a pamphlet, compiled from notes taken down in the courtroom at the time, was published shortly before the arrest of Temperance Lloyd, Susanna Edwards and Mary Trembles.[49] Its revelations of the bewitchment of children, the uttering of curses, tales of counter-charms and familiar spirits provided potent examples of witchcraft; while the courses pursued by the local authorities in Suffolk in order to detect the witches, might well have provided a ready-made blueprint for the witch-hunters of North Devon. Amy Denny (or 'Duny') and Rose Cullender had reputations for being bad tempered and sharp-tongued, and both had had previous brushes with the law and experienced long-running feuds with their neighbours, whose livestock had subsequently died in mysterious circumstances, whose carts overturned, and whose persons became infected with lice. Six, or perhaps seven years before, Amy Denny had acted as a wet nurse to a child who subsequently began to suffer from fits, and the charges rapidly widened to include allegations of the bewitchment of seven more people. One of the children affected, Jane Bocking, was said to have vomited crooked pins and a nail, which were presented to the court, and – according to the testimony of her mother, had seen spectres of the witches during her seizures. An attempt at counter-magic, suggested by the local cunning man, saw a toad thrown onto the fire. The poor creature sizzled and then exploded, and the next day Amy Denny was seen to have scorch marks on her face and body and appeared to establish the link between her physical form and that of her familiar spirit.[50] If you hurt one, you struck at the other.

Unlike the Bideford Witches, both women 'confessed nothing' and, as a consequence, the local magistrate appointed six local women (including the mother of one of the afflicted children) to search the bodies of the accused for the witch's mark. We do not know if Amy Denny consented to be strip-searched in her home, but Rose Cullender did, and the women soon discovered:

> in her privy parts three more excrescences or teats, but smaller than the former [that they had found on the lower part of her stomach, and which like that of Temperance Lloyd had also measured an inch long] ... [and] that in the long teat at the end thereof there was a little hole, and it appeared unto them as if it had been lately sucked, and upon the straining of it there issued out white milkie matter.[51]

However, the deadly novelty contained within the case was the willingness of the court under Sir Matthew Hale to permit the evidence of spectral apparitions as being legally valid and, also, the reliance upon expert testimony, most notably that given by Sir Thomas Browne (1605–82) as one of the foremost physicians and men of science of his day. Like Hale, he stood at the apogee of his career, and delivered decisive evidence that sought to provide a reasoned, empirical and even scientific, explanation for the operation of magic and evil spirits.[52] For Browne:

> he was clearly of [the] opinion, that the persons were bewitched; and said, that in Denmark there had been lately a great discovery of witches who used the very same way of afflicting persons, by conveying pins into them, and crooked as these pins were, with needles and nails. And his opinion was, that the Devil in such cases did work upon the Bodies of Men and Women, upon a Natural Foundation (that is) to stir up and excite such humours

super-abounding in their Bodies to a great excess, whereby he did in an extraordinary manner afflict them with such distempers as their bodies were most subject to, as particularly appeared in these children; for he conceived, that those swooning Fits were Natural, and Nothing but wall they call the Mother [ie. hysteria], but only heightened to a great excess by the subtilty of the Devil, co-operating with the Malice of these which we term Witches, at whose Instance he doth these Villainies.[53]

Thus, the Devil accentuated what were known medical complaints, manipulating science and the natural world, within their boundaries, to his own advantage. Sir Matthew Hale, in his summing up of the case for the jury, went further. It has been suggested that he was reluctant to direct the jurymen at Bury St Edmunds and that he left the balance of probability to rest with them, but when we look at his words it is hard to see evidence of anything more but a bold and unambiguous injunction:

That there were such Creatures as Witches he made no doubt at all; For First, the Scriptures had affirmed so much. Secondly, The wisdom of all Nations had provided Laws against such Persons, which is an Argument of their confidence of such a Crime. And such hath been the judgment of the Kingdom as appears by that Act of Parliament which hath provided Punishments proportionate to the quality of the Offence. And desired them {ie. the jury], strictly to observe their Evidence; and desired the great God of Heaven to direct their Hearts in this weighty thing they had in hand: For to Condemn the Innocent, and to let the Guilty go free, were both an Abomination to the Lord.[54]

It would be a brave or a particularly headstrong juryman who would choose to acquit upon such advice.[55] Yet, Hale did not have matters all his own way, with one of his fellow judges on the circuit, Sir John Keeling, being heard to observe that he was 'much unsatisfied' as to the women's guilt for if spectral evidence was permitted in all cases from those who had suffered visions and fits, 'no person can be in safety'.[56] Such a notion was a novelty in English witchcraft cases in the 1660s and it is possible that, some twenty years later, Dorcas Coleman's gesturing towards the spot where she believed Susanna Edwards stood before her, and Joane Jones' suggestion that the Devil had 'oftentimes carry about' Susanna Edward's spirit, were motivated by this idea and were attempts to enlarge upon it.[57]

Rose Cullender went to the gallows largely upon Sir Matthew Hale's willingness to permit evidence of assaults in spirit, as opposed to corporeal form, upon two of the young girls who were held to be bewitched. The trouble with this, as Keeling immediately understood and even Cotton Mather tentatively grasped, was that it defied any form of empiricism. Either the individual experiencing spirit attacks, or the apparition of witches, is lying (or possibly deluded) or they are telling the truth. The normal rules of evidence break down and it becomes a simple, binary matter of belief or disbelief. As a consequence, the admission of spectral evidence sustained and informed the witch trials at Salem, Massachusetts, in 1692, but when it was judged inadmissible, by Governor Phips, the cases and the convictions quickly dried up.[58] Unsurprisingly, the pamphlet account of Judge Hales' verdict at Bury St Edmunds was cited approvingly during the Salem outbreak by the Rev. Cotton Mather, New England's leading theorizer of witchcraft. 'We may see', he wrote, 'the Witchcrafts here most exactly resemble the Witchcrafts there', and that the pamphlet account of *A Tryal of Witches*, published a decade earlier, established the case as one that was 'much considered by the Judges of New-England'.[59] Given the frequency and comparative rapidity of the flow of commerce and information between the North American colonies and Bideford there may be grounds to speculate upon the cross-fertilization of themes and experiences of witchcraft between Massachusetts and North Devon. Economically, culturally, linguistically and theologically the largest thing to separate these communities was the more than three and a half thousand miles of Atlantic Ocean that separated New England from old. Thus, the Hale judgement – taken together with Sir Thomas Browne's testimony as a leading medical professional – provided clear legal precedent and the apparent conjunction of intellectual and temporal authority. There has been a tendency to see the prosecution of the Bideford Witches as being driven from below. To an extent this is true, but the picture is more nuanced than that, as the Eastchurches and the Colemans believed that they were acting in accordance with the best legal and scientific advice on offer. Far from being a tale of ignorance and superstition, the tragedy of the Bideford Witches was that they became the victims, in an increasingly unequal society, of their own powerlessness and the intellectual conceit of others.

Thus, their own flaws were turned against them; as evidence of guilt as opposed to innocence, and as proofs of their strength as opposed to weakness. It was Sir Matthew Hale's view that: 'Afflictions are most certainly fruits and effects of sin: and worldly crosses and calamities do as naturally flow from precedent sins, as the crop doth from the seed that is sown'.[60] Therefore, it followed that the disfigured, the poor, and the chronically sick were not to be the objects of pity but of suspicion and blame, for their sufferings were a manifestation of God's displeasure and their own sinfulness. It was a comforting vision for the wealthy and self-reverential, like Hale, and for Bideford's nascent capitalist class, who could choose to read divine sanction into their success in trampling upon and exploiting others less fortunate, or commercially astute, than themselves. In a similar fashion, the melancholia – or depression – that was noted eating away at Temperance Lloyd, Susanna Edwards and Mary Trembles during their imprisonment and trial at Exeter came to be viewed, largely through the writings of Joseph Glanvill, not as an extenuating factor that gave rise to wishful fantasies and delusions born out of an empty belly, but as further symptoms of demonic suggestion. The idle 'discourse of the sleepy chimney' piece, where the elderly and infirm would huddle for warmth and swop drowsy stories wreathed by pipe and woodsmoke were to be overlaid by the suspicion that it was precisely in these settings that truth was told and where diabolical plots were hatched and spells were cast.[61]

If the legal underpinning of witch prosecution was restated by Sir Matthew Hale, then its corresponding basis in academic debate was championed by the major intellectual offensive launched by the Anglican divine, Joseph Glanvill (1636–80) who had sought to defend the core tenets of witch-belief and the necessity for persecution. His interest in witchcraft was no mere academic, or esoteric, pursuit but a major theological – and by extension, political – attack upon not just witchcraft, but the practice of natural magic and the adherents of religious nonconformity and Whiggism. A Fellow of the Royal Society and Chaplain in Ordinary to King Charles II, Glanvill was another figure who does not conform to our modern stereotypes of witch-hunters as being marginal, credulous, and inarticulate. He was plausible and dangerous on account of his learning, his proximity to power, and his thirst for scientific experiment. This sense that the pursuit of 'pure' science can lead otherwise than to 'pure' reason, has recently troubled revisionist academics. 'How could,' asked Thomas Harmon Jobe, 'the cautious, skeptical, and empirically minded Glanvill defend witchcraft, even in its most popular version, and the occultist Webster [whom Glanvill consistently wrote against] seek to abolish the belief entirely?'[62] Just as with Sir Matthew Hale, Joseph Glanvill appears as an individual whose career – when viewed in terms of its role in sustaining witch-hunting – seems to strike at comforting beliefs in the linear progression of reason through the 'scientific revolution' and the prejudice of social elites that holds that educated, wealthy, and powerful men might be less subject to irrationality and blind hatred than the masses.

The growing threat to religious belief and social order posed by Cartesian science and Hobbesian materialism had prompted Glanvill to publish *A Blow at Modern Sadducism*, in 1668, which linked together Sadducism (which in this case was equated to a sceptical attitude towards witches) with atheism, 'sacriledge, rebellion and witchcraft'.[63] In effect, the denial of spirits or witches was portrayed as the first step towards denying the reality of God, Himself, and the embrace of corrosive godlessness and atheism.[64] Glanvill had become fascinated by an outbreak of witchcraft at the hall at Tedworth, in Wiltshire, owned by John Mompesson. Shortly after apprehending a vagrant, who had formerly served as a drummer in the Cromwellian army, Mompesson's home became subject to all sorts of unexplained happenings – the ripping of bolsters, the scratching of nails across the floor, the delivering of blows from unseen assailants and a remorseless drumming above the roof – that today we might ascribe to poltergeists, but which were then perceived to be rooted in the operation of evil spirits, directed by witchcraft.[65] It was noted that once the vagrant had been forcibly removed from the community, sentenced and transported to the colonies, the drumming suddenly ceased. However, once he had returned – with or without official permission – the mysterious tattoo began to beat again in the heavens. For Glanvill, who had personally examined Tedworth house, from the cellars to the roof spaces, and found no evidence of fraud, or natural explanation for the strange and disturbing occurrences, just as for Robert Hunt, his original source; this seemed *prima facea* proof of the reality and efficacy of witchcraft.[66] He then began to compile a vast casebook of incidents of witchcraft – to be completed and published after his death by Henry Moore and Anthony Horneck, in 1681, as *Saducismus Triumphatus* – which attempted to provide a new, empirical and therefore 'scientific' basis for the old art of witch-hunting.[67]

Glanvill was a master of Orwellian 'double think', by which he argued that the sheer improbability of the witches' confessions was actually a smokescreen raised by the Devil to encourage disbelief in his designs and the depredations of his agents.[68] Imagination, as opposed to 'Knowledge' was to be distrusted as a sign of the Devil, as 'heightened and prepared by Melancholy and Discontent' it prepared the witch to take service with her dark master.[69] Similarly, the venting of 'Malice, Envy, and Desire of Revenge' – all those characteristics more likely to be found within the make-up of those cheated in life and found begging on the streets, rather than with society's elites – were thought by Glanvill to prepare the way for the Devil's approach.[70] He provided his readership with a concise definition of a witch, as being:

> one, who can do, or seems to do strange Things, beyond the known Power of Art and ordinary Nature, by virtue of a Confederacy with evil Spirits . . . The strange Things are really performed, and are not all Impostures and Delusions. The Witch occasions, but is not the principal Efficient; she seems to do it, but the Spirit performs the Wonder . . . And these Things are done by vertue of a Covenant, or Compact, betwixt the Witch and an evil Spirit.[71]

If the idea of the demonic pact, enshrined by the Continental witch theorists like Remy and Bodin was still held to be valid, then so was the particularly English conception of the familiar spirit, as:

> 'tis not impossible, but the Familiars of Witches are a vile Kind of Spirits, of a very inferior Constitution and Nature, and none of those, that were one of the highest Hierarchy, now degenerated into the Spirits we call devils.[72]

Yet the ethereal hierarchy also had to be defended and maintained. Glanvill made it clear that all of these spirits existed only upon the sufferance of God who could 'annihilate' them 'at his Pleasure'.[73] If familiars existed then, so too, did the witch's mark. It seemed probable to Glanvill that:

the Familiar doth not only suck the Witch, but, in the Action, infuseth some poisonous Ferment into her, which gives her Imagination and Spirits a magical Tincture, whereby they become mischeviously influential ... that the evil Spirits having breathed some vile Vapour, into the Body of the Witch, it may taint her Blood and Spirits with a noxious Quality; by which her infected Imagination, heightened by Melancholy ... may do much Hurt upon Bodies, that are impressible by such Influences. And 'tis very likely, that this Ferment disposeth the Imagination of the Sorceress to cause ... the Separation of the Soul from the Body; and may, perhaps, keep the Body in fit Temper for its Re-entry, as also it may facilitate Transformation, which, it may be, could not be effected by ordinary and unassisted Imagination.[74]

Furthermore:

the Devil is a Name for a Body Politick, in which there are very different Orders and Degrees of Spirits, and, perhaps, in as much Variety of Place and State, as among ourselves; so that 'tis not one and the same Person, that makes all the Compacts with those abused and seduced Souls, but they are divers ... of the meanest and basest Quality in the Kingdom of Darkness.[75]

Herein, Glanvill attempted to provide a reasoned rationale for the Devil and his powers that was the mirror image of God's majesty and ability to work miraculous wonders. It seemed to him to be but a short step from denying the power of witches to harm to denying the presence of an imminent God, who could cure. Thus, a lengthy biblical exegesis was mounted in order to defend the proposition that the ailments and possessions suffered by the victims of witchcraft were not diseases but afflictions that stemmed directly from malefic magic and the operation of demons. To do otherwise would, he thought, compromise the integrity of the gospels and threaten 'the Truth and Credit of the whole [of Christian] History'.[76] Consequently, we can see that he was playing for what he, rightly, regarded as high stakes. In addition, the opinion of Bideford's apothecaries and physicians in attributing symptoms beyond their understanding or remedy to witchcraft was neither so craven nor ill-informed as might have been first thought. If they were reading Glanvill – and, as Jonathan Barry has shown, his particular referencing of West Country cases of witchcraft and possession is suggestive of a regionalized appeal – then they were reading an up-to-date source, that appeared authoritative, and which had a direct bearing upon their professional knowledge.

Amid a climate of Tory political reaction, Glanvill appeared as an ideal spokesman for the Crown and for the proto-absolutist state, while his nemesis, the former surgeon to a regiment in Cromwell's army and religious radical, John Webster (1610–82), appeared as 'the Squire' or 'Advocate' 'of his beloved Hags'.[77] The irony, therefore, lay in the fact that a considerable body of evidence already existed, both in terms of Reginald Scot's *Discoverie of Witchcraft*, published in 1584 – which Glanvill, like James VI & I before him, excoriated – and Webster's *The Displaying of Supposed Witchcraft*, probably begun in the early 1670s but published in 1677, that fundamentally challenged the core tenets of witch-belief.[78] The trouble was that, certainly within the context of North Devon in the 1670s–80s, no one in the professions or in a place of political authority appeared to be reading the critical texts. It may have seemed, as Henry More was quick to point out when editing Glanvill's manuscripts, that the pen of John Webster appeared 'rude' and far beneath the standards of 'Charity and good Manners' that Glanvill had appealed to in one of his more patrician passages.[79] The fact, however, remained that even though Webster's intellectual contribution to the repeal of the witchcraft acts has often been denigrated or overlooked, while the representatives of authority, high culture and learning championed witch-belief and the judicial murder of 'Hags'; an anarchic, and often fiery mystic, who rejected formal academia, consistently maintained a sceptical attitude towards the existence of demonic witches, who could shape-change and do harm through magic.[80] While the academics heard the voices of devils in the cry of the night owl; the rural physician gently mocked the improbability of the feast at Hoarstones, in Lancashire , whereby the reputed witches 'were carried away upon [the backs of] Dogs, Cats or Squirrels'.[81]

Webster – a marginal man, who championed marginal causes and marginal women – was risking a lot in entering into the controversy, as his opponents were cosmopolitan and well-connected, and operating within the mainstream of the restored, monarchical regime. Moreover, they were quick to level the charge of 'Atheism' against him, that (like witchcraft) carried the death penalty, and did not scruple at attempting to bring him down through attacking him as a practitioner of magic, the very 'Paraclete of Sorceresses', who masked the activities of witches because he was in league with the Devil, himself.[82] Being the 'Hag's Advocate' carried risks. Yet, for Webster, the learned 'science' of demons was no science at all. For:

> Though there be a numerous company of Authors that have been written of Magick, Witchcraft, Sorcery, Inchantment, Spirits, and Apparitions, in sundry ages, of divers Countrys, and in various languages: yet have they for the most but borrowed from one another, or have transcribed what others had written before them.[83]

As a consequence of simply parroting received wisdoms, without checking their sources, demonologists had created a perfect system of solipsistic thought, whereby 'a multitude of vain and lying stories, [had been] amassed up together in the Writings of Demonographers and Witchmongers of strange and odd Apparitions, Feats, Confessions, and such like'.[84] The seemingly impressive compendia of case studies, compiled by writers like Glanvill, were therefore hardly worth the paper that they were written upon, while Glanvill's 'story of the Drummer [of Tedworth], and his other[s] of Witchcraft', were in Webster's eyes 'as odd and silly as can be told or read'.[85] This was an author engaged in fighting a bitter rear-guard action in defending witch-belief, and Webster was quick to employ military metaphors – culled from his time in the Parliamentarian army – to exploit the idea that he was being driven back, further and further, from the core assumptions of King James and Bodin into the margins, and blind alleys, of debate. The tide of learned opinion appeared to be turning in his favour. 'Now', Webster argued:

> we know they use to do in this case, as Souldiers use, who when they are beaten forth of some Out-work or Trench, they then retreat into another that they think more strong and safe. And being driven from their weak Hold of a bare affirmation without proof ... then they flye to this assertion: That the Confessions of so many Witches in all Ages, in several Countries,

at divers times and places, all agreeing in these particulars, are sufficient evidence of the truth of these matters.[86]

However, the evidence gained from the confessions of witches was 'not of credit and validity to prove these things; but are in themselves null and void, as false, impossible, and forged lyes', as they were extracted either under duress, and threat of torture, or were the products of simple frenzy or deep-seated mental illness.[87]

Webster distinguished between two different types of individual who had consistently been identified, and convicted, as witches. Firstly, there were those who pretended to be able to harness demonic power, who were merely 'Impostors, Cheaters, and active Deceivers'; and, secondly, there were 'those that are but under a mere passive delusion through ignorant and superstitious education, a melancholy temper and constitution, or led by the vain credulity of inefficacious Charms, Pictures, Ceremonies and the like, traditionally taught them'.[88] It was the duty of magistrates and justices to exercise 'much judgment, caution, care and diligent inspection' in order to distinguish between the two, for in all 'things of this nature great heed ought to be taken of the conditions, qualities, ends and inventions of the Complainants and Informers, who are often more worthy of punishment, than the persons accused. For many [come] forth of a meer deluded fancy, envious mind, ignorance and superstition do attribute natural diseases, distempers, and accidents to Witches and Witchcraft, when in truth there is no such matter at all'.[89] There was, indeed, guilt to be adjudged, but it sprang from cheap, worldly deception; and not from the flames of hell, wrought by witches and demons. Consequently, according to Webster's distinction: 'The one sort of which deserves to be punished for couzening of the people, and taking upon them, and pretending to bring to pass things that they have neither skill nor power to perform; but the other sort rather merit pity and information, or the Physician's help than any punishment at all.'[90]

The discrediting of the reality of the demonic pact was at the kernel of the book's argument. However, Webster approached the subject in a number of novel ways that reveal not only his background as schoolmaster and physician, but also his realization that misogyny and the projection of sexual fantasies onto the suspects were factors that drove the identification, and prosecution, of witches forward. Thus, he took exception to the methods of identifying the witch's mark and noted from his medical practice that:

> there are divers Nodes, Knots, Protuberances, Warts, and Excrescences that grow upon the bodies of men and women, is sufficiently known to learned Physicians and experienced Chirurgions. Some have them from their mothers wombs, some grow afterwards, some proceed from internal causes, some from external hurts, some are soft, some hard, some pendulous, some not, some fistulous, and issue matter, some hollow and indolent … And these are more frequent in some persons, by reason of their Complexion and Constitution, in others by reason of their Age, Sex, and other accidents and circumstances, especially in Women that are old, and their accustomed purgations staid, or by reason of Child-birth, and the like. Now if all these were Witch-marks, then few would go free, especially those that are of the poorer sort, that have the worst diet, and are but nastily kept. And for their being indolent, it doth argue but ignorance for many sorts of Tumors and Excrescences are without pain, as well as fistulous and hollow Warts. And it is a wo[e]ful error, to make that a sign and mark of a diabolical Contract, that hath natural causes for its production … where is the coherence, connexion, or just consequence?[91]

Once again, he combined a sense of observation with scientific understanding and an awareness that persecution tended to be age-, gender- and class-specific. Furthermore, he understood that many of the intrusive examinations of women for the witch's mark, and the accompanying humiliations that suspects were forced to endure, had a pornographic component, or exalted in a perverse and sadistic sense of the erotic. The violent stripping of women and the forcible – and forceful – examination of their genitalia, enacted as part of a public ritual, was no more than an exercise in voyeurism and an essentially masturbatory act. In Webster's words, the 'pricking' of witches – suggestive then, as now – 'can have nothing in it more than the stirring up of the imaginative faculty, and thereby to move titillation in the members fitted for the act of generation, which is a thing that happens to many both and women' through auto-eroticism.[92]

He held that witches did 'not make a visible Contract with the Devil', that the Devil 'doth not suck upon their bodies, [and that] they have not carnal Copulation with him'.[93] Rather 'they become so deluded and besotted in their Phantasies, that they believe the Devil doth visibly appear unto them, suck upon them, have carnal copulation with them, that they are carried in the Air to feastings, dancings, and such Night-revellings; and that they can raise tempests, kill men or beasts, and an hundred such like fopperies and impossibilities, when they do not suffer any thing at all, but in their depraved and deceived imaginations'.[94] Therefore, their 'delusion is internal' rather than the product of external, corporeal forces and beings.[95] Part of the solution lay in an enhanced role for education and critical thinking, on a popular level, so that 'such as have an humble, lowly, and equal mind, that they [might] commonly read Books to be informed, and to learn those truths of which they are ignorant, or to be confirmed in those things they partly knew before'.[96] Thus, writes Webster, the pedagogue, that the common people 'ought to be clear and free from those imbibed notions of Spirits, Hobgoblins, and Witches, which have been instamped upon their Phantasies from their very young years, through ignorant and superstitious education', as once their youthful education was overlooked 'but very few that get themselves extricated from those delusive Labyrinths, that parents and ignorance have instilled into them'.[97]

The move to consider the nature of evil as an internal, metaphysical, phenomena rather than as a predatory, external presence was a new and revolutionary proposition, which had an immediate and transformative impact upon the way in which seventeenth-century men and women thought about their place in the world and the preternatural. For Webster, the Devil became – at the most conservative reading – a transcendent force in human affairs, at the most radical, he was reduced to the role of a metaphor, as the philosophical embodiment of the essence of evil. Consequently, the power of the Devil, just like that of the witch, was downgraded, while – in true Puritan fashion – the totality of God's power and insight was emphasized. Consequently, wrote Webster, 'to ascribe to the Devil the efficiency of those operations we do not clearly understand, is to allow him a kind of Omnipotency, and to rob God and Nature of that which belongeth unto them'.[98] Moreover, the 'Devil cannot by his own power or will, either appear visibly in what shape he please, neither can he when he will, nor as he will, perform these strange tricks, because he is under restraint, and can act nothing but as the will of God orders and determines'.[99] He could not 'afflict Job, until that God's hand was laid upon him, and God ordered him to be an instrument in that affliction'.[100] Thus, 'he cannot execute any evil, but as he is ordered of God, and that God doth not let him loose but for just causes and reasons; then can it not be that the Devil doth visibly appear and make Leagues with Witches, nor work such strange things for them, because there is no just or reasonable end that can be assigned, why God should order him to do these things; and therefore a visible League with Witches is merely false and fraudulent'.[101] The divine will was designed, essentially, for the good and for the progress of man: to enable the transition from a fallen state to that of salvation. Webster's vision was, therefore, essentially an optimistic one. However, there is also the sense that he – even in the pages of *The Displaying of Supposed Witchcraft* – still, at heart, promoting a form of Grindletonianism (the 'heretical' sect within Anglicanism that he had championed in his youth) that held that heaven might be created upon earth. That utopia is only made possible if man's capacity to commit evil is owned as a natural – if unpalatable – part of the human condition, rather than outsourced and projected onto a preternatural 'other'. Within this framework, there was a place for the betterment of humanity through educational and scientific progress; marking a truly revolutionary – and potentially earth-shattering – break with deference, and a uniting, immutable 'Great Chain of Being', of the type beloved by proto-absolutists of the stamp of King James VI and I and Jean Bodin. A struggle over the nature and importance of demons, thus disguised a far more fundamental political and individual divide, between – on the one hand – Glanvill, who would seek to place limits upon the scope of intellectual endeavour; and Webster, who conceived of the human potential as being limitless.

Webster's expression of humanism might have been thought to have had a direct appeal to Bideford's potters, sailors and tradesmen: men like John Abbott and Gabriel Beale, and women like Sarah Dennis and Susan Davy. Certainly, by the time that Daniel Defoe visited the town, a generation later, this notion of mutability, change, endeavour and invention as underpinning an improvement in human affairs had taken root. However, while Glanvill's work became a best-seller, running through four fresh editions and twelve print-runs into the first half of the eighteenth century, the sales of *The Displaying of Witchcraft* were slight by comparison.[102] Thus, while Webster's book remained something of a lone voice, the only significant challenge to Glanvill's restatement of witch theory, the Anglican demonologists were able to rally and marshal their forces behind the monumental *Saducismus Triumphatus*, and through Benjamin Camfield's *A Theological Discourse of Angels* – that was published in 1678 under the imprimatur of the Archbishop of Canterbury – launched a direct attack upon Webster's scholarship.[103] In struggling to regain their doctrinal and political supremacy at the heart of the English state, the Anglican clergy – confronted by the reality of schism with the non-conformist sects and the certainties offered by their traditional Roman Catholic critics – had felt compelled to take the definition of spirits, and the limitations of God's powers, extremely seriously, indeed. It was this that served to redefine and promote witch theory in the 1670s–80s as an integral part of natural philosophy, and which permitted Glanvill's blueprint for political and theocratic absolutism to dominate the intellectual landscape. The danger for the unaware and un-reflexive is that they risk being buffeted by storms that they are incapable of understanding. This was certainly the case of the Bideford Witches who could not comprehend that their struggles for subsistence and street corner quarrels could be magnified by those in authority to appear as matters of state, which touched upon both the Crown of Charles II and the heavenly majesty and magistracy of God. Ignorance, for them offered neither defence nor a state of bliss, as Temperance Lloyd shivered away her life in the dungeons underneath Exeter Castle, and as Susanna Edwards and Mary Trembles faced a fresh round of allegations and interrogation at Bideford town hall.

8

The politics of death

The stench of the Devil's breath was everywhere. He was held to have whispered into the ears of the old women, to have walked beside them, and to have become their lover. From the reports of conversations had, and overheard, at the town jail, Thomas Gist and John Davie already had a fair conception of the nature and scope of Susanna Edwards', and Mary Trembles' dealings with the Devil long before the two women were brought to the town hall for questioning, on Tuesday 18 July 1682.[1] Neither appear to have had any trouble confessing their guilt, incriminating the other, or placing the striking of the demonic pact at the heart of their profession of witchcraft. Certain lines of questioning are apparent in their depositions, as taken down by John Hill, with the nature of the pact returned to and clarified. Susanna Edwards referenced her begging and her deference to authority, explaining that when she thought she spied a gentleman approaching her across the field known as Parsonage Close she had opportuned him for a coin and curtseyed to him 'as she did use to do to Gentlemen'.[2] Her poverty was of great interest to the Devil who asked her, explicitly:

> whether she was a Poor woman? unto whom she answered, that she was a Poor woman; and that thereupon the Devil in the shape of the Gentleman did say unto her, that if this Examinant [ie. Susanna Edwards] would grant him one request, that she should neither want for Meat, Drink nor Clothes.[3]

Unfortunately, at that point, Susanna managed to bungle the deal. Instead of naming her price she used the name of God and asked: 'what is it shall I have?'. As a consequence, 'the said Gentleman vanished clear away from her'.[4] Whether she really did meet someone out in the broom field or whether the whole event was simply an imagining, what is revealing is the fact that Susanna Edwards was not an individual who was ever given a choice. The offer of 'Meat, Drink' or 'Clothes' – let alone riches – was so alien to her that she had no idea how to respond, falling back upon deference and letting the 'Gentleman' or devil make the choice for her. So used to want, and to not receiving that which she desired, even in her imagination she could not conceive of attaining plenty. The confession of Mary Trembles was mainly concerned with her daily round of begging and her pursuit of food. She described her hunt for bread, meat and tobacco and even suggested that her failure to kill Grace Barnes at the Devil's behest was the result of her dropping some of 'the Meat she was then carrying unto the ... [common] Bakehouse'.[5] The communal fire provided, therein, for cooking and baking appears central to Mary Trembles' existence and her daily routine to the extent that an incantation, or spell, forged with demonic assistance could be interrupted in order to scrabble about the street in search of spilled scraps. Hunger, in this case, was a more potent and immediate master than the Devil.

It is striking that, in terms of the wording of her compact with the Devil, Mary Trembles used the same words as Susanna Edwards. The difference lies in that, whereas the Devil had approached Susanna directly, it is she – as an already practised witch – who came to Mary with the Devil's temptation in her mouth. Unlike her erstwhile partner, Mary Trembles had no difficulty in conceiving of an opportunity that she 'should do very well' and added 'Money' to the head of the list of the comforts that had been offered.[6] What is strange, from a purely theoretical view of demonology, was that she did not claim to have struck the pact with the Devil but with Susanna Edwards, as his intermediary. Only when she had agreed to serve Susanna and made 'this Bargain' did 'the Devil in the shape of a Lyon (as she conceived it) ... come to this Examinant, and lay with her, and had carnal knowledge of her Body'.[7] Setting aside John Hill's condescension that her familiar spirit was something 'like' a lion, it is worth noting that the justices did not pursue the novel idea that Susanna Edwards, as a witch, had the power to buy souls and sign covenants in her own right. Instead, they chose to return – time and again, with both women – to their preoccupation with the nature of the Devil's sexual assaults and the length of time that they had spent in his service. Thus, Mary Trembles confessed that she had practised witchcraft 'about three years last past' even though all of the instances of her involvement were drawn from a relatively brief and more recent period, stretching from 18 May to 16 July 1682.[8] As soon as her pact had been struck, presumably in the spring of 1679:

> the Devil had had carnal knowledge of her Body, that he did suck her in her Secret parts; and that his sucking was so hard, which caused her to cry out for the pain thereof . . . besides the time above-mentioned . . . the Devil hath had carnal knowledge of her Body three other times; and that the last of the said three times, was upon the said 16th day of July as she was going towards the common Bakehouse.[9]

For her part, Susanna Edwards testified that her initial meeting with the gentleman in black apparel had occurred 'about two years ago', that is in the summer of 1680, more than a year after she supposedly tempted Mary Trembles.[10] Yet no one, before or since, seemed to mind the slip in the chronology. Doubtless Thomas Gist and John Davie were far more interested in her meetings with the Devil, for they also permitted her to glide over the issue of whether or not she struck a bargain with him. It is assumed to have taken place but, unlike Temperance Lloyd, Susanna Edwards did not seek to define its terms. Her use of God's name had frightened the Devil away, once, but then he – or more likely a familiar spirit – returned to visit her. 'Afterwards', she thought:

> there was something in the shape of a little Boy, which she thinks to be the Devil, came into her house and did lie with her, and that he did suck at her breast. And [she] confesseth, that she did afterwards meet him in a place call'd Stambridge-Lane in this Parish of Biddiford, leading towards Abbotisham (which is the next Parish on the west of Biddiford aforesaid) where he did suck bloud out of her breast.[11]

Both women, therefore, seemed hazy about the formal conclusion of their pacts with the Devil and conflated his person with the traditional witch's familiar spirit, whether as a creature that Mary Trembles attempted to describe as best she could, and which John Hill approximated as a lion, or with Susanna

Edwards experience of 'a little Boy'. It is to be wondered whether Susanna explicitly referred to her black-clad 'Gentleman' as being the Devil in corporeal form, or if this was the court's interpretation of her words as set down by John Hill. At the close of her confession, he was clear to distinguish that he is assigning the name of the Devil to that entity which Susanna Edwards 'called by the Appellation of a Gentleman'.[12] Whatever the case, Susanna added a further detail that appeared to corroborate the evidence provided by Mary Trembles, in that:

> the said Mary Trembles was a servant unto her . . . in like manner as she . . . was a Servant unto the Devil.[13]

This was an exceptionally foolish admission. It may have reflected no more than the one time in her life that Susanna Edwards thought herself more important than another living soul, or it might have been born out of the squabble between the two women that was eavesdropped by Joane Jones, with each seeking to drag the other down with her. However, in attempting to play to – and please – the justices, Susanna Edwards merely succeeded in making things far worse for herself and her unfortunate accomplice. And things did suddenly, and expectedly, become worse amid the theatre of the courtroom. When pressed to describe how she actuated her magic, Susanna made the further mistake of attempting to oblige, describing how – just like Temperance Lloyd – she and Mary Trembles 'did prick and pinch . . . Grace Barnes with their fingers, & put her to great pain and torment'.[14] Thus, when Anthony Jones – the husband of Joane – observed Susanna while under questioning 'to gripe and twinkle her Hands upon her own Body, in an unusual manner', he assumed the worst and spoke harshly and, presumably, loudly to her, saying: 'Thou Devil, thou art now tormenting some person or other'.[15] At this, she shot back a curse without thinking, saying: 'Well enough, I will fit thee'.[16] Precise, cutting and threatening it had all the marks of a witch's torment and, sure enough, the words grew through the day in Anthony Jones' mind. The town hall was packed and the justices wanted it cleared upon any pretext in order to physically remove the crowd from the scene of an altercation, and to give them some time for their tempers to cool. Consequently, Jones was sent, together with the parish constables and 'some others' to bring Grace Barnes from her home, a few hundred yards across town, in order to give her own testimony. Unfortunately, this only served to make matters worse. Anthony Jones arrived at Grace Barnes' home to find her relapsed, struck with pain at the precise moment – or so he thought – that Susanna Edwards had 'griped' and 'twinkled' her fingers. If she could do that, he reasoned, then he – according to her curse – was surely next.

The crowd bearing Grace Barnes swept through the streets and into the town hall, where Susanna Edwards spun around to regard them as they clattered up the stairs that led to the council chamber. She looked Anthony Jones straight in the eye while he was helping Grace Barnes up the steps. Immediately, he let go of her and cried out: 'Wife, I am now bewitched by this Devil Susanna Edwards!'[17] According to Joane Jones' account, her husband was 'forthwith . . . taken in a very [sad] condition . . . and . . . leapt and capered like a Madman, and fell a shaking, quivering, and foaming, and lay for the space of half an hour like a dying or dead man'.[18] Despite the commotion, Anthony Jones was eventually revived and was well enough to swear a statement, on the following day, echoing that given on the 18 July 1682 by his wife, and that further accused Susanna Edwards of bewitching both himself and Grace Barnes while she stood before the court. The incident surrounding his apparent possession, while bearing testimony to the power of suggestion in the human psyche, also sheds considerable light upon the conduct of the case. The court testimonies are brief and laconic but here we have the sense that the questioning of the women was undertaken amid an atmosphere more akin to a bear-pit than a courtroom, where a press of people were continually jockeying for position, running in and out of the building, and barracking the defendants. Furthermore, it seems more than coincidental that the confession eventually taken from Susanna Edwards, on Tuesday 18 July, was practically identical to that overheard – and reported – by Joane Jones. The earlier exchange with John Dunning and the words that allegedly passed between Susanna Edwards and Mary Trembles were, thus, reworked in the forms of confessions given to the two women to acknowledge. Clearly, Joane Jones proved a far more effective and single-minded figure in driving forward the charges against the two women than either John Coleman or Grace Barnes. Unfortunately, we know next to nothing about her other than her husband was a small-scale farmer like

William Wakely and the elder William Herbert.[19] Like Dunning, with whom she consorted, she slips in and out of the trial records with little explanation and no obvious connection to the accused or the other accusers. Her grudge, though unexplained in a way that those of Dorcas Coleman's or Grace Barnes' were not, seems to run all the deeper on account of its lack of articulation. She clearly believed in the efficacy of witchcraft, did not hesitate to identify its source in Bideford and was one of the most active compilers of evidence against the women, attempting to shoehorn their words to fit particular demonological patterns and precedents. Moreover, she was prepared, like William Edwards, to press the idea of spectral evidence upon the court. At the same time as Grace Barnes was being helped across town, William Edwards (a blacksmith, who does not appear to have been related to Susanna) was confiding the substance of yet another conversation overheard between Mary Trembles and Susanna Edwards while they were in jail. This restated Susanna Edwards' admission that 'the Devil had carnal knowledge of her Body; and that he had suckt her in her Breast and in her Secret Parts' but added the fresh detail that the two witches had allegedly taken on the forms of spectres and 'did appear hand in hand invisible in John Barnes's house' in order to torment his wife and to attempt 'to make an end of her'.[20] If the court now appeared to be in danger of drowning amid a sea of evidences of different forms of maleficia, then what was clear-cut – just as in the case of Temperance Lloyd – was the preparedness of Gist and Davie to, in the ugly parlance of today's market economy, 'outsource' the operation of justice in the town and to entrust the primary job of the collection of testimonies and confessions to the women's accusers. As a consequence, the overwhelming majority of the allegations brought against Susanna Edwards and Mary Trembles were simply hearsay, compiled from the eavesdropping upon their conversations over a relatively brief period, of not more than twenty-four hours, between 17 and 18 July. The problem was that the women were guileless enough to agree to all that was set before them and to give their assent to the idea that they had concluded demonic pacts and that they had endeavoured to kill both Dorcas Coleman and Grace Barnes through the means of witchcraft. This was more than enough to send them both to the gallows and compelled Thomas Gist and John Davie to despatch them, under guard, to Exeter to await the summer assizes.

They did so with haste, as Susanna Edwards and Mary Trembles were already on the road to the county town before Anthony Jones had chance to present further evidence against them. Once again, there is a sense that the Justices of the Peace were hoping that the physical removal of the two women would ease tensions and permit the governance of Bideford to return to something that might pass for normality. It was certainly an exercise in expediency that smacked of an attempt to make the women someone else's problem and to absolve the justices from the consequences of their own actions. They had undoubtedly empowered a certain section of the townsfolk – foremost among whom were Thomas Eastchurch and Joane Jones – to take the law into their own hands in order to settle long-standing scores. As a result, the witch-hunt in Bideford might have gone even further. On Friday 21 July, John Hill noted the contents of a letter sent to him from John Gist in Exeter, where the pre-trial assessments of the assizes' cases were being made by the county's grand jury. This referenced two more cases of witchcraft in Bideford, concerning Mary Beare and Elizabeth Caddy, who were further suspects. The implication appears to be that at the same time as allegations were being made against Susanna Edwards and Temperance Lloyd, they were also being made by a fresh set of accusers against these two other women. It is clear, therefore, that Bideford between 1 and 19 July had been the scene of no less than four distinct allegations of witchcraft (namely: the individual cases against Temperance Lloyd, Mary Beare and Elizabeth Caddy, and the joint case taken against Susanna Edwards and Grace Trembles). The difficulty lies in the lack of evidence that survives about the attempts to prosecute Mary Beare and Elizabeth Caddy. This amounts to no more than Hill's registering of the mayor's letter in the *Bideford Sessions Book*, and it seems that the authorities attempted to stifle these particular allegations.[21]

The mechanics of witchcraft prosecution worked very differently in the cases involving Beare and Caddy, to those which had been permitted to dominate the actions against Lloyd, Edwards, and Trembles. Caddy and Beare do not appear on the lists of the poor chargeable to the parish or in the payments made by the Andrew Dole. It is just possible that Elizabeth Caddy had links to the Conventicle movement in Bideford, but both women clearly were of some means and had friends, or family, to speak for them.[22] As a result, Thomas Gist was reluctant to move against Mary Beare at all. We do not know who levelled charges against her, although there were 'several informations' noted. Similarly, we do not know what the allegations of witchcraft entailed, or even the identity of a possible victim, or victims. However, what we do know is that on this occasion, the justices were quick to ensure that 'there was no prosecution' and to draw the matter to a close as swiftly as possible. Elizabeth Caddy was not quite so fortunate as there was enough evidence presented by Mary Weekes, 'wife of Robert Weekes of Bideford', to ensure that the pre-trial papers were forwarded for consideration by the grand jury at Exeter. Unlike Temperance Lloyd, Susanna Edwards, and Mary Trembles, she was not remanded in the town jail – so none of her accusers could get near her – but, instead, she was bailed and returned home to await the judgement from Exeter as to whether or not she had a case to answer. The fact that she was capable of meeting the bail requirements further suggests that she had ready access to money and that she was well above the threshold of poverty. Dealing with the propertied classes under the law, as Thomas Gist knew full well, was a very different proposition than dealing with the indigent poor. He had travelled to Exeter, shortly after the removal of Susanna Edwards and Mary Trembles, having heard William Edwards' evidence; and he appears to have made it his business to steer the witchcraft cases through the meeting of the grand jury. Here the contention that Bideford's justices conceived of the cases as an adjunct to questions of the paying of the poor rate and control of the town's beggars, breaks down. For, Gist was prepared to act decisively in halting the proceedings against Elizabeth Caddy at the pre-trial stage while permitting the actions against Temperance Lloyd, Susanna Edwards and Mary Trembles to run their course. A major factor in channelling the official response in a different direction was, also, the simple fact that Elizabeth Caddy, like Mary Beare – but unlike Temperance Lloyd, Susanna Edwards and Mary Trembles – had had the wit and resourcefulness to simply deny all the charges levelled against her. At the grand jury stage, there was precious little that could be done to help those who had already confessed to crimes but a good case could be made for those who held themselves innocent. Therefore, it seems that Thomas Gist was able to marshal a plausible defence of Elizabeth Caddy that quickly won round the county jurymen to the view that she had no case to answer. His letter to John Hill was to signal the swift termination of action against her in Bideford and the return of her bail bond. With that, she slipped quietly out of the frame and history, just as the mayor had intended.

The same was not the case for Temperance Lloyd, Susanna Edwards or Mary Trembles. However, the grand jury does not seem to have had the easiest of jobs in settling upon their indictments. The morass of hearsay evidence proved problematic and time consuming in order to edit it down into neat charge headings. Furthermore, despite her admission of guilt, Temperance Lloyd had already been tried – and acquitted – for the murder of William Herbert the elder. Under English common law she could not stand trial for the same crime, a second time. Therefore, that capital charge had to be dropped, however much it might enrage the victim's son. She could, though, be charged for the murder through *maleficia* of Lydia Burman and for the bewitching of Grace Thomas. A similar problem faced the grand jury over how to handle the multiple confessions of Susanna Edwards and Mary Trembles. As John Hill noted at the time:

> Susanna Edwards & Mary Trembles having severally confessed upon their Examinations that they had bewitched Grace Barnes they could not be indicted for the same crimes severally, wherefort Mary Trembles was Indicted only for practising witchcraft upon Grace Barnes, And the said Susanna was severally Indicted for practising witchcraft upon the body of the said Dorcas Coleman.[23]

Official uncertainty persisted. Witchcraft had always been viewed as an 'exceptional' crime and with prosecutions declining nationally throughout the Restoration period, the Western Circuit had seen a long list of acquittals for the crime running from 1670 to 1680. The exceptions to this were to be found in the case involving two women, Judith Witchall and Anna Tillinge, who had been convicted of 'Feloniously lameing Thomas Webb by witchcraft' at the Wiltshire Assizes and left for execution, in March 1672.[24] This is a tantalizingly under-researched case, especially as the presiding judge, Sir Richard Rainsford (1605–80), was far from credulous and the 'prime suspect', Elizabeth Peacock, who had previously been accused of witchcraft, in 1670, and was now indicted on multiple counts of murder, walked free, after it was revealed that the fits suffered by a child witness were feigned.[25] The case against these 'Malmesbury Witches' seems to have been part of an attempt to head off a wider witch-hunt in the area, as up to fourteen suspects had been initially identified as witches in the pre-trial hearings. If a major outbreak had been averted and Elizabeth Peacock, who seems to have been universally disliked and mistrusted, was acquitted of murders, bewitchment and the far less common charge of killing fifteen horses, then it seems somewhat anomalous that her accomplices, Judith Witchall and Anna Tillinge, were hanged for the lesser charge of laming a man, for which Peacock was also arraigned but acquitted.[26]

Set against these two convictions, there were nineteen acquittals, during the ten-year period in question, including that of Temperance Lloyd for the bewitching to death of Lydia Burman in 1679. The cases seem to follow a particular pattern of maleficia and bewitchment, resulting in the incapacity, possession and death of victims, with Elizabeth Peacock's specific destruction of property – the eight geldings and seven mares worth £150 – being exceptional, probably pursued on account of their high monetary value, as Prof. Jim Sharpe has suggested.[27] Increasingly, the standard practice was for assize judges to steer juries away from the delivering of guilty verdicts or, if this ploy failed, to grant a reprieve for the convicted witch. Even in Exeter where, as Prof. Mark Stoyle has pointed out in the course of his study, there was a 'deep-rooted tradition of popular witch-belief', trials of suspected witches were far more likely to result in an acquittal than a conviction.[28] Indeed, the last witch to have hanged at Exeter, before 1682, was a labourer, Richard Wilkyns, who was convicted of bewitching his neighbours, and had been executed as long ago as July 1610.[29]

It would be entirely wrong, therefore, to see the trials of witches in North Devon as being normative or to assume that their convictions were assured. This may have prompted the Bideford justices to take further statements from John and Dorcas Coleman, and Thomas Bremincombe on Wednesday 26 July, a week after the transportation of the witches to Exeter and five days after the meeting of the grand jury had decided upon the charges that they would stand trial for at the assizes. These fresh statements were clearly conceived in the light of the decision to prosecute Susanna Edwards, solely, for the bewitchment of Dorcas Coleman and to let the allegations against Mary Trembles drop. As a consequence, it is Susanna – alone – who features in these new testimonies as the source of Dorcas Coleman's afflictions with all reference to Mary Trembles being struck out of the final document. Very much a reflexive afterthought, these papers seem to have been put on top of the existing file of transcriptions by John Hill and remained in that order when the papers were taken to Exeter and sent on from there to London, for publication. This explains the otherwise strange chronology offered by *A True and Impartial Relation of the Informations Against Three Witches*, with the last testimonies presented first and out of context with the general thrust of the pamphlet. It seems reasonable to suggest that when Freeman Collins took possession of the papers, he simply printed them in the order that they had been presented to him, without any further editorial thought or, perhaps, without having read them beyond a cursory glance in order to establish their content.[30] If he had paid them any attention, then it is likely that he would have begun the text with Grace Thomas' evidence that set the scene for all that was to follow, rather than these later, more partial, and less readily understood accounts. As it was, the swearing of fresh evidence at Bideford town hall, on 26 July 1682, demonstrates that the Justices of the Peace were willing to pursue the conviction of the women. Had Thomas Gist wanted to frustrate the prosecution, then by simply failing to pursue the legal ramifications of the decision to charge Susanna Edwards and Mary Trembles on separate counts of attempted murder by means of witchcraft, he might have muddied the waters enough to secure Edwards' acquittal and perhaps even that of Trembles, too. However, he did not and the sense that he, in probable conjunction with John Hill, was prepared to make the pre-trial depositions available for publication in an attempt to validate witch-belief and the actions taken to combat it for a Tory readership, suggests that he and Hill sat easily within the authoritarian cosmology described by Joseph Glanvill, whereby rebellious spirits acted through the disaffected and dispossessed upon earth in pursuit of God's ruin.

The fear that the women may have had cause to escape the noose may well have caused the Rev. Francis Hann to visit them in prison. The comparative rarity of witch trials and the notoriety that stemmed from the leaked tales of the evidence presented at Bideford had turned them into figures of celebrity in Exeter, with Roger North (an eyewitness at their trial) recalling that: 'The stories of their acts were in everyone's mouth' and that 'the city rang with tales of the preternatural exploits' of the alleged witches.[31] Once, a pamphleteer wrote, 'the report' of their witchcraft and apprehension 'spread abroad [there] came many from all parts to see this grand Witch', Temperance Lloyd, and her companions in misfortune.[32] Never in their lives had they been subject to such attention, with the crowds paying the jailers in order to have sight of them through the bars of their cell and to hear, first-hand, their stories. If they played up to their designated roles and gave the crowds the performance that they wanted to see, then they can hardly have been blamed. The trouble, in Exeter as at Bideford, was that their stories fed back to the courtroom and fuelled the popular hatred against them, leading to fresh suspicions and accusations. As a result, the accusations against them mutated, once they had moved to Exeter, and became far grander in their scope and intent. Now, it was suggested, that they also killed cattle, caused tempests and storms to rise upon the oceans, made a boy lose his footing on the topmast of a ship and plummet to his death, and caused several great ships to be sunk out at sea.[33] Even their contact with familiar spirits and the Devil appeared grander, as he now went 'with them on nights in several Shapes, sometimes like a Hound, who Hunted before them' for souls.[34] For the first time, the three women took on a group identity as the 'Bideford Witches' and were perceived as having acted in concert, in a manner that had never been alleged while they were questioned by Thomas Gist. Undoubtedly, the city had other priorities, concerns and fears about witchcraft than the busy port town and the sense that their crimes were being enlarged to fit with specific maritime accidents and misfortunes became a significant new weapon to be used against them. Temperance Lloyd, however, remained at the centre of everyone's attention and there is no doubt that she was the dominant personality among the three: the one who was held to be the primary cause of the trouble and the main recipient of the Devil's favour and stolen power. Well might she be styled as the 'grand Witch' by those who came to gawp at her from a comfortingly safe distance.[35]

Such attention took its toll. A familiar face among the crowds seemed a blessing: and this seems to be how she viewed the sudden appearance of Francis Hann in her cell. The author of *The Life and Conversation of . . . Three Eminent Witches*, a pamphlet which clearly attempted to make the Rev. Hann the central, heroic figure, thought that at the sight of him amid the press of many others:

> she seemed Extraordinary Joyful, and desired to Touch his Hands; which the Minister refused not, and having him by the Hand she told him she knew not but that his advice and prayers might do her good'.[36]

Desperate and friendless, Temperance literally reached out to a man whom she believed had the capacity to save both her life and her soul. Her intention was to show meekness and that she was, despite all that had been said against her, a godly Christian woman. Yet again, though, she spectacularly misjudged her approach and the interpretation that might be placed upon her actions. It is clear that, as with her over-the-top approach to Grace Thomas in the street, her intent to appear as being kindly and concerned over the fate of the minister spectacularly misfired. Furthermore, as she had nothing to give to others – outside of good wishes and grovelling deference – she seems to have had a fatal tendency to boast of things, and preternatural powers, that permitted her to appear as somebody who could positively assist the lives of others. Thus, she reminded the Rev. Hann of a time when riding:

> between Banton and Taunton wherein the midst of the Water, his Horse would neither go forward nor backward, untill she used these, or words to this effect, Well Satan thou hast not long time to continue a Torment to human Nature before thou shalt be chained up ... at which words the Devil fled away in the Shape of a Bull, and roaring most terribly: And told him then she was there thou invisible.[37]

What she seemed to be suggesting was that she had admonished the Devil, in conventional Christian language, reminding him of his final fall on the day of judgement, and that she had rescued the minister from a potential assault by him. Unfortunately, her pretence of holding power over the Devil – which she could not resist making – and her added coda to the story that she had been witness to the scene, though in spectral form, was a spectacularly stupid admission. It confirmed the substance of Grace Thomas' evidence against her – in as much as she could make herself invisible at the Devil's behest – seemed to imply her complicity in a demonic pact that would bestow that magical power upon her and affirmed that she communicated, with some familiarity, with the Devil. She was, therefore, a woman who when dealing with her neighbours, or anyone in authority, misread signals, tramped across social boundaries and norms, and with pathetic and repetitive regularity got everything that mattered wrong. She attempted to sound godly but appeared demonic. She threatened when she should have retreated or apologized; she stood on ceremony when she should have deferred; and she abased herself when she should have shown a touch of pride. Worse still, she may also have attempted to shift the blame onto her co-accused. Francis Hann also visited Susanna Edwards and Mary Trembles (it may be that all three were all held together in a communal cell) and during the course of their interview, as well as possibly garbling another attempt to say the Lord's Prayer together, it seemed as if Susanna had something bundled up 'under her Coats'.[38] Temperance Lloyd suggested to him that this 'something' was actually the Devil suckling away at her, and that he had been there with the two women 'but is now fled'.[39] Again, it did nothing to rescue her predicament but everything to worsen theirs, as Hann remembered and circulated her fresh allegations.

Unfortunately, we lack the trial record for the Exeter assizes. The account printed in William Cobbett's *Complete Collection of State Trials* simply comprises the testimonies taken at Bideford which had originally been published in pamphlet form as *A True and Impartial Relation of the Informations Against Three Witches*.[40] It may be that the actual trial at Exeter Castle was very brief and not even an enterprising bookseller thought to take notes of the proceedings. Of the three pamphlet sources, two – *The Life and Conversation of . . . Three Eminent Witches* and *The Tryal, Condemnation, and Execution of Three Witches* – touch upon it briefly, while the third, *A True and Impartial Relation of the Informations Against Three Witches*, ignores it entirely. All three are far more interested in the gallows scene than in the legal argument that delivered the women there. We do, however, have accounts written by two influential and extremely well-placed eyewitnesses to the trial: namely, the letter written by one of the two circuit court judges, Sir Francis North (1637–85), on the day after the trial; and two much later reminiscences penned by his brother, Roger North (1653–1734), in defence of his conduct and career.[41] The trial, itself, though, fell to the oversight of Sir Thomas Raymond (c.1626–83) probably on account of the fact that Sir Francis North 'dreaded the trying of a witch' and did all that he could to pass on the responsibility to his colleague.[42] Despite the posthumous publication of a law book, full of examples of precedents that he had collected and collated on everything from riots, to the swearing of oaths, the conduct of churchwardens, the breaking down of fences, and the stealing of deer, Sir Thomas Raymond did not see fit to publicly pronounce upon the crime of witchcraft and left no written record of his involvement in the trial of the Bideford Witches.[43] This is unfortunate as his motivations and actions have, by default, been filtered through the views of the North brothers, neither of whom appear to have been particularly well-disposed to him or generous in their estimation of his talents. What we can say, though, is that both Sir Thomas Raymond and Sir Francis North were united in their service of the Crown and in the defence of its prerogative. They were part of a generation of young and highly ambitious lawyers who had made their names, and fortunes, in utilizing the law in order to directly implement royal policy, whether (in North's case) through ensuring the conviction of Stephen College – a prominent Whig activist – of high treason, on the flimsiest of evidence, or through the willingness of both to break the opposition to Charles II's hold upon municipal government, through revoking the charters of the major towns and purging their administration. Highly politicized, intelligent and cultured, these were also men who had risen rapidly, who felt that they had much further to go, and who had been shaped by the civil wars and their aftermath to brook neither religious nor societal dissent. Indeed, Sir Francis North's account of the trial of the three old women from Bideford is a masterpiece of dry cynicism, self-interest and an overriding concern for the *realpolitik*. As it is the closest thing we have to a primary account of the trial it is worth examining both his letter of 19 August 1682 and the rationale that lay behind his writing of it to the Secretary of State, Sir Leoline Jenkins, in some detail.

The summer assizes of 1682 permitted the king's agents to tour the counties and test the political temperature in the wake of the collapse of the Oxford Parliament, the fracturing of the Whig offensive, the exile of the Duke of Monmouth, and the resurgent Tory assault upon the boroughs. As a consequence, the first part of Sir Francis North's letter was entirely concerned with the politics of packing the grand juries of the West Country with loyal

Figure 17 *Sir Francis North (1637–85) is one of the major sources for the trial of the Bideford Witches (Author's Collection). However, his account is far from impartial and is coloured by cynicism and the calculation of political, and personal, gain.*

Tory gentlemen who would vote as directed and his suggestion that the 'firm and zealous' should be used selectively, with the best saved in order to try important cases of 'sedition' instead of being burdened with routine cases which 'I fear they will quickly weary of'.[44] In both Devon and Cornwall, the high sheriffs had effectively purged the localities and secured control of the jurymen. In Wiltshire, North had made contact with the young Henry Baynton (or Bayntun), the possessor of 'a very considerable estate' centred upon Broham, who had been assiduously courted by the Whig opposition but who now offered 'some very handsome expressions . . . of his loyalty and good affections to the King's service'.[45] If the Tory reaction was to take hold in the provinces, then the winning over of wealthy individuals like Baynton whose family had deep roots in the governance of the county was essential and, as North knew only too well, patronage and venality were the ways to do it. Thus, he asked the Secretary of State to let Charles II know of Henry Baynton's good intentions and, by way of a return, let him 'by some means know the King has a good opinion of him'.[46] The favour of the monarch appears to have been forthcoming and Baynton was rewarded with a seat, as MP for Chippenham, in James II's

Figure 18 *The Hanging Judge: Sir Thomas Raymond (1626/7–83) (oil on canvas, possibly by John Riley, c. early 1670s, by kind permission of Gray's Inn). Cultured and conscientious, he was blamed by the North brothers for bowing to the will of the mob and permitting the execution of the witches at the Exeter Assizes.*

parliament of 1685. From this evidence of quiescent gentlemen, a broken and demoralized opposition, and packed juries, it might not appear – contrary to what Sir Francis' brother, Roger, would later come to write – that the judges should have had too much to worry about in terms of convicting or acquitting whomever they wanted. The attempt, therefore, of both brothers to shift the responsibility for the outcome of the case onto the jury and the balance of public opinion seems more than a little disingenuous. After all, either the Tories controlled the levers of judicial power in the West Country, or they did not. However, as a lawyer to the last, Sir Francis North was prepared to argue both positions just as his own need arose and this is exactly what he did, after beginning and ending his letter with accounts of Tory triumphs. What threatened the king's hold upon the West Country was not, as might be suspected, religious dissent, underground networks of Whig supporters and green Ribbon Clubs connecting Monmouth, Shaftesbury and the Prince of Orange with provincial radicals, but the threat to order posed by the possible acquittal of the three Bideford women which, if sanctioned, might bring the whole house of cards crashing down upon them.

The fate of the women is, thus, not considered within the letter according to their merits, or demerits, or to lengthy legal argument. Instead, it is framed within the wider political struggle in the county between the Whig and Tory factions. This obscured, as it was intended to, the nature of their crimes and the probability of their guilt. It also reduced the Bideford women to the status of pawns in a game designed and played by others. Thus, North's letter is a model of expediency, which disguises a clinical and callous purpose with cheery, clubbable, language. Sir Francis North was not in the courtroom, himself, as he would have been employed with the trying of other assize cases, so therefore his account, as he admitted, was second hand. He could only tell Secretary Jenkins 'what I had from my brother [judge] Raymond, before whom they were tried'.[47] Why then was it not Raymond rather than North who was providing the information to central government? The answer would, again, seem to lie in the realm of politics as opposed to law. North was acting as the eyes and ears of the Secretary of State, gathering intelligence and forging contacts on his travels that were of use to the Crown. Moreover, he also seems to have been keeping a watch upon his fellow judge. His letter is particularly subtle as it slips in its main business – whether or not there was room for a pardon or a reprieve for the alleged witches – within other information and a wider discussion of the case. At the same time, the fate of the women was everything and nothing. Thus, North suggests to Jenkins: 'Your curiosity will make you enquire of their circumstances.'[48] This confiding tone establishes the idea that the case is novel and intriguing in as much as it involves magic, and magical belief, but by the same token it devalued its importance and meaning. It is 'curiosity' that impels comment and explanation, rather than a necessity of business that requires judgement. Sir Francis then went on to provide what he suggested is a paraphrasing of the words with which Sir Thomas Raymond used to describe the women and the case, to him:

> they were the most old, decrepid, despicable, miserable creatures that he ever saw. A painter would have chosen them out of the whole country for figures of that kind to have drawn by.[49]

Crucially:

> The evidence against them was very full and fanciful, but their own confessions exceeded it. They appeared not only weary of their lives but to have a great deal of skill to convict themselves. Their descriptions of the sucking devils with saucer eyes were so natural that the jury could not choose but to believe them.[50]

This is the best account of the trial that we possess. From it, it is clear that the matter of Temperance Lloyd's meeting with the toad-like gambolling devil was reprised in the Exeter courtroom and that all three women admitted congress with familiar spirits, or the Devil himself. It is not surprising that the experience of frequent cross-questioning and imprisonment over the course of the previous month had left them disorientated, depressed, frightened and highly suggestable. The desire to please was their constant undoing. The word 'no', uttered as a denial in order to close off a line of investigation never seems to have occurred to them and appears to have been the hardest word that they ever had to say. A blanket denial establishes a line that can be maintained. The continual concession of ground, even by the most articulate, leads to potential disaster through further incrimination. With no one to counsel them, or to speak for their cause, the three were effectively, as Sir Francis North suggested, talking themselves to the gallows.

The other corroborative evidence for the trial is more partial. Roger North penned his lengthy defences of his brother's conduct a generation later, in the light of the Glorious Revolution and changing ideas about the efficacy of witchcraft, and as a response to the barbs of his many political enemies. In the case of the Bideford Witches, the passage of time had occluded his memory. Although Roger North had accompanied his brother on the circuit to Exeter and was sufficiently interested in the witch trial to look in on the hearings and rifle through the file of depositions sworn at Bideford, by the time he came to write his two separate accounts of the trial he could neither recall the correct number of those accused, nor their fates.[51] Indeed, he thought that only two witches stood accused and that one of them might even have been reprieved from the noose.[52] As a result, it is probably wise to treat his accounts in their other particulars with a degree of caution. What is clear from his recollections is that he had nothing but contempt for the women who stood accused of the crime of witchcraft. 'These', he wrote:

> were two miserable old creatures, that, one may say, as to sense or understanding, were scarce alive; but were overwhelmed with melancholy, and waking dreams, and so stupid as no one could suppose they knew either the construction or consequence of what they said.[53]

It is tempting to speculate as to whether he had a copy of his brother's letter to Secretary Jenkins before him, when he fashioned his memoirs, as his later accounts certainly accorded with its major themes and characterizations of the women. He thought that the evidence of the women, themselves, was the key element guiding the course of the trial, as that of the stream of witnesses who testified against them 'was trifling'.[54] He came across Thomas Eastchurch's evidence, amid the file of pre-trial depositions, and later recalled the story of the mysterious 'Braget cat' and that 'This informant saith he saw a cat leap in at her (the old woman's window), when it was twilight; and this informant farther saith, that he verily believeth the said cat to be devil'.[55] 'The evidence', that proved decisive, 'was their own confession, the rest of the stuff was mere matter of fancy, as pigs dying and the like', while 'the confession of the women', itself, 'was mean and ignorant, the proceed of poverty and melancholy, and in the style of the vulgar traditions of sucking teats etc.'.[56] However, it was, he alleged, the conduct of Judge Raymond and, in particular, 'his passive behaviour' in refusing to direct the jury, that was decisive in influencing the outcome of the trial.[57] Roger North alleged that:

> The judge made no nice distinctions, as how possible it was for old women in a sort of melancholy madness, by often thinking in pain, and want of spirits, to contract an opinion of themselves that was false; and that their confession ought not to be taken against themselves, without a plain

evidence that it was rational and sensible, no more than that of a lunatic, or distracted person; but be left the point upon the evidence fairly (as they call it) to the jury.[58]

Roger North, just like his elder brother, despised and mistrusted jurymen even when, as in this case, they were handpicked. However, it is interesting to note that in his emphasis upon the role played by depression in forming the women's self-destructive testimonies, he was echoing the views already advanced by Weyer, Scot and Webster. The crucial difference that set apart elite opinion in the early eighteenth century from that of the seventeenth was that these ideas, though far from new, had now seeped incrementally into the mainstream consciousness of an increasingly 'polite' society, which sought to embrace rationalism and sneered at anything that smacked of popular culture or folk belief. The mischance of the Bideford Witches was that they sat upon the cusp of that watershed in intellectual fashion and manners and that, when viewed from the safety of the other side, Roger North could see little credit in defending the actions of any of those involved in condemning the women. As a result, he heaped opprobrium upon Sir Thomas Raymond in an attempt to excuse the role of his brother in the trial. Yet, there is evidence in one of the pamphlet accounts of the trial that Raymond had sought to sway the jury towards the grounds that would favour an acquittal, for it was said that he 'gave his Opinion that these three poor Women (as he supposed) were weary of their Lives, and that he thought it proper for them to be carried [back] to the Parish from whence they came, and that the Parish should be charged with their Maintenance; for that he thought their oppressing Poverty had constrained them to wish for Death'.[59] This was a line of argument that had proved particularly useful, and effective, in drawing a halt to the Scottish witch-hunt of 1662 when the Privy Council in Edinburgh had warned against convicting those who through their depression sought their own deaths, as this would in effect be a form of aiding and abetting suicide.[60] However, it cut no ice with the crowds who had pressed into the courtroom:

Whereupon several Neighbours, who had been great Sufferers by their diabolical Practices, moved that if these Witches went home in peace, none of them could promise themselves a minutes Security, either of their Persons or Estates.[61]

Presumably Thomas and Elizabeth Eastchurch, and possibly Joane and Anthony Jones, were at the forefront of these threats and catcalls. If Judge Raymond did, indeed, display passivity and showed 'neither dexterity nor spirit to oppose a popular rage' it was in the context of his handling of public opinion and the conduct of those who came to spectate at the trial or to give evidence to it.[62] However, in this, he was not alone. The North brothers were equally fearful of the trial's potential impact upon public order in Exeter and Bideford. Roger North thought that Exeter was a hotbed of resistance to the Crown characterized by 'defection and revolution'.[63] Though on the one hand, he thought that the circuit through the Western counties had to date been nothing short of a triumph, as 'we were very welcome in the west, and my brother was extremely caressed in all places, because he was the first clear loyalist of a judge that had come amongst them since the [civil] wars', there was still the potential for trouble.[64] He thought that the Whigs 'upon fanatic causes contrived to tease him both by their factious counsel at the bar and factious gentlemen in his chamber'.[65] And, of course, the most fanatical and factious cause of all was witchcraft. Thus, the crime became something of a political football, with the Whigs and religious dissenters refashioned as 'sectarian impostures' who sought to 'cultivate the credulity as to witches, and both triumph over Satan in their several ways of exorcitation, and in the meantime hold the people deceived when only they will work zealously to their corrupt and ambitious ends'.[66] Furthermore, Roger North alleged that they knowingly brought the three Bideford women 'to the assizes with as much noise and fury of the rabble against them' as could be thought possible.[67] There may be some truth in this and, indeed, the two most recent academic considerations of the trial have chosen to see it in largely political terms as either – in the view of Jonathan Barry – an opportunist use of 'the popular rage' by local Whigs to reinvigorate the opposition to the Crown, or – according to Stephen Timmons' pioneering study – as a device by which central government, helped along by Glanvill's theories, Tory pamphleteers and Bideford's ruling elite, could hope to break the back of the radical, dissenting community.[68] The presence of Rev. Hann in

Exeter, schooled in the same demonological sources as Richard Baxter and Cotton Mather, does appear to indicate a particular low church involvement with the question of witchcraft and the staging of the trial. Yet, the leaders of Bideford's radical dissenting community, such as Gabriel Beale, Susan Davy, and Samuel Johns were entirely absent from the stage, while the Justices of the Peace who controlled the prosecution were Tories, and more likely to be influenced by the potent new wave of Anglican writers on witchcraft, such as Glanvill, Caubason and Camfield. Those who made the initial accusations were, as far as we can tell, drawn from across the political spectrum. Thomas Eastchurch was a Tory, while his wife and sister-in-law came from a background of Dissent. If the populace surged around the castle walls in Exeter and barracked the judge, then it is as well to remember that the dissenting minister, John Bartlett, had also suffered hard knocks at the hands of the city's mob. Two of the trial pamphlets appear to have come from Whig printers, the other – lengthier account – was emphatically Tory in its origins. A belief in witchcraft, it seems, was no respecter of factional lines or religious divides, and appears more as an index of fear than as a barometer of political ideology. Yet, within this context it is possible to see the trial, as Stephen Timmons has done, as reflecting the sudden collision of competing priorities, namely 'the expanding powers of the state, village poverty, and political party conflict'.[69]

What shocked Roger North, however, was not that the country folk believed the charges but that the townspeople should so readily take them up and amplify them.[70] This may well have been the product of the constant stream of visitors who had come to see the alleged witches before their trial and the further spread of their fame that seems, primarily, to have been the work of the Rev. Hann. Temperance Lloyd's story about the Devil halting the minister's horse, mid-stream, seems to have been widely circulated and came back to haunt her on the first day of the assizes. According to Roger North, 'miracles were fathered upon' the witches and it was said that their charms had caused the horses harnessed to the judges' coach to stop, stock still upon the castle bridge and refuse to take another step forward towards the scene of the trial.[71] This sounds very much like an interpretation projected onto an event with full knowledge of the earlier preternatural tale. Exeter's citizens were familiar with the witches' supposed spectral projections and the idea that they might possess the power to make themselves invisible to frighten the judges' horses, thereby attempting to prevent the trial from taking place, or to slip out of their holding cells and venture about the castle on the lookout for mischief gained a wide circulation. According to one of the pamphlet writers, the verdict turned upon an admission of spectral evidence, possibly in the course of evidence given by Grace Thomas or Thomas Eastchurch, over Temperance Lloyd's gaining access to a chamber in their house. As part of evidence a witness 'alledging a door to be shut, one of the Three cryed out, that is false, for the door was open; which tacitly implied that she was then an Actor, and consequently convinced both Judg and Jury that she was guilty, and so of the other two'.[72] This may sound more like housebreaking to us than the stuff of spirit-walking and apparitions, and Temperance Lloyd's frenzied attempts to convince Minister Hann at Heavitree that she could not have possibly passed through a keyhole in the Eastchurch house but could quite easily push open a door do seem to be related to the same incident and line of questioning. Similarly, her confession that the 'Devil did lead me up the Stairs' in the house seems to be no more than Temperance acknowledging a state of guilt rather than the corporeal existence of the Devil.[73] For once, at least, she appeared far more nuanced than her learned interrogators, who were prepared to confuse – perhaps even willingly – a figure of speech with a literal occurrence.

Due to the lack of an official trial record we cannot know how many of the later allegations rehearsed in the cells at Exeter Castle and reprised by the Rev. Hann on the scaffold at Heavitree were addressed at the trial of the women. It may well be that none of them were and that Judge Raymond simply concentrated upon the already copious dossier of evidence collected against them at Bideford. It seems the surest and most likely course for a judge whom, whatever the Norths said about him, had established his career through his painstaking attention to detail and recapitulation of both evidence and precedent. As a result, the wilder claims that Temperance Lloyd 'used often to put to sea (in an Egg-shell as she affirmed) where she has been the destruction of many Ships' and that which 'she most repented was that she once threw overboard a Pretty Youth whose shape and Beauty; she spoke of with great commendation' can be seen as the result of Francis Hann's promptings, rather than as anything that was raised as formal evidence at her trial.[74] Similarly, the desire to make Hann the hero of the story and Temperance Lloyd the main villain (for reasons of space and narrative clarity) has served to obscure many of the features of the evidence brought against all three women. Consequently, in some of the pamphlet literature the dramatic tension is heightened, with Temperance Lloyd remaining 'perfectly Resolute', while in custody, 'not minding what should become of her Immortal Soul' and refusing to confess to anything until her interview with the Rev. Hann at which she was prevailed upon by the minister to make 'a free confession' of all her crimes and sins against God, together with 'many more exploits to incert' here.[75] In similar fashion, Hann seems to have injected a further idea into the trial: namely, that while the Devil accompanied the three women to 'the Prison Door . . . there he left them', abandoning them to their fate despite all of his promises to aid them. It was a deft literary touch that left the reader in no doubt that, in keeping with the theories expounded by the major demonological texts, the Devil was 'a very Bad Master', 'the Author of Lies' and an 'unsatisfied deceiver'.[76]

The women's confessions of their intent to harm Dorcas Coleman, Grace Barnes and Grace Thomas by means of witchcraft, together with Temperance Lloyd's additional admission of her guilt for the killing of Lydia Burman, were more than enough to secure their convictions by the Exeter jury. Indeed, without a firm direction from the judge directing them otherwise – by reason of the women's incapacity, delusion or melancholia – it is difficult to see how the jurymen might have called the case otherwise. After all, the confessions to their guilt had been recorded on multiple occasions and freshly restated in the courtroom at Exeter Castle. Judge Raymond's pronouncement of the death sentence upon them might not, however, have been thought to have been an end to matters. In cases of witchcraft – as in other cases of murder, or attempted murder – stays of execution, that sometimes became indefinite once passions had cooled, or reprieves from the gallows, were commonplace. This was precisely the contingency that Sir Francis North was subtly warning against, when he wrote his letter to Sir Leoline Jenkins on 19 August 1682. He was particularly careful to address the counter-argument made by the 'virtuosi' – as he styled those intellectuals who did not believe in the reality of witchcraft – that the case was flawed through means of 'confederacy' (either of the witnesses against them, or through the women's collective fantasies), 'melancholy or delusion'.[77]

Furthermore, he was also quick to address the question of the women's advanced age and illness as being at the root of their conviction, floating and then discarding the charge 'that young folks are altogether as quicksighted as those who are old and infirm'.[78] It was a crafty ploy that, although North would not have countenanced it in such terms, owed much to the Jesuitical line of persuasion that employed the logic of an enemy in order to undermine his own arguments. Having effectively done just this, Sir Francis delivered the crucial blows. With:

> the country so fully possessed against them ... we cannot reprieve them without appearing to deny the very being of witches, which, as it is contrary to law, so I think it would be very ill for his Majesty's service, for it may give the faction [ie. the Whigs] occasion to set afoot the old trade of witch finding, that may cost many innocent persons their lives, which this justice will prevent.[79]

It does not take much to see that this is a deeply political statement that contains, hidden within it, more than an element of blackmail. It is apparent that Sir Francis North did not personally believe in witches, and the same can be inferred to hold true for Sir Leoline Jenkins. However, the letter of the law said otherwise and might not be contradicted, while the weight of public opinion – as evidenced by the mob on the streets of Exeter – expected and demanded a hanging to conclude the process. Furthermore, political expediency demanded that the recourse to private justice – through the 'rabble' and employment of witch-finders – might be denied to the Whigs, so that the Crown might solidify its hold upon the implementation of the law. Lastly, as a salve to the Secretary of State's conscience, there was an attempt at relativism, suggesting that a greater injustice might be prevented through permitting a small one: as by satisfying the mob with the deaths of the three Bideford women a future, much larger witch-hunt might be prevented. Whatever one thinks about his argument for the law to operate upon the basis of the *realpolitik*, there are certain grounds upon which we might question North's fundamental premises.

Firstly, he appears to contradict himself over the balance of power in the Western Counties. Either the Tories had control over the judicial mechanisms, as he confidently boasted in the opening passages of his letter, or they had not. If they had, then there were plenty of legal weapons at the disposal of the local authorities that could be deployed to discourage the extra-legal depredations of the would-be witch-hunters. The rationale offered by his brother, echoing his own words, that 'if these women had been acquitted, it was thought that the country people would have committed some disorder' appears as an abrogation of justice rather than its robust defence.[80] It may well be that the king's men in the West were rather more nervous of their hold upon power than they were prepared to admit to the Secretary of State sitting in Whitehall. Secondly, North's identification of witch-hunting as the political tool of the Whig party would seem to be, at best, simplistic and at worst mendacious. As we have already seen, attempting to tie party tags to people and events involved in Bideford's outbreak of witchcraft is a tenuous pursuit as so many of the major figures, with the exception of John Hill and the Justices of the Peace, either left no clear record of their personal allegiances or were, as in the case of Francis Hann, deeply ambiguous and capable of speaking for no one other than themselves. It might well be that, in the aftermath of Monmouth's visit to Exeter and the resulting Tory backlash, the Whigs were seeking to cloak themselves in the agitation against the witches in order to critique Charles II's government. However, it is just as likely that North was attempting to throw mud at his political opponents and to equate one source of disorder with another. Providing a political rationale for a legal decision that, whichever way you looked at it, was cowardly was a means of saving face with Whitehall and dressed up a decision that was reached through expediency to look as if it was taken for the highest ideological reasons and for the better service of the king and state. Finally, North's dilemma as a judge over the growing divide that separated the letter of the witchcraft statutes from sceptical opinion among society's elites was, indeed, a very substantial problem. That is why his brother recalled that he was 'never more puzzled than when a popular cry was at the heels of a business; for then he had his jury to deal with, and if he did not tread upon eggs, they would conclude sinistrously, and be apt to find against his opinions'.[81] However, other judges did succeed in finding creative and practical ways around the statute book in order to prevent the execution of witches with, as we shall see, Sir John Holt skilfully combining directions to jurymen that permitted religious faith and even the law's acceptance of the validity of witch-belief with measures to seek acquittals through the raising of questions of reasonable doubt and the unmasking of fraudulent cases of possession. Thus, the two judges overseeing the Western Assizes in the summer of 1682 were far from straightjacketed by the law and could have sought to secure either an acquittal or a reprieve had they so desired. The truth of the matter, however, was that Judge Raymond appeared half-hearted in his attempts to lead the jury while Judge North did everything in his power, behind the scenes, to deny the three women of Bideford a stay of execution.

With such forces arrayed against them, these victims of circumstance never really stood a chance. Six days – the time it took for arrangements to be made and for a despatch rider to carry North's letter to Whitehall and return with an answer – separated Sir Francis's sealing his account from the day appointed for the execution, by hanging, of the women. We know nothing about their last week though it is to be wondered whether their entrepreneurial jailers did not attempt to squeeze the last elements of advantage out of their predicament by charging other curious onlookers to intrude upon the scene of their despair. They certainly remained a source of popular interest, conversation, and debate as demonstrated by the large crowds that assembled to witness their hanging at Heavitree, the tradition site of execution in Exeter, on a low rise less than two miles from the castle walls, on Friday 25 August 1682.[82]

The reality of the situation hit Mary Trembles hard, that last morning. She was reported to have been 'very obstinate, and would not go, but lay down, insomuch that they [ie. the prison guards and city constables] were forc'd to tye her upon a Horse-back, for she was very loath to receive her deserved Doom'.[83] By way of contrast, 'the Old Witch Temperance Floyd went all the way' to Heavitree, 'Eating, and was seemingly unconcerned'.[84] Food, or rather the lack of it, had dominated her life and, as it neared its end, the largesse of her jailers provided in the form of the last meal of the condemned offered her the chance to experience a varied diet and the unfamiliar feel of what it was like, for once, to have a full stomach. Unused to plenty, she intended that none of the precious foodstuffs should go to waste and scooped up some of the scraps – possibly left on the plate by her companions whose appetites had failed them – and, practical to the last, saved them for her final journey.

The importance of making a 'good' and uplifting death at the scaffold, complete with fulsome confessions, admonitory prayers, and the begging of

God's forgiveness, was generally understood in the seventeenth century.[85] Yet the words placed into Temperance Lloyd's mouth seem far too polished and eloquent, as she offered her repentance and desperately sought to safeguard her soul: 'as I know my own Heart that were I to live my Days over again, I would lead such a Life, as should have no room for Doubt; but, seeing my Minutes are but few, I can do no more than can be done in such a Time' but surrender herself to God's mercy in the hope that 'all my former Iniquities, shall be blotted out'.[86] They appear to reflect what a London pamphleteer thought that she *should* have said, rather than what she did utter in extremis. Reality seems to have been somewhat different. Notes appear to have been made 'at the time and place of their Execution; or as fully as could be taken in a Case liable to so much noise and confusion', where tempers ran high and the crowd hooted its derision and called for blood.[87] The Rev. Francis Hann was beside the three as they mounted the scaffold and conducted a halting last interview with, and said prayers for, the condemned women. Yet, even this did not go according to plan. If Hann wished to make his name as a godly foe of the Devil, and the agent of destruction of witches, then his stratagem miscarried. While, if the seething crowd expected more lurid stories and abject confessions then, they were also to be disappointed. In their last minutes, all three women seemed to have gained a sense of dignity and resolve. Each in turn denied sexual congress with the Devil or having had familiars that sucked at their teats.[88] Though they all admitted having met the Devil in various shapes and forms – Mary Trembles held to her story that he had appeared to her as a 'Lyon', Susanna Edwards conceded that she had seen a 'black' man, and Temperance Lloyd said that took on a 'woful shape' – they stayed away from admitting their guilt in inflicting witchcraft against Grace Barnes, Dorcas Coleman and Lydia Burman, and refused all suggestion that the Devil had even taken their blood. Understandably, amid all the confusion, some things, as the pamphlet writer admitted, may seem to have been lost but their testimonies and identities seem also to have been once more jumbled together. It was Temperance Lloyd who had supposedly stopped the minister's horse mid-stream and had met the 'short black man, about the length of you[r] arm'. But these deeds were now, respectively, attributed to Mary Trembles and Susanna Edwards.[89] It might have been that whoever was taking down their statements simply got their names wrong, or even that the Rev. Hann could not remember their pre-trial testimony clearly and conflated the events. Whatever the case, it is on a par with the rest of their doleful story that even their last words were misremembered and distorted, and that their individual identities should be so completely submerged in their collective identity as 'Bideford Witches' whereby the utterances of one, might be held to signify that of another. Hann appeared prolix, while the women were terse. Mary Trembles after being forcibly bound and carried to the gallows was now resigned, making it plain that 'I have spoke as much as I can speak already, and can speak no more', while Susanna Edwards said little at all that was thought worth recording.[90] It was left to Temperance Lloyd to play the role as 'Grand Witch' to the very end and was designated as the last to be sent up the ladder to be hanged. She, too, was no longer given to any flights of fancy and her denials were flat and concise. She had 'never hurt any Ship, Bark or Boat in my life'; 'the Child took an Apple from me . . . but the Child died of the Small Pox'; 'No' she had not bruised or squeezed Grace Thomas 'till the bloud came out of her Mouth and Nose', and 'No' to a completely new charge that she had bewitched the child of Mr Lutteril.[91] Had she answered in such a way at her hearing at Bideford or before the judge and jury at Exeter Castle, then her fate – and those of her compatriots – might have been very different.

Even her account of the meeting with the Devil now took on the form of an interior dialogue, focusing upon her guilt over her treatment of Grace Thomas, rather than as an external physical presence. Her sin actuated the evil deed but was, after all, that sin analogous with the Devil? Anyone who actually took the trouble to listen to her words above the shouts and murmurs of the crowd would have been hard pressed to decide upon which interpretation to put upon what was now said. Though there was 'no Discourse or Treaty' with the Devil, he had 'caused me to go and do harm' and 'I did hurt a Woman sore against my Conscience', and because she had refused to kill her 'the Devil beat me about the Head grievously'.[92] Then an almighty squabble broke out upon the scaffold between two of the women. The pamphleteer attributes the row to Temperance Lloyd and Susanna Edwards but the details recorded make little sense within the context of what we know about their relationship and the charges levelled against them. Moreover, it seems to be a reprise of the argument overheard in Bideford jail by Joane Jones. In this light, it appears much more likely that the angry words were exchanged between Susanna Edwards and Mary Trembles and that, once again, in the heat of the moment the identities of the women became mixed up. If this was so, then it was Mary Trembles who, when reacting to an allegation that she had damaged ships and boats and that she had ridden 'over an Arm of the Sea on a Cow', snapped back 'no, Master, 'twas she, meaning Susan'.[93] Thereupon, Susanna Edwards rounded on her and said: 'she was the cause of her bringing to die: for she said when she was first brought to Gaol, if that she was hanged, she would have me hanged too; she reported I should ride on a Cow before her, which I never did'.[94] We know that Temperance Lloyd was not in jail in Bideford at the same time as Mary Trembles and Susanna Edwards and so, again, the reference to being 'first brought to Gaol' cannot refer to her. Now, it is conceivable that Exeter rather than Bideford was being referenced but this seems less likely and there is no evidence for the two sets of evidence (the one for Temperance Lloyd, and the other for Susanna Edwards and Mary Trembles) cross-contaminating. There was no reason for Temperance Lloyd to seek to pull one of the other women down with her, but we do know from the testimony of Joane Jones that these threats had already been made against one another by Susanna Edwards and Mary Trembles. For the spectators gathered around the gallows and spilling back down the road towards Exeter, it must have made a confusing and unedifying spectacle as the pair bickered and blamed away their last minutes upon earth.

At some point, the Rev. Hann was able to restore an element of order to the proceedings but he had singularly failed in his prime purpose in order to induce the women to make a full confession to everything that was put before them. This they had not done and, with the exception of Temperance Lloyd's remorse about the hurt that she had caused to Grace Thomas and attempt to demonstrate how her sympathetic magic had worked, 'laying her two Hands to her Sides' – just as she had shown Thomas Eastchurch little more than a month before – there was precious little that was salacious or which might confirm the existence of witches and the deadly efficiency of their craft.[95] Even Hann's prayer for the souls of the women, a final admonition and the summation of his thoughts upon their lives and deeds went unrecorded, lost beneath the clamour and rising noise of the crowd. With its loss went his opportunity to stamp his own mark upon the case and his attempt to be remembered as the man who had laid low the Bideford Witches. Susanna Edwards had made a last request to have sung a 'part' of the 40th Psalm and this the Rev. Hann led, before making way for the county sheriff who would preside over the actual executions. It is unfortunate that we do not know which verses of the psalm were sung by them, though the following might have been particularly fitting:

> For innumerable evils have compassed me about: mine iniquities have taken hold upon me, so that I am not able to look up; they are more than the hairs of mine head: therefore my heart faileth me.

> Be pleased, O LORD, to deliver me: O LORD, make haste to help me.

> Let them be ashamed and confounded together that seek after my soul to destroy it; let them be driven backward and put to shame that wish me evil.

> Let them be desolate for a reward of their shame that say unto me . . .

> But I am poor and needy; yet the Lord thinketh upon me: thou art my help and my deliverer; make no tarrying, O my God.

It suggests a reflexivity that we have not yet had chance to detect within Susanna Edwards. Time was pressing and she must be away to another place but despite her poverty and all the evils that had beset her, she hoped that she was not entirely forsaken.

That might have been a good end of it, and of them, had not the sheriff now attempted to revisit the avenues of questioning which the Rev. Hann had already laboriously explored with them on the steps of the gallows. Uncalled for and by now thoroughly unnecessary, this prolonged the women's wait while he seems to have lectured them as their hands were being bound. Susanna Edwards was the first to die. She climbed up the ladder and, if the pamphleteer is to be believed, her new-found eloquence did not leave her after the last words of Psalm 40 died away upon her own and the lips of the crowd. Though, she told the multitude, 'my sins be as red as Scarlet, the Lord Jesus can make them as white as Snow'.[96] She was then pushed off her perch on the ladder or crossbeam and left to swing and choke as Mary Trembles followed her up the rungs. While her two companions twisted high above her, Temperance Lloyd found that the sheriff had by no means finished with her. The tedious questioning began again in a last attempt to force out the 'right' confession and the 'right' account of the Devil's workings from a woman surrounded by a baying crowd, who had just seen her co-accused go to their deaths, and who was expected to follow them within seconds or at best a few minutes. Indeed, it appears that her last words – probably uttered as she set foot upon the ladder – were interrupted by his renewed questions. There was little dignity left and little, or nothing, to be gained through this particularly callous final interrogation. Yet, still the sheriff persisted and took the chance to berate her for being 'lookt on as the woman that has debauch the other two' and who had 'served a very bad Master'.[97] Temperance Lloyd ventured nothing that was new and, save for the hurt that she had caused to Grace Thomas, denied everything of substance that was put before her. Finally, having attested to her belief in God and Jesus, she begged a pardon for her sins before she, too, stepped off the ladder, plummeting downwards before being jerked backwards with a snap of the rope to swing and sway over those, both great and small, who had known only of her reputation, and who had come to despise her and to desire to witness her end.

'So,' wrote Roger North in laconic fashion, 'they were convict and died.'[98]

9

Disenchantment

There was to be no salvation for the witches. Their bodies were cut down and thrown into a common pit that lay a little distance from the gallows. Denied a burial in consecrated ground, their separation from mainstream society in the present and from any hope of God's mercy in the hereafter was underscored by the treatment of their bodies.[1] They were considered to be damned, excluded from life eternal, and deserving of nothing but contempt and opprobrium for their exceptional crimes. After all, they had not only murdered the godly but sold themselves to the Devil, murdering their own souls (in terms of a redemptive afterlife) and attempting by their wiles to deprive others of their chance of heavenly immortality.

Yet, if their physical remains were thrown away like scraps of rubbish on the roadside, then their stories were far from forgotten. The plain truth was that witchcraft sold and the printers of Exeter and London were more than happy to meet the demand for new tales of devilry, enchantment and murder. As a result, the three women who had been of so little interest and account for most of their lives, became national celebrities through their convictions and deaths. Ironically, the very judicial process and societal pressures that were intended to obliviate and excoriate the memories of the women resulted in their memorialization and celebration. Within weeks of their hanging, two – and possibly three – anonymous pamphlet accounts of their lives were published and were followed soon after by a ballad setting their story to music.[2]

Significant modern scholarly attention has been paid to these sources in order to contextualize the literature and to determine its varying political bias.[3] In light of the work of Stephen Timmons, Jonathan Barry and Peter Elmer, it is reasonable to suggest that *A True and Impartial Relation of the Informations against Three Witches*, was printed in London by Freeman Collins, and sold in Exeter by Charles Yeo. This work had the strongest connections to West Country authorship, was pro-Tory and combined Thomas Hill's transcriptions of the pre-trial evidence sworn at Bideford town hall with a separate account of the hangings at Heavitree taken down at the scene by a spectator in the crowd who was close enough to hear their dying statements but who did not know the women beforehand. Running to some forty pages, it is the fullest account of the case against the women and the most authoritative. It must have been sanctioned, in some form, by Thomas Gist and John Hill and gives the lie to the idea that the local authorities in Bideford were passive actors in deciding the fates of the women. Gist had moved against them at the meeting of the grand jury in Exeter, in marked contrast of his handling of the charges against Mary Beare and Elizabeth Caddy, and desired – or at the very least – facilitated their deaths. He, together with John Hill, seem to have viewed the account contained within *A True and Impartial Relation of the Informatons against Three Witches* as a vindication of their conduct and governance of the town.[4]

The other two pamphlet sources are far briefer and more problematic, in terms of both their veracity and the political complexion of their unknown authors. *The Tryal, Condemnation, and Execution of Three Witches*, printed by John Deacon 'at the sign of the Rainbow, a little beyond St. Andrews Church, in Holborn' placed Francis Hann and Temperance Lloyd centre stage, as adversaries locked in a dualistic struggle between the forces of light and dark, and ignores or conflates the roles and identities of the other two women. Aimed at celebrating Hann's role as the detector and victor over the forces of the witches and their devilish master, the seven-page account may well have been aimed at a Dissenting or Whig audience, and certainly intended to establish the minister as an expert witch-hunter and to spark fresh prosecutions.[5] It combined populism, with the promise of 'many Wonderful Things, worth your Reading' with an essentially theocratic and moralistic tale that emphasized the importance of Temperance Lloyd as a lascivious weather witch, who killed livestock and devastated Bideford's maritime trade through the sinking of ships at sea.[6] Furthermore, it established the fallacious view that the witches acted in concert, much like Shakespeare's archetypal sisterhood in *Macbeth*, with something akin to a coven-like structure and with differences in rank and authority.[7] On the one hand, this served to consolidate the fame of the 'Bideford Witches' as a unitary group but, on the other, the pamphlet failed in its primary aims of stimulating a fresh wave of persecution and establishing Hann as a national figure. In a bitter irony, the women gained the posthumous fame that he did not.

The third of the trial pamphlets, *The Life and Conversation of ... Three Eminent Witches*, a brief account running to just six pages, makes no pretence of dealing with all three women and focuses, instead, on the figure of Temperance Lloyd (or 'Floyd' as she is styled) as a fully demonized witch figure, the wrecker of ships, commerce and lives. Although Hann is not directly named, he appears in the misleading guise of the 'Minister of the Parish' who brings the women to justice, while the author (who appears to have been working largely from hearsay and the earlier accounts) was unclear – as even the title of the pamphlet shows – about the names and relationship between the three women, even managing to mix up the identities of their principal victims.[8] The 'J.W.' who printed the work cannot be identified with any certainty, as there no fewer than eight London printers who – as Stephen Timmons has shown – used those initials at the time, though John Weld who operated from Fleet Street and published on both witchcraft and Scottish affairs appears as the most likely suspect.[9] The pamphlet was angled towards a Scottish audience, presumably with an eye to initiating a fresh witch-hunt north of the border.[10] In this it signally failed, though it did keep memories of the case fresh in the popular consciousness and provided a topical restatement of witch-belief. The blurring of the date set upon the title page means that it can either be read as being published in 1682 or 1687. Jonathan Barry has favoured the former date, Stephen Timmons the latter, and while both are as valid as each other on account of the unfortunate ink smudge, I have chosen to follow Jonathan Barry's dating as it seems to fit with the topicality of the case and what we know of the sources appearing to cluster around the aftermath of the trial and feeding upon one another.[11] What, however, seems certain is that it is going too far to dismiss all three accounts as being purely 'fictitious'.[12] If we compare the taking of evidence as recorded in *A True and Impartial Relation of the Informations against Three Witches* with the surviving depositions in manuscript form for the breaking up of conventicles in Bideford, it is apparent that in form, style and approach both sources come from the hand of John Hill.[13] Moreover, the unevenness of the gallows speeches recorded in the same pamphlet, complete with omissions and the uncertainties of who was saying what amid the din and clamour of the Exeter crowd, does suggest a true eyewitness account being at its root. If the other two pamphlet sources are more fanciful and flawed, then they at least are suggestive of the priorities of Francis Hann in refashioning the tales to fit demonological theory and his own desire for self-promotion.[14]

Less discussed is the ballad source for the trial, *Witchcraft Discovered and Punished*, that was once again published anonymously and though undated probably also hails from the mid-1680s. It professed to discuss 'Witchcraft, that Old Wicked Sin' and reworked both its illustrative woodcut and the tune to which it was set from earlier, well-known sources.[15] The accompanying image of the horned, cloven-hooved devil, candle, and broomstick in hand, surrounded by a magical circle, dancing witches, owls, and an over-sized cat was well-chosen by the printer as it was suggestive of both the subject matter and the promise of a dark musical experience. The Devil appears to be trampling the ground in time to the rough country music provided by a horn or trumpet player, the female and male witches have paired off into dancing couples, the cat seems to be swaying in time to the tune – paws raised, in either celebration or supplication – the birds start up into the air, roused by the sound, and a flagon of ale suggests that a good time is on offer to all: whether those engaged in the scene or those about to purchase and perform the ballad to the delight of their friends. Yet, the reworking of the woodcut, taken from the frontispiece to John Collier Payne's 1628 edition of *Robin Good-Fellow, His Merry Prankes and Merry Jests* (or from one of its many subsequent reprintings during the seventeenth century) subtly reversed and reworked the image; denuding it of its sexuality and adding, instead, a more overt sense of the demonic. Thus, the erect phallus of Robin Goodfellow is banished, hidden away underneath the fringes of a hairy apron that the less skilled woodcutter has substituted for the original's shaggy, goat-like thighs. The faerie is no longer a 'harmless Spirit' engaged upon household mischief and the giving of gifts of silver and 'pretty toys' as favours, but the Devil, himself, tempting and deceiving souls, and visiting death upon the virtuous.[16] In a similar fashion, the dance tune chosen to fit the topical words around was a familiar and highly popular air, known from the late 1580s onwards as *Doctor Faustus* or *Fortune my Foe*.[17] This was a melody that, by 1682, had long been associated with songs celebrating God's providence, or lamenting poverty, murder, criminality and witchcraft. As Sarah F. Williams has shown, it had been reworked within this context no less than 18 times between 1590 and 1680, and had already been connected to witchcraft through the publication of the broadside *Truth Brought to Light*, in 1662.[18] While historians concerned primarily with trial literature have tended to be dismissive of *Witchcraft Discovered and Punished*, it is notable that Dr Williams – in looking at the performative interplay between words, music, and dance – singles it out for particular praise as 'perhaps the finest example of a ballad accusing witches'.[19]

Figure 19 *The Devil is in the Detail: the bowdlerized version of John Goodfellow used to illustrate the ballad of the Bideford Witches in* Witchcraft Discovered and Punished *(Author's Collection). The faerie child has been reconfigured as the embodiment of the Devil, while the erect phallus which caused offence on the publication of a 1628 pamphlet has been erased.*

The anonymous, London-based author of the ballad, clearly had access to the accounts of the trial and attempted to combine the image of the fully demonized witch with the idea of the Devil as a treacherous figure, and what was known from the trial pamphlets concerning the Bideford Witches, their victims, their 'marks', and their employment of familiar spirits. It is not unreasonable to suggest that the ballad was written in the early autumn or winter of 1682, as the scene is set: 'At the last Assizes held at Exeter'.[20] Consequently, echoing the text of *The Tryal, Condemnation, and Execution of Three Witches*, we learn that 'For Satan, having lull'd their Souls asleep / Refuses Company with them to keep' in order 'that so they may / Be plung'd in Hell, and there be made his Prey'.[21] The Devil proves himself to be a 'known deceiver', as having promised Temperance Lloyd that he would preserve her despite the great 'Crouds of People' who cried out for justice against her, and 'bid her be strong', he finally forsakes her at 'the Prison Door', disappearing to return no more, and abandoning her to her fate upon the gallows.[22] The author seems to have some knowledge of the wider circumstances surrounding the charging of the women at Bideford, as he alludes to those who 'Roar in cruel sort, and loudly cry / Destroy the Witch and end our misery' and is highly critical of those who sought to bring in witch-hunters or employ counter-magic, decrying: 'Some [who] used Charms by *Mountabanks* set down / Those cheating *Quacks*, that swarm in every Town'.[23] Thus, the ballad is more nuanced and powerful than it appears at first sight. It confirms the reputation of Temperance Lloyd, Susanna Edwards and Mary Trembles as famously notorious and powerful witches and effectively compresses their lives and careers in the service of the Devil into the form of popular song. Given the wide dissemination and easy transmission of song in a society which still relied upon oral culture for its news and information, it is worth quoting from this substantial ballad in some detail.

Having outlined the trial at Exeter, the Devil's malignity and the witches' predilection for harming 'Sweet Innocents' and shedding their 'harmless blood', the author provides – in true ballad-monger style – all the news about the witches that is fit to sing:

For it appear'd they Children had destroy'd,
Lamed Cattel, and the Aged much annoy'd.

Having Familiars always at their Beck,
Their Wicked Rage on Mortals for to wreck;
It being proved they used Wicked Charms,
To Murther Men, and bring about sad harms.

And that they had about their Body's strange
And Proper Tokens [ie. supernumerary teats and witch marks]
   of their Wicked Change:
As Pledges that, to have their cruel will,
Their Souls they gave unto the Prince of Hell.

The Country round where they did live came in,
And all at once their sad complaints begin;
One lost a Child, the other lost a Kine,
This his brave Horses, that his hopeful Swine.

One had his wife bewitch'd, the other his Friend,
Because in some things they the Witch offend.[24]

The denouement, in the form of God's judgement, is, however, swiftly delivered
and Temperance Lloyd is left to reflect with bitterness and regret upon her
many sins, as:

... all's in vain, no rest at all they find,
For why? All Witches are to cruelty enclin'd;
And do delight to hear sad dying groans,
And such laments as wou'd pierce Marble Stones.

But now the Hand of Heaven has found them out.
And they to Justice must pay Lives, past doubt;
One of these Wicked Wretches did confess,
She Four Score Years of Age was, and no less.

And that she had deserved long before
To be sent packing to the *Stigian* shore;

For the great mischiefs she so oft had done,
And wondered that her life so long had run.[25]

The ballad managed to combine newsworthiness with entertainment and is likely to have reached as many ears, as the published trial accounts. The Rev. Sabine Baring-Gould, one of the great folk-song collectors of the late nineteenth and early twentieth centuries certainly believed that Barnstaple and Bideford imbibed a culture where popular song thrived among the taverns and warehouses.[26] One wonders if copies of the ballad made it back to the quayside at Bideford and if the hawkers and street vendors sung the air in the market and along the High Street. Did it rekindle memories, prompt feelings of pride or regret in the hearts of the principal actors in the events of the summer of 1682 who, after the catharsis of the denunciations and the trial returned home to lives that were far from transmuted by the deaths of the women and remained shaped by the same concerns over good trade, wealth and physical well-being?

The town remained bitterly divided between its Tory and Whig factions, the raids on the conventicles gathered pace and the authorities sought to further clamp down upon political and religious dissent in the wake of the Rye House Plot, paying informers and keeping a close watch upon those travelling through the port bound for Ireland and northern England.[27] On 3 August 1683, Margaret Johnson was 'bound to ... good behaviour' for using 'seditious language' against the Crown.[28] There were searches for arms, allegedly being stored by radicals, the holding of an official 'day of Thanksgiving' at the church and town hall for the preservation of 'his Majestie, and his Royal Highnesse, the Duke of Yorke, from a damnable conspiracy', and the implementation of further measures sent down by the county Quarter Sessions to combat the 'seditious practices of sertaine phanatikes'.[29] The loyal declaration following the Rye House Plot was not, perhaps, the triumphant demonstration of Toryism that Thomas Gearing and John Hill had envisaged, as only 86 townsfolk signed the document. It was a thin return, given the effort that Hill had lavished upon it. Significantly, the Rev. Michael Ogilby had not thought to sign it and, save for John Barnes – who signed well down the list – none of the men associated with the levelling of charges against the Bideford Witches had done so, either.[30] This seems to reinforce the idea that if the charges against the women were generated from among those on the fringes of the dissenting community then they were actuated by the town's Tory leadership. As might be expected, Thomas Gist and John Davie signed the loyal address, as the fourth and fifth names, respectively.[31]

However, the voluntary surrender of Bideford's charter for renewal to the Crown, through the intervention of the Earl of Bath, went awry. The king 'was sick and indisposed' on the designated day that the Earl intended to petition him for the charter's favourable restitution, further loyal addresses following his death and the accession of James II also fell flat, and a clash with central government threatened to pull down the new king's natural allies in the town. In the wake of the Monmouth Rising, Whitehall had moved a writ of *Habeus Corpus* upon a suspect questioned by Bideford's Justices of the Peace. However, no one did anything to acknowledge the writ sent from the judges of the King's Bench or to send the suspect for examination, as requested, in London. The result was ill-disguised fury on the part of the both the judiciary and the king. Bideford's Tory elites then turned in upon themselves in a blame game, where various excuses for their failure to obey the will of the Crown were offered. The new mayor, John Darracott, was perhaps the most self-serving as, when called to give an account of his actions at Whitehall, he pleaded that he could not read the legal documentation as it was written in Latin and had 'delivered it to the Town Clerk' who had failed in his duty to act upon it. This effectively shifted the blame onto the shoulders of John Hill, as Darracott was discharged 'his ignorance' in the matter 'not reaching to a contempt' and Hill was ordered to be 'brought up' for questioning before the King's Bench.[32] Judge Jeffreys' lawyers were in no mood for understanding or for reaching an accommodation with the local elites and seem to have read the actions of this implacable Tory as being deliberately obstructive of the aims and objectives of royal government and 'they prayed liberty to prosecute the Town Clerk'.[33]

Doubtless, Gabriel Beale, Samuel Johns and Margaret Johnson had good reason to rejoice at the fall from grace of their chief persecutor but, in the aftermath of the failure of Monmouth's West Country rebellion, Bideford's dissenters (as opposed to suspected witches) were under the lash of what, increasingly, appeared to resemble arbitrary government. Though no one from Bideford was convicted for their part in the rising and North Devon had failed to stir, Judge Jeffreys was still intent upon sending a clear message to the town's many religious nonconformists and political radicals, and decreed that the quartered remains of one unfortunate rebel, boiled in pitch, should be hung in chains from the Long Bridge as a constant reminder of the fruits of rebellion.[34] If, today, commemoration and restitutive justice are – as we shall see in the course of the following chapter – often deployed in an attempt to 'correct' instances of historical injustice and cruelty, then one might do well by comparing witchcraft to the effects of Jeffreys' Western Assize of autumn 1685 whereby some 4,000 suspects were rushed through the courts and sentenced to whipping, public execution or transportation as slaves to the West Indies. If English law did not burn witches at the stake, like Scotland or Germany, then it did reserve that punishment for traitors to the Crown and Dame Alice Lisle, who had harboured fugitives from the battle of Sedgemoor, was condemned to the flames at the Winchester Assizes. Her sentence was commuted to beheading and the elderly woman, who had frequently nodded off during the hearing and fifteen-minute deliberation of the jury, was executed on 2 September 1685.[35] Equally unedifying was the frantic squabble between the governors and merchants of Jamaica, Barbados and the Leeward Isles in a bidding war to secure their stakes in the new human property that might be used to work their plantations.[36] The fact that George Jeffreys acquitted Jane Vallett on the charges of bewitching Grace Badcock and Anne Fossett, at the Exeter Assizes held in September 1685, perhaps reflects less upon his attitude towards human rights or the reality of witchcraft, than upon his focus upon other targets and his desire to swiftly clear other judicial business that had been sandwiched between the trials of two large batches of Monmouth's soldiers and sympathizers.[37]

Back in Bideford, the accession of James II had seen a further flourish of loyal declarations and petitions celebrating both the person and the policies of the new king. Once again, the popular response was, at best, lukewarm and not a single member of the nonconformist community, centred around Gabriel Beale and Samuel Johns, thought fit to sign the public document welcoming James II to the throne. Those who did sign were, overwhelmingly members of the town council, office holders and placemen, together with a number of highly committed Tory partisans resident in the locality. As a consequence, it provides an interesting insight into the combination of political principle and naked self-interest that drove Bideford's social elites. Thomas Eastchurch's name sits as the fourteenth on the list, two places higher than both the Rev. Michael Ogilby and John Hill, consciously and conspicuously reflecting his growing status and wealth as a gentleman of the town.[38] John Barnes and John Coleman added their names, while Robert Galworthy (or Galsworthy) and George Wakely signed together, suggesting that the families of the women who respectively searched and accused Temperance Lloyd of witchcraft, in 1679 and 1682, were on close terms.[39] Tantalizingly, another member of the Winslade family also signed the declaration which suggests that not all of that family were on the margins of literacy or penury, while the names of Bartholemew and John Blackmore, who also signed, might have been kinsmen to the pauperized John Blackamoore who received outdoor relief in the parish during the early years of the Restoration, and hint – if so – that social mobility in Bideford was open to people of North African as well as Devonian descent in the latter part of the seventeenth century.[40] Morgan Thomas appears as the only individual of obvious Welsh background, while that inveterate bully and bruiser, Peter Bagelhose, chose to add his signature to the end of the document in display of his Tory allegiances.[41] Politics and religion evidently cut across families, as Thomas Eastchurch already knew, with Lawrence Gay signing both declarations welcoming the foiling of the Rye House Plot and the succession of James II, while his kinsman William Gay, who had married the daughter of the dissenting preacher John Hanmer, did not.[42]

It is reasonable to conclude that this group, led by those stalwarts of local government (William Titherley, Thomas Gearing, John Davie and Thomas Gist) approved of the further attempts to break the conventicles operating within the town in the spring and summer of 1685. On 26 April 1685, Henry Parsons preached at the house of Samuel Johns before at least twenty townsfolk, resulting in a fresh rash of committals and fines, while a month later Gabriel Beale was once again fined for holding a conventicle in his house. In a particularly spiteful move, William Titherly, who was then mayor of Bideford, and Thomas Gearing, the former mayor then serving in the capacity as one of the aldermen, went back through the past records of prosecutions in order to establish if any of those who stood accused of attending the illegal prayer meetings were guilty of previous offences. As a result, James and John Garrett – the rope-makers – had their fines increased when it was discovered that they had attended a prayer meeting convened at Gabriel Beale's home more than a decade earlier.[43] As late as 13 April 1687 – almost a fortnight after the issuing of James II's Declaration of Indulgence to religious dissenters – Elizabeth Bartlett was brought before John Darracott for harbouring a preacher.[44] Indeed, the continuation of Darracott's mayoralty over an unprecedented two successive terms, stretching from 1685 to 1687, seems to indicate a concern among Bideford's ruling Tories to maintain a continuity of personnel and office at a time when the king's new and innovative religious policies were seeming to hold the possibility of toppling them from power. Darracott, like John Hill before him, had publicly clashed with the Rev. Ogilby, who – according to a number of witness testimonies sworn before the justices on 25 November 1685 – had abused and struck the mayor.[45] It is quite possible that as with the 'great disturbance' in the parish church in May 1682, religious tensions were once more at the root of the conflict. Yet, as with the case of John Hill, possession of the 'right' political and religious persuasion did not always equate with being placed above the law. In this respect, John Coleman found himself in trouble with the authorities in both 1685 and 1709, while Peter Bagelhose remained a running sore in the side of the forces of law and order throughout the period, acquiring a notorious reputation in the town and accumulating a large tally of convictions and fines for all manner of petty crimes, disorders and derelictions.[46]

However, the one person who could no longer trouble the authorities was Grace Thomas. Despite the destruction of the witches, she does not ever seem to have recovered her health, remaining an invalid and dying in March 1685.[47] If the deaths of Temperance Lloyd, Susanna Edwards and Mary Trembles offered her any reprieve or peace of mind, then it was of a remarkably brief duration. With her own passing, the prosecution of John Hill followed by his political eclipse in 1688–9, and the failure of Francis Hann to seize the public imagination as an expert demonologist: the triumvirate most closely associated with the prosecution of the Bideford Witches disappeared into the grave, disgrace and obscurity. Yet, if Thomas Eastchurch, Thomas Gist or Dorcas Coleman ever had any doubts about the guilt of the three women they had helped to hang, they never seem to have voiced them and witch-belief continued in both Bideford and across the West Country long after the executions at Heavitree. Indeed, the committal rate does not seem to have appreciably fallen off across the South West in the period between 1683 and 1707. What did change, however, was the attitude of the judiciary with only two convictions returned during that period despite twenty-seven women being charged with a variety of forms of bewitchment resulting in murder, the wasting of bodies, the laming of limbs, the 'consuming' with sickness, spectral appearances and the physical possession of individuals resulting in their fitting and vomiting of all manner of pins, straw, and feathers.[48]

If what looks very much like an attempt to spark a major hunt in Somerset, in March 1685, failed when four women were acquitted of bewitching Thomas Atwell at Taunton Castle; then Alice (or Alicia) Molland was less fortunate in being convicted at the Exeter Assizes, held in the same month, for practising 'witchcraft on the bodies of Joane Snow, Wilmott Snow and Agnes Furze'.[49] The presiding judge, Sir William Montagu (c.1618–1706), then Chief Baron of the Exchequer, sentenced Molland to death and left her for execution. However, the trouble with this case – unlike that of the Bideford Witches – is that it is unsupported by any pamphlet literature and remains as a blunt statement of judicial fact in the gaol delivery book, defying all those who have tried to look into it to elaborate any further. It would appear significant that the conviction was, again, returned at Exeter little more than eighteen months after the executions of the Bideford women and that – just like Sir Thomas Raymond – Sir William Montagu felt himself under political threat and was to be removed from his post by James II, in 1686, for failing to give unqualified support to the power of the royal prerogative. His judicial record is a mixed one. If he was prepared to display religious tolerance in the case of a Dominican priest caught preaching in England in 1680 and successfully pressed for his banishment rather than execution, then – at least at face value – it seems strange that he, as opposed to Jeffreys, would have shown a heavy handedness when it came to the consideration of witchcraft. The answer may lie in the particular local circumstances in Exeter and that Montagu, like Raymond before him, did not wish to incite the mob to violence through returning an acquittal. It may be, though, that unlike Sir Francis North, he was prepared to defer the execution of the victim and to privately lobby for a reprieve or discharge once the furore had died down. Without the survival of any further documentation it is impossible to say for sure, but it would seem unlikely that the hanging of a further witch at Heavitree should not have elicited an account in a contemporary diary, letter, chapbook, pamphlet, or ballad. Bearing this in mind, it is possible to suggest that Alice Molland did not hang but was quietly released from the dungeon underneath Exeter Castle and slipped back into the quiet, but welcome, obscurity from which she had come. It is a less dramatic view of events but one that makes some sense from the paucity of evidence surrounding the case.[50]

Such a scenario was enacted following the trial of Margareta Young at the Wiltshire Assizes in July 1689. Following a run of acquittals for the crime on the Western Circuit, she was found guilty by the jury for bewitching William Mundy and sentenced to death by Sir Robert Atkyns (1621–1710), Montagu's eventual successor as Chief Baron of the Exchequer. As with Alice Molland she was 'left for execution' but in her case we know that she was eventually granted a reprieve and freed.[51] If we are in doubt as to whether Alice Molland or the Bideford Witches were the last women to be executed for the crime of witchcraft in England, then we are in no doubt that Margareta Young was the last woman to be convicted on the Western Circuit. However, the solipsistic problem remained at the heart of witch persecution, as Roger North perceptively summarized:

> if a judge is so clear and open as to declare against that impious vulgar opinion that the Devil himself has power to torment and kill innocent children, or that he is pleased to divert himself with good people's cheese, butter, pigs and geese, and the like errors of the ignorant and foolish rabble, the countrymen (the triers) cry, this judge hath no religion, for he doth not believe witches; and so, to show they have some, hang the poor wretches.[52]

Bideford, itself, had experienced one last flurry of witchcraft accusations in an attempt to secure a prosecution, in 1686. 'Severall informations' were lodged against Abigail, the wife of Robert Handford, 'concerning the suspicion of witchcraft', revealing that belief in witchcraft was still strongly held in the port town.[53] However, as in the cases of Mary Beare and Elizabeth Caddy, no further action was taken. With no other supportive evidence (as the depositions sworn against Abigail Handford have not survived) we have no means of knowing what tensions generated the charges or how they were resolved, other than through the case being quietly shelved. This said, the simple fact that Abigail Handford was a married woman and had somebody to speak for her, set her apart from Temperance Lloyd, Susanna Edwards and Mary Trembles. The simplest recourse to a defence or to the 'protective colouring' offered by marriage – let alone the possession of money – may have been enough to deter further inquiries. Once again, the abjectness of the Bideford Witches' deprivation and desertion is emphasized through the comparison with those prosecutions for the crime that were allowed by the authorities to fall at the first hurdle.

This said, while the witchcraft acts remained on the statute book, judges – however sceptical they might have been – were still confronted by the need to bend or circumvent the letter of the law in order to consistently deliver acquittals.[54] If the history of witchcraft often seems like a dismal catalogue of misogyny, double-dealing and cruelty, then it is also worth remembering that it was illuminated by rare and decent individuals who were prepared to break with prevalent opinion, self-interest or intellectual fashion and to embark upon courses of action solely because they believed them to be right. One of these, whose influence upon bringing about the end of witch persecution has been accorded less consideration than it deserves, was Sir John Holt (1642–1710) who, in 1696, found himself trying Elizabeth Horner on charges of killing Alice Corbett by means of witchcraft, in the same courtroom where the Bideford Witches had been sentenced by Raymond in 1682.[55]

Holt's exceptional role in bringing the values of the proto-Enlightenment has been obscured for a number of reasons. Unlike Sir Matthew Hale, he did not turn his hand to the writing of legal treatises; his eighteenth-century biographer and the compilation of his trial rulings are heavy, stodgy materials that make no mention of his judgements on the witch trials and occlude his progressive attitudes towards domestic violence, militarism and slavery.[56] At the height of the Tory reaction of the 1680s, his politics seem – probably purposely – opaque. On the one hand, he was prepared to support the assaults of the Crown upon the Whig corporations but, on the other, he defended, alike,

Figure 20 *Sir John Holt from his funerary monument, St Mary's Church, Redgrave, Suffolk, 1710 (photograph by Michael Garlick, Creative Commons). Flanked by the embodiment of Justice, the statue of the judge was based upon a portrait by Richard van Bleeck which was destroyed in the Blitz of 1940. An opponent of cruelty, political absolutism and militarism, Holt was instrumental in ending witchcraft prosecutions in England.*

ordinary Whig political activists and political grandees like Lord William Russell, who stood accused of treason after the revelation of the Rye House Plot. In acting as counsel to Russell, in the face of a vengeful Crown, after Monmouth and Shaftesbury had fled to Holland, their fair weather friends had deserted them, and the popular movement had collapsed, required some considerable reserves of courage, self-belief and resource.[57] Again, unlike Hale, he lacks a modern biographer. This said, the anonymous – and near contemporary – author behind *The Life of the Right Honourable Sir John Holt* was unstinting in his praise of his defence of the 'Lives, Rights, Liberties and Properties of the People'.[58] Holt had lost his position as Recorder of the City of London, in 1686, after saving the life of a soldier discovered asleep at his sentry post by establishing the point that while James II might press soldiers into service during peacetime, for his rapidly expanding army, through the use of the Royal Prerogative, he could only subject them to civil as opposed to martial law. The ruling effectively meant that the king could not discipline his conscripts and effectively struck at the growing use of arbitrary power by the sovereign and the ability of the Crown to maintain a standing army that was independent of parliamentary scrutiny.[59] Similarly, in 1705, he delivered a verdict that curtailed the possibility of the growth of the slave trade in England itself, and opened up the possibility that if an African slave could jump ship and reach the English shore then they should be treated as a free woman or man. The case revolved around a Black slave, purchased in Virginia and brought to England, who was then to be resold in the London Parish of St Mary le Bow. Holt ruled that the laws of colonies became void in England, and that 'As soon as a Negro comes to England, he becomes free' as 'one may be a Villein in England, but not a Slave'.[60]

Bearing these approaches in mind, we can see the way in which he attempted to effectively not only side-step but to fundamentally challenge the witchcraft laws, during his employment as a circuit judge between 1690 and 1701. By the time he sat in judgement at Exeter Castle, he had already gained a reputation for showing scepticism when confronted with the case of Mary Hill, a young woman from Beckington by Frome, who at the Taunton Assizes, in April 1690, had claimed to be possessed by an elderly woman, Elizabeth Carrier, who visited her in spectral form during her night terrors and caused her to vomit forth hundreds of pins, nails and spoon handles.[61] Six years later, at Exeter, Sir John Holt heard evidence concerning the alleged bewitchment of three young sisters by another old woman, Elizabeth ('Bett') Horner, who they felt had threatened them. In some respects, the genesis of the case mirrors that of the outbreak at Bideford in as much as the allegations of witchcraft stemmed from the opinion of the local physicians that they could find 'no natural cause' for the worsening stomach pains that took hold of Alice, the youngest child, and killed her within five days. Her sisters, Mary and Sarah, similarly sickened, exhibiting pinch and bite marks on their arms and cheeks, and vomiting crooked pins and small stones. Mary, a ten-year-old, 'her body being strangely distorted and her legs twisted like the screw of a gun' was often observed by her parents Thomas and Elizabeth Bovet, sitting beside the fire with her eyes clamped shut, moaning that 'Bett Horner drove her in'.[62] Sarah Bovet testified that she had been scratched by a cat as she lay in bed and that the animal was really Elizabeth Horner who had shifted her form and 'whom she described exactly in the apparel she had on, though the child had not seen her in six months'.[63] The girls' mother gave evidence that they were unable to say their prayers having been threatened by the witch and could not eat as the witch's spirit had infiltrated their bodies and occupied their stomachs. As at Bideford, Sarah Bovet claimed that the old woman had killed her sister by squeezing all the breath out of her body, and both children alleged that she had forged a compact with the Devil and received his mark, in the form of a supernumerary teat upon her left shoulder, that was suckled by her familiar spirits who came to her in the form of toads. Neighbours presented evidence of both the rough justice meted out to Bett Horner in an attempt to break her spells and of her alleged spectral powers. John Fursey said that he had seen her rising as an apparition out of the ground on three successive occasions; while Margaret Armiger claimed that although the suspected witch was imprisoned in Exeter Castle at the time, she had still met her – in spirit form – upon a country lane. We can see, as consequence, that the same dynamics of allegation, belief and prosecution that appeared at Bideford were still live issues for a significant number of people in West Devon and were capable of manifesting themselves, again, in a capital case almost thirteen years later. Just like Temperance Lloyd, Bett Horner was forced to say the Lord's prayer as part of the evidence to determine her witchery and compact with the Devil. She halted 'a little' before saying 'Forgive us our trespasses' but 'and went on' repeating the creed without a fault.[64] In this she certainly helped herself, but the attitude of the judge to other strands of the evidence brought against her was to prove conclusive. When she revealed her left shoulder there was, indeed, a mark upon it: the significance and purpose of which was very much in the eye of the beholder. However, Holt was quick to declare that it was a wart or a mole, rather than the Devil's teat, rendering the blemish mundane as opposed to preternatural or threatening.

In a similar fashion, the judge focused the attention of the jury upon the claims of Sarah Bovet's mother that the child had walked up a nine foot high wall, several times over, backwards and forewords, 'her face and fore part of her body parallel to the ceiling of the room, saying at the time that Bett Horner carried her up'.[65] For Sir John Holt the claims were risible and in contravention of both common sense and the laws of physics. Now this might seem to be a fairly straightforward statement (at least for those reared in the empirical atmosphere of the European Enlightenment) but within the context of Early Modern England, where for demonological writers of the stamp of Glanvill and More, the ability of the Devil to manipulate physical reality was at the heart of his dark science, this was an altogether more radical proposition which went to the heart of the controversy over the legal 'proofs' of witchcraft. The judgements of Sir Matthew Hale, and the supportive professional evidence of Sir Thomas Browne, had – as we have already seen – opened the way for the admission of spectral evidence and for the view that natural science might be purposely manipulated by demons during the act of possession. Holt's bold contention that all this was simply the product not of godly learning but of simple credulity, provided legal precedent to counteract persecution, swept away the basis of spectral evidence in English law, and sought to bind considerations of witchcraft to an uncompromising rationalism. If Sir Thomas Raymond had appeared unsure of his hold upon his jurymen, and Sir Francis North had been contemptuous of them; then Sir John Holt had used his authority, embodied in his office, his learning and his patrician background, to confide to his jury that he *knew* the evidences of Sarah Bovet to be ridiculous and that he expected them, as sensible men of property, to think likewise.

There is nothing that works so well to dispel terror as laughter and this increasing sense that belief in witchcraft was the preserve, not of the godly, the insightful and the intellectual, but of the unlettered commonality, was deployed to great effect at Exeter Castle, on 1 April 1696, when the jurymen – after a short deliberation – acquitted Bett Horner of all charges.[66] One contemporary observer of the trial recorded, in a letter to the Bishop of Exeter, that 'by his questions and manner of hemming up the evidence, [Holt] seemed to me to believe nothing of witchery at all'.[67]

Another landmark and far more complex case came his way, in July 1701, when long-running tensions boiled over between Richard Hathaway, a young Southwark apprentice who believed himself bewitched, and Sarah Moordike (or Morduck), the aged wife of a Thames waterman from the same parish. Moordike, a seemingly quiet and inoffensive woman of good character, had been accused of bewitching the blacksmith and of breaking his health over a period of more than a decade. If her neighbours seemed to think well of her, then the juvenile street gangs did not and Hathaway – who seems to have envisaged himself as a populist hero – possessed a ready charisma, had the mob on his side and before Easter 1701, determined to take the law into his own hands. Cornered and almost lynched, Moordike was bloodied, beaten and had clumps of her hair torn out, when her house was stormed and she was thrown to the ground and stamped upon by a gang of youths.[68] As Francis Hutchinson recorded, they threatened to throw her 'into a Horse-pond, to be tried by Swimming, and [she] very hardly escaped with her Life' after the intervention of Dr Martin, a Southwark minister, who at once became a similar object of fury for the mob and was, himself, targeted for rough treatment.[69] Against this background, Hathaway was emboldened to seek Moordike out, after she fled her home and sought sanctuary across the river, in the anonymity of the City's streets. He had her followed and, with a mob in tow, broke into her new lodgings beside Paul's Wharf, repeatedly drawing blood from her, scratching her face and arms in order to break the curse, and subsequently strip-searching her for supernumerary teats, watched approvingly by a band of apprentices and soldiers, and with the connivance of both parish constables and London aldermen. Sir Thomas Lane, who had given Hathaway permission – in the manner of the Bideford justices in 1682 – to conduct searches, interrogations, and the gathering of evidence at will, committed the cut, battered and bruised woman to prison, charged afresh with witchcraft and left there for several months, with bail refused, to wait upon the sitting of the assizes.[70]

In the meantime, Hathaway collected a large amount of evidence supportive of his charges of witchcraft, from sixteen of his friends and neighbours (including six women), while undeterred by abuse and threats of a beating, Dr Martin noted down the nature of the assaults launched upon Moordike and the allegations made against her in the street.[71] From the perspective of Richard Hathaway and his supporters, the trial – held before Sir John Holt at the Guildford Assizes, on 28 July 1701 – was about witchcraft. He was said to have foamed at the mouth, vomited 'great Numbers of Pins', passed 'a Lump of Hair, loose Pins, a Stump of a Nail, half a Nutshel, and Two or Three Pieces of Stone' in a stool, to have been rendered dumb and blind, and to have gone for a period of some ten weeks without eating a morsel.[72] In the depths of his possession:

His Head was bent to the Reins of his Back; and he went sometimes almost upon his Ankles. He would lie as if he was dead, and once was brought to himself by Cupping-Glasses. Screeking and other Noises were heard in the Bed, and about the House; and Charms were applied to him, and were said to do him good. It was also deposed, That he barked like a Dog; and in his Fits burnt like a flame of Fire.[73]

Unfortunately, unlike the subsequent trial in March 1702, the records of the Guildford Assizes are relatively sketchy. What does seem apparent, is that Holt did not address directly the belief, or disbelief, in witches but concentrated upon the medical evidence surrounding Hathaway's supposed possession and his role as a fraudster. However shaken Sarah Moordike had been by her experiences at the hands of the mob, and subsequently in jail, she retained her composure in order to deny everything that was laid against her, enabling Holt to secure a swift acquittal despite a popular outcry against 'both judges, and Jury, and Witnesses' who were 'slandered as if they had not done fairly'.[74] However, Sir John Holt in his judgement intended to go further than a simple acquittal of the suspected witch. He ruled that all of her fees should be paid and that her accuser should be arrested and locked up in the Marshalsea prison, on charges of perjury: 'Without any reason or colour' for his allegations against Moordike, and for 'pretending himself to be bewitched', while his accomplices were to be imprisoned and charged with common assault.[75] This was strong and unexpected action that challenged the ability of malicious persons to bring charges of witchcraft and effectively broke the power of the mobs on the South Bank of the Thames.

Richard Hathaway's counter-trial was held in Southwark, 'the Place in which the Fact was best known, and where any Witnesses might appear without Charge', on 25 March 1702, with Sir John Holt again presiding. During the course of the trial, which again turned on the judge's direction upon the question of imposture rather than the crime of witchcraft, a number of specialist witnesses drawn from the medical profession testified – in very different terms to Sir Thomas Browne a generation before – as to the veracity of Hathaway's state of possession by demons. Mr Kensy, a surgeon who had examined him in November 1701, with the help of his maidservant, had witnessed that:

> He ate and drank any Thing she gave him, Ale, Brandy, Fish, Pudding, Mutton etc. [And] Once he was drunk, and spew'd, and covered his Vomit with Ashes: But if either Mr. Kensy, or any one else, offered him any, he refused to take it, and when he had eaten heartily, he would show them his Belly clung up to his Back, as though there had been nothing in it ... He ate in this manner for Eleven Days together, and yet pretended to continue his Fast.[76]

The indefatigable Dr Martin 'on purpose for an Experiment' to discern whether Hathaway's condition and blindness really were relieved upon drawing blood from the alleged witch, had him scratch:

> another Woman, [and] when he thought he had scratch'd this Sarah Morduck; and upon that he opened his Eyes, but being told he had scratch'd the wrong Woman, he pretended to be blind and dumb again. And the manner of his doing it was such, as shewed him a crafty Fellow, taking Care of himself, for he felt her Arm Four Times over, before he would scratch her.[77]

To seal off the last line of inquiry, a Mr Bateman gave evidence that he had noted that Hathaway's 'vomiting Pins was by a Trick', as:

immediately after he had vomited great Numbers, in appearance, upon the Ground, and was going to vomit more, care being taken that he should vomit into a Chamber-pot, and his Hands being kept down below it, there was not a Pin in the Pot, but a great many crooked ones in his Pockets, in readiness to have play'd his Tricks.[78]

The strange noises that came from his bed 'were shewed to be made by his own Feet, scratching the Bed-post' while a financial motive for his actions was suggested, as besides his celebrity and 'what he got by Gifts and Collections, it was proved, that he tried to make a Gain, by printing a Narrative of his own Case'.[79] In order to press home the point about the Devil's inability to possess individuals, during his summing up of the case, Holt suggested to the jurymen that 'Tricks the Devil may play, but not work a miracle, it is not to be thought that God would let him loose so far'.[80] This saw the power of the Devil diminished from that of God's adversary – capable of destroying, withering and corrupting individuals – to a cheap fraudster, whose sleight of hand was similar to that of Hathaway, himself. If one no longer feared the Devil, then it followed that no one should have cause to fear the witch. The jury were certainly convinced and, in record time, 'without going from the bar' brought in a guilty verdict on Hathaway.[81] The case appears to have combined all those elements – namely, the privatization of violence by the mob, the disorder and swagger of military men, domestic violence and the irrationality of witch-belief – in the conduct of society that Holt seems to have hated most. As a consequence, Richard Hathaway could expect exemplary treatment as a warning to other 'Cheats and Impostors'. He was ordered to pay a fine of 100 marks, to stand in the pillories in Southwark and the City of London, and then to be whipped at the house of correction, where he would serve a sentence of six months' hard labour.[82] As such, the two trials of July 1701 and March 1702 registered highly significant verdicts in the history of witch persecution as they registered, respectively, not just the acquittal of an accused witch but the prosecution and punishment of her persecutor as a deterrent to others who might have been tempted to levy similar charges in the future. If the European witch trials are often used to demonstrate the cruelty and prejudices of individuals and host societies, then it is also worth pausing a moment here to consider that they might also, as in this case, reveal something of the hard-nosed will required in order to obtain justice, to break the tyranny of the crowd, and to establish a new age in which an enlightened reason might flourish. Sarah Moordike, Dr Martin and Chief Justice Holt, it seems, needed no lessons in that.

The theological shift, in the watershed that lay between the cosmologies of the late seventeenth and early eighteenth centuries, that saw God become a transcendent as opposed to an imminent figure, was accompanied by generational and cultural changes that degraded the operations of spirits and demons to the realm, as John Gay put it, of 'nurse-invented lies'.[83] It had been noted, early on, by Roger North after the acquittal of a man on charges of witchcraft at Taunton Dean in 1676. 'As the judge [Francis North] went down stairs, out of the court,' he wrote, 'a hideous old woman cried, "God bless your lordship." "What's the matter, good woman?" [replied Francis North] "My lord," said she, "forty years ago, they would have hanged me for a witch, and they could not; and, now, they would have hanged my poor son."'[84] This encounter, as we know, did nothing to lodge in the mind and compel Sir Francis North to step in to save the Bideford Witches six years later but it is indicative evidence that at least some of those who felt themselves to be the potential victims of allegations of witchcraft were informed and reflexive enough to understand that the attitudes of the judiciary and society's elites were changing.[85] Within this context, the theorization of the witch appeared an increasingly marginal intellectual pursuit. However, it still had its adherents. The publication by Richard Boulton in 1715–16 of two highly detailed casebooks of witch trials that purported to provide empirical evidence for witchcraft, represented an attempt to bolster Glanvill's thesis, to unite it with a form of Lockean political ideology, and to establish a case for the retention of the crime upon the statute books. In the course of his compiling of supportive instances of outbreaks of witchcraft, Boulton devoted a large amount of space in his work to reprinting the pre-trial hearings at Bideford and the account of the hangings of Temperance Lloyd, Susanna Edwards and Mary Trembles that had originally appeared in 1682 as *A True and Impartial Relation of the Informations Against Three Witches*.[86] It certainly may have served to refocus local attention at the popular level on the Bideford Witches but, strangely, the reprinting of the account was not accompanied by any attempt by Boulton at a form of exegesis or restatement of the validity of the verdicts found against them at Exeter Castle. As a result, the account stands as a lengthy historical filler, that is supposed to be taken at simple face value, sandwiched between discussions of the auguries of classical and Egyptian magicians, on the one hand, and a short account of spectral evidence from a murder case of 1687 and a lengthy recapitulation of Sir Matthew Hale's witchcraft trial at Bury St Edmunds, in 1662, upon the other.[87] The trouble for Boulton was that, in large measure, his designated readership – among the jurists, professions, academics and clergy – were simply no longer interested in a restatement of witch theory that, as Ian Bostridge has shown, was after 'the rage of party' seen as being anachronistic and largely eviscerated by the revelation of successive fraudulent examples of demonic possession.[88] While the belief in witches, continued long after at the popular level – not just in village communities but also in urban environments, as the case of Moordike and Hathaway reveals – Boulton's arguments framed neither the right medium nor message to garner significant notice among the masses.

By way of contrast, the rebuttal to his work, published in 1718 by Francis Hutchinson, appeared as a timely breath of fresh air that collated together examples of injustice and legal arguments – such as those advanced by Sir John Holt – for the ending of witch persecution, together with a dialogue between a Scottish clergyman and an English juryman on the reality of witches that consciously mirrored that provided by King James VI and I in his *Daemonologie*. Although Hutchinson devoted a full chapter to a discussion of witches' marks, to the Salem outbreaks, and the judgement of Sir Matthew Hale at Bury St Edmunds, he did not tackle Boulton directly over his citation of the Bideford Witches. Rather, he simply observed that 'Susan Edwards, Mary Trembles, and Temperance Lloyd, hanged at Exeter, confess'd themselves Witches, but died with good Prayers in their Mouths' and noted, laconically, that 'I suppose these are the last Three that have been hanged in England'.[89] While Hutchinson had succeeded in producing a concise, rationalist rebuttal of the reality of witchcraft which would stand as a model for educated thought in the eighteenth century, within the context of the society and culture of North Devon, his decision not to directly engage with the Bideford case established the symbolic act of the hanging of the 'last' witches above a wider discussion of the ills that had brought them to their deaths. This served to colour the treatment of the women in the subsequent historiography of witchcraft in England and, also, quite possibly unwittingly acted to permit the survival of witch-belief in Bideford, itself, as a distinct subculture functioning at the margins of its society.

Yet, even here, much had changed. The Revolution of 1688–9 had provided a comprehensive religious and political settlement that was increasingly felt to have satisfied the concerns of large sections of interest within the political nation. The last of the great smallpox epidemics had burned itself out by the close of the century, finance and trade remained buoyant despite the wars with Louis XIV's France, the supply of and demand for consumer goods was steadily expanding, and with wind and water power yet to be supplanted by steam the environment remained unpolluted. When Daniel Defoe visited Bideford, in the early years of the eighteenth century, he witnessed a town that had experienced significant change since the witches had been sent to the gallows. The quay had been further extended, and the surrounding warren of old streets, yards and gardens cleared away to create the new development of Bridgeland. In the wake of the passing of the Act of Toleration that ended the persecution of Dissenters, 'a very large, well-built, and well-finished meeting-house' had been built, with the financial help of Gabriel Beale.[90] Defoe was struck by the industry and elegance of the port town, and by its strong attachment to religious nonconformity, which he thought had become its defining feature. While the 'people of the best fashion' attended Anglican services at St Mary's, he thought that 'all the town had gone thither' when he saw 'the multitude of the people' come out of the meeting house.[91] In a sign of the changing times, Defoe chanced – or perhaps contrived – to meet with William Bartlett, the son and grandson of the persecuted ministers. He was now:

> the person who officiates at the meeting-house ... and found ... to be not only a learned man, and master of good reading, but a most acceptable and gentlemanly person, and one who, contrary to our received opinion of these people, had not only good learning and good sense, but abundance of good manners and good humour – nothing sour, cynical, or morose in him, and in a word, a very valuable man ... so I found this gentleman was very well received in the place, even by those whom he differed from in matters of religion, and those differences did not, as is usual, make any breach in their conversing with him.[92]

No longer hunted and reviled, Bideford's Dissenters – useful, industrious, wealthy and seemingly increasingly good company – had come into their own. Little more than a generation had separated John Strange and John Abbott, but in terms of the manner in which they sought to be represented to posterity their lives spoke of rapid cultural change and markedly shifting priorities and values. While Strange's portrait, from the 1640s, attempts to recount the course of his life through a series of pictograms reflecting the workings of God's providences towards him, Abbott's portrait, painted in the late 1680s or early 1690s, is a statement of individual, human, skill and personality. God is, literally, absent from the frame, as John Abbott flourishes his plasterer's 'rifler' or scalpel,

Figure 21 *John Abbott of Frithelstock, master craftsman, c.1685–90 (oil on canvas by an anonymous artist, by kind permission of Exeter Museum). Though separated by a gulf of wealth, social connections and personal talent from the Bideford Witches, Abbott would have known the women by sight. The worldly celebration of his individual artistry stands in contrast to John Strange's stark cosmology. As such, it marks a watershed in European thought that, after 1660, increasingly separated the Early Modern from the Modern.*

as the tool of his trade that has made his fortune. He stands within an arcadian landscape, with a setting sun illuminating the red flash of his cap and the folds of his cloak; but if he can afford the costly black dye for his coat, then he has eschewed the wearing of a fashionable gentleman's cravat and wig. He is justly proud of his artistry and gift for creation but, though enjoying the trappings of wealth and the good things in life, he has no desire to appear to be anything other than he is and stands before us as a craftsman, rather than as a would-be gentleman, ashamed of his origins. Those confident, regarding, eyes speak to us of a curiosity in – and an engagement with – the world around him that is secular, materialistic and wholly open to the potentialities of human endeavour, discovery and imagination. The ships that crowd Bideford's quayside in the portrait of John Strange seemed reliant upon God's provision of bounty from the Americas, and continuing favour in harnessing the winds and the waves. By way of contrast, it is suggested that John Abbott's fortune was secured by his own, personal, intelligence and art.

Abbot was a man who would have known, or at least would have certainly passed by, the Bideford Witches in the street, yet his horizons and lived experience were entirely different.[93] If he missed seeing the first staging of *The Beggar's Opera* by a few short months, then it is likely that he would have been far more in sympathy with the spirit of its English dance tunes than with Handel's Italianate opera, *Rinaldo*, that premiered in London's Haymarket theatre in 1711. The idea of the efficacy of witches in undermining Christianity through their workings of love magic with the Turks was probably far more remote from his conception, than the downgrading of the name of the 'witch' to become the sport of the nursery as evidenced by the fable, written by John Gay – who had grown up as his neighbour – wherein a chorus of half-starved cats mocked 'to serve a hag', complained that they were believed to be her 'imps' and thought even 'her broom a nag'.[94] Given that the writer spent his youth in Barnstaple, and his family had links to both Frithelstock and Bideford, it is tempting to speculate that stories of the Bideford Witches circulated and implanted themselves to fashion his vision of:

A wrinkled Hag, of wicked fame,
Beside a little smoaky flame

Sat hov'ring, pinch'd with age and frost;
Her shrivell'd hands, with veins emboss'd,
Upon her knees her weight sustains,
While palsy shook her crazy brains:
She mumbles forth her backward pray'rs,
An untam'd scold of fourscore years.[95]

Even if the verses, destined to be repeated in the playrooms of the children of King George II, spoke to an established archetype – as opposed to the folk memory of a specific case – then the shift in the paradigm that took the witch from being the enemy of God to being an object of pity, mirrored the cultural triumph of materialist over idealistic, or theocratic, modes of thought.

10

At the house of the White Witch

When John Watkins came to compile his *History of Bideford*, in 1792, he was caught between his own Anglican beliefs and the rationalist spirit of the age. In discussing the fate of Temperance Lloyd, Susanna Edwards and Mary Trembles, he ventured that when it came to witchcraft:

> That there are not invisible, nefarious beings, cannot well be denied by any who believe the sacred scriptures; or are versed in the histories of different countries, antient and modern. But the oeconomy of that order of intelligence lies enveloped in impenetrable darkness; and though we are, unquestioningly, to believe, that the Supreme Disposer of all things has the wisest ends in permitting their influence and operations in the world, yet it would be derogating infinitely from his exalted excellence to suppose, that he permits any mere wanton acts of evil ... it is not to be supposed that he would design the everlasting destruction of a few mortals, for an everlasting benefit to others. But it is entirely upon such a supposition, that the hypothesis of witchcraft, or of a union between human beings and evil spirits, depends for its support. To believe in such a doctrine is, therefore, lessening the dignity, narrowing the power, confining the benevolence, and degrading all the glorious attributes of the Deity.[1]

In effect, Watkins was attempting to have his cake and to eat it. Witchcraft existed on a theoretical level, as evidenced by the Bible, but its prosecution – which had been removed from the statute books in 1736 – was sordid and the preserve of the stupid and ill-educated. 'To the honour of this age', he adds with more than a touch of hubris, 'such miserable bigotry and absurd superstition have lost a considerable degree of their influence, and the enlightening cheering rays of generous truth and sensible benevolence seem to be gladly received by almost all orders of persons.'[2] Here, it is worth stressing the qualifications he used and that while it might *seem* to have disappeared as a belief system among *almost all* of Bideford's citizens, it still clung on in some dark corners. Watkins clearly held that the belief in witchcraft had 'remained very general in this town and neighbourhood' as late as the 1770s, more than a full generation since the repeal of the legislation governing the prosecution of witches and that, even in the 1790s, although 'pretty much worn away' the notion still remained as a palpable terror and threat in the lives of some of his poorer neighbours.[3] This might be thought of as being no more than a touch of romantic hyperbole, on Watkins' part, had we not supportive evidence from the local press of the remarkable durability of witchcraft in Bideford and its environs. On 10 March 1853, the *North Devon Journal* reported the death of Martha Lee, 'better known as "Old Matty"', who – it was said – had reached the age of 105. If this was indeed the case – and it is far from certain as popular memory and records of the poor were far from exact – then, 'Old Matty' would have been in middle age at the time that the Rev. Watkins was composing his history and might just have known, in her turn, elderly people when she was a young girl who had first-hand memory of the Bideford Witches. Coming from Monkleigh, which lies three and a half miles south-east of the port town, she spent her early years in the company of her grandmother who, in the 1730s, was held to be 'the most formidable personage in all the neighbourhood (not excepting the parsons)' on account of her reputation as a witch. A little more than a decade later, grandmother and granddaughter:

> residing in an uneducated and thinly-populated neighbourhood . . . declared themselves to be in the especial confidence of the powers of evil, and persuaded the timid and credulous to give heed to their teachings. For their own pecuniary benefit Matty and her grandmother exacted a sort of black mail from the better to-do portion of their neighbours, who, by this offering, escaped from their witchery, thereby securing protection and prosperity to their persons as well as their piggeries.[4]

Soon enough:

> Matty having witnessed the ascendancy her grandmother gained over the minds of the ignorant, resolved to inherit the empire her ancestress had held with undisputed sway, and accordingly initiated herself into all the mysteries of the dark profession, until, by repeated deception, she appears to have become the dupe of her own deceivings, for up to the last year of her existence she made it no secret but frequently boasted of the spell she had thrown over many a superstitious wiseling.[5]

However, though her fame spread and with it the profits of the blackmailer's art, there was still a price to be paid. Though the judiciary were no longer interested in combatting witchcraft, the mob was and fell upon her to scratch her and effect 'a little blood-letting for the purpose of breaking her charm, and on one occasion a party of desperadoes actually stuck her upon a spit and commenced roasting her before a blazing fire'.[6] Her case, as related to us in the pages of the *North Devon Journal* appears in many of its respects, not least through the counter-measures taken against her 'magic' and the grinding poverty amid which Matty Lee eked out her existence, very close to that of the three original Bideford Witches. The difference lay in the denouement, through changing official responses to dealing with the elderly and the indigent poor. Whereas the Bideford Witches had been in receipt of 'out door' poor relief, paid out to them in the churchyard of St. Mary's from the parish rates or through individual grants from charitable institutions such as the Andrew Dole, after the passing of the New Poor Law of 1834 a nationwide system of 'indoor relief' was established through the workhouses, which effectively served to remove potential witch figures from their local communities. This is exactly what happened to the aged Matty Lee, who falling upon hard times and infirmity was admitted to the Bideford Union Workhouse at the end of her span of her years. As the account of her life makes plain, in terms of homilies, the workhouses acted not only to 'punish' the poor for their plight but also to 'reform' the manners of the lower orders. Consequently, we are told:

> Notwithstanding the state of heathenism in which she had passed the greater part of a long life, it is worthy of remark that during the last year of her

existence she had entirely renounced her former acts of wickedness, and, turning her back on her old refuge of lies, became a great lover of the bible, and manifested the most sincere desire to have its truths read in her hearing. She appeared sensible of the kindness shown her by the Master, Matron, Chaplain, and Surgeon of the Workhouse, the latter of whom constantly supplied her with what she considered a great comfort – namely, a little snuff.[7]

A similar tale was told, and fate recorded, for the better-known Devonian figure of Mary Ann Voaden, a beggar woman from Bratton Clovelly, who came to the attention of the Rev. Sabine Baring-Gould over the course of the last two decades of the reign of Queen Victoria. It was he who made famous, and significantly reworked her story, and settled the more picturesque name of 'Marianne' upon her. The reverend, who consistently exaggerated her age, thought that 'She must have been handsome in her day, with a finely-cut profile,

Figure 22 *Mary Ann Voaden and the tumbled-down cottage of the 'White Witch', Bratton Lane, Devon, c.1890 (Author's Collection). Rural poverty was a continuing feature of Victorian society, but the witch figure was increasingly being removed from the community and consigned to the workhouse.*

and piercing dark eyes', and described her as usually wearing 'a red kerchief about her head or neck and an old scarlet petticoat'.[8] However, he also noted that 'she was dirty – indescribably so. Her hands were the colour of mahogany' and that 'It was six years since she bought a bar of yellow or any other soap'.[9]

She was born in Bratton Clovelly, Devon, in 1827 and, as far as we can tell, never left the confines of her village until she was forced out by the parish constable and the officers of the poor law. Her home is listed as 'Voaden Cottage' and then as the 'Cottage in Bratton Lane' in the respective census returns for 1881 and 1891, and at one point seems to have been a substantial, two-storied cob and thatch cottage with two brick chimneys, and surrounded by a quarter of an acre of land in which to grow a supplementary crop of food. In 1881, Mary Ann was still at work as a seamstress; however, in the course of the following decade she stopped working and slipped, quietly, into the ranks of the rural poor. Soon after, the thatch started to give way in several places and the rain got into the fabric of the building. The Rev. Baring-Gould thought that she could have sought help from her neighbours to make the necessary repairs, as 'the farmers offered her straw, and a thatcher would have done the work for her gratis, or only for her blessing. She would not. "God made the sky," she said, "and that is the best roof of all."'[10] The way that he tells it, overlooking the heavy insurance rates placed upon thatch and the fact that the tired and worn – but it should be emphasized far from elderly – woman may well have been falling prey to mental illness, Baring-Gould weaves a picturesque and faintly gothic tale of decay from the bare bones of her misery.

When the roof fell in, 'the proprietress obtained shelter for her head by stuffing up the chimney of the bedroom fireplace with a sack filled with chaff, and pushing her bed to the hearth and sleeping with her head under the sack'.[11] Surely enough, the staircase rotted away and 'the walls were exposed, rain and frost told on them, and also on the beam ends sustaining the floor, and the next stage was that one side of the floor gave way wholly' and in its collapse 'the floor blocked the fireplace and the doorway'.[12] The glass was broken in half of the window frames and the gaps patched and stopped with rags. Without a fire for at least three winters, including the bitterly cold one of 1893–4, she buried herself away under layers of fallen cob and building debris, 'her only means of egress and ingress [being] through the window' and 'finally took refuge in an old oak chest, keeping the lid up with a brick' in order to escape the winds and dripping rain.[13]

It was, therefore, unsurprising that the sight of 'a venerable dame, in an old bacon box in a fallen cottage' left a powerful imprint upon the reverend's imagination. When he came to write his novel, *Arminell* – subtitled a 'Social Romance', in 1891, she served as the model for 'Patience Kite', 'the white witch' who saves the eponymous heroine from a fall from a rock ledge and spirits her back to the safety of her tumbledown cottage, where a pet raven pecks at the bars of its cage and there is a 'perversity in all things'.[14] Yet, Baring-Gould did not choose, initially, to describe Mary Ann as a witch, of either 'black' or 'white' variety or to associate her with witchcraft of any kind. Rather, in the first of his three accounts of her life, he used her particular plight in order to highlight the attachment of the English to their homes and property. Having discovered her distress, he wrote that 'I went back to Marianne and said, "Now, tell me why you will go on living in this ruin?" "My dear," she said, "us landed proprietors must hold on to our houses and acres. Tes a thing o' principle."'[15] In this way, her lack of reflexivity and preparedness to confide in the propertied gentleman as though she were his equal becomes, due to the invidious nature of the English class system, the cause of a polite – and it has to be said very faint – comedy of manners.

When Baring-Gould came to write of her once again, a decade later in 1908, he explicitly framed her as a 'White Witch', as opposed to a 'Cunning Woman', and discussed at length her 'book of charms' – which she promised to give him but never did – that contained her various cures for everything from burns, scalds and sprains, to whooping cloth, toothache and the staunching of the flow of blood from a wound. In case of a burn the following words were, she said, to be recited over the injury:

There were three Angels who came from the North,
One bringing Fire, the other brought Frost,
The other he was the Holy Ghost.
In Frost, out Fire![16]

Angels seemed to have formed a distinct part of Mary Ann's cosmology as she told the rector of Bratton that she believed that two of them sat watching over her each night, so that the house timbers did not fall upon her and to make sure that she was safe from intruders. The charm to cure a sprain took the form of a story turned to chant, to be repeated trice times over:

> As Christ was riding over the Crolly Bridge, His horse slid and sprained his leg. He alighted and spake the words: Bone to bone, and sinew to sinew! And blessed it and it became well, and so shall . . . become well.[17]

The local resetting of the life of Jesus together with the dominant framework of Christian prayer in the sealing of her charms, similarly appear to have been integral to her world view and her conception of her ability to manipulate the order of nature about her. Baring-Gould was certainly intrigued by her skill and repeated his belief that, like any good cunning person:

> Marianne had the gift of stanching blood even at a distance. On one occasion when hay was being cut, a man wounded himself at Kelly, some eight miles distant, and the blood flowed in streams. At once the farmer bade a man take a kerchief dipped in his blood and gallop as hard as he could to the tumble-down cottage, and get Marianne to bless the blood. He did so, and was gone some three hours. As soon as the old woman had charmed the kerchief the blood ceased to flow.[18]

So far, this all seems closer to village healing, cloaked in a slightly garbled and unconventional but still avowedly Christian form of piety, rather than anything that might have been regarded as 'witchery'. She seems to have gleaned a living from her ability to 'bless bad knees and stop the flow of blood, and show where stolen goods are hidden, and tell who has ill-wished any one'.[19] Furthermore, she did not seek to embellish her insights, or to hint at the possession of arcane knowledge that she did not, in truth, possess. Thus, when the Rev. Baring-Gould asked her opinion of the 'witches' ladder' that had been recently discovered and was making academic headlines, in the hope that as a 'White Witch' she might provide a link to an underground, oral tradition of magic working, Mary Ann replied bluntly that the apparatus looked more like a net for stringing together garden beans and for frightening away thieving birds than for assisting in spellcraft. In this she was, as modern scholars have affirmed, closer to the truth in her judgement than many Victorian folklorists who took the 'ladder' to be a new and important discovery in the archaeology of witchcraft.[20]

However, two instances from her story draw parallels with the predicament of the Bideford Witches and suggest how Mary Ann Voaden might have found herself in considerable trouble had she been born two centuries earlier: the first concerns the giving of charity, the second upon her using her reputation as a witch to intimidate her neighbours in the expectation of gain. It seems that Mary Ann had a reciprocal view of begging, and of the act of charity, and would attempt to reward those who had shown her kindness with a gift as well as a kind word.[21] The trouble was that the only thing of any value that she had to give was a piece 'of fine old lace' – that she had probably made, herself, in better days – and that she knew she would not be able to replace. Thus, when Baring-Gould's daughter gave her a basket of food, the aged woman presented her with the lace but as she took her leave Mary Ann called out after her asking for the gift to be returned, as 'my dear, I shall want that lace again. If any one else be so gude as to give me aught, I shall want it to make an acknowledgement of the kindness.'[22] It does not take too much imagination to see how misunderstandings over the nature of Mary Ann's 'giving' might arise, as two different conceptions of ownership: one rooted in the idea of acquisition and possession made general by the capitalist, industrial age, and the other harking back to the symbols and commonalities of pre-industrial, agrarian communities, where the act of giving was as important as the substance of the gift, itself. Less benign was Mary Ann's willingness, when all else had failed, to turn to threats and extortion in order to make ends meet. 'How she subsisted,' considered Baring-Gould, 'was a puzzle to the whole parish. But, then, she was generally feared. She received presents from every farm and cottage.'[23] He then provides a chilling example of how the 'strangeness in her manner' and the sudden shift to 'a savagery in the woman's tone' might be deployed to force charity from among her neighbours.[24] 'Sometimes,' he wrote:

> she would meet a child coming from school, and stay it, and fixing her wild dark eye on it, say, 'My dear, I knawed a child just like you – same age, red rosy cheeks, and curlin' black hair. And that child shrivelled up, shrumped like an apple as is picked in the third quarter of the moon. The cheeks grew

white, the hair went out of curl, and she jist died right on end and away'. Before the day was out, a chicken or a basket of eggs as a present from the mother of that child was sure to arrive.[25]

This was exactly the sort of practice that had resulted in the death of Temperance Lloyd and the bloodying of Matty Lee. However, the presence of the local constable and the overseers of the poor law appear to have acted as a transmission belt, placing a check upon local fears, and encouraging a sense of deference to the authority of law and local government that made the recourse to private score-settling far less likely, efficacious and respectable. There seem to have been growing attempts by the local authorities to evict her from her home and send her to the workhouse but, in 1890–1, the Rev. Baring-Gould reported that Mary Ann was 'At the present . . . defying all the authorities. They have come to a dead lock. She has resisted orders to leave for three years, and is in hourly peril of her life. The only person who can expel her is the landlord', who, it seems, was reluctant to move against her, either through fear or genuine concern for her well-being.[26] In a semi-fictionalized exchange, the reverend has Mary Ann explain – in a far more eloquent and rational manner than she was probably capable – her predicament and motivation, as the local authorities:

can order me to go, but they cannot force me to go. The policeman says they can fine me ten shillings a day if I remain and defy them. Let them fine me. They must next get an order to distrain to get the amount. They may sell my furniture, but they won't be able to turn me out . . . I've nowhere else to go to. I will not go into the union [ie. the workhouse], and I will not live in a house with other folk. I am accustomed to be alone. I am not afraid. Here I am at liberty, and I will here die rather than lose my freedom.[27]

Yet, in the end, Mary Ann did lose her freedom. Her fall, though, happened through accidental misfortune rather than through the official malice of the sanitary officer, the board of guardians or the magistrates. As Baring-Gould related:

The huntsmen were wont, whenever passing her wretched house, to shout 'Marianne! Marianne!' and draw up. Then from amidst the ruins came a muffled response, 'Coming, my dears, coming!' Presently she appeared. She was obliged to crawl out of her window that opened into the garden and orchard at the back of the house, go round it, and unlace a gate of thorns she had erected as a protection to her garden; there she always received presents. One day as usual the fox-hunters halted and called for her; she happened at the time to have kindled a fire on the floor of her room to boil a little water in a kettle for tea, and she left the fire burning when she issued forth to converse with the gentlemen and extend her hand for half-crowns. Whilst thus engaged the flames caught some straw that littered the ground, they spread, set fire to the woodwork, and the room was in a blaze. Everything was consumed, her chest-bed, her lace, her book of charms.[28]

'After that,' the reverend noted as the coda to her story, 'she was conveyed to the workhouse, where she is still [1908], and now is kept clean.'[29] As with the case of Matty Lee, one can see the stress upon the New Poor Law as an exercise in public health and moral reform. The rural dirt was scrubbed away and with it the sense of individuality that made Mary Ann Voaden noteworthy in the first place. Yet, again, Baring-Gould was stretching the limits of his tale. By 1908, his anti-heroine was long dead. She had been removed to the Okehampton workhouse which had been just been extended and rebuilt after the publication of a withering report on conditions there by the commission of the British Medical Journal in 1894. Ironically, given her own attempts to staunch the rain that had washed away her own home, in February 1900, the banks of the West Okement River burst and flooded the work house grounds, ensuring that Mary Ann had to swab and scrub away at the mud and flood water that gushed into her cell-like room. She did not survive the collective experience of the workhouse long and is listed as dying at the beginning of 1902, at Okehampton, though curiously her age is given as eighty-three rather than seventy-nine. Though the Rev. Baring-Gould willingly sought her out, dramatized her life, and made money from his telling of her oddities and misadventures it does not seem that he ever considered a reciprocal gesture of payment in order to make her last years more comfortable. Rather, he seems to have lost interest in her the moment that her book of charms burned, and the workhouse door swung closed behind her.

With the silencing and removal of the witch figure from the community, as a by-product of the New Poor Law, discussions of witchcraft shifted – by and large – from consideration of the subject as a dead, rather than a living art. Increasingly the witch was perceived to be the victim of injustice and requiring understanding and pity, rather than as an object of hatred, derision and fear. She could also be commercialized, as evidenced by works of the Rev. Baring-Gould as well as by the growth of the greetings cards and advertising that accompanied the celebration of Hallowe'en, in North America, from the 1890s onwards.[30] The burgeoning tourist industry in North Devon also made use of the witch, with the thatched cottages at the top of Higher Gunstone Lane becoming associated with the names of the Bideford Witches, recorded in photographs and prints, and acquiring the status of a local visitor attraction.[31] By 1904, the tourist guide to the town and surrounding area remarked upon the 'stupid, yet fatal, superstition of witchcraft' and devoted considerable attention to their lives, alongside the more familiar accounts of North Devon's role in the expeditions of Elizabethan seafarers, of the stamp of Sir Richard Grenville of *The Revenge*.[32] Yet, witchcraft still cast a strange and unexpected canker over the town.

When Arthur H. Norway (1859–1938) came to write his travelogue to the *Highways and Byways in Devon and Cornwall*, which was first published in November 1897, he left the reader in no doubt that he believed in the efficacy of witchcraft and that the hanging of Temperance Lloyd, Susanna Edwards and Mary Trembles had been warranted and was entirely just. An eclectic – and it has to be said somewhat eccentric – author, he had written on everything from a popular guidebook to *Naples, Past and Present* to a study of Dante's *Divine Comedy* and a less than riveting *History of the Post-Office Packet Service, between the years 1793–1815*.[33] His best-selling guidebook combined poetry (with Kipling appearing a keen favourite), with history (in the manner of J.A. Froude), and popular novels (such as Kingsley's *Westward, Ho!*), together with accounts of rambles through the countryside of Devon and Cornwall undertaken by the author and his dog. However, though its commercial success – that saw the book run to nine editions between 1897 and 1919 – was founded upon an age of industry, the steamship and the freedom to holiday brought about by the coming of the railway, he was keen – as no one else had been since Richard

Boulton – to establish the Bideford Witches as a test case that 'proved' the validity of witch-belief. He had read the 1682 pamphlet, *The Tryal, Condemnation, and Execution of Three Witches*, and considered that it might be useful reference material 'for any one afflicted with doubts as to the existence of witches to study carefully'.[34] As a consequence, the three suspected witches appear as 'bad old women', and 'companions in guilt', who 'were very justly hanged'.[35] The corporeal reality of the demonic pact is restated, while the Rev. Hann – as precisely had been intended by the original source – was taken to be the focus of their rage, whereby as 'a matter of mere spite' they made 'his cows give blood instead of milk'. Similarly, even though her companions were 'almost equally wicked', the witches observe a strict hierarchy, with Temperance Lloyd appearing as the foremost and by far the most dangerous.[36] However, his main authority for the malign efficacy of witchcraft was not, as might be supposed the Bideford trial account or its surrounding literature, but the opinion given by Sir Thomas Browne at Bury St. Edmunds, in 1662. He paraphrases Browne as follows:

'For my part,' said Sir Thomas Browne, 'I have ever believed, and do now know, that there are witches.' That settles the matter. I am both too humble and too deeply imbued with West Country prejudices to feel any disposition to differ with the silver tongued physician of Norwich ... Sir Thomas has convinced us.[37]

Such a declaration, and strident appeal to local 'prejudices', is startling but Norway goes much further setting the case of the Devon witches alongside much more recent tales of Cornish cunning folk, and the author's own accounts 'of the transactions now taking place from day to day between the peasants and those white witches in whom, for the most part, they had a confidence far exceeding that which they bestow on any doctor'.[38] He focuses upon the story of an unfortunately unnamed young girl 'of poor parents' who had been seized by epileptic fits, in 1887. Unable to find a cure for her seizures, the assistance of a local 'white' witch was sought by her father and mother and the woman quickly and authoritatively pronounced that 'the case was serious, and in all probability the girl had been bewitched by somebody'.[39] Norway then tells his readership that it was considered that, before 'the week was up the witch's intelligent suggestion had produced its effect', as:

The girl began to dream every night of a stout elderly woman with a very red face, who approached her in a very threatening manner, and the parents hurried off to report this new and alarming symptom to the witch. Of course, the witch was triumphant. There could not be a doubt that the red-faced elderly lady of the girl's dream had wrought the mischief.[40]

A likely suspect was quickly identified as being a near neighbour:

an old widow lady, charitable, popular, and highly respected, but stout, and having an unfortunately red face. No one had ever suspected her of any but kind and benevolent actions; but this fact, the witch argued, really made the case against her stronger, since it was well known that all persons who practised magic were extremely apt at diverting suspicion from themselves ... Besides, if the old lady had not bewitched the girl, what was she doing in her dream?[41]

Unable to swim the witch the girl's parents resorted to the form of counter-magic advocated by the 'white' witch and determined that 'the next best way was to go by night to the old lady's house, take a stone from her garden wall, and put it into the kitchen fire at the girl's home. When it was charred away the fits would cease'. To make doubly sure, the finger of a man who had hanged himself 'that very week' in a neighbouring hamlet was also procured and hung around the afflicted girl's neck, 'as the witch directed' and, we are told, 'the fits ceased almost immediately'.[42] The trouble with the story is that it is, largely, unverifiable as the author did not see fit to record either the location of these events or the identity of both the accused and the afflicted. The passage occurs between descriptions of the country between Truro and Newquay, so it seems reasonable to suggest that the events occurred somewhere along the road north, close to the villages of Treviscoe and St. Michael. It is possible that the entire story is a fabrication but Arthur H. Norway's brooding certainty over the continuity of witchcraft belief and folk magic across the South West, suggests that even when set against the backdrop of Victorian empire, the factory system, and scientific certainties, the witch had not been entirely removed from the intellectual and physical landscape of England. All of a sudden, the values of the European Enlightenment appeared to run perilously skin-deep.

Coda: Where are the witches?

The Bideford Witches came to Parliament. Reviled or ignored in life, they had become emblematic in death. The Witchcraft Statute of 1736 had in many respects captured the spirit of the Enlightenment and enshrined the approach taken by Sir John Holt, in as much as it persecuted the pretence of bewitching, by either accuser or defendant, rather than the act of harmful magic. However, it had, by the first decades of the twentieth century begun to be used as a 'catch all' for the prosecution of gypsy fortune tellers, spiritualists, astrologers and village cunning folk.[1] This had been reinforced, at village level, by the passing of a new Vagrancy Act in 1824, which had strengthened the hand of the authorities, and later that of the national police force, in targeting beggars and professional diviners, alike. Consequently, an extended campaign led the National Spiritualists Union but drawing together figures from the esoteric movement – including Gerald Gardner, the founder of modern Wicca, who proved to be an indefatigable and adept lobbyist – and winning support among both establishment figures (including Lord Dowding, the hero of the Battle of Britain) and a number of junior ministers in the Labour Government, for the repeal of the Witchcraft Act. It is notable that many of those who forwarded the debates in the House of Commons were marked by a background in religious nonconformity as well as by an affinity with progressive causes and radical politics. This was certainly the case with James Chuter Ede (1882–1965), the Home Secretary, trade unionist and one-time municipal schoolteacher, who had initially made his name campaigning for the extension of educational opportunities and the abolition of the death penalty. Although it was to be a free vote on a Private Member's Bill, with no whip along party lines, Chuter Ede chose to introduce and, in large measure, to shape the parameters of the debate.[2] At the second reading of the Fraudulent Mediums Bill, on 1 December 1950, he announced that:

> This Bill sets out to repeal the Witchcraft Act ... in its entirety, and to exempt persons purporting to possess spiritualistic powers from prosecution under Section 4 of the Act of 1824 ... It may seem surprising to some that the spiritualists of today should be in any way embarrassed by two such ancient and differing Acts as the Witchcraft Act of 1735 and the Vagrancy Act of 1824 but anyone who has perused the late Sir James Frazer's *Golden Bough* will realise how prevalent all over the world among all races has been a belief in spirits.[3]

Figure 23 *Three Poor Women of Bideford: pottery jug by Harry Juniper, 2018 (Collection of Gill Clayton). One of a series of splendid jugs made by the renowned Bideford potter that began with a prize-winning entry to a local design competition held at Exeter Museum, in 1966. The witches were now firmly established as being persecuted rather than persecutor, objects of pity rather than of hatred.*

The appeal to the authority of Frazer's *Golden Bough*, the great synthesis of late Victorian anthropology, Classical scholarship and the attempt to recover the substance of Europe's pre-Christian, pagan belief systems and cosmologies, was significant as the massive compendium made a powerfully attractive academic argument for the existence of an a priori nature religion, which contained within it elements of witchcraft.[4] The witch, herself, was moving from being a figure of opprobrium, mockery or condescension, to one that might elicit educated study and comment, pity and perhaps even admiration. This sense of witchcraft as being part of a larger, now lost, pagan religion sat in tension with the rationalist argument that denied the ability of magic to harm, or for that matter to help. Furthermore, it emphasized the plight of the innocent woman wrongly accused of a wholly improbable crime. James Chuter Ede chose to pursue both lines of attack during his parliamentary speech, stressing that:

> As anyone who has browsed over the accounts of the witchcraft trials can discover for himself the Witchcraft Act, 1735 [sic], closed a very disreputable part of British history. One unfortunate woman called Temperance Lloyd in 1682 was charged with bewitching Lydia Burman while this lady was brewing ale in the house of a gentleman at Bideford. The verdict of the jury was 'Guilty', which is evidence of the public opinion of the day, and Temperance Lloyd was hanged.[5]

Thus, Temperance Lloyd – who could never have imagined such a thing in life and had been denied the right of an appeal to Whitehall – became the matter of parliamentary sympathy and debate long after her death. Yet, in keeping with Roger North's garbling of their identities and stories, the Home Secretary managed to effectively sketch the outlines of Temperance Lloyd's case while emphasizing one aspect (namely, the slaying of Lydia Burman through witchcraft) over another (the breaking of Grace Thomas' health through enchantment), and for the sake of clarity chose to ignore the fates of Susanna Edwards and Mary Trembles altogether. Thus, Temperance Lloyd again became the 'foremost' of the Bideford Witches and was set upon a stage as representative of both the 'last' witches to hang in England, under the legislation of 1604, and as a symbol of cruelty, irrationality and injustice.

With the carrying of the bill and its enactment into law, a whole range of prohibitions against magical belief and practice that had existed, in one form or another, for almost three hundred years, fell away. In so doing, it permitted, as an unforeseen by-product, the reclaiming of the name and identity of the witch herself. However, the legacy of the Bideford Witches did not initially find a secure purchase within revived witchcraft until the second wave of Feminism, which gained ground from the early 1970s to the early 1980s. Wicca increasingly emphasized the role of the goddess over the horned god, and conjoined its religious practice with ideas and approaches taken from the flourishing environmentalist and Women's movements.[6] 'The term *Witch*,' wrote Starhawk, 'has negative connotations. It is a word that scares people, a word that shocks or elicits nervous, stupid laughter … Yet I prefer the word *Witch* to prettier words, because the concept of a Witch goes against the grain of the culture of estrangement. It *should* rub us the wrong way. If it arouses fear or negative assumptions, then those thought-forms can be openly challenged and transformed.'[7] In this way, the witch suddenly carried the power of everywoman and the goddess, who was 'not one image but many – a constellation of form and associations – earth, air, fire, water, moon and star, sun flower and seed, willow and apple, black, red, white, Maiden, Mother, and Crone.'[8] Viewed within this light, Temperance Lloyd, 'the Crone', was capable of reinvention as a darkly powerful, and knowing, source of female power and empowerment as an aspect of the divine.

The witch suddenly turned sexual rebel and ecological activist *par excellence*. Within a British context, the integration of witchcraft with Green politics and political activism found a forceful expression, in the spontaneous establishment, in 1983, of a 'Women's Peace Camp' at Greenham Common, Berkshire. Intended as a protest against the escalation of the arms race by NATO and the siting of US cruise missiles on English soil that was, in theory at least, publicly owned, it swiftly developed its own dynamic and served as one of the decade's most striking – and visible – expressions of female driven protest and Feminist empowerment. Though there was no 'typical' Greenham woman or anti-nuclear protestor, it seems fair to suggest that for all those who came to protest at the air force base weapons were no longer an abstract but a 'vividly present' symptom of a Cold War that was, increasingly, threating to turn hot.[9] Furthermore, for many, 'Cruise [had] become a symbol of nuclear terror, male domination and imperialist exploitation'. The phallocism of the warheads was often noted and linked to a sense of violence and patriarchy.[10] Among the protestors taking part in non-violent direct action, culminating in a series of mass incursions, were individual pagan women together with members of P.A.N. (Pagans Against Nukes), a group founded in 1980 by Philip and Kate Cozens that was strongly influenced by Starhawk's best-selling book, *The Spiral Dance*.[11]

Amid the mud and wire at Greenham, there was a shrine to the goddess at the 'Orange Gate' featuring 'a moulded figurine of a pregnant woman, full size', with an altar 'at her feet which was continuously replenished with offerings of fruit, shells' and brightly burning candles'.[12] The name of Temperance Lloyd, among that of other women persecuted as witches, hung upon the protestors' lips and was incised upon the scraps of paper containing prayers and drawings that were tied to the perimeter fence. When they appealed to Newbury District Council in order to protest at attempts to use an old, and largely redundant, law against vagrancy to clear the Peace Camp, the women began by reminding the councillors that:

> They used to burn witches and the law of the time endorsed it . . . When laws clash with the developing moral standards of the time then these laws are put aside – ignored. Human beings make, break, change laws and ignore laws that are morally wrong.[13]

If no English witch had ever been burned at the stake, as opposed to hanged from a gibbet, it did nothing to prevent the parallels from being drawn or from the poignancy of past sufferings. One of the women protestors, sheltering from the rain that drummed down incessantly against a plastic sheet, heard the voice of a US soldier 'loud and clear', saying that 'If it was up to me I'd pour gasoline over them and burn them'.[14] In this way, the imaginative links appeared both vivid and valid.[15] Floating over the wire, the sentry posts and the dull grey silos, was the chanted call, asking:

> Where are the witches?
> Where do they come from?
> Maybe your great-great-grandmother was one
> Witches are wild, wise women they say,
> There's a lot of witch in every woman today.[16]

Increasingly equated with freedom, independence and opposition to patriarchal society, the fully feminized witch had become a powerful symbol for the protestors and was also making inroads into wider society, on both sides of the Atlantic, within the context of debates on women's sexual, political and economic liberation. If, along the way, her figure became commercialized, dumbed down, or sanitized within popular culture – whether as *Sabrina the Teenage Witch*, the Halliwell sisters in *Charmed*, or as the misfit High School protagonists of *The Craft* – then there also were crone figures, such as Temperance Lloyd, who still defied all attempts to strip away all that was 'wild', frightening and disconcerting from the witch. As a consequence, Temperance Lloyd could appear more vital than ever. Her recovery, and subsequent memorialization, was due in large measure to the interest and researches of Frank Gent, a local historian of Bideford and a W.E.A. tutor, who became interested in the witches while renovating an old cottage in the town's Rope Walk Street.[17] It was an atmospheric setting in which to begin writing *The Trial of the Bideford Witches*, an engaging labour of love and a model of engaged – and engaging – local history, based upon solid research and judgement. His work first appeared in self-published form in 1982 – shortly before the establishment of the Greenham Camp – as a pamphlet and was then republished, in enlarged book form, some twenty years later by a Bideford-based company.[18] To a far greater degree than the account of the women given in Antonia Fraser's best-selling *The Weaker Vessel*, published in 1984 by the major publishing company of George Weidenfeld and Nicolson, Gent's work succeeded in tying the women to the landscape of North Devon and in evoking the sense of late seventeenth-century Bideford as a dynamic, yet troubled place where fortunes rose and fell, and where disorder threatened at every turn.[19]

It certainly captured the imagination of Judith Noble, a film maker who had been empowered by the Punk scene in London and Nottingham in her youth, and had come to consider witchcraft through the lens of Dion Fortune's esoteric writings, with their strong focus on women and the divine, and the fantasy novels of Alan Garner, where the worlds of the faerie and human children collide. Having moved to Devon in the early 1980s, she was one of the protestors at Greenham Common and a member of Cruisewatch, becoming 'totally inspired by the Goddess Movement' and describing herself as 'a Radical Feminist who also wanted a spirituality'.[20] Witchcraft seemed to fit the bill, perfectly. During her time working for the regional

Arts Council, in Exeter, she was keen to encourage the participation of women not just in the film making process but in the control of film distribution and marketing, without which 'nothing could change' in the industry. Against this background, she found herself occupying an office that overlooked the Rougemont Gardens that now formed part of the site once occupied by Exeter Castle. However, she never had cause to make the connection between the place, itself, and the Bideford Witches until, one day in the early 1990s, she met up with an old friend for lunch. Paul Laity was a Cornish judge who – just like Sir Francis North or Sir Thomas Raymond – sat upon cases heard at the circuit court. Judith recalls that he 'used to try cases from time to time in Exeter, and ... was a great raconteur who loved to have someone to tell his stories to, which were always about the law ... He was quite a surprising character because he was very anti-establishment, and always on the side of the underdog, which isn't how I'd expected judges to be!'[21] Pausing beside the ruined walls and castle gateway, he observed that it was there that the Bideford Witches had been tried a little more than three hundred years before. That revelation, in Judith's words, 'was the beginning of so many things for me', prompting 'a gut female decision' that something needed to be done in order to commemorate their lives, and pitiful deaths, in a city that was packed full of 'colonial statues'.[22] That night she dreamed about Temperance Lloyd – 'who really enjoyed being a bad witch' – and awoke, shaken and tearful, but determined, with the support of her own, small 'Anarcho-Syndicalist' coven, 'that there should be a permanent public memorial to the witches at the site of the trial in Exeter, so that they could not be forgotten.'[23]

At the spring equinox 1995, they began a publicity campaign around the witches by leaving a large, anonymous bouquet to the women's memory at the site of their deaths, three miles to the south-east of the city centre. Heavitree is now a busy road junction, somewhat run-down and defined by the bulk of a Texaco garage and by the 'Gallows Corner' bus stop that provided the only tangible link with the site's original, grim purpose. The curiosity of the local media was piqued, in part 'because they couldn't find out who we were' says Judith, and the story ran on regional tv and radio programmes for a couple of weeks, and made the front pages of the Exeter *Express* and *Echo*, gathering along the way much positive support for the idea of a permanent memorial to Temperance Lloyd, Susanna Edwards and Mary Trembles. A committee had been founded for the purpose, with Judith Noble as the secretary, and it quickly began the process of fundraising. In the meantime, the group had been contacted by Judy Molland, who suggested that her reputed ancestor Alice Molland should also be included on the projected monument.[24] For her, like the other women involved, the campaign was proving to be both inspirational and life changing. Her participation certainly opened a lot of doors locally, as her father had been a senior cleric at Exeter Cathedral and her family were well-known in the city.[25] Professor Ronald Hutton and Frank Gent both lent their generous and timely support, as respectively the leading national and local authorities on witchcraft and the Bideford case. An inspiration, of sorts, for the memorial was provided by the late nineteenth century fountain designed by John Duncan in memory of witches burned in Edinburgh. Standing at the top of the Royal Mile, it captures a sense of the dualistic notion of witchcraft with her appearing in the design as both an enraged, harmful figure and as a sorrowful victim, with the accompanying figure of a serpent coiled about a spray of wild foxgloves.

However, perhaps the deciding factor that secured permission for the Exeter monument was the responsibility for the cost. Once the city council had realized that the committee was prepared to fund-raise and foot the bill, itself, any objections swiftly ceased. Indeed, as the donations – raised primarily through the wider pagan community, nucleated around the Pagan Federation, its annual conference and journal – the Planning Committee met and approved a design for a slate plaque to go on the castle walls at Rougemont Gardens with remarkable rapidity.[26] Fears that the council might tone down the pagan content, phrase the inscription so that it was 'anti-witches', or that the plaque might be targeted by fundamentalist Christian groups all proved to be unfounded and the whole exercise appears as a model of reasoned, effective co-operation between an enlightened local government and a campaigning community group.[27] The South West Arts Council suggested the services of a local stone carver, Ben Jones who delivered a crisp, contemporary grey slate plaque that commemorated:

The Devon Witches ... The Last People in England to be Executed for Witchcraft. Tried Here & Hanged at Heavitree. In the hope of an end to persecution & intolerance.[28]

The memorial was unveiled on the afternoon 14 September 1996, in a simple pagan ceremony, though disappointingly for the organizers the promised local

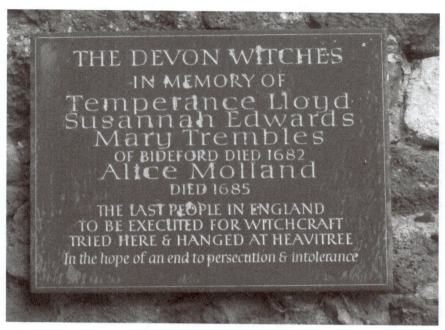

Figure 24 *The Last English Witches: memorial plaque to Temperance Lloyd, Susanna Edwards, Mary Trembles and Alice Molland, in Rougemont Gardens, Exeter, November 2019 (Author's Photograph). There can be few more remarkable changes to historical reputation, and the emphasis on particular societal groups, than that evidenced by this commemoration.*

press and tv cameras failed, this time, to put in a promised appearance. For its part, the Pagan Federation hoped 'that the plaque in Exeter will be the first of many, and that it will raise people's awareness of witchcraft possibly as a Human Rights issue and strengthen the case for legislation against religious discrimination'.[29] Judith Noble felt that:

> The celebration of the Plaque was great. It's become a part of Exeter life now, and there have been lots of good comments about it. The museum people and the tourist authorities love it! I feel good every time I walk past it, just knowing that they are remembered.[30]

Seen as a quiet, contemplative place – and even as a 'new sacred space for Pagans' – it quickly established itself on the routes of the city's Red Badge tourist guides and was quickly supplemented by a nearby mural, by local artist Andrew Alleyway, that

Figure 25 *The Bideford Witches huddle around a cauldron in Andrew Alleyway's mural of 1996, depicting the pageant of Exeter's history (Author's Photograph). Though the depiction of the women as stereotypical, storybook witches divided opinion, this colourful example of figurative public art sits comfortably with the surrounding maze of alleys, characterized by New Age shops selling crystals, Tarot cards and even broomsticks.*

depicted the witches as three, pointy-hatted crones, crouched besides a bubbling cauldron.[31] Though not to the taste of all, as it played upon accepted stereotypes of the storybook witch, the portrayal of the women in Exeter's 'Historical Pageant' alongside knights, fine ladies and explorers, was a powerful demonstration of the manner in which they had moved from the outer fringes of history to occupying the literal and metaphorical centre ground of civic – and popular – memory. They provided the inspiration for Judy Molland to begin writing a novel about her ancestor, whereby a modern-day inhabitant of Exeter 'keeps having visions, flashes of Alice' in the streets of the city, while the three Bideford Witches appeared in both a radio drama by Heidi Stephenson that was aired on the BBC's Devon service, on 28 August 2006, and a full-length novelization of the life of Temperance Lloyd by B. Chris Nash, that was published in Canada six years later.[32]

In Bideford, itself, there were both official and unofficial commemorations that took their leads from the pattern established in Exeter by Judith Noble and her group of friends. In 2012, Peter Christie – a Green Party Councillor and local historian, whose popular guidebooks and scholarly monographs on the history and architecture of the town had provided models of their kind for more than two decades – had convinced the local council, again without any significant opposition, to erect a plaque on the side of the Victorian town hall commemorating the witches. Taking its inspiration directly from the memorial in Rougemont Gardens it similarly records the fates of Temperance Lloyd, Susanna Edwards (here spelled with an added 'h' to her Christian name) and Mary Trembles, and that they were 'all of Bideford'. However, in contrast to the Exeter inscription, here they are unequivocally stated to be 'the last to be executed in England for the crime of witchcraft'.[33] This is understandable within the context of a specific commemoration of the town's witches and given the equivocal fate of Alice Molland. Despite her own chase after the life of the historical witch through the county records offices and the West Country Library in Exeter, Judy Molland had earlier been forced to conclude, with a palpable air of sadness, that there was 'always nothing' to be found within the archives aside from the assize record of her sentence.[34] Despite all her best efforts, and those of other researchers, Alice Molland remains an enigma. Just as significant in terms of providing an appreciation of those considered to be marginal within society is Peter Christie's telling observation that the plaque to the three Bideford Witches is 'the only memorial to women in the town'.[35] This was a point that was not wasted upon a local coven of modern pagans, who attempted to commemorate and reclaim the witches, in their own way, through ritual, as emblematic figures not just for the new creative synthesis of Wicca and 'magickal practice' but as testaments to 'the scapegoating, for the sacrifice of women, for the crushing of those who gave birth to us, for turning away from the feminine, the collective, for our own cruelty and ignorance and stupidity'.[36] In this way, a red rose thrown from the Long Bridge – that twists and turns in the darkness of evening, until 'it hits the mud beside the skeleton form of a shopping trolley' half-buried in the riverbed of the Torridge – stands as its own memorialization, linking place, historical memory and a fresh religious inspiration.[37]

The witch was now both profoundly counter-cultural and emphatically political. In this light, the campaign to launch a petition to seek a judicial pardon of the women, begun in August 2013, brought together progressive politics – in large measure shaped by the scientific revolution and the European Enlightenment – and practitioners of a gamut of esoteric and magical traditions, for whom witchcraft appeared a worthy and viable practice both in the seventeenth century and in the world of today. As a consequence, when surveying the recent re-imaging of the Bideford Witches two contrasting – and, on the face of it, incompatible – views of witchcraft present themselves. The first, as articulated by Chris Nash – the author of the novelized account of the life of Temperance Lloyd, who was the initial driving force behind the petition – restated the innocence of the women as they 'certainly did not do any of the things they were accused of, one of which was turning into a magpie'. 'Quite clearly', she told BBC News, 'they were not witches'.[38] At the other end of the spectrum, there were modern pagans and witches who wish to celebrate the lives of Temperance Lloyd, Susanna Edwards and Mary Trembles precisely because they *were* witches, though not guilty of the specific, demonically inspired crimes, levelled against them. If this, at times, made for some mudded thinking, then, it did at least create a wide umbrella group for the campaign, and one which was capable of bringing together a number of very different, and highly creative, interpretations of the women and their lives. One early champion of the petition was the Exeter MP, Ben Bradshaw, a bright and engaging former journalist who had served as the Secretary of State for Culture, Media and Sport in the Labour government from 2009 to 2010. Being interested in the history of his constituency, he had 'known about the Exeter witches for a long time' and 'it seemed obvious from this case and other studies of the persecution of "witches" that whatever it was these women were supposed to have done or been involved with, they became victims of a superstitious and vindictive society and were punished unjustly or completely out of proportion to their actions'.[39] Though critics might have sneered at attempts to 'retro-fit' justice or to approach historical processes solely through the prism of a modern, humanist morality, the MP is steadfast in his defence of toleration and respect for human rights, and held that the granting of the petition would send out a clear message to the present. 'It rights a historic wrong,' he writes, 'but it also encourages us to think about what actions or norms our current society supports, sanctions or tolerates that people in the future will be astonished by.'[40]

However, if the online petition appeared newsworthy and garnered favourable reports in quality newspapers such as the *Independent*, *The Times* and *Daily Telegraph*, it did little to garner public support. With only 426 signatures, it fell far short of securing the 10,000 names needed to secure a parliamentary response, let alone the 100,000 required to trigger a full parliamentary debate. This was surprising given the holding of a high-profile 'Witches' Grand Tea Party' in Rougemont Gardens, on 31 August 2014, the nearest Sunday to the anniversary of the deaths of the three Bideford Witches. Part commemoration, part ritual, part picnic: it was the brainchild of Jackie Juno, a charismatic musician, writer and professional tarot card reader, who

Figure 26 *The Last Witches? A mother and daughter at the 'Grand Witches' Tea Party', Rougemont Gardens, August 2014 (photograph by Jim Bachelier-Moore). If the lives of the Bideford Witches were uniformly miserable, degraded and hopeless, then their legacy has been anything but. Their names have been reclaimed through celebration, creativity and activism, entertaining and engaging a new generation for whom witchcraft has positive connotations.*

moved down to Devon at the age of twenty and has remained there ever since, revelling in the stark scenery of Dartmoor and regularly convening retreats and workshops aimed, primarily, at women looking to find a spiritual path. Though she eschews the term 'Wicca', she was originally inspired by 'wild witchy women' and is deeply influenced by Shamanic practices and by native American belief systems. Conjoined to the gaining of signatures for the serious matter of the petition to parliament was a far more playful attempt to break the world record for the most witches gathered together in one place, at one time. 'To qualify for the official record', it was announced that 'you must wear a black pointy witches' hat, black cloak and carry a broom'. ''Tis time,' declared the accompanying press release, 'to rev up your broomsticks, dust off your hats and ... get together.' Unsurprisingly, the call divided opinion. Some members of the Pagan Federation felt that it lacked gravitas, and reinforced hackneyed and negative stereotypes. At the same time, Christian fundamentalists – alerted by all the publicity – threatened to picket the event. 'If they did,' muses Jackie Juno, 'we never saw them on the day, there were too many of us.'[41]

The day itself was a great success on a number of different levels. In the baking August heat, around 350–400 women, men and children gathered at the gardens at the stroke of noon, beside three wicker figures that had been set up to represent the three Bideford Witches 'and all of the Witches before and after' them. At their base was an iron cauldron into which people were encouraged to put scraps of paper containing their thoughts, wishes and prayers. There was something of a carnival atmosphere but there was also a space for poignancy and remembrance. During the minute's silence held to remember the women, when most of the crowd was sheltering from the sun underneath the canopy of trees, it was said that you could hear a pin drop. Then, suddenly and seeming out of nowhere, a fierce wind whipped up, whistling through the trees and chilling the spectators just as the names of Temperance Lloyd, Susanna Edwards and Mary Trembles were read out. Nervous glances were exchanged, some tears were shed and coats were hastily pulled around bare shoulders: most seem to have been deeply moved.[42] More fantastical than any supposed 'magic' that the Bideford Witches harnessed during their lives: their legacies wove themselves – through the appeals to justice, to an end to war, to women's rights and self-empowerment – into the consciousness of the present through the unlikely medium of 'a fun and friendly picnic'.[43] Herein lies the nature of their posthumous triumph. Their names were remembered and carried on the breeze when those of their powerful detractors (such as the North brothers) are largely forgotten by all save a handful of students of legal history and precedent. Bideford town hall takes no civic pride in recalling the persecutions of John Hill and Thomas Gist; yet the names of the three witches are now carved into its cornerstone. If in life, Temperance Lloyd, Susanna Edwards and Mary Trembles enjoyed precious little rest, notice, or contentment and sparked only hatred, resentment and fear in those about them: then, the patterns of their modern commemoration – which have been spontaneous, irreverent, and joyous – suggest that against all the odds a victory, of sorts, was to be found in the laughter of their sisters and their children.

Notes

Prologue

1 Anon., *A True and Impartial Relation of the Informations Against Three Witches* (London: Freeman Collins, 1682), p.7. Grace Thomas' identity is confused with that of Elizabeth Eastchurch in another of the pamphlet accounts of the case; see: Anon., *The Life and Conversation of Temperance Floyd, Mary Lloyd, and Susanna Edwards, Three Eminent Witches* (London: J.W., 1682), p.3.

2 Anon., *A True and Impartial Relation of . . . Three Witches*, p.23.

3 Devon Heritage Centre, Exeter, Bideford, North Devon, Parish Register, Vol.III, Marriages (1653–1678), f.62.

4 Devon Heritage Centre, Exeter, Bideford, North Devon, Parish Register, Vol.III, Marriages (1653–1678), f.59.

5 Anon., *A True and Impartial Relation of . . . Three Witches*, pp.7–8.

6 Anon., *A True and Impartial Relation of . . . Three Witches*, pp.11–12.

7 R. Briggs, *Witches & Neighbors. The Social and Cultural Context of European Witchcraft* (London & New York: Penguin Books, 1996 rpt. 1998), pp.398–402, 406, 408–9; A. Macfarlane, *Witchcraft in Tudor and Stuart England. A Regional and Comparative Study*, intro. J. Sharpe, second edition (London: Routledge, 1970 rpt. 1999), pp.201–6; P.K. Monod, *Solomon's Secret Arts. The Occult in the Age of the Enlightenment* (New Haven & London: Yale University Press, 2013), pp.7, 9, 16–17, 190–6, 202–3; D. Purkiss, *The Witch in History. Early Modern and Twentieth-Century Representations* (London & New York: Routledge, 1996 rpt. 2003), pp.7–8, 15–20, 26; J. Sharpe, *Instruments of Darkness. Witchcraft in England, 1550–1750* (London: Penguin Books, 1996 rpt. 1997), pp.5–7; K. Thomas, *Religion and the Decline of Magic. Studies in Popular Beliefs in Sixteenth- and Seventeenth-Century England* (London: Penguin Books, 1971 rpt. 1991), pp.681–4, 689–4, 696–8; F. Valletta, *Witchcraft, Magic and Superstition in England, 1640–70* (Aldershot: Ashgate, 2000), pp.218–22.

Chapter 1

1 North, R., *The Lives of the Right Hon. Francis North, Baron Guilford; the Hon. Sir Dudley North; and the Hon. And Rev. Dr. John North*, ed. A. Jessop (London: George Bell & Sons, 1890), Vol.I p.167; Anon., *The Life and Conversation of Temperance Floyd, Mary Lloyd, and Susanna Edwards, Three Eminent Witches*, p.1; *The Tryal, Condemnation, and Execution of Three Witches, Viz. Temperance Floyd, Mary Floyd, and Susanna Edwards* (London: J. Deacon, 1682), p.i; F.H. Blackburne Daniell (ed.), *Calendar of State Papers Domestic, January 1st – December 31st 1682* (London: HMSO, 1932), pp.347–8.

2 J. Ashton (ed.), *A Century of Ballad, Illustrative of the Life, Manners and Habits of the English Nation during the Seventeenth Century* (London: Elliot Stock, 1887), pp.79–81. See also: J.W. Ebsworth (ed.), *The Roxburghe Ballads* (Hertford: The Ballad Society / Stephen Austin & Sons, 1887), Vol.VI Part II pp.706–8.

3 Anon., *The Life and Conversation of . . . Three Eminent Witches*; Anon., *The Tryal, Condemnation, and Execution of Three Witches*; Anon., *A True and Impartial Relation of . . . Three Witches*; North Devon Records Office, Barnstaple Library: 1064Q / 501/184, Liber Session Pacis, 1659–1709 (Bideford Sessions Book); National Records Office, Kew: Assi 21/1, Exeter Assizes, 1670–1677.

4 Anon., *A True and Impartial Relation of . . . Three Witches*, pp.ii, 37–40; Anon., *The Life and Conversation of . . . Three Eminent Witches*, p.6; Anon., *The Tryal, Condemnation, and Execution of Three Witches*, pp.2–4.

5 Anon., *The Life and Conversation of . . . Three Eminent Witches*, pp.2, 6; Anon., *The Tryal, Condemnation, and Execution of Three Witches*, pp.2, 4.

6 Anon., *The Tryal, Condemnation, and Execution of Three Witches*, pp.2–4.

7 A Temperance Babacombe was baptized at Bideford on 20 April 1589 but there is no record of her marriage and much less to a Lloyd. One might argue that she might have married in another parish but, even then, she would have been ninety-three at the time of her trial. As a consequence, we can firmly discount her in our search for Temperance Lloyd. See: Devon Heritage Centre, Exeter: Bideford Parish Register, Vol.I, Bideford Baptisms, f.25.

8 D. Nokes, *John Gay. A Profession of Friendship. A Critical Biography* (Oxford: Oxford University Press, 1995), pp.21–3; J. Watkins, *An Essay Towards A History of Bideford in the County of Devon* (Bideford: The Lazarus Publishing Company, 1792 rpt. 1993), p.57.

9 Devon Heritage Centre, Exeter: Bideford Parish Register, Vol.II, Bideford Baptisms, f.98; Vol.II Bideford Burials, f.82.

10 Devon Heritage Centre, Exeter: Bideford Parish Register, Vol.II, Bideford Baptisms, ff.98, 99, 101, 104, 106, 108, 109, 111, 112, 113; Bideford Parish Register, Vol.III, Bideford Baptisms, ff.118, 120; Bideford Parish Register, Vol.II, Bideford Burials, f.82.

11 Devon Heritage Centre, Exeter: Bideford Parish Register, Vol.II, Bideford Baptisms, ff. 108, 111, 113; Vol.II, Bideford Burials, ff.70; 75, 78, 84.; Vol.II, Bideford Marriages, ff.28, 29, Vol.III, Bideford Baptisms, ff.118, 120; Vol.III, Bideford Burials ff. 90, 127.

12 Devon Heritage Centre, Exeter: Bideford Parish Register, Burials Vol.II, f.75; Marriages Vol.II, f.28.

13 Devon Heritage Centre, Exeter: Bideford Parish Register, Marriages Vol.II, ff.28, 29.

14 Anon., *Life and Conversation of Temperance Floyd, Mary Lloyd and Susannah Edwards*, p.7; Anon., *Tryal, Condemnation and Execution of Three Witches*, pp.2–3.

15 R.W. Cotton, *Barnstaple and the Northern Part of Devonshire during the Great Civil War, 1642–1646* (Chilworth & London: Unwin Brothers, 1889), pp.126, 195–6, 206–7, 217, 297.

16 W.H. Thornton, 'The Plague at North Bovey', *Devon and Cornwall Notes and Queries*, Vol.VI (January 1910 – October 1911), pp.198–9.

17 Granville, *History of Bideford*, p.54.

18 Devon Heritage Centre, Exeter: Bideford Parish Register, Vol.II, Bideford Burials, f.79. See also: Watkins, *History of Bideford*, p.42.

19 Watkins, *History of Bideford*, p.43.

20 Cotton, *Barnstaple and the Northern Part of Devonshire during the Great Civil War*, p.533.

21 Devon Heritage Centre, Exeter: Bideford Parish Register, Vol.II, Bideford Burials, ff.72–9.

22 Devon Heritage Centre, Exeter: Bideford Parish Register, Vol.II, Bideford Burials, f.78.

23 Devon Heritage Centre, Exeter: Bideford Parish Register, Vol.II, Bideford Burials, f.75.

24 Devon Heritage Centre, Exeter: Bideford Parish Register, Vol.II, Bideford Baptisms, ff.111, 113. Here, for ease, clarity and sense, I have rendered 'Ffloyd' or 'Ffloyde' as Lloyd, and 'Rice' or 'Rise' as Rhys. The recording of Welsh names in the register is both haphazard and extremely fluid.

25 Devon Heritage Centre, Exeter: Bideford Parish Register, Burials Vol.II, f.84.

26 A. Grant, *North Devon Pottery: The Seventeenth Century* (Exeter: University of Exeter, 1983), p.43.

27 North Devon Records Office, Barnstaple Library, B1003, Records of the Andrew Dole Charity: John Andrew Dole Trust Book, 1626–1809, f.114.

28 John Andrew Dole Trust Book, f.120.

29 Devon Heritage Centre, Exeter: Bideford Parish Register, Vol.II, Bideford Baptisms, f.109. Mostyn, the son of Evens Morgan, was baptized at St Mary's Church, Bideford, on 15 June 1648. However, the name of his mother is not recorded. Women, in the Early Modern period, were not only unheard but also largely unrecorded.

30 John Andrew Dole Trust Book, ff.116, 117, 120.

31 T.L. Stoate (ed.), *Devon Hearth Tax Return, Lady Day 1674* (Bristol: T.L. Stoate, 1982), p.99.

32 John Andrew Dole Trust Book, ff.113, 115, 117, 120, 122, 123, 149, 152.

33 John Andrew Dole Trust Book, f.136. Mary Umbles had been in receipt of parish relief for over twenty years when she was scheduled for a payment of the dole in January 1671 but died before ever receiving her customary sixpence.

34 John Andrew Dole Trust Book, f.153.

35 John Andrew Dole Trust Book, ff.114, 117, 137, 147.

36 John Andrew Dole Trust Book, f.116.

37 John Andrew Dole Trust Book, ff.150, 151.

38 John Andrew Dole Trust Book, f.153.

39 John Andrew Dole Trust Book, ff.153–9.

40 John Andrew Dole Trust Book, f.159.

41 Devon Heritage Centre, Exeter: Bideford Parish Register, Vol.I, Bideford Baptisms, f.51.

42 Devon Heritage Centre, Exeter: Bideford Parish Register, Vol.I, Bideford Baptisms, ff.52, 59.

43 Devon Heritage Centre, Exeter: Bideford Parish Register, Vol.II, Bideford Baptisms, f.78.

44 Devon Heritage Centre, Exeter: Bideford Parish Register, Vol.II, Bideford Baptisms, ff.66, 83, 115.

45 G.R. Quaife, *Wanton Wenches and Wayward Wives. Peasants and Illicit Sex in Early Seventeenth Century England* (New Brunswick, New Jersey: Rutgers University Press, 1979), pp.89–91, 202–3; L. Stone, *The Family, Sex and Marriage in England, 1500–1800* (London: Penguin Books, 1977 rpt. 1988), pp.30, 325, 389, 400.

46 J. Kermode & G. Walker, *Women, Crime and the Courts in Early Modern England* (London: UCL Press, 1994), p.39; Quaife, *Wanton Wenches and Wayward Wives*, pp.89, 107; Stone, *The Family, Sex and Marriage in England*, p.401.

47 Devon Heritage Centre, Exeter: Bideford Parish Register, Vol.II, Bideford Marriages, f.24.

48 Devon Heritage Centre, Exeter: Bideford Parish Register, Vol.II, Bideford Baptisms, f.104,108, 112; Bideford Parish Register, Vol.III, Bideford Baptisms, ff.118, 124. Respectively: Robert, baptized 12 March 1645; Elizabeth, baptized 10 October 1647; Roger, baptized 17 April 1650; Katheryn, born 19 November and baptized 8 December 1653; and Richard, born 21 January 1657. There is no baptism record for Susan Edwards but her burial as a 'childe' on 1 October 1646 is registered in: Devon Heritage Centre, Exeter: Bideford Parish Register, Vol.II, Bideford Burials, f.78.

49 Devon Heritage Centre, Exeter: Bideford Parish Register, Vol.III, Bideford Baptisms, f.118.

50 John Andrew Dole Trust Book, ff.138, 140, 142, 144, 146, 148, 151, 153.

51 John Andrew Dole Trust Book, ff. 126, 128, 130, 132, 134, 136, 138, 140, 142, 144, 146, 148, 151, 153; Stoate (ed.), *Devon Hearth Tax Return*, p.99.

52 John Andrew Dole Trust Book, f.133.

53 Devon Heritage Centre, Exeter: Bideford Parish Register, Vol.II, Bideford Burials, f.78.

54 Devon Heritage Centre, Exeter: Bideford Parish Register, Vol.III, Bideford Burials, f.96.

55 Devon Heritage Centre, Exeter: Bideford Parish Register, Vol.III, Bideford Burials, ff.98, 108.

56 Devon Heritage Centre, Exeter: Bideford Parish Register, Vol.III, Bideford Burials, f.129.

57 J. Ashton (ed.), *A Century of Ballads, Illustrative of the Life, Manners and Habits of the English Nation during the Seventeenth Century* (London: Elliot Stock, 1887), p.81.

58 Stone, *The Family, Sex and Marriage*, p.402.

59 John Andrew Dole Trust Book, ff.109, 119, 120.

60 John Andrew Dole Trust Book, f.151.

61 John Andrew Dole Trust Book, ff.153, 155.

62 John Andrew Dole Trust Book, f.155.

63 John Andrew Dole Trust Book, ff.112, 114, 115.

64 John Andrew Dole Trust Book, ff.125, 126.
For Meg, or Margaret Rork, see: John Andrew Dole Trust Book, ff.133, 135, 147, 149.

65 John Andrew Dole Trust Book, ff. 113, 115, 117, 123, 146, 151, 153, 155.

66 North, *Lives*, Vol.I p.167.

67 It has been argued that she was part of the wider familial network of the Umbels or Umbles, a family who appear frequently in the parish registers. However, the problem is that the name Umbles is not, no matter what you might wish or make it appear, analogous with Trembles. Even allowing for the vagaries of seventeenth-century handwriting, there are only two clear – and they are very distinct – references to individuals with the surname Trembles in the parish registers between 1600 and 1685. The same is true of the John Andrew Dole Book, where Mary Umbles and Grace Umbles, the family of Trudging Trembles, are clearly differentiated. See: Devon Heritage Centre, Exeter: Bideford Parish Register, Vol.III, Bideford Burials, ff.116, 118; John Andrew Dole Trust Book, ff.112, 114, 116, 117, 122, 124, 125, 127, 129, 130, 131, 136, 137, 138; Gent, *Trial of the Bideford Witches*, p.128.

68 John Andrew Dole Trust Book, f.131.

69 John Andrew Dole Trust Book, ff.130, 131.

For Justinian Prance, see: John Andrew Dole Trust Book, ff.108, 111, 114, 115, 117, 122, 123, 125, 127, 128, 130, 132.

70 John Andrew Dole Trust Book, ff. 133, 135, 137.

71 Devon Heritage Centre, Exeter: Bideford Parish Register, Vol.III, Bideford Burials, f.116; John Andrew Dole Trust Book, f.138.

72 John Andrew Dole Trust Book, f.140.

73 Devon Heritage Centre, Exeter: Bideford Parish Register, Vol.III, Bideford Burials, ff.116, 118.

74 John Andrew Dole Trust Book, f.142.

75 John Andrew Dole Trust Book, f.144, 146, 148.

76 John Andrew Dole Trust Book, f.154.

77 John Andrew Dole Trust Book, f.155.

78 A. Farquharson-Coe, *Devon's Witchcraft* (St. Ives: James Pike Ltd., 1975), p.6.

79 M. Ashley, *The Battle of Naseby and the Fall of King Charles I* (Stroud: Alan Sutton, 1992), p.90; G. Foard, *Naseby. The Decisive Campaign* (Guildford: Pryor Publications, 1995), pp.288–9; D. Purkiss, *The English Civil War. A People's History* (London: HarperCollins, 2006), p.430; P. Young, *Naseby, 1645. The Campaign and the Battle* (London: Century Publishing, 1985), pp.270–1.

Chapter 2

1 R.P. Chope (ed.), *Early Tours in Devon and Cornwall*, intro. A. Gibson (Newton Abbot: David & Charles, 1967), p.5; F.E. Whiting & P. Christie, *The Long Bridge at Bideford*, fourth edition (Bideford, Lazarus Press, 1945 rpt. 2006), p.8; North Devon Records Office, Barnstaple Library: 1064Q/501, Liber Session Pacis (Bideford Sessions Book) 1659–1709, f.6.

2 R.N. Worth, 'Notes from the Autobiography of Dr. James Yonge, FRS', *Report and Transactions of the Devonshire Association*, Vol.13 (1881), pp.338–9.

3 D. Defoe, *A Tour Thro' the Whole Island of Great Britain*, Vol.I (London: Peter Davies, 1927), p.261; Goaman, *Old Bideford*, p.20; Western Express, *Tedrake's Illustrated Guide to Bideford and North Devon* (Bideford, 1904), p.14.

4 A. Grant, *North Devon Pottery: The Seventeenth Century* (Exeter: University of Exeter, 1983), pp.7, 10.

5 J. Ogilby, *Britannia, Volume the First: or an Illustration of the Kingdom of England and Dominion of Wales: By a Geographical and Historical Description of the Principal Roads thereof* (London: John Ogilby, 1675), plate 68.

6 Worth, 'Notes from the Autobiography of Dr. James Yonge', p.341.

7 Defoe, *Tour Thro' Great Britain*, Vol.I p.261.

8 W.N. Sainsbury (ed.), *Calendar State Papers Colonial Series, America and the West Indies, 1675–1676* (London: HMSO, 1893), p.425.

9 Sainsbury (ed.), *Calendar State Papers Colonial Series, America and the West Indies, 1675–1676*, p.198; R.G. Lounsbury, *The British Fishery at Newfoundland, 1634–1763* (London: Archon Books, 1934 rpt. 1969), pp.109–12.

10 Lounsbury, *The British Fishery at Newfoundland*, pp.248–9; Sainsbury (ed.), *Calendar State Papers Colonial Series, America and the West Indies, 1675–1676*, pp.198–9.

11 Lounsbury, *The British Fishery at Newfoundland*, p.119.

12 Watkins, *History of Bideford*, p.65.

13 J.A. Fraser, *Spain and the West Country* (London: Burns Oates & Washbourne Ltd., 1935), p.246.

14 A. Gant & P. Christie, *The Book of Bideford* (Buckingham: Barracuda Books, 1987), p.28.

15 D. Nokes, *John Gay. A Profession of Friendship* (Oxford: Oxford University Press, 1995), fn.19 p.17.

16 Grant, *North Devon Pottery*, pp.121–3.

17 I. Rogers, *A Record of Wooden Sailing Ships and Warships built in the Port of Bideford from the year 1568 to 1938, with a Brief Account of the Shipbuilding Industry in the Town* (Bideford: self-published, 1947), pp.6, 14 & 22; Western Express, *Tedrake's Illustrated Guide to Bideford*, p.13.

18 A.T. Vaughan, *Transatlantic Encounters: American Indians in Britain, 1500–1776* (Cambridge: Cambridge University Press, 2006), pp.26–7.

19 A.P. Middleton, *Tobacco Coast. A Maritime History of Chesapeake Bay in the Colonial Era* (Baltimore & London: The John Hopkins University Press, 1953 rpt, 1984), p.141.

20 N. Matar, *British Captives from the Mediterranean to the Atlantic, 1563–1760* (Leiden & Boston: Brill, 2014), pp.258–65.

21 John Andrew Dole Trust Book, ff. 113, 115, 120, 122, 123, 125, 128, 130, 132, 135, 137, 143, 144.

22 Liber Session Pacis (Bideford Sessions Book) 1659–1709, f.193 verso.

23 Liber Session Pacis, ff.4, 7, 11, 84 verso – 85 verso; A.P. Middleton, *Tobacco Coast. A Maritime History of Chesapeake Bay in the Colonial Era* (Baltimore & London: The John Hopkins University Press, 1953 rpt. 1984), p.115.

24 Stoate (ed.), *Devon Hearth Tax Return, Lady Day 1674*, pp.91, 98. At least three other properties were bigger, paying tax on eleven, twelve and fourteen hearths. However, because of the lost folio(s) for the Bideford return, there may have been even more mansions in the town. For John Davie, see: Grant & Christie, *Book of Bideford*, p.28.

25 A.G. Duncan, *The Long Bridge of Bideford and Bideford under the Restored Monarchy* (Bideford: self-published, 1930), p.68; Liber Session Pacis, ff.84 verso – 85 verso.

26 Duncan, *The Long Bridge of Bideford*, p.68.

27 Anon., *The Life and Conversation of . . . Three Notorious Witches*, p.2; Anon., *A True and Impartial Relation . . . Against Three Witches*, pp.13–14.

28 Grant, *North Devon Pottery*, pp.4, 9.

29 Grant, *North Devon Pottery*, pp.1, 79, 87, 119.

30 Grant & Christie, *Book of Bideford*, p.28.

31 Grant, *North Devon Pottery*, p.4.

32 R.J. Kerr & I.C. Duncan (eds.), *The Portledge Papers, being Extracts from the Letters of Richard Lapthorne, Gent. of Hatton Garden London, to Richard Coffin Esq. of Portledge, Bideford, Devon from December 10th 1687 – August 7th 1697* (London: Jonathan Cape, 1928), pp.5, 7, 12, 21, 26–7, 32–3, 44.

33 R.P. Chope, 'John Abbott, Plasterer', *Devon & Cornwall Notes and Queries*, Vol.XIV (January 1926 – October 1927), pp.289–90; Granville, *History of Bideford*, p.60; M. Hearn, *Frithelstock. Past and Present* (Frithelstock: Frithelstock Book Group, 2004), pp.30, 55, 118, 158; B.W. Oliver, 'The Early Seventeenth-Century Plaster Ceilings of Barnstaple, *Report and Transactions of the Devonshire Association*, Vol.XLIX (1917), p.195. See also, the wonderful postgraduate project by Glenn Adamson archived in a blog: https://www.vam.ac.uk/blog/sketch-product/john-abbott-portrait-plasterworker.

34 Grant, *North Devon Pottery*, p.8.

35 Rogers (ed.), *Report on Documents belonging to the Feoffees*, p.17.

36 Bideford Parish Register, Vol.II, Bideford Burials, ff. 71, 73, 88, 90.

37 Liber Session Pacis, f.8.

38 Kerr & Duncan (eds.), *The Portledge Papers*, p.31.

39 Liber Session Pacis, f.8.

40 Duncan, *Long Bridge*, p.49; Gent, *Trial of the Bideford Witches*, pp.20–1; Thompson, *Wives, Widows, Witches & Bitches*, pp.60, 62.

41 Stoate (ed.), *Devon Hearth Tax Return, Lady Day 1674*, pp.98–9.

42 Duncan, *Long Bridge at Bideford*, p.51; Liber Session Pacis, ff.84 verso – 85 verso.

43 Duncan, *Long Bridge at Bideford*, p.50; Liber Session Pacis, ff.4, 11, 84 verso – 85 verso.

44 Duncan, *Long Bridge at Bideford*, p.50.

45 A.G. Duncan, 'Early Brick Buildings in Devon and Cornwall', *Devon Notes and Queries*, Vol.XI (1920–1), p.141; Duncan, *Long Bridge of Bideford*, pp.49, 51 & 53–4; Western Express, *Tedrake's Guide to Bideford*, p.15; Liber Session Pacis, ff.4, 11, 84 verso – 85 verso.

46 North Devon Records Office, Barnstaple Library, BBT A1/b Bundles 31, 35, 39, Bideford Bridge Trust Documents; BBT add/2; BBT add/28A–28B; BBT add/37; BBT add/67.

47 BBT A1/b Bundles 4, 31, 35, 39, 93; BBT add/28A–28B, BBT add/37, BBT add/65, BBT add/67.

48 BBT add/67; BBT A/1/b Bundle 42.

49 Duncan, *The Long Bridge of Bideford*, pp.62–3, 66–7; Liber Session Pacis, ff.4, 5.

50 Chope (ed.), *Early Tours in Devon and Cornwall*, p.172; Defoe, *Tour Thro' Great Britain*, Vol.I p.260.

51 Duncan, 'Early Brick Buildings', p.141; Duncan, *Long Bridge*, p.8; Goaman, *Old Bideford*, p.26.

52 Gent, *Trial of the Bideford Witches*, pp.118–19; R. C. Nash, *Temperance Lloyd, Hanged for Witchcraft in 1682* (Victoria, British Columbia: Friesen Press, 2012), p.53.

53 Anon., *Tedrake's Illustrated Guide to Bideford and North Devon* (Bideford: Western Express Office, 1904), p.70.

54 Anon., *Life and Conversation of . . . Three Eminent Witches*, p.2.

55 Anon., 'Witchcraft', *The North Devon Journal* (14 August 1851), p.5. I am grateful to Julian Vayne for this reference.

56 Thompson, *Wives, Widows, Witches & Bitches*, p.58.

57 Thompson, *Wives, Widows, Witches & Bitches*, pp.60 & 62.

58 Thompson, *Wives, Widows, Witches & Bitches*, pp.59, 61; Duncan, *Long Bridge of Bideford*, pp.54 & 58.

59 Thompson, *Wives, Widows, Witches & Bitches*, pp.58–9.

60 Thompson, *Wives, Widows, Witches & Bitches*, p.61; Duncan, *Long Bridge of Bideford*, p.54.

61 Duncan, *Long Bridge of Bideford*, p.54.

62 F.H. Blackburne Daniell (ed.), *Calendar State Papers Domestic, Charles II, 1682*, Vol.23 (London: HMSO, 1932), p.180.

63 Blackburne Daniell (ed.), *Calendar State Papers Domestic, Charles II, 1682*, p.180.

64 Liber Session Pacis, ff.6, 7, f.78 verso.

65 Liber Session Pacis, f.160.

66 Liber Session Pacis, f.167.

67 Liber Session Pacis, ff. 170, 173, 194.

68 Liber Session Pacis, ff. 5, 6, 7, 8; Thompson, *Wives, Widows, Witches & Bitches*, p.62.

69 Thompson, *Wives, Widows, Witches & Bitches*, p.62.

70 Liber Session Pacis, ff. 4, 6.

71 Liber Session Pacis, ff. 9, 10.

72 Liber Session Pacis, ff. 11, 15.

73 Liber Session Pacis, ff. 4, 6.

74 P. Slack, *Poverty and Policy in Tudor and Stuart England* (London & New York: Longman, 1988), pp.24, 32.

75 P.A. Fideler, *Social Welfare in Pre-Industrial England. The Old Poor Law Tradition* (Houndmills, Basingstoke: Palgrave Macmillan, 2006), pp.81, 103, 110, 112—114, 120, 132; B. Hill, *Women Alone. Spinsters in England, 1660–1850* (New Haven & London: Yale University Press, 2001), p.94; J. Pound, *Poverty and Vagrancy in Tudor England* (London: Longman, 1971 rpt. 1973), pp.25–6; J.A. Sharpe, *Early Modern England. A Social History, 1550–1760* (London & New York: Edward Arnold, 1987 rpt. 1992), pp.217–18; Slack, *Poverty and Policy*, pp.40, 71–80.

76 Pound, *Poverty and Vagrancy*, pp.53–7; Sharpe, *Early Modern England*, p.217; Slack, *Poverty and Policy*, pp.1–2; Fideler, *Social Welfare in Pre-Industrial England*, pp.99–101.

77 Slack, *Poverty and Policy*, p.7.

78 Devon Heritage Centre, Exeter: O.M. Moger (ed.), *Quarter Sessions, Devonshire – Civil War Petitions from 1645–1685*, unpublished manuscript, Vol.I (Devon & Cornwall Record Society, April 1983), pp.69, 75, 95.

79 Moger (ed.), *Quarter Sessions, Devonshire – Civil War Petitions*, Vol.I p.95.

80 Moger (ed.), *Quarter Sessions, Devonshire – Civil War Petitions*, Vol.I p.95.

81 Moger (ed.), *Quarter Sessions, Devonshire – Civil War Petitions*, Vol.I pp.69, 95.

82 Liber Session Pacis, f.15.

83 Gribble, *Memorials of Barnstaple*, pp.69–74, 78–80, 83, 89–103.

84 HMSO, *Endowed Charities (County of Devon). Parish of Bideford* (Eyre and Spottiswoode Ltd., 1908), pp.2, 18.

85 HMSO, *Endowed Charities*, pp.13–14, 39; John Strange's Gift of Annuitie, 20 October 1626; Rogers (ed.), *Report on Documents belonging to the Feoffees*, p.33.

86 HMSO, *Endowed Charities*, pp.14, 15–16, 39, 41; BBT add/114; Rogers (ed.), *Report on Documents belonging to the Feoffees*, p.31.

87 HMSO, *Endowed Charities*, pp.13, 38–9; John Andrew Dole Trust Book, ff.150, 151, 156.

88 Liber Session Pacis, f.7.

89 Liber Session Pacis, f.8.

90 Liber Session Pacis, f.8.

91 Liber Session Pacis, f.8.

Chapter 3

1   Duncan, *Long Bridge of Bideford*, pp.48, 65, 69; P.W. Jackson, *Nonconformists and Society in Devon, 1660–1689*, unpublished PhD thesis (Exeter: University of Exeter, 1986), pp.25, 138; Timmons, 'Witchcraft and Rebellion', pp.307–12, 328–30; Watkins, *History of Bideford*, pp.44, 47, 123, Western Express, *Tedrake's Illustrated Guide*, p.62.

2   A. Browning (ed.), *English Historical Documents, 1660–1714* (London: Eyre & Spottiswoode, 1966), pp.377–84; P. Seaward, *The Cavalier Parliament and the Reconstruction of the Old Regime, 1661–1667* (Cambridge: Cambridge University Press, 1989), pp.163–4, 166, 171, 179–83, 187–94; J. Spurr, *The Restoration Church of England, 1646–1689* (New Haven & London: Yale University Press, 1991), p.43; Liber Session Pacis, ff.4, 6.

3   Grant, *North Devon Pottery*, p.6; Watkins, *History of Bideford*, p.119.

4   Watkins, *History of Bideford*, p.117; E. Calamy, *The Nonconformists Memorial*, second edition (London: Alexander Hogg, 1778), Vol.I p.340.

5   W.P. Athers, 'William Bartlett of Bideford', *Devon and Cornwall Notes and Queries*, Vol. XXXI Part II (April/July 1968), p.64.

6   Jackson, *Nonconformists and Society in Devon*, pp.50–2; A. Brockett, *Nonconformity in Exeter, 1650–1875* (Manchester: Manchester University Press, 1962), pp.23, 26, 29, 42.

7   Devon Heritage Centre, Exeter, Devon QS 74/5/2–4; 74/5/10; 74/5/12–13; Devon Q/S 74/15/17.

8   Devon Heritage Centre, Exeter, Devon Q/S 74/5/5–9, 13 f.4.

9   Boulton, *A Compleat History of Magick, Sorcery, and Witchcraft*, Vol.II p.36.

10 R. Raines, *Marcellus Laroon* (London: Routledge & Kegan Paul, 1966), pp.5–6.

11 Gent, *Trial of the Bideford Witches*, p.26.

12 P.J. Helm, *Jeffreys* (London: Robert Hale, 1966), pp.122–3; R. Milne-Tyte, *Bloody Jeffreys. The Hanging Judge* (London: Andre Deutsch, 1989), pp.91–2.

13 The additional verse, added by another hand, attempts to link the scene more specifically to the Scottish Covenanters who were in arms at that time against the governments of Charles II and James II in what became known as the 'Killing Times' in Lowland Scotland. An anti-Scots diatribe mocks 'that race from when England's woes

proceed', symbolized through both their women's unbridled lust and their attachment to the humble bagpipes. However, amongst all the symbols – and pornographic asides – that Laroon manages to include within his picture, there is nothing to tie it (as opposed to the verse) to Scotland. We might, therefore, conclude that the later diatribe was added for topical measure when the work was engraved and sold at the 'Eagle and Child' in the Strand in 1686. It is worth noting that Laroon had already produced a satire on Quaker women preaching and an image of a monk scourging a girl. Pierre Tempest, his printer, merely described this latest work as 'a Presbyterian Meeting', in a letter of 9 January 1686. See: Raines, *Marcellus Laroon*, pp.17–18.

14 Blackburne Daniell (ed.), *Calendar State Papers Domestic, Charles II, 1682*, p.180.

15 Raines, *Marcellus Laroon*, p.17.

16 Gent, *Trial of the Bideford Witches*, p.127.

17 British Library, Add. MSS. 18992 f.340, letter from John Granville to Prince Maurice, 23 December 1644; Clarendon, E. Hyde, Earl of, *The History of the Rebellion and Civil Wars of England* (Oxford: Oxford University Press, 1849), Vol.III (Book VIII 160), p.452; Vol. VI (Book XVI 165–6), pp.217–19; R. Granville, *The History of the Granville Family* (Exeter: William Pollard & Co., 1895), pp.346, 349–50, 366–7; A.C. Miller, *Sir Richard Grenville of the Civil War* (London & Chichester, 1979), p.4; Stucely, *Sir Bevill Grenville*, pp.147–9.

18 G. Burnet, *History of His Own Time*, ed. M.J. Routh (Oxford: Oxford University Press, 1833), Vol.I p.98; Duncan, *Long Bridge*, pp.48–9; Granville, *History of the Granville Family*, pp.349–51, 364, 367, 388, 390; R. Hutton, *Charles II: King of England, Scotland and Ireland* (Oxford: Clarendon Press, 1989), pp.131, 139, 142, 148; R.C. Latham & W. Matthews (eds.), *The Diary of Samuel Pepys*, Vol.X Companion (London: Harper Collins, 1971 rpt. 1995), p.161; H.C.G. Matthew & B. Harrison (eds.), *Oxford Dictionary of National Biography* (Oxford: Oxford University Press, 2004), Vol.23, pp.732–3.

19 Chope, 'John Abbott, Plasterer', p.290; Granville, *History of Bideford*, p.77.

20 D. Spurr, *Devon Churches. Vol.I Bideford, Barnstaple and the Hartland Peninsula* (Braunton, Devon: Merlin Books Ltd., 1983), p.19.

21 Matthew & Harrison (eds.), *Oxford Dictionary of National Biography*, Vol.23, p.733; Burnet, *History of His Own Time*, Vol.III p.626.

22 A. Browning (ed.), *English Historical Documents, 1660–1714* (London: Eyre & Spottiswoode, 1966), pp.384–5.

23 Gent, *Trial of the Bideford Witches*, p.23; Jackson, *Nonconformists and Society in Devon*, p.138.

24 Devon Heritage Centre, Exeter, Devon Q/S 74/5/2.

25 Devon Heritage Centre, Exeter, Devon Q/S 74/5/3.

26 Devon Heritage Centre, Exeter, Devon Q/S 74/5/5.

27 Devon Heritage Centre, Exeter, Devon Q/S 74/5/6.

28 Devon Heritage Centre, Exeter, Devon Q/S 74/5/7–8.

29 J. Besse, *Sufferings of Early Quakers: South West England, 1654 to 1690*, intro. M. Gandy (York: Sessions Book Trust, 1753 rpt. 2004), p.169; Duncan, *Long Bridge*, p.69; Liber Session Pacis, ff.8–9.

30 Besse, *Sufferings of Early Quakers: South West England*, pp.169, 171, 578, 580–1; W.C. Braithwaite, *The Beginnings of Quakerism to 1660* (York: William Sessions Ltd., 1912 rpt. 1981), pp.386–7. It is conceivable that John Budd was attempting to forge transatlantic links from Bideford to the Chesapeake. His kinsman, Thomas, embarked on just such a project during the more tolerant decade of the 1690s. See: W.C. Braithwaite, *The Second Period of Quakerism* (York: William Sessions Limited, 1919 rpt. 1979), pp.483, 485.

31 Jackson, *Nonconformists and Society in Devon*, pp.60, 270.

32 Watkins, *History of Bideford*, pp.121–2; Brockett, *Nonconformity in Exeter*, p.35.

33 Watkins, *History of Bideford*, pp.121–2.

34 Devon Heritage Centre: Devon Q/S 74/5/13 ff.1–2; Gent, *Trial of the Bideford Witches*, p.25.

35 Granville, *History of Bideford*, fn. p.68.

36 Granville, *History of Bideford*, fn.p.67, p.71; Calamy, *Nonconformists Memorial*, Vol.I p.372. Authers, 'William Bartlett of Bideford', p.65. The careers of father and son intertwined so closely that their identities have been confused and conflated, see: Brockett, *Nonconformity in Exeter*, pp.4, 11, 21, 37.

37 Blackburne Daniell (ed.), *Calendar State Papers Domestic, Charles II, 1682*, pp.25, 179–80.

38 Blackburne Daniell (ed.), *Calendar State Papers Domestic, Charles II, 1682*, p.25; Jackson, *Nonconformists and Society in Devon*, p.144.

39 Liber Session Pacis, f.8.

40 Liber Session Pacis, ff.9, 171 verso.

41 Liber Session Pacis, f.171 verso.

42 A. Brockett (ed.), *The Exeter Assembly. The Minutes of the Assemblies of the United Brethren of Devon and Cornwall, 1691–1717, as Transcribed by the Reverend Isaac Gilling* (Torquay: The Devonshire Press Ltd./Devon & Cornwall Record Society, 1963), p.xiii.

43 Brockett (ed.), *The Exeter Assembly*, p.xiii; Watkins, *History of Bideford*, p.124.

44 Brockett (ed.), *The Exeter Assembly*, pp.16, 21, 28, 38, 42.

45 Devon Heritage Centre, Exeter, Devon Q/S 74/5/13; Jackson, *Nonconformists and Society in Devon*, p.368; Liber Session Pacis, ff.11, 16.

Chapter 4

1 Barry, *Witchcraft and Demonology in South-West England*, pp.74, 84–5; Elmer (ed.), *English Witchcraft, 1560–1736*, Vol.V p.364; Timmons, 'Witchcraft and Rebellion', p.302; Liber Session Pacis, f.192 verso.

2 Barry, *Witchcraft and Demonology in South-West England*, pp.82, 99; Jackson, *Nonconformists and Society in Devon*, pp.103, 356; Timmons, 'Witchcraft and Rebellion in Late Seventeenth-Century Devon', p.311.

3 Barry, *Witchcraft and Demonology in South-West England*, p.99.

4 Jackson, *Nonconformists and Society in Devon*, p.140.

5 Barry, *Witchcraft and Demonology in South-West England*, p.99.

6 Jackson, *Nonconformists and Society in Devon*, p.356.

7 No one, it appears, had a good word to say about Nathaniel Eaton. Indeed, one historian writing on the seventeenth-century growth of the colony of Massachusetts concluded that he was 'a martyr to puritan bigotry and malice' and that 'he turned Episcopalian and came to a bad end'. See: Morison, *Builders of the Bay Colony*, p.192.

8 Granville, *History of Bideford*, p.76.

9 Watkins, *History of Bideford*, p.109.

10 Elmer (ed.), *English Witchcraft, 1560–1736*, Vol.V p.363; Fielder, *History of Bideford*, p.39; Liber Session Pacis, ff.7, 154–154 verso, 155, 171.

11 Liber Session Pacis, ff.7, 160.

12 Jackson, *Nonconformists and Society in Devon*, p.138; Elmer (ed.), *English Witchcraft, 1560–1736*, Vol.V p.363.

13 Duncan, *Long Bridge . . . And Bideford Under the Restored Monarchy*, p.66; Fielder, *History of Bideford*, p.39; Liber Session Pacis, f.154.

14 Jackson, *Nonconformists and Society in Devon*, pp.262–3.

15 Duncan, *Long Bridge . . . And Bideford Under the Restored Monarchy*, pp.65–6; Liber Session Pacis, ff.154–5.

16 Duncan, *Long Bridge . . . And Bideford Under the Restored Monarchy*, p.66.

17 Bideford Parish Register, Vol.IV, Bideford Burials, f.133.

18 Liber Session Pacis, ff.183 verso, 192 verso; Elmer (ed.), *English Witchcraft, 1560–1736*, Vol.V p.364.

19 Elmer (ed.), *English Witchcraft, 1560–1736*, Vol.V p.364.

20 Burnet, *History of His Own Time*, Vol.I p.108.

21 Elmer (ed.), *English Witchcraft, 1560–1736*, Vol.V p.362.

22 Anon., *A True and Impartial Relation of the Informations Against Three Witches*, p.7.

23 Anon., *A True and Impartial Relation of the Informations Against Three Witches*, p.7.

24 Anon., *A True and Impartial Relation of the Informations Against Three Witches*, pp.7–8.

25 H. Dean, *Begging Questions. Street-Level Economic Activity and Social Policy Failure* (Bristol: The Policy Press, 1999), p.8.

26 Anon., *A True and Impartial Relation of the Informations Against Three Witches*, p.8.

27 Dean, *Begging Questions*, p.134.

28 Anon., *A True and Impartial Relation of the Informations Against Three Witches*, p.8.

29 Anon., *A True and Impartial Relation of the Informations Against Three Witches*, p.8.

30 Anon., *A True and Impartial Relation of the Informations Against Three Witches*, p.8.

31 Anon., *A True and Impartial Relation of the Informations Against Three Witches*, pp.14, 18, 21.

32 Anon., *A True and Impartial Relation of the Informations Against Three Witches*, pp.11–12.

33 Anon., *A True and Impartial Relation of the Informations Against Three Witches*, pp.18, 20, 38–40.

34 Anon., *A True and Impartial Relation of the Informations Against Three Witches*, p.39.

35 Anon., *A True and Impartial Relation of the Informations Against Three Witches*, pp.13–19, 38–40; Liber Session Pacis, f.171 verso.

36 O. Davies, *Popular Magic. Cunning-Folk in English History* (London & New York: Hambledon Continuum, 2003 rpt. 2007), pp.9–12; C. Phythian-Adams, 'Rural Culture' in: G.E. Mingay (ed.), *The Victorian Countryside*, Volume 2 (London, Boston & Henley: Routledge & Kegan Paul, 1981), pp.616–17, 620–1.

37 K. Thomas, *The Ends of Life. Roads to Fulfilment in Early Modern England* (Oxford: Oxford University Press, 2009), pp.13–16, 20–3, 226, 229, 241.

38 Anon., *A True and Impartial Relation of the Informations Against Three Witches*, pp.38–40.

39 Bideford Parish Register, Vol.III, Bideford Burials, f.113.

40 Anon., *A True and Impartial Relation of the Informations Against Three Witches*, pp.23–4.

41 Bideford Parish Register, Vol.III, Bideford Burials, f.115.

42 Anon., *A True and Impartial Relation of the Informations Against Three Witches*, p.24.

43 Gent, *Trial of the Bideford Witches*, p.31.

44 National Archives, Kew, Exeter Assizes, PRO Assi 21/1 (1670–1677).

45 Anon., *A True and Impartial Relation of the Informations Against Three Witches,*
pp.24–5.

46 Anon., *A True and Impartial Relation of the Informations Against Three Witches,* p.19.

47 Liber Session Pacis, ff.4, 7, 11.

48 Anon., *A True and Impartial Relation of the Informations Against Three Witches,* pp.19,
23–4; Gent, *Trial of the Bideford Witches,* pp.31, 125; Liber Session Pacis, ff.84 verso –
85 verso.

49 National Archives, Kew, Exeter Assizes, PRO Assi 21/1 (1670–1677).

50 Anon., *A True and Impartial Relation of the Informations Against Three Witches,* p.24.

51 Bideford Parish Register, Vol.III, Bideford Burials, f.117.

52 J. Sharpe, *Instruments of Darkness. Witchcraft in England, 1550–1750* (London: Penguin
Books, 1996 rpt. 1997), pp.159–60.

53 K. Thomas, *Religion and the Decline of Magic. Studies in Popular Beliefs in Sixteenth-
and Seventeenth-Century England* (London: Penguin Books, 1971 rpt. 1991),
pp.633–4.

54 O. Davies, *Witchcraft, Magic and Culture, 1736–1951* (Manchester & New York:
Manchester University Press, 1999), pp.106–19.

55 Liber Session Pacis, f.141; Anon., *A True and Impartial Relation of the Informations
Against Three Witches,* p.17.

56 P. Crawford, 'Attitudes to Menstruation in Seventeenth-Century England', *Past &
Present,* Vol.91 (1981), pp.61–3, 65, 67–9, 71; M. Daly, *Gyn/Ecology: The Metaethics of
Radical Feminism* (London: The Women's Press, 1978 rpt. 1979), pp.xiii, 17, 187, 189; A.
Dworkin, *Woman Hating* (New York: E.P. Dutton & Co., 1974), pp.24, 45, 48;
Ehrenreich & English, *Witches, Midwives, and Nurses,* pp.1–2, 5–6, 15–18; J. Sharpe,
'Witchcraft and Women in Seventeenth Century England: Some Northern Evidence',
Continuity and Change, Vol.VI (1991), pp.179–82, 187–8, 192–5.

57 Elmer (ed.), *English Witchcraft, 1560–1736,* Vol.V pp.363–4; Barry, *Witchcraft and
Demonology in South-West England,* p.74.

58 Anon., *A True and Impartial Relation of the Informations Against Three Witches,*
pp.11–12; Liber Session Pacis, ff.141, 171 verso.

59 Liber Session Pacis, f.141 verso.

60 Anon., *A True and Impartial Relation of the Informations Against Three Witches,* p.39.

61 Liber Session Pacis, f.141 verso.

62 Bideford Parish Register, Vol.IV, Bideford Burials, f.134.

63 Duncan, *Long Bridge . . . And Bideford Under the Restored Monarchy,* p.66.

64 Bideford Parish Register, Vol.IV, Bideford Burials, ff.133, 135.

65 Anon., *A True and Impartial Relation of the Informations Against Three Witches*, pp.8–9.

66 Anon., *A True and Impartial Relation of the Informations Against Three Witches*, p.9.

67 Anon., *A True and Impartial Relation of the Informations Against Three Witches*, p.9.

68 Anon., *A True and Impartial Relation of the Informations Against Three Witches*, p.13; Gent, *Trial of the Bideford Witches*, pp.76–7.

Chapter 5

1 Anon., *A True and Impartial Relation of the Informations Against Three Witches*, pp.34–5; F.H. Blackburne Daniell (ed.), *Calendar of State Papers Domestic, January 1st – December 31st 1682* (London: HMSO, 1932), p.348.

2 Anon., *A True and Impartial Relation of the Informations Against Three Witches*, pp.34–5.

3 Anon., *A True and Impartial Relation of the Informations Against Three Witches*, p.35.

4 Anon., *A True and Impartial Relation of the Informations Against Three Witches*, p.35.

5 Anon., *A True and Impartial Relation of the Informations Against Three Witches*, p.35.

6 Anon., *A True and Impartial Relation of the Informations Against Three Witches*, p.27.

7 Liber Session Pacis, ff.9, 15, 141.

8 W. Behringer, *Witches and Witch-Hunts. A Global History* (Cambridge & Malden, Massachusetts: Polity Press, 2004), p.87, 143; Elmer (ed.), *English Witchcraft, 1560–1736*, Vol.V p.362; B.P. Levack, *The Witch-Hunt in Early Modern Europe*, second edition (London & New York: Longman, 1987 rpt. 1995), 110, 139–41; L. Roper, *Witch Craze. Terror and Fantasy in Baroque Germany* (New Haven & London: Yale University Press, 2004), pp.9–10, 32–3, 141, 173; Sharpe, *Instruments of Darkness*, pp.174–5, 181, 184; Thomas, *Religion and the Decline of Magic*, pp.125, 593, 640–2, 653–4, 685–6, 693. For the seminal account of the witch as midwife and folk-healer, see: B. Ehrenreich & D. English, *Witches, Midwives and Nurses: A History of Women Healers* (London, 1973).

9 R. Briggs, *Witches & Neighbors. The Social and Cultural Context of European Witchcraft* (New York & London: Penguin Books, 1996 rpt. 1998), pp.77–8; D. Purkiss, *The Witch in History. Early Modern and Twentieth-Century Representations* (London & New York, 1996 rpt. 2003), pp.8, 21 & 19; P.G. Maxwell-Stuart (ed. & trans.), *The Malleus Maleficarum* (Manchester & New York, 2007), pp.33, 92–3, 144–5, 249, 252; L. Roper, *Oedipus and the Devil. Witchcraft, Sexuality and Religion in Early Modern Europe* (London, 1994), p.201; Sharpe, *Instruments of Darkness*, pp.172–3.

10 Liber Session Pacis, f.171 verso; Anon., *A True and Impartial Relation of the Informations Against Three Witches*, pp.11–12.

11 Anon., *A True and Impartial Relation of the Informations Against Three Witches*, p.27.

12 Anon., *A True and Impartial Relation of the Informations Against Three Witches*, pp.27–8.

13 Anon., *A True and Impartial Relation of the Informations Against Three Witches*, pp.25–6.

14 Anon., *A True and Impartial Relation of the Informations Against Three Witches*, pp.14–15.

15 Anon., *A True and Impartial Relation of the Informations Against Three Witches*, p.26.

16 Anon., *A True and Impartial Relation of the Informations Against Three Witches*, pp.26, 28.

17 Anon., *A True and Impartial Relation of the Informations Against Three Witches*, pp.26, 28.

18 Anon., *A True and Impartial Relation of the Informations Against Three Witches*, p.29.

19 Anon., *A True and Impartial Relation of the Informations Against Three Witches*, pp.29, 31.

20 Anon., *A True and Impartial Relation of the Informations Against Three Witches*, pp.1–2.

21 Elmer (ed.), *English Witchcraft, 1560–1736*, Vol.V p.362; & Gent, *Trial of the Bideford Witches*, p.127.

22 Anon., *A True and Impartial Relation of the Informations Against Three Witches*, pp.2–3.

23 Elmer (ed.), *English Witchcraft, 1560–1736*, Vol.V p.362.

24 Ady, writing in 1656, quoted in: Thomas, *Religion and the Decline of Magic*, p.640.

25 F. Valletta, *Witchcraft, Magic and Superstition in England, 1640–70* (Aldershot, 2000), pp.244–56; I. Bostridge, *Witchcraft and Its Transformations, c.1650–c.1750* (Oxford, 1997 rpt. 2003), pp.73–7; A. MacFarlane, *Witchcraft in Tudor and Stuart England. A Regional and Comparative Study*, second edition, Intro. J. Sharpe (London, 1970 rpt. 1999), pp.135, 142, 179–84; Sharpe, *Instruments of Darkness*, pp.40–1, 59–60, 65.

26 Anon., *A True and Impartial Relation of the Informations Against Three Witches*, p.3.

27 *A True and Impartial Relation*, pp.3 & 5; R. Merrifield, *The Archaeology of Ritual and Magic* (London, 1987), p.170; Sharpe, *Instruments of Darkness*, pp.160 & 230; & Thomas, *Religion and the Decline of Magic*, pp.633–4 & 649.

28 *A True and Impartial Relation*, pp.3–6.

29 *A True and Impartial Relation*, pp.2, 4 & 6.

30 Namely, Temperance Lloyd taken on 1 July; Mary Trembles taken on 18 July; and Mary Beare and Elizabeth Caddy on 21 July. Susanna Edwards had been arrested at the same time as Mary Trembles, but was not accused by the Coleman family until 26 July. See: Liber Session Pacis, f.171 verso.

Chapter 6

1   Anon., *A True and Impartial Relation of the Informations Against Three Witches*, p.17.

2   Anon., *A True and Impartial Relation of the Informations Against Three Witches*, p.10.

3   Anon., *A True and Impartial Relation of the Informations Against Three Witches*, pp.20–2.

4   Anon., *A True and Impartial Relation of the Informations Against Three Witches*, p.11.

5   A. Somerset, *Unnatural Murder. Poison at the Court of James I* (London: Weidenfeld & Nicolson, 1997), pp.123–4; D. Lindley, *The Trials of Frances Howard. Fact and Fiction at the Court of King James* (London & New York: Routledge, 1993 rpt. 1996), pp.109–13; B. White, *Cast of Ravens. The Strange Case of Sir Thomas Overbury* (London: John Murray, 1965), pp.41–2.

6   Sharpe, *Instruments of Darkness*, pp.143–4; Macfarlane, *Witchcraft in Tudor and Stuart England*, p.137.

7   C. Cabell, *Witchfinder General. The Biography of Matthew Hopkins* (Thrupp, Nr. Stroud: Sutton Publishing, 2006), pp.170, 173.

8   Cabell, *Witchfinder General*, pp.174, 176–8.

9   Cabbell, *Witchfinder General*, p.173.

10 A. Huxley, *The devils of Loudun* (London: Readers Union, Chatto & Windus, 1954), pp.131–2.

11 Anon., *A True and Impartial Relation of the Informations Against Three Witches*, p.11.

12 Anon., *A True and Impartial Relation of the Informations Against Three Witches*, p.11.

13 Anon., *A True and Impartial Relation of the Informations Against Three Witches*, pp.3–6, 10. See also: B.P. Levack, *New Perspectives on Witchcraft, Magic and Demonology. Volume 4: Gender and Witchcraft* (London & New York: Routledge, 2001), pp.1–2, 6, 11–12, 15–16, 22–3, 25, 41–2, 48, 143–5, 153–4, 161–2, 168–9, 274; Y.G. Brown & R. Ferguson (eds.), *Twisted Sisters. Women, Crime and Deviance in Scotland since 1400* (East Linton, East Lothan: Tuckwell Press, 2002), pp.16–17, 19–20, 27; D. Willis, *Malevolent Nurture. Witch-Hunting and Material Power in Early Modern England* (Ithaca, USA, & London: Cornell University Press, 1995), pp.5–6.

14 Anon., *A True and Impartial Relation of the Informations Against Three Witches*, pp.11–12.

15 L. Roper, *Oedipus and the Devil. Witchcraft, Sexuality and Religion in Early Modern Europe* (London & New York: Routledge, 1994), p.20.

16 Macfarlane, *Witchcraft in Tudor and Stuart England*, pp.139–40; Thomas, *Religion and the Decline of Magic*, pp.617–18.

17 Anon., *A True and Impartial Relation of the Informations Against Three Witches*, pp.13–14.

18 Anon., *A True and Impartial Relation of the Informations Against Three Witches*, pp.14–15.

19 Anon., *A True and Impartial Relation of the Informations Against Three Witches*, p.22.

20 Anon., *A True and Impartial Relation of the Informations Against Three Witches*, pp.11–12, 14.

21 Anon., *A True and Impartial Relation of the Informations Against Three Witches*, p.15.

22 Anon., *A True and Impartial Relation of the Informations Against Three Witches*, p.14.

23 Anon., *A True and Impartial Relation of the Informations Against Three Witches*, p.14.

24 Anon., *A True and Impartial Relation of the Informations Against Three Witches*, p.22.

25 Anon., *A True and Impartial Relation of the Informations Against Three Witches*, p.14.

26 Anon., *A True and Impartial Relation of the Informations Against Three Witches*, p.16.

27 Anon., *A True and Impartial Relation of the Informations Against Three Witches*, p.17.

28 Anon., *A True and Impartial Relation of the Informations Against Three Witches*, p.24.

29 Anon., *A True and Impartial Relation of the Informations Against Three Witches*, p.24.

30 Anon., *A True and Impartial Relation of the Informations Against Three Witches*, pp.24–5.

31 Anon., *A True and Impartial Relation of the Informations Against Three Witches*, p.24.

32 Anon., *A True and Impartial Relation of the Informations Against Three Witches*, p.18.

33 Anon., *A True and Impartial Relation of the Informations Against Three Witches*, p.10.

34 Anon., *A True and Impartial Relation of the Informations Against Three Witches*, p.10.

35 Anon., *A True and Impartial Relation of the Informations Against Three Witches*, p.18.

36 Anon., *A True and Impartial Relation of the Informations Against Three Witches*, p.18.

37 Anon., *A True and Impartial Relation of the Informations Against Three Witches*, p.18.

38 Anon., *A True and Impartial Relation of the Informations Against Three Witches*, p.18.

39 Anon., *A True and Impartial Relation of the Informations Against Three Witches*, pp.18–19.

40 Anon., *A True and Impartial Relation of the Informations Against Three Witches*, p.19.

41 Elmer (ed.), *English Witchcraft, 1560–1736*, Vol.V p.363; Gent, *The Trial of the Bideford Witches*, p.127.

42 Anon., *A True and Impartial Relation of the Informations Against Three Witches*, pp.19, 22.

43 Anon., *A True and Impartial Relation of the Informations Against Three Witches*, p.19.

44 Anon., *A True and Impartial Relation of the Informations Against Three Witches*, p.19.

45 Anon., *The Tryal, Condemnation, and Execution of Three Witches*, p.3; Anon., *The Life and Conversation of . . . Three Eminent Witches*, pp.4–5.

46 Anon., *The Life and Conversation of . . . Three Eminent Witches*, pp.4–7.

47 Anon., *The Life and Conversation of . . . Three Eminent Witches*, pp.6–7.

48 Anon., *The Life and Conversation of . . . Three Eminent Witches*, pp.3–4.

49 Anon., *The Life and Conversation of . . . Three Eminent Witches*, p.5.

50 Anon., *The Life and Conversation of . . . Three Eminent Witches*, p.2.

51 Anon., *The Life and Conversation of . . . Three Eminent Witches*, p.2.

52 Anon., *The Life and Conversation of . . . Three Eminent Witches*, p.3.

53 J. Bodin, *On the Demon-Mania of Witches*, trans. R.A. Scott (Toronto: Centre for Reformation & Renaissance Studies, 2001), pp.112–20, 130–3, 156; K.M. Briggs, *Pale Hecate's Team. An Examination of the Beliefs on Witchcraft and Magic among Shakespeare's Contemporaries and His Immediate Successors* (London: Routledge and Kegan Paul, 1962), p.26; S. Clark, *Thinking with Demons. The Idea of Witchcraft in Early Modern Europe* (Oxford: Oxford University Press, 1997 rpt. 1999), pp.80–1, 297, 310, 462; N. Cohn, *Europe's Inner Demons. The Demonisation of Christians in Medieval Christendom*, revised edition (London: Pimlico, 1975 rpt. 1993), pp.112, 144–5; James VI & I, *Daemonologie (1597); News from Scotland (1591)*, ed. G.B. Harrison (London & New York: John Lane, The Bodley Head, 1924), pp.23, 32–4, 36; Macfarlane, *Witchcraft in Tudor and Stuart England*, pp.81, 89–91; Sharpe, *Instruments of Darkness*, pp.142–7; H. Trevor-Roper, *The European Witch-Craze of the 16th and 17th Centuries* (Harmondsworth, Middlesex: Penguin Books, 1967 rpt. 1969), pp.64, 69–70, 79, 86.

54 Anon., *The Life and Conversation of . . . Three Eminent Witches*, p.3.

55 Anon., *The Life and Conversation of . . . Three Eminent Witches*, pp.3–4.

56 Anon., *The Life and Conversation of . . . Three Eminent Witches*, pp.3–4.

57 Anon., *The Life and Conversation of . . . Three Eminent Witches*, p.5.

58 Barry, *Witchcraft and Demonology*, pp.291–2; Elmer (ed.), *English Witchcraft*, Vol.V p.1; Timmons, 'Witchcraft and Rebellion', pp.325–6.

59 J. Goodacre (ed.), *The Scottish Witch-Hunt in Context* (Manchester & New York: Manchester University Press, 2002), pp.146–52, 155, 161–5, 175, 178–80.

60 S. Macdonald, *The Witches of Fife: Witch-Hunting in a Scottish Shire, 1560–1710* (East Linton, East Lothian: Tuckwell Press, 2002), p.181.

61 Anon., *The Life and Conversation of . . . Three Eminent Witches*, p.5.

62 Anon., *The Tryal, Condemnation, and Execution of Three Witches*, pp.i, 4. One may wonder how Grace Thomas felt about this revelation as she was still very much living and breathing when the pamphlet was published in Holborn.

63 Anon., *The Tryal, Condemnation, and Execution of Three Witches*, p.4.

64 Anon., *The Tryal, Condemnation, and Execution of Three Witches*, p.3.

65 Anon., *The Tryal, Condemnation, and Execution of Three Witches*, p.3.

66 Clark, *Thinking with Demons*, pp.162–3, 171, 234, 240–1, 245–8.

67 Anon., *The Tryal, Condemnation, and Execution of Three Witches*, pp.1–2.

68 Anon., *The Tryal, Condemnation, and Execution of Three Witches*, p.4.

69 Anon., *The Tryal, Condemnation, and Execution of Three Witches*, p.4.

Chapter 7

1 Anon., *A True and Impartial Relation of the Informations Against Three Witches*, p.27.

2 Anon., *A True and Impartial Relation of the Informations Against Three Witches*, p.30.

3 Barry, *Witchcraft and Demonology*, p.87; Elmer (ed.), *English Witchcraft*, Vol.V p.364; Gent, *Trial of the Bideford Witches*, pp.86, 88–9, 127.

4 Stoate (ed.), *Devon Hearth Tax Return, Lady Day 1674*, pp.144, 146, 166.

5 Stoate (ed.), *Devon Hearth Tax Return, Lady Day 1674*, pp.142, 143.

6 Anon., *A True and Impartial Relation of the Informations Against Three Witches*, p.30.

7 Anon., *A True and Impartial Relation of the Informations Against Three Witches*, p.32.

8 Anon., *A True and Impartial Relation of the Informations Against Three Witches*, p.30.

9 Anon., *A True and Impartial Relation of the Informations Against Three Witches*, pp.31–2.

10 Anon., *A True and Impartial Relation of the Informations Against Three Witches*, p.31.

11 Anon., *A True and Impartial Relation of the Informations Against Three Witches*, pp.34–5.

12 Anon., *A True and Impartial Relation of the Informations Against Three Witches*, p.31.

13 D. Cressy, 'Literacy in Seventeenth-Century England: More Evidence', *The Journal of Interdisciplinary History*, Vol.8 No.1 (Summer 1977), pp.146–8, 150.

14 F. Hutchinson, *An Historical Essay Concerning Witchcraft* (London: R. Knaplock, 1718), p.41.

15 J. Glanvill, *Saducismus Triumphatus: Or, A Full and Plain Evidence, Concerning Witches and Apparitions* (London: A. Bettesworth & J. Batley, W. Mears & J. Hooke, 1668 rpt. 1676), p.391.

16 Glanvill, *Saducismus Triumphatus*, p.391.

17 Glanvill, *Saducismus Triumphatus*, pp.392–4.

18 Glanvill, *Saducismus Triumphatus*, p.395.

19 Glanvill, *Saducismus Triumphatus*, p.391.

20 Anon., *A True and Impartial Relation of the Informations Against Three Witches*, p.iii.

21 L. Daneau, *A Dialogue of Witches* (London: T. East for R. Watkins, 1575); H. Holland, *A Treatise Against Witchcraft* (Cambridge: John Legatt, 1590).

22 J. Bodin, *On Sovereignty. Four Chapters from The Six Books of the Commonwealth*, ed. & trans. J.H. Franklin (Cambridge University Press, Cambridge, 1992), p.xii. See also: J.P. Sommerville (ed.), *King James VI & I. Political Writings* (Cambridge University Press, Cambridge, 1994), p.xxviii.

23 E.W. Monter, 'Inflation and Witchcraft: The Case of Jean Bodin', in T.K. Rabb & J.E. Seigel (eds.), *Action and Conviction in Early Modern Europe. Essays in Memory of E.H. Harbison* (Princeton University Press, Princeton, New Jersey, 1969), p.375.

24 S. Anglo (ed.), *The Damned Art. Essays in the Literature of Witchcraft* (Routledge & Kegan Paul, London, Henley & Boston, 1977 rpt. 1985), pp.76–7.

25 Normand & Roberts (eds.), *Witchcraft in Early Modern Scotland*, p.11; J. Wormald, 'James VI and I: Two Kings or One', *History*, Vol.68 (1983), pp.187–209.

26 R. Scot, *The Discoverie of Witchcraft* (London: William Brome, 1584); J. Weyer, *De Praestigiis Daemonum* (Basle: Oporinus, 1563).

27 James VI & I, *Daemonologie*, pp.xi–xii, 28.

28 James VI & I, *Daemonologie*, pp.5, 54–5.

29 James VI & I, *Daemonologie*, p.2.

30 James VI & I, *Daemonologie*, p.35.

31 James VI & I, *Daemonologie*, pp.43–4.

32 James VI & I, *Daemonologie*, pp.44–7 & 59.

33 James VI & I, *Daemonologie*, pp.17, 20 & 32.

34 James VI & I, *Daemonologie*, p.23.

35 James VI & I, *Daemonologie*, p.23.

36 James VI & I, *Daemonologie*, p.41.

37 James VI & I, *Daemonologie*, p.32.

38 James VI & I, *Daemonologie*, pp.32–3.

39 James VI & I, *Daemonologie*, p.30.

40 James VI & I, *Daemonologie*, pp.33–4.

41 James VI & I, *Daemonologie*, pp.19 & 23.

42 Thomas Potts, clerk to the court at Lancaster in 1612, wrote of one of the Lancashire witches, Isobel Robey: 'What hath the Kings Majestie written and published in his

Daemonologie, by way of premonition and prevention, which hath not here by the first or last beene executed, put in practice or discovered?'

See: S. Pumfrey, 'Potts, plots and politics: James I's *Daemonologie* and *The Wonderfull Discoverie of Witches*' in: R. Poole (ed.), *The Lancashire Witches. Histories and Stories* (Manchester University Press, Manchester & New York, 2002), pp.23, 27 & 32–3; T. Potts, *The Wonderfull Discoverie of Witches in the Countie of Lancaster*, intro. A. Stuttard (Carnegie Publishing Ltd., Lancaster, 2003), pp.153–4; E. Peel & P. Southern, *The Trials of the Lancashire Witches* (Hendon Publishing, Nelson, 1969), p.34; & J. Lumby, *The Lancashire Witch-Craze. Jennet Preston and the Lancashire Witches, 1612* (Carnegie Publishing Ltd., Preston, 1995), pp.23, 54, 67, 75 & 188 fn.80.

43 Robertson (ed.), *Goodnight, My Servants All*, pp.53–4. See also: J. Goodacre (ed.), *The Scottish Witch-Hunt in Context* (Manchester University Press, Manchester & New York, 2002), p.130; & B.P. Levack, *Witch-Hunting in Scotland. Law, Politics and Religion* (Routledge, New York & London, 2008), p.22.

44 Quoted in: R.H. Robbins, *Encyclopaedia of Demonology and Witchcraft* (Crown Publishers, London & New York, 1959), p.279.

45 James VI & I, *Daemonologie*, pp.80–1.

46 M. Gaskill, *Witchfinders. A Seventeenth-Century English Tragedy* (John Murray, London, 2005 rpt. 2006), pp.41, 105–7, 217 & 258–9; P.G. Maxwell-Stuart, *Witch Hunters. Professional Prickers, Unwitchers & Witch Finders of the Renaissance* (Tempus, Stroud, Gloucestershire, 2003 rpt. 2006), pp.161–8; & Sharpe, *Instruments of Darkness*, pp.218–19.

47 C. L'Estrange Ewen, *Witch Hunting and Witch Trials. The Indictments for Witchcraft from the Records of 1373 Assizes held for the Home Circuit, A.D. 1559–1736* (London: Kegan Paul, Trench, Trubner & Co. Ltd., 1929), pp.98–113; A. Macfarlane, *Witchcraft in Tudor and Stuart England. A Regional and Comparative Study*, second edition, intro. J. Sharpe (London: Routledge, 1970 rpt. 1999), pp.23–30, 57–8, 60–3; Sharpe, *Instruments of Darkness*, pp.105–27.

48 Clark, 'King James's Daemonologie', p.161; Larner, 'James VI and I and Witchcraft', pp.81 & 87–8.

49 Anon., *A Tryal of Witches, at the Assizes held at Bury St. Edmonds for the County of Suffolk; on the Tenth day of March, 1664. Before Sir Matthew Hale Kt. Then Lord Chief Baron of His Majesties Court of Exchequer* (London: William Shewsbery, 1682).

50 Anon., *A Tryal of Witches, at the Assizes held at Bury St. Edmonds*, pp.2–6.

51 Geis & Bunn, *A Trial of Witches*, pp.73–4.

52 J.S. Finch, *Sir Thomas Browne. A Doctor's Life of Science & Faith* (New York: Henry Schuman, 1950), pp.214–15, 217.

53 Anon., *A Tryal of Witches, at the Assizes held at Bury St. Edmonds*, pp.29–30.

54 Kitteredge, *Witchcraft in Old and New England*, pp.332–3; Sharpe, *Instruments of Darkness*, p.226; Anon., *A Tryal of Witches, at the Assizes held at Bury St. Edmonds*, p.40.

55 A. Cromartie, *Sir Matthew Hale, 1609–1676. Law, Religion and Natural Philosophy* (Cambridge: Cambridge University Press, 1995 rpt. 2003), pp.238–9; M. Hale, *A Collection of Modern Relations of Matter of Fact, Concerning Witches & Witchcraft* (London: John Harris, 1693), pp.1–8. Unfortunately, Hale did not finish his own treatise on witchcraft and it was subsequently printed as part of a compendium of cases that seemed to point towards the veracity of witchcraft. Nevertheless, his writings echo the judgement that he handed down at Bury St Edmunds.

56 Kitteredge, *Witchcraft in Old and New England*, p.364.

57 Anon., *A True and Impartial Relation of the Informations Against Three Witches*, pp.2, 4, 31.

58 E.G. Breslaw, *Tituba, Reluctant Witch of Salem. Devilish Indians and Puritan Fantasies* (New York & London: New York University Press, 1996), pp.172–4, 178–9; M.K. Roach, *Six Women of Salem. The Untold Story of the Accused and their Accusers in the Salem Witch Trials* (Boston, Massachusetts: Da Capo Press, 2013), p.355; S. Schiff, *The Witches. Salem, 1692. A History* (London: Weidenfeld & Nicolson, 2015 rpt. 2016), pp.350–5; K. Silverman, *The Life and Times of Cotton Mather* (New York: Columbia University Press, 1970 rpt. 1985), pp.98–9, 113, 118.

59 C. Mather, *On Witchcraft* (New York: Dorset Press, 1991), p.92.

60 Geis & Bunn, *A Trial of Witches*, p.111.

61 Glanvill, *Saducismus Triumphatus*, 'Second Part', p.iii.

62 T.H. Jobe, 'The Devil in Restoration Science: The Glanvill-Webster Witchcraft Debate', *ISIS*, Vol.72 (1981), p.343. In part, this view stems from Lecky's brief treatment and reluctance to own Webster as one of his heroes of the proto-Enlightenment. See: W.E.H. Lecky, *History of the Rise and Influence of the Spirit of Rationalism in Europe* (Longmans, Green and Co., London, Bombay & Calcutta, 1910), p.119.

63 J. Glanvill, *A Blow at Modern Sadducism in Some Philosophical Considerations about Witchcraft* (London: E.C. for James Collins, 1668), 'First Part' p.x.

64 Glanvill, *A Blow at Modern Sadducism*, pp.vii–x.

65 Glanvill, *A Blow at Modern Sadducism*, pp.97–125.

66 J. Barry, *Witchcraft and Demonology in South-West England, 1640–1789* (Palgrave Macmillan, Houndmills Basingstoke, 2012), pp.17–24, 26 & 51–7. See also: S. Clark, *Thinking with Demons. The Idea of Witchcraft in Early Modern Europe* (Oxford University Press, Oxford, 1997 rpt. 1999), pp.296–7.

67 J. Glanvill, *Saducismus Triumphatus: Or, a Full and Plain Evidence, Concerning Witches and Apparitions* (A. Bettersworth & J. Batley, & W. Mears & J. Hooke, fourth edition, London, 1681 rpt. 1726). The book, running to more than 500 dense pages of text, was divided into two parts. The first examined the 'Possibility' of witches and apparitions, while the second – which comprised the case studies – considered their 'Real Existence'.

68 Glanvill, *Saducismus Triumphatus*, p.6.

69 Glanvill, *Saducismus Triumphatus*, p.18.

70 Glanvill, *Saducismus Triumphatus*, p.22.

71 Glanvill, *Saducismus Triumphatus*, pp.225–6.

72 Glanvill, *Saducismus Triumphatus*, p.12.

73 Glanvill, *Saducismus Triumphatus*, p.122.

74 Glanvill, *Saducismus Triumphatus*, p.10.

75 Glanvill, *Saducismus Triumphatus*, p.21.

76 Glanvill, *Saducismus Triumphatus*, pp.238–9.

77 Glanvill, *Saducismus Triumphatus*, pp. 'Postscript' 21–2, 27, 34, & 'Part Two' 225–6.

78 J. Webster, *The Displaying of Supposed Witchcraft* (London: J.M., 1677).

79 Glanvill, *Saducismus Triumphatus*, 'Postscript' p. 30 & 'Part One' p.20.

80 R. Neill, *Witch Bane*, p. 222; H.R. Trevor-Roper, *The European Witch-Craze of the 16th and 17th Centuries* (Harmondsworth: Penguin Books, 1967 rpt. 1978), p.97.

81 Webster, *Displaying of Witchcraft*, p.276.

82 Jobe, 'The Devil in Restoration Science', p.348.

83 Webster, *Displaying of Witchcraft*, pp.ix–x.

84 Webster, *Displaying of Witchcraft*, p.65.

85 Webster, *Displaying of Witchcraft*, p.11.

86 Webster, *Displaying of Witchcraft*, p.66.

87 Webster, *Displaying of Witchcraft*, p.66.

88 Webster, *Displaying of Witchcraft*, p.v.

89 Webster, *Displaying of Witchcraft*, pp.v–vi.

90 Webster, *Displaying of Witchcraft*, p.v.

91 Webster, *Displaying of Witchcraft*, pp.82–3.

92 Webster, *Displaying of Witchcraft*, p.68.

93 Webster, *Displaying of Witchcraft*, p.37.

94 Webster, *Displaying of Witchcraft*, p.74.

95 Webster, *Displaying of Witchcraft*, p.76.

96 Webster, *Displaying of Witchcraft*, p.ix.

97 Webster, *Displaying of Witchcraft*, p.61. See also: op.cit. p.32, in a similar vein.

98 Webster, *Displaying of Witchcraft*, p.18.

99 Webster, *Displaying of Witchcraft*, p.77.

100 Webster, *Displaying of Witchcraft*, p.77.

101 Webster, *Displaying of Witchcraft*, p.78. See also: op.cit. pp.196–7.

102 W. Notestein, *A History of Witchcraft in England from 1558 to 1718* (The American Historical Association, Washington, 1911), p.303; Elmer, *Library of Dr. John Webster*, p.14; & Webster, *From Paracelsus to Newton*, p.96.

103 B. Camfield, *A Theological Discourse of Angels, and their Ministries. Wherein their Existence, Nature, Number, Order and Offices, are Modestly Treated ... Also an Appendix Containing Some Reflections upon Mr. Webster's Displaying Supposed Witchcraft* (London: R.E. for Henry Brome, London, 1678), pp.170, 172, 197, 200–1, 213.

Chapter 8

1 Anon., *A True and Impartial Relation of the Informations Against Three Witches*, pp.34–7. The pamphlet source cites the date of Susanna Edwards' questioning as 10 July but from internal evidence contained within that confession it is clear that she gave her confession at the same time as Mary Trembles, eight days later.

2 Anon., *A True and Impartial Relation of the Informations Against Three Witches*, p.36.

3 Anon., *A True and Impartial Relation of the Informations Against Three Witches*, p.36.

4 Anon., *A True and Impartial Relation of the Informations Against Three Witches*, p.36.

5 Anon., *A True and Impartial Relation of the Informations Against Three Witches*, pp.34–5.

6 Anon., *A True and Impartial Relation of the Informations Against Three Witches*, p.34.

7 Anon., *A True and Impartial Relation of the Informations Against Three Witches*, p.34.

8 Anon., *A True and Impartial Relation of the Informations Against Three Witches*, pp.34–5.

9 Anon., *A True and Impartial Relation of the Informations Against Three Witches*, pp.34–5.

10 Anon., *A True and Impartial Relation of the Informations Against Three Witches*, p.36.

11 Anon., *A True and Impartial Relation of the Informations Against Three Witches*, p.36.

12 Anon., *A True and Impartial Relation of the Informations Against Three Witches*, p.37.

13 Anon., *A True and Impartial Relation of the Informations Against Three Witches*, p.37.

14 Anon., *A True and Impartial Relation of the Informations Against Three Witches*, p.37.

15 Anon., *A True and Impartial Relation of the Informations Against Three Witches*, pp.32–3.

16 Anon., *A True and Impartial Relation of the Informations Against Three Witches*, pp.32–3.

17 Anon., *A True and Impartial Relation of the Informations Against Three Witches*, pp.32–4.

18 Anon., *A True and Impartial Relation of the Informations Against Three Witches*, p.32.

19 Elmer (ed.), *English Witchcraft*, Vol.V p.364.

20 Anon., *A True and Impartial Relation of the Informations Against Three Witches*, p.29.

21 Liber Session Pacis, f.171 verso.

22 Barry, *Witchcraft and Demonology in South-West England*, p.74.

23 Liber Session Pacis, f.171 verso.

24 Inderwick, *Side-Lights on the Stuarts*, pp.190–2.

25 L'Estrange Ewen, *Witchcraft and Demonism*, pp.355–7.

26 L'Estrange Ewen, *Witchcraft and Demonism*, pp.442–3.

27 Sharpe, *Instruments of Darkness*, p.121.

28 Stoyle, *Witchcraft in Exeter, 1558–1660*, p.55.

29 Stoyle, *Witchcraft in Exeter, 1558–1660*, pp.21–2.

30 Anon., *A True and Impartial Relation of the Informations Against Three Witches*, pp.1–6.

31 Jessop (ed.), *Lives*, Vol.III p.130; Jessop (ed.), *Lives*, Vol.I p.167.

32 Anon., *The Life and Conversation of . . . Three Eminent Witches*, p.6.

33 Anon., *The Tryal, Condemnation, and Execution of Three Witches*, pp.4–5.

34 Anon., *The Tryal, Condemnation, and Execution of Three Witches*, p.5.

35 Anon., *The Life and Conversation of . . . Three Eminent Witches*, p.6.

36 Anon., *The Life and Conversation of . . . Three Eminent Witches*, p.6.

37 Anon., *The Life and Conversation of . . . Three Eminent Witches*, p.6.

38 Anon., *A True and Impartial Relation of the Informations Against Three Witches*, p.38.

39 Anon., *A True and Impartial Relation of the Informations Against Three Witches*, p.38.

40 W. Cobbett (ed.), *State Trials*, Vol.III (London: T.C. Hansard, 1810), pp.1018–39.

41 *CSPD 1682*, pp.347–8; Jessop (ed.), *Lives*, Vol.I pp.167–8; Jessop (ed.), *Lives*, Vol.III pp.130–1.

42 Jessop (ed.), *Lives*, Vol.I p.166.

43 T. Raymond (ed.), *Reports of Divers Special Cases, Adjudged in the Courts of King's Bench, Common Pleas, and Exchequer, in the Reign of Charles II*, third edition (Dublin: James Moore, 1793), pp.212, 374, 439, 386, 440, 444–5, 458, 487.

44 *CSPD 1682*, p.347.

45 *CSPD 1682*, pp.347–8.

46 *CSPD 1682*, p.348.

47 *CSPD 1682*, p.347.

48 *CSPD 1682*, p.347.

49 *CSPD 1682*, p.347.

50 *CSPD 1682*, p.347.

51 Jessop (ed.), *Lives*, Vol.I p.167.

52 Jessop (ed.), *Lives*, Vol.I pp.167–8.

53 Jessop (ed.), *Lives*, Vol.I p.167.

54 Jessop (ed.), *Lives*, Vol.I p.167.

55 Jessop (ed.), *Lives*, Vol.I p.167.

56 Jessop (ed.), *Lives*, Vol.III p.131.

57 Jessop (ed.), *Lives*, Vol.I p.167.

58 Jessop (ed.), *Lives*, Vol.I pp.167–8.

59 Anon., *The Life and Conversation of . . . Three Eminent Witches*, p.7.

60 P.H. Brown (ed.), *The Register of the Privy Council of Scotland*, Third Series, Vol.I (Edinburgh: General Register House, 1908), p.243.

61 Anon., *Life and Conversation of Temperance Floyd, Mary Lloyd and Susannah Edwards*, p.7.

62 Jessop (ed.), *Lives*, Vol.III p.131.

63 Jessop (ed.), *Lives*, Vol.III p.130.

64 Jessop (ed.), *Lives*, Vol.III p.133.

65 Jessop (ed.), *Lives*, Vol.III p.133.

66 Jessop (ed.), *Lives*, Vol.III p.132.

67 Jessop (ed.), *Lives*, Vol.III p.130.

68 Barry, *Witchcraft and Demonology*, pp.63, 78–9, 102; Timmons, 'Witchcraft and Rebellion', pp.298, 307–10, 312, 317, 322–5, 328–30.

69 Timmons, 'Witchcraft and Rebellion', p.298.

70 Jessop (ed.), *Lives*, Vol.III p.130.

71 Jessop (ed.), *Lives*, Vol.III p.130.

72 Anon., *The Life and Conversation of . . . Three Eminent Witches*, pp.7–8.

73 Anon., *A True and Impartial Relation of the Informations Against Three Witches*, p.39.

74 Anon., *Life and Conversation of Temperance Floyd, Mary Lloyd and Susannah Edwards*, pp.6–7.

75 Anon., *The Tryal, Condemnation, and Execution of Three Witches*, p.4; Anon., *The Life and Conversation of ... Three Eminent Witches*, p.5.

76 Anon., *A True and Impartial Relation of the Informations Against Three Witches*, p.40; Anon., *The Tryal, Condemnation, and Execution of Three Witches*, p.5.

77 *CSPD 1682*, p.347.

78 *CSPD 1682*, p.347.

79 *CSPD 1682*, p.347.

80 Jessop (ed.), *Lives*, Vol.III pp.130–1.

81 Jessop (ed.), *Lives*, Vol.I p.166.

82 Anon., *The Tryal, Condemnation, and Execution of Three Witches*, p.1. I am grateful to Prof. Mark Stoyle for confirming the opinion that it was Heavitree, one of two city gallows, where the witches perished. Mark Stoyle, email to the present author (14 December 2020).

83 Anon., *The Tryal, Condemnation, and Execution of Three Witches*, p.6.

84 Anon., *The Tryal, Condemnation, and Execution of Three Witches*, p.6.

85 V.A.C. Gatrell, *The Hanging Tree. Execution and the English People, 1770–1868* (Oxford: Oxford University Press, 1994 rpt. 1996), pp.33–40; P. Linebaugh, *The London Hanged. Crime and Civil Society in the Eighteenth Century*, second edition (London & New York: Verso, 2003 rpt. 2006), pp.72–3, 88–9, 123, 280–1.

86 Anon., *Life and Conversation of Temperance Floyd, Mary Lloyd and Susannah Edwards*, p.8.

87 Anon., *A True and Impartial Relation of the Informations Against Three Witches*, p.37.

88 Anon., *A True and Impartial Relation of the Informations Against Three Witches*, p.38.

89 Anon., *A True and Impartial Relation of the Informations Against Three Witches*, pp.38–9.

90 Anon., *A True and Impartial Relation of the Informations Against Three Witches*, pp.37–9.

91 Anon., *A True and Impartial Relation of the Informations Against Three Witches*, pp.38–9.

92 Anon., *A True and Impartial Relation of the Informations Against Three Witches*, pp.38–9.

93 Anon., *A True and Impartial Relation of the Informations Against Three Witches*, p.39.

94 Anon., *A True and Impartial Relation of the Informations Against Three Witches*, p.39.

95 Anon., *A True and Impartial Relation of the Informations Against Three Witches*, p.39.

96 Anon., *A True and Impartial Relation of the Informations Against Three Witches*, p.40.

97 Anon., *A True and Impartial Relation of the Informations Against Three Witches*, p.40.

98 Jessop (ed.), *Lives*, Vol.III p.131.

Chapter 9

1 In 1926 and 1973, a number of skeletons were dug up at the intersection of the Sidmouth and Honiton Roads and were thought to be the remains of some of those executed at Heavitree. See: C.S. Barber, *The Lost City of Exeter* (Exeter: Obelisk Publications, 1982), p.85.

2 Anon., *The Life and Conversation of . . . Three Eminent Witches*; Anon., *The Tryal, Condemnation, and Execution of Three Witches*; Anon., *A True and Impartial Relation of the Informations Against Three Witches*; Ashton (ed.), *A Century of Ballad*, pp.79–81; Ebsworth (ed.), *The Roxburghe Ballads*, Vol.VI Part II pp.706–8.

3 Timmons, 'Witchcraft and Rebellion, pp.314–30; Barry, *Witchcraft and Demonology in South-West England*, pp.76–102; Elmer (ed.), *English Witchcraft, 1560–1736*, Vol.5 pp.1–2.

4 Elmer (ed.), *English Witchcraft, 1560–1736*, Vol.5 pp.1–2.

5 Anon., *Life and Conversation of Temperance Floyd, Mary Lloyd and Susannah Edwards*, p.5.

6 Anon., *The Tryal, Condemnation, and Execution of Three Witches*, p.1.

7 Briggs, *Pale Hecate's Team*, pp.77–80, 86–8; H.N. Paul, *The Royal Play of Macbeth* (New York: The Macmillan Company, 1950), pp.60–74; M. Murray, *The Witch-Cult in Western Europe. A Study in Anthropology* (Oxford: The Clarendon Press, 1921), pp.34, 66, 95; R. Hutton, *The Triumph of the Moon. A History of Modern Pagan Witchcraft* (Oxford: Oxford University Press, 1999), pp.195–6. Murray, just like the aristocratic North brothers, entirely forgot about Mary Trembles and wrote of 'both' the Bideford Witches, see: op.cit. p.66.

8 Anon., *The Life and Conversation of . . . Three Eminent Witches*, pp.1, 3–6.

9 Timmons, 'Witchcraft and Rebellion, p.325.

10 Anon., *Life and Conversation of . . . Three Eminent Witches*, p.5.

11 Timmons, 'Witchcraft and Rebellion', pp.314, 325–7; Barry, *Witchcraft and Demonology*, pp.78, 291–2.

12 Timmons, 'Witchcraft and Rebellion', p.298.

13 Anon., *A True and Impartial Relation of the Informations Against Three Witches*, pp.1–37; Devon Heritage Centre, Exeter, Devon QS 74/5/2–6; QS 74/5/13; QS 74/15/13.

14 Anon., *A True and Impartial Relation of the Informations Against Three Witches*, pp.37–40.

15 Ashton (ed.), *A Century of Ballads*, p.79.

16 K. Briggs, *The Anatomy of Puck. An Examination of Fairy Beliefs among Shakespeare's Contemporaries and Successors* (London: Routledge and Kegan Paul, 1959), pp.40–1; J.P. Collier (ed.), *The Mad Pranks and Merry Jests of Robin Goodfellow: Reprinted from the Edition of 1628* (London: The Percy Society, 1841), pp.vi, x–xii, xv, 20, 30; D. Purkiss, *At*

the Bottom of the Garden. A Dark History of Fairies, Hobgoblins and Other Troublesome Things (New York: New York University Press, 2000 rpt. 2001), p.164.

17 S.F. Williams, *Damnable Practices. Witches, Dangerous Women and Music in Seventeenth Century English Broadside Ballads* (Farnham & Burlington, Vermont, USA, 2015), p.65.

18 Williams, *Damnable Practices*, pp.68–9.

19 Williams, *Damnable Practices*, p.67. Writing primarily to condemn witch persecution, the Rev. Sabine Baring-Gould delivered an entirely different verdict considering the ballad to be 'wretched doggerel'. See: S. Baring-Gould, *Devonshire Characters and Strange Events*, First Series (London: John Lane the Bodley Head Limited, 1908 rpt. 1926), p.277.

20 Ashton (ed.), *A Century of Ballads*, p.79.

21 Ashton (ed.), *A Century of Ballads*, p.80.

22 Ashton (ed.), *A Century of Ballads*, p.81.

23 Ashton (ed.), *A Century of Ballads*, p.81.

24 Ashton (ed.), *A Century of Ballads*, p.80.

25 Ashton (ed.), *A Century of Ballads*, p.81.

26 S. Baring-Gould, *Devonshire Characters and Strange Events*, Second Series (London: John Lane the Bodley Head Limited, 1908 rpt. 1926), p.13.

27 F.H. Blackburne Daniell & F. Bickley (eds.), *Calendar State Papers Domestic, July 1 to September 30 1683* (London: HMSO, 1934), pp.61, 76, 106–7; *Liber Session Pacis*, f.ix, ff.183 verso – 184.

28 *Liber Session Pacis*, f. viii.

29 *Liber Session Pacis*, ff.viii–ix.

30 *Liber Session Pacis*, ff.183 verso – 184.

31 *Liber Session Pacis*, f.184.

32 HMSO, *Calendar State Papers Domestic, James II, Vol.I, February – December 1685* (London: HMSO, 1960), no. 1840, p.371.

33 *CSPD, February – December 1685*, no.1862 p.377.

34 I. Roots (ed.), *The Monmouth Rising. Aspects of the 1685 Rebellion in the West Country* (Exeter: Devon Books, 1986), pp.67–75; Watkins, *History of Bideford*, p.47.

35 W.M. Wigfield (ed.), *The Monmouth Rebels, 1685* (Gloucester: Alan Sutton Publishing Ltd., 1985), p.104.

36 Wigfield (ed.), *The Monmouth Rebels*, pp.viii–ix, xix–xx.

37 L'Estrange Ewen, *Witchcraft and Demonianism*, p.444; Inderwick, *Side-Lights on the Stuarts*, pp.174, 193.

38 *Liber Session Pacis*, f.192 verso.

39 *Liber Session Pacis*, f.193.

40 *Liber Session Pacis*, ff.193–4.

41 *Liber Session Pacis*, ff.193 verso – 194.

42 *Liber Session Pacis*, ff.184 verso, 192 verso.

43 Devon Heritage Centre: Devon Q/S 74/5/7.

44 *Liber Session Pacis*, f.263 verso.

45 *Liber Session Pacis*, f.xvi.

46 *Liber Session Pacis*, ff.223, 282.

47 Bideford Parish Register, Vol.IV, Bideford Burials, f.149.

48 Inderwick, *Side-Lights on the Stuarts*, pp.192–3.

49 L'Estrange Ewen, *Witchcraft and Demonianism*, p.444. Frederick Andrew Inderwick records her surname as 'Welland' as opposed to Molland. See: Inderwick, *Side-Lights on the Stuarts*, p.173.

50 Sharpe, *Instruments of Darkness*, pp.121, 226.

51 Inderwick, *Side-Light on the Stuarts*, pp.173, 193; L'Estrange Ewen, *Witchcraft and Demonianism*, p.445.

52 Jessop (ed.), *Lives*, Vol.I p.166.

53 Duncan, *The Long Bridge of Bideford and Bideford under the Restored Monarchy*, p.64; Gent, *Trial of the Bideford Witches*, p.117.

54 C. L'Estrange Ewen (ed.), *Witch Hunting and Witch Trials. The Indictments for Witchcraft from the Records of 1373 Assizes held for the Home Circuit A.D. 1559–1736* (London: Kegan Paul, Trench, Truener & Co. Ltd., 1929), pp.18–21.

55 Notestein, *History of Witchcraft in England*, pp.321–2; Inderwick, *Side-Light on the Stuarts*, p.194.

56 Anon. ('J.R.'), *The Life of the Right Honourable Sir John Holt, Knight, Lord Chief Justice of the Court of King's-Bench* (London: 'J.R.', sold by J. Worrall, 1764); Anon. (ed.), *A Report of all the Cases Determined by Sir John Holt, Knt., from 1688 to 1710, during which Time he was Lord Chief Justice of England* (London: E. & R. Nutt and R. Gosling, 1738). It is possible that both of these publications appeared under the aegis of the Raymond family. Sir Robert Raymond, 1st Baron Raymond (1673–1733) was the son of Sir Thomas Raymond and had been a protégé of Sir John Holt's. This would certainly fit with the praise accorded to the judge of the Bideford Witches and the downplaying of Holt's radicalism. See: Anon. ('J.R.'), *Life of the Right Honourable Sir John Holt*, p.3.

57 G.H. Artley, *Law and Politics under the Later Stuarts: Sir John Holt, the Courts, and the Constitutional Crisis of 1688*, unpublished PhD dissertation (Oxford: Lincoln College,

University of Oxford, 2019), pp.2, 6–7, 11, 20, 31, 41–4, 45–6; P.D. Halliday, 'Sir John Holt (1642–1710)', in: H.C.G. Matthew & B. Harrison (eds.), *Oxford Dictionary of National Biography*, Vol.27 (Oxford: Oxford University Press, 2004), pp.830–1; Anon. ('J.R.'), *Life of the Right Honourable Sir John Holt*, pp.3–4.

58 Anon. ('J.R.'), *Life of the Right Honourable Sir John Holt*, p.xi. This said, a recent doctoral thesis offers a wealth of biographical detail, see: Artley, *Law and Politics under the Later Stuarts*, op.cit.

59 G. Lane, 'Lord Chief Justice Holt', *Graya*, No.93 (1990), p.18; Anon. ('J.R.'), *Life of the Right Honourable Sir John Holt*, pp.3–4.

60 Anon. (ed.), *A Report of all the Cases Determined by Sir John Holt*, p.495.

61 L'Estrange Ewen, *Witchcraft and Demonianism*, p.376.

62 L'Estrange Ewen, *Witchcraft and Demonianism*, p.377.

63 L'Estrange Ewen, *Witchcraft and Demonianism*, p.377.

64 L'Estrange Ewen, *Witchcraft and Demonianism*, p.378.

65 L'Estrange Ewen, *Witchcraft and Demonianism*, p.378.

66 L'Estrange Ewen, *Witchcraft and Demonianism*, p.378; Notestein, *History of Witchcraft in England*, pp.321–2.

67 Notestein, *History of Witchcraft in England*, p.322.

68 F. Hutchinson, *An Historical Essay Concerning Witchcraft* (London: R. Knaplock, 1718), p.225; Anon., *The Tryal of Richard Hathaway, Upon an Information for Being an Impostor, For Endeavouring to Take Away the Life of Sarah Morduck for being a Witch* (London: Isaac Cleave, 1702), pp.1–3, 27–9.

69 Hutchinson, *Historical Essay Concerning Witchcraft*, p.225; Anon., *The Tryal of Richard Hathaway*, pp.5–6, 8.

70 L'Estrange Ewen, *Witchcraft and Demonianism*, p.380; Anon., *The Tryal of Richard Hathaway*, p.5.

71 L'Estrange Ewen (ed.), *Witch Hunting and Witch Trials*, p.264; Hutchinson, *Historical Essay Concerning Witchcraft*, p.226.

72 Hutchinson, *Historical Essay Concerning Witchcraft*, p.224; Anon., *The Tryal of Richard Hathaway*, pp.10–11.

73 Hutchinson, *Historical Essay Concerning Witchcraft*, pp.224–5.

74 Hutchinson, *Historical Essay Concerning Witchcraft*, p.226.

75 Hutchinson, *Historical Essay Concerning Witchcraft*, p.226; L'Estrange Ewen (ed.), *Witch Hunting and Witch Trials*, p.265.

76 Hutchinson, *Historical Essay Concerning Witchcraft*, p.227.

77 Hutchinson, *Historical Essay Concerning Witchcraft*, p.226.

78 Hutchinson, *Historical Essay Concerning Witchcraft*, p.226.

79 Hutchinson, *Historical Essay Concerning Witchcraft*, p.227.

80 Inderwick, *Side-Light on the Stuarts*, p.184.

81 Notestein, *History of Witchcraft in England*, p.323; Anon., *The Tryal of Richard Hathaway*, p.27.

82 Inderwick, *Side-Light on the Stuarts*, p.184.

83 J. Gay, *Poems on Several Occasions*, Vol.II (London: J. & R. Tonson et al., 1767), p.62.

84 Jessop (ed.), *Lives*, Vol.I p.169.

85 L. Bordelon, *A History of the Ridiculous Extravagancies of Monsieur Oufle*, intro. J. Grieder (New York & London: Garland Publishing Inc., 1711 rpt. 1973), p.8; D. Outram, *Panorama of the Enlightenment* (Los Angeles: The J. Paul Getty Museum / Thames and Hudson, 2006), pp.13–15.

86 R. Boulton, *A Compleat History of Magick, Sorcery, and Witchcraft*, Vol.I (London: E. Curll at the Dial and Bible, J. Pemberton at the Buck & Sun, and W. Taylor at the Ship, 1715), pp.216–54.

87 Boulton, *Compleat History of Magick, Sorcery, and Witchcraft*, Vol.I pp.210–15, 254–62.

88 I. Bostridge, *Witchcraft and Its Transformations, c.1650–c.1750* (Oxford: Clarendon Press, 1997 rpt. 2003), p.141.

89 Hutchinson, *Historical Essay Concerning Witchcraft*, p.41.

90 Pearse Chope (ed.), *Early Tours in Devon and Cornwall*, p.172.

91 Pearse Chope (ed.), *Early Tours in Devon and Cornwall*, p.172.

92 Pearse Chope (ed.), *Early Tours in Devon and Cornwall*, p.172.

93 R. Pearse Chope, 'John Abbott, Plasterer', *Devon and Cornwall Notes and Queries*, Vol. XIV (January 1926 – October 1927), pp.289–90.

94 J. Gay, *Fables* (London: J. Buckland et al, 1775), p.70. See also: M.J. Willin, *Witchcraft, Music and the Paranormal* (Ely: Melrose Books, 2005), p.181; Nokes, *John Gay*, p.78; A. Dickson, '"To Lash the Age": John Gay and the Beggar's Opers', accessed at: https://www.bl.uk/restoration-18th-century-literature/articles/to-lash-the-age-john-gay-and-the-beggars-opera.

95 Gay, *Fables*, p.69.

Chapter 10

1 Watkins, *History of Bideford*, pp.46–7.

2 Watkins, *History of Bideford*, p.47.

3   Watkins, *History of Bideford*, p.247.

4   Anon., 'Death of Martha Lee, the Centenarian', *North Devon Journal* (10 March 1853), p.8. I am grateful to Peter Christie for supplying the reference to this article.

5   Anon., 'Death of Martha Lee, the Centenarian', p.8.

6   Anon., 'Death of Martha Lee, the Centenarian', p.8.

7   Anon., 'Death of Martha Lee, the Centenarian', p.8.

8   Baring-Gould, *Devonshire Characters*, First Series, pp.75–6.

9   Baring-Gould, *Devonshire Characters*, First Series, pp.73, 76.

10 National Archives, Kew, RG11/2222 Bratton Clovelly Parish f.9 (Devon Census 1881); National Archives, Kew, RG12/1753 Bratton Clovelly Parish f.16 (Devon Census 1891); Baring-Gould, *Devonshire Characters*, First Series, p.74.

11 S. Baring-Gould, *An Old English Home and its Dependencies* (London: Methuen & Co., 1898), p.1.

12 Baring-Gould, *An Old English Home*, p.2.

13 Baring-Gould, *An Old English Home*, pp.2, 5; Baring-Gould, *Devonshire Characters*, First Series, p.75.

14 Baring-Gould, *Arminell*, p.46.

15 Baring-Gould, *An Old English Home*, p.5.

16 Baring-Gould, *Devonshire Characters*, First Series, p.77

17 Baring-Gould, *Devonshire Characters*, First Series, p.77.

18 Baring-Gould, *Devonshire Characters*, First Series, p.78.

19 Baring-Gould, *Arminell*, p.50.

20 S. Page, M. Wallace, O. Davies, M. Gaskill & C. Houlbrook, *Spellbound. Magic, Ritual & Witchcraft* (Oxford: Ashmolean Museum, 2018), pp.85–7; C. Wingfield, 'A Case Re-opened: the Science and Folklore of a "Witch's Ladder"', *Journal of Material Culture*, Vol.15 no.3 (2010), pp.302–22.

21 Baring-Gould, *Devonshire Characters*, First Series, pp.78–9.

22 Baring-Gould, *Devonshire Characters*, First Series, p.75.

23 Baring-Gould, *Devonshire Characters*, First Series, p.74.

24 Baring-Gould, *Arminell*, p.48.

25 Baring-Gould, *Devonshire Characters*, First Series, p.74.

26 Baring-Gould, *Arminell*, f.n. p.50.

27 Baring-Gould, *Arminell*, pp.49–50.

28 Baring-Gould, *Devonshire Characters*, p.76.

29 Baring-Gould, *Devonshire Characters*, p.76.

30 R. Hutton, *The Stations of the Sun. A History of the Ritual Year in Britain* (Oxford & New York: Oxford University Press, 1996), pp.379–84; N. Rogers, *Halloween. From Pagan Ritual to Party Night* (Oxford: Oxford University Press, 2002 rpt. 2003), pp.52–7, 67, 74, 76; C. Savage, *Witch. The Wild Ride from Wicked to Wicca* (London: The British Museum Press, 2000), pp.99, 109.

31 S. Norris, *Tales of Old Devon* (Newbury, Berkshire: Countryside Books, 1991), p.104.

32 Anon., *Tedrake's Illustrated Guide to Bideford and North Devon* (Bideford: Western Express Office, 1904), p.14.

33 A.H. Norway, *History of the Post-Office Packet Service, Between the Years 1793–1815* (London: Macmillan & Company, 1895); A.H. Norway, *Naples. Past and Present*, 2 vols. (New York: Frederick A. Stokes & Company, 1901); A.H. Norway, *Dante, The Divine Comedy: Its Essential Significance* (London: Student Christian Movement Press, 1931).

34 A.H. Norway, *Highways and Byways in Devon and Cornwall* (London: Macmillan & Co. Ltd., 1897 rpt. 1919), p.373.

35 Norway, *Highways and Byways*, p.372.

36 Norway, *Highways and Byways*, pp.372–3.

37 Norway, *Highways and Byways*, pp.372–3.

38 Norway, *Highways and Byways*, p.321.

39 Norway, *Highways and Byways*, p.321.

40 Norway, *Highways and Byways*, p.321.

41 Norway, *Highways and Byways*, p.322.

42 Norway, *Highways and Byways*, p.322.

Coda

1 O. Davies, *Witchcraft, Magic and Culture, 1736–1951* (Manchester & New York: Manchester University Press, 1999), pp.72–3.

2 Hansard, *Parliamentary Debates*, Fifth Series, Vol.481, p.1522.

3 Hansard, *Parliamentary Debates. House of Commons Official Report Session, 1950–51*, Fifth Series, Vol.481 (London: Hansard, 1950), p.1491.

4 J.G. Frazer, *The Golden Bough: A Study in Comparative Religion*, 2 vols. (London: Macmillan & Co., 1890).

5 Hansard, *Parliamentary Debates*, Fifth Series, Vol.481, pp.1492–3.

6   Starhawk, *Dreaming the Dark. Magic, Sex & Politics* (Boston: Beacon Press, 1982), pp.8, 151–2, 168–72, 179, 189–99; Starhawk, *The Spiral Dance. A Rebirth of the Ancient Religion of the Great Goddess*, tenth anniversary edition (New York & San Francisco: HarperSanFrancisco, 1979 rpt. 1989), pp.7–8, 11, 19, 207.

7   Starhawk, *Dreaming the Dark*, p.25.

8   Starhawk, *Dreaming the Dark*, p.9.

9   D. Fairhall, *Common Ground. The Story of Greenham* (London: I.B. Tauris, 2006), p.10.

10 B. Harford & S. Hopkins, *Greenham Common: Women at the Wire* (London: The Women's Press, 1984), p.1. See also: M. Sjoo, 'Women's Dream-Journeying Across Salisbury Plain Reclaiming Earth our Mother from the Military', *The Pipes of P.A.N.*, no.20 (Lughnasadh 1985), pp.5–6.

11 R. Parfitt, 'Pagans Against Nukes', *The Cauldron*, no.136 (May 2010), p.17; Anon., *The Pipes of P.A.N.*, no.2 (Imbolc 1981), p.1; Anon., *The Pipes of P.A.N.*, no.6 (Imbolc 1982), pp.1, 5; Anon., 'P.A.N. Lughnasadh Sabbat', *Pipes of P.A.N.*, no.12 (Lughnasadh 1983), supplement f.1; C. Eve, 'Green Gathering 1983 – Some Experiences and Feelings', *Pipes of P.A.N.*, no.13 (Samhain 1983), p.6; Anon., *Pipes of P.A.N.*, no.16 (Lughnasadh 1984), p.1.

12 Ros, 'Greenham Gathering', *Pipes of P.A.N.*, no.17 (Samhain 1984), p.8; Parfitt, 'Pagans Against Nukes', p.17.

13 Hartford & Hopkins, *Greenham Common: Women at the Wire*, p.30.

14 Hartford & Hopkins, *Greenham Common: Women at the Wire*, p.45.

15 Hartford & Hopkins, *Greenham Common: Women at the Wire*, pp.50–1, 94, 119–20, 166; Ros, 'The Greenham Gathering', *Pipes of P.A.N.*, no.17 (Samhain 1984), p.8; Anon., 'A Ring of Fire', *Pipes of P.A.N.*, no.13 (Samhain 1983), pp.7–8; Fairhall, *Common Ground*, p.24.

16 Anon., 'Chants from Greenham Common', *Pipes of P.A.N.*, no.17 (Samhain 1984), p.4.

17 Gent, *Trial of the Bideford Witches*, p.11.

18 The first edition is: F.J. Gent, *The Trial of the Bideford Witches* (Bideford: Frank J. Gent, 1982).

19 A. Fraser, *The Weaker Vessel. A Woman's Lot in Seventeenth-Century England* (London: George Weidenfeld & Nicolson Ltd., 1984; rpt. Mandarin, 1994), pp.125–9.

20 Interview with Judith Nobel by the current author, 1 June 2018.

21 Interview with Judith Nobel by the current author, 1 June 2018.

22 Interview with Judith Nobel by the current author, 1 June 2018.

23 Interview with Judith Nobel by the current author, 1 June 2018.

24 Judy Molland, letter to Levannah Morgan, 13 February 1995, ff.1–2; L. Morgan, 'Remembering the Exeter Witches', *The Cauldron*, no.153 (Summer 2014), pp.12–14.

25 Judy Molland, letter to John Clarke (14 December 1995), f.1.

26 L. Morgan, *Exeter Witches' Memorial Appeal*, unpublished article (1997), f.1. John Clark, letter to Judith Higginbottom, 2 February 1996; Judith Higginbottom, letter to John Clark (22 May 1996), f.1; Judith Higginbottom, letter to Ben Jones (22 May 1996). f.1; John Clark, letter to Judith Higginbottom (14 May 1995), f.1.

27 Danielle Marsden, letter to Judith Noble, undated c. May 1995.

28 J. Higginbottom, *A Brief History of the Exeter Witches' Memorial in Rougemont Gardens*, unpublished manuscript (13 April 2007), f.1; Morgan, 'Remembering the Exeter Witches', pp.12–14.

29 Wendy and Pete Musker, letter to Judith Higginbottom (25 October 1996), f.1.

30 Judith Higginbottom, letter to Wendy and Pete Musker (16 October 1996), f.1.

31 L. Morgan & Judy Molland, letter to Jem, Editor of *Pagan Dawn* (27 August 1997), f.1.; Morgan, *Exeter Witches' Memorial Appeal*, f.1.

32 Judy Molland, letter to Judith Noble, 17 March (undated, presumably 1996), f.1.

33 P. Christie, *Secret Bideford* (Stroud, Gloucestershire: Amberley Publishing, 2015), p.91.

34 Judy Molland, letter to Judith Noble, 25 April 1995, ff.1–2.

35 Christie, *Secret Bideford*, p.90.

36 J. Vayne, *Magick Works. Stories of Occultism in Theory and Practice* (Oxford: Mandrake, 2008), p.96.

37 Vayne, *Magick Works*, p.96.

38 BBC News, 10 June 2013, accessed at: https://www.bbc.co.uk/news/uk-england-devon-22840560.

39 Ben Bradshaw MP, email to the present author, 21 January 2020.

40 Ben Bradshaw MP, email to the present author, 21 January 2020.

41 Jackie Juno, interview with the present author, 29 November 2019.

42 Jackie Juno, interview with the present author, 29 November 2019; H. Greene, 'The Grand Witches Tea Party: A Call to Women Worldwide' (3 September 2014), accessed at: https://wildhunt.org/2014/09/the-grand-witches-tea-party-a-call-to-women-worldwide.html; S. de Bruxelles, 'Witches Brew Up a Tea Party in Memory of Hanged Sisters', *The Sunday Times* (29 August 2019), accessed at: https://www.thetimes.co.uk/article/witches-brew-up-a-tea-party-in-memory-of-hanged-sisters-czphdkhcm9d.

43 Jackie Juno, interview with the present author, 29 November 2019; Greene, 'The Grand Witches Tea Party'.

Bibliography

Primary Sources

a) Archival

Devon Heritage Centre, Exeter

Q/S 74/5/1–13   Bideford, presentments for individuals taking part in conventicles, 1670–85.

2178A/PO/4/C/1   Walter Stadden, 1677, Tedburn St Mary.

Bideford Parish Register, Vol I (Marriages 1561–1621; Baptisms 1561–1622; Burials 1561–1621).

Bideford Parish Register, Vol II (Marriages 1623–1653; Baptisms 1622–1653; Burials 1623–1653).

Bideford Parish Register, Vol III (Marriages 1653–1678; Baptisms 1653–1678; Burials 1653–1678).

Bideford Parish Register, Vol I (Marriages 1679–1750; Burials 1679–1726).

Moger, O.M. (ed.), *Quarter Sessions, Devonshire – Civil War Petitions from 1642–1685*, unpublished mss., 2 vols. (Devon & Cornwall Record Society, April 1983).

North Devon Records Office, Barnstaple Library

BBT A1 / b   Bideford Bridge Trust Documents, Bundles, 4, 6, 17, 20, 31, 35, 39, 42, 78, 93, 101.

BBT add   Bideford Bridge Trust Documents, documents 2, 28A–28B, 37, 65, 67, 114.

B1003   Records of the Andrew Dole Charity: John Andrew Dole Trust Book, 1626–1809.

184A/PF/1/1/2/15 John Strange's Grant of Annuitie, 20 October 1626.

1064Q / 501/184   Liber Session Pacis, 1659–1709 (Bideford Sessions Book).

National Records Office, Kew

Assi 21/1   Exeter Assizes, 1670–1677.

b) Printed

Anon., *His Grace the Duke of Monmouth Honoured in His Progress in the West of England in an Account of a Most Extraordinary Cure of the King's Evil* (London: Benjamin Harris, 1680).

Anon., *A True Narrative of the Duke of Monmouth's Late Journeys into the West in a Letter from an Eye-witness thereof, to his Correspondent in London* (London: Printed illegally and anonymously, 1680).

Anon., *A True and Impartial Relation of the Informations Against Three Witches, Viz. Temperance Lloyd, Mary Trembles, and Susanna Edwards* (London: Freeman Collins, 1682).

Anon., *The Tryal, Condemnation, and Execution of Three Witches, Viz. Temperance Floyd, Mary Floyd, and Susanna Edwards* (London: J. Deacon at the Sign of the Rainbow, 1682).

Anon., *The Life and Conversation of Temperance Floyd, Mary Lloyd, and Susanna Edwards, Three Eminent Witches* (London: J.W., 1682).

Anon., *A Trial of Witches, At the Assizes held at Bury St. Edmund's in the County of Suffolk, On the Tenth Day of March 1664, Before Sir Matthew Hale, Knt. then Lord Chief Baron of His Majesty's Court of Exchequer* (Bury: P. Deck, 1682 rpt. 1771).

Anon., *The Tryal of Richard Hathaway, Upon an Information for being a Cheat and Impostor, For endeavouring to take away The Life of Sarah Morduck, For being a Witch at Surrey Assizes* (London: Isaac Cleave, 1702).

Anon., 'Death of Martha Lee, the Centenarian', *North Devon Journal* (10 March 1853), p.8.

Anon. ('J.R.'), *The Life of the Right Honourable Sir John Holt, Knight, Lord Chief Justice of King's Bench* (London: 'J.R.' sold by J. Worrall, 1764).

Anon. (ed.), *A Report of all the Cases Determined by Sir John Holt, Knt. From 1688 to 1710, during which Time he was Lord Chief Justice of England* (London: E. & R. Nutt & R. Gosling, 1738).

Ashton, J. (ed.), *A Century of Ballads. Illustrative of the Life, Manners and Habits of the English Nation during the Seventeenth Century* (London: Elliot Stock, 1887).

Besse, J., *Sufferings of Early Quakers: South West England, 1654 to 1690*, intro. M. Gandy (York: Sessions Book Trust, 1753 rpt. 2004).

Bordelon, L., *A History of the Ridiculous Extravagancies of Monsieur Oufle*, intro. J. Grieder (New York & London: Garland Publishing Inc., 1711 rpt. 1973).

Boulton, R., *A Compleat History of Magick, Sorcery, and Witchcraft*, 2 vols. (London: E. Curll at the Dial, J. Pemberton at the Buck and Sun, & W. Taylor at the Ship, 1715–16).

Boyer, P.; & Nissenbaum, S. (eds.), *Salem-Village Witchcraft. A Documentary Record of Local Conflict in Colonial New England* (Boston: Northeastern University Press, 1993).

Brockett, A. (ed.), *The Exeter Assembly. The Minutes of the Assemblies of the United Brethren of Devon and Cornwall, 1691–1717, As Transcribed by the Reverend Isaac Gilling* (Torquay: Devon & Cornwall Record Society / The Devonshire Press Ltd., 1963).

Calamy, E., *The Nonconformists Memorial: Being an Account of the Ministers who were Ejected or Silenced after the restoration particularly by the Act of Uniformity, which took Place on Bartholomew Day, Aug. 24 1662*, ed. S. Palmer, Vol.I (Alexander Hogg: London, 1778).

Camfield, B., *A Theological Discourse of Angels, and their Ministries . . . Also an Appendix Containing Some Reflections upon Mr. Webster's Displaying Supposed Witchcraft* (London: R.E. for Henry Brome, 1678).

Chope, P.R., *Early Tours in Devon and Cornwall*, intro. A. Gibson (Newton Abbot: David & Charles, 1918 rpt. 1967).

Cobbett, W. (ed.), *Complete Collection of State Trials,* Vol.VIII (London: T.C. Hansard, 1810).

Collier, J.P. (ed.), *The Mad Pranks and Merry Jests of Robin Goodfellow: Reprinted from the Edition of 1628* (London: The Percy Society / C. Richards, 1841).

Defoe, D., *A Tour Thro' the Whole Island of Great Britain,* Vol.I (London: Peter Davies, 1927).

Ebsworth, J.W. (ed.), *The Roxburghe Ballads,* Vol.VI Part II (Hertford: Stephen Austin and Sons, 1887).

Elmer, P. (ed.), *English Witchcraft, 1560–1736. Vol. 5: The Later English Trial Pamphlets* (London: Pickering & Chatto, 2003).

Gibson, M. (ed.), *Witchcraft and Society in England and America, 1550–1750* (London: Continuum, 2003).

Glanvill, J., *A Blow at Modern Sadducism in Some Philosophical Considerations About Witchcraft* (London: E.C. for James Collins at the King's Head, 1668).

Glanvill, J., More, H., & Horneck, A., *Sadducismus Triumphatus: Or, A Full and Plain Evidence Concerning Witches and Apparitions* (London: A. Bettesworth & J. Bailey, & W. Mears & J. Hooke, 1681 rpt. 1726).

HMSO, *Endowed Charities (County of Devon). Parish of Bideford* (London: Eyre and Spottiswoode Ltd., 1908).

Hutchinson, F., *An Historical Essay Concerning Witchcraft* (London: R. Knaplock, 1718).

Kerr, R.J., & Coffin Duncan, I. (eds.), *The Portledge Papers being Extracts from the Letters of Richard Lapthorne, Gent. Of Hatton Garden, London, to Richard Coffin, Esq. of Portledge, Bideford, Devon, from December 10th 1687 – August 7th 1697* (London: Jonathan Cape, 1928).

Larner, C., Lee, C.H., & McLachlan, H.V. (eds.), *A Source-Book of Scottish Witchcraft* (Glasgow: The Grimsay Press, 1977 rpt. 2005).

Levack, B.P. (ed.), *The Witchcraft Sourcebook* (New York & London: Routledge, 2004 rpt. 2006).

Mather, C., *On Witchcraft: Being the Wonders of the Invisible World* (New York: Dorset Press, 1692 rpt. 1991).

Mather, C., *Memorable Providences Relating to Witchcraft and Possessions* (Boston, New England, & Edinburgh: Andrew Anderson, 1697).

North, R., *The Lives of the Right Hon. Francis North, Baron Guilford; the Hon. Sir Dudley North; and the Hon. And Rev. Dr. John North,* ed. A. Jessop, 3 Vols. (London: George Bell & Sons, 1890).

Ogilby, J., *Britannia, Volume the First: or, An Illustration of the Kingdom of England and Dominion of Wales: By a Geographical and Historical Description of the Principal Roads thereof* (London: John Ogilby, 1675).

Raymond, T., *Reports of Divers Special Cases, Adjudged in the Courts of King's Bench, Common Pleas, and Exchequer, in the Reign of King Charles II,* 3rd Edition (Dublin: James Moore, 1793).

Stoate, T.L. (ed.), *Devon Hearth Tax Return, Lady Day 1674* (Bristol: T.L. Stoate, 1982).

Wawman, R. (ed.), *Never Completely Submerged. The Story of the Squarson of Lewtrenchard as revealed by 'The Diary of Sabine Baring-Gould'* (Guildford, Surrey: Grosvenor House Publishing Ltd, 2009).

Webster, J., *The Displaying of Supposed Witchcraft* (London: J.M., 1677).

Wescote, T., *A View of Devonshire in MDCXXX with a Pedigree of its Gentry,* eds. G. Oliver & P. Jones (Exeter: William Roberts, 1845).

Wylie, J.H., & Wylie, J. (eds.), *Reports of the Records of the City of Exeter* (Hereford: HMC/ The Hereford Times Ltd., 1916).

Yonge, J., *Plymouth Memoirs,* ed. J.J. Beckerlegge (London: Jonathan Cape Ltd., 1951).

Secondary Sources

Ankarloo, B., & Henningsen, G. (eds.), *Early Modern Witchcraft. Centres and Peripheries* (Oxford: Oxford University Press, 1990 rpt. 2001).

Anon., *Tedrake's Illustrated Guide to Bideford and North Devon* (Bideford: Western Express Office, 1904).

Artley, G.H., *Law and Politics under the Later Stuarts: Sir John Holt, the Courts, and the Constitutional Crisis of 1688,* unpublished doctoral thesis, Lincoln College, University of Oxford, 2019.

Authers, W.P., 'William Bartlett of Bideford', *Devon and Cornwall Notes & Queries,* Vol.XXX1 Part II (April/July 1968), pp.64–5.

Barber, C., *The Lost City of Exeter* (Exeter: Obelisk Publications, 1982).

Baring-Gould, S., *Arminell. A Social Romance,* 3rd edition (London: Methuen & Co., 1891).

Baring-Gould, S., *An Old English Home and its Dependencies* (Methuen & Co.: London, 1898).

Baring-Gould, S., *Devonshire Characters and Strange Events,* First Series (London: John Lane, The Bodley Head Limited, 1908 rpt. 1926).

Barry, J., *Witchcraft and Demonology in South-West England, 1640–1789* (Palgrave Macmillan: Houndmills, Basingstoke, 2012).

Bostridge, I., *Witchcraft and Its Transformations, c.1650-c.1750* (Oxford: Clarendon Press, 1997 rpt. 2003).

Briggs, R., *Witches & Neighbors. The Social and Cultural Context of European Witchcraft* (London & New York: Penguin Books, 1996 rpt. 1998).

Brockett, A., 'The Attack on Nonconformists in Exeter after the Withdrawal of the Declaration of Indulgence', *Transactions of the Congregational Historical Society,* Vol.18 No.3 (1958), pp.89–93.

Brockett, A., *Nonconformity in Exeter, 1650–1875* (Manchester: Manchester University Press / The University of Exeter, 1962).

Brockett, A. (ed.), *The Devon Union List (D.U.L.). A Collection of Written Material Relating to the County of Devon* (Exeter: The University Library, 1977).

Brown, K.M., *Good Wives, Nasty Wenches, and Anxious Patriarchs. Gender, Race, and Power in Colonial Virginia* (Chapel Hill & London: University of North Carolina Press, 1996).

Brown, T., '66th Report on Folklore: I. Witches and Witchcraft', *The Devon Association,* Vol. 101 (1969), pp.281–2.

Camporesi, P., *Bread of Dreams. Food and Fantasy in Early Modern Europe* (Cambridge & Oxford: Polity Press, 1989).

Carroll, W.C., *Fat King, Lean Beggar. Representations of Poverty in the Age of Shakespeare* (Ithaca, USA, & London: Cornell University Press, 1996).

Carswell, J., *The Old Cause. Three Biographical Studies in Whiggism* (London: The Cresset Press, 1954).

Chope, R.P., 'The Bideford Witches', *Devon and Cornwall Notes & Queries*, Vol.VII (January 1912 – October 1913), pp.37–40.

Chope, R.P., 'John Abbott, Plasterer', *Devon and Cornwall Notes & Queries*, Vol.XIV (January 1926 – October 1927), pp.289–90.

Christie, P., *Secret Bideford* (Stroud, Gloucestershire: Amberley Publishing, 2015).

Clark, A., *Working Life of Women in the Seventeenth Century* (London & New York: George Routledge & Sons Ltd and E.P. Dutton & Co, 1919).

Clark, P., & Slack, P. (eds.), *Crisis and Order in English Towns, 1500–1700. Essays in Urban History* (London: Routledge & Kegan Paul, 1972).

Clifton, R., *The Last Popular Rebellion. The Western Rising of 1685* (London & New York: Maurice Temple Smith & St. Martin's Press, 1984).

Cotton, R.W., *Barnstaple and the Northern Part of Devonshire during the Great Civil War, 1642–1646* (Chilworth & London: Unwin Brothers, 1889).

Cox, T., 'Devonshire', from: *Magna Brittania Antiqua & Nova: Or, a New, Exact, Comprehensive Survey of the Ancient and Present State of Great-Britain* (London: C. Ward & Chandler, 1738), pp.465–547.

Cromartie, A., *Sir Matthew Hale, 1609–1676: Law, Religion and Natural Philosophy* (Cambridge: Cambridge University Press, 2003).

Cromartie, A., 'Sir Matthew Hale 1609–1676' in: H.C.G. Matthew & B. Harrison (eds.), *Oxford Dictionary of National Biography*, Vol. 24 (Oxford: Oxford University Press, 2004), pp.533–40.

Darnton, R., *The Great Cat Massacre and Other Episodes in French Cultural History* (London: Allen Lane / Penguin Books Ltd., 1984).

Davies, O., *Witchcraft, Magic and Culture, 1736–1951* (Manchester & New York: Manchester University Press, 1999).

Davies, O., *Popular Magic. Cunning Folk in English History* (London & New York: Hambledon Continuum, 2003 rpt. 2007).

Davies, O., & White, S., 'Witchcraft and the Somerset Idyll. The Depiction of Folk Belief in Walter Raymond's Novels', *Folklore*, Vol.126 no.1 (April 2015), pp.53–67.

Duncan, A.G., *The Long Bridge of Bideford and Bideford under the Restored Monarchy* (Bideford: self-published, 1930).

Earle, P., *Monmouth's Rebels. The Road to Sedgemoor 1685* (London: Weidenfeld and Nicolson, 1977).

Erickson, A.L., *Women and Property in Early Modern England* (London & New York: Routledge, 1993 rpt. 1995).

Farquharson-Coe, A., *Devon's Witchcraft* (St. Ives: James Pike Ltd., 1975).

Feraro, S., 'Playing the Pipes of PAN: Pagans Against Nukes and the Linking of Wiccan-Derived Paganism and Ecofeminism in Britain, 1980–1990', in: Feraro, S., & Doyle White, E. (eds.), *Magic and Witchery in the Modern West. Celebrating the Twentieth*

Anniversary of 'The Triumph of the Moon' (Cham, Switzerland: Palgave Macmillan / Springer Nature, 2019), pp.45–63.

Fideler, P.A., *Social Welfare in Pre-Industrial England. The Old Poor Law Tradition* (Houndmills, Basingstoke: Palgrave Macmillan, 2006).

Fielder, D., *A History of Bideford* (Chichester: Phillimore & Co. Ltd., 1985).

Finch, J.S., *Sir Thomas Browne. A Doctor's Life of Science & Faith* (New York: Henry Schuman, 1950).

Fraser, A., *The Weaker Vessel. A Woman's Lot in Seventeenth Century England* (London: Mandarin, 1984 rpt. 1994).

Fraser, J.A., *Spain and the West Country* (London: Burns Oates & Washbourne Ltd., 1935).

Geis, G., & Bunn, I., *A Trial of Witches. A Seventeenth-Century Witchcraft Prosecution* (London & New York: Routledge, 1997 rpt. 1998).

Gent, F., *The Trial of the Bideford Witches* (Bideford: Frank Gent/self-published, 1982).

Gent, F., *The Trial of the Bideford Witches,* 2nd edition (Bideford: Edward Gaskell Publishers, 2002).

Goaman, M., *Old Bideford and District* (Bristol: E.M. Cox & A.G. Cox, 1968).

Goodare, J. (ed.), *The Scottish Witch-Hunt in Context* (Manchester & New York: Manchester University Press, 2002).

Grabe, M., *As I Walked Out. Sabine Baring-Gould and the Search for the Folk Songs of Devon and Cornwall* (Oxford: Signal Books, 2017).

Grant, A., *North Devon Pottery: The Seventeenth Century* (Exeter: University of Exeter, 1983).

Grant, A., & Christie, P., *The Book of Bideford* (Buckingham: Barracuda Books Ltd., 1987).

Granville, R., *The History of Bideford* (Bideford: W. Cosbie Coles, 1883).

Granville, R., *The History of the Granville Family* (Exeter: William Pollard & Co., 1895).

Gray, T., 'Witchcraft in the Diocese of Exeter: Dartmouth, 1601–1602', *Devon and Cornwall Notes & Queries,* Vol.XXXVI Part VII (Spring 1990), pp.230–8.

Gray, T., *Not One of Us. Individuals Set Apart by Choice, Circumstances, Crowds or the Mob in Exeter, 1451–1952* (Exeter: The Mint Press/Exeter Local History Society, 2018).

Gray, T., Rowe, M., & Erskine, A. (eds.), *Tudor and Stuart Devon. The Common Estate and Government* (Exeter: University of Exeter Press, 1992).

Gregory, A., *Rye Spirits. Faith, Faction and Fairies in a Seventeenth Century English Town* (London: The Hedge Press, 2013).

Halliday, P.D., 'Sir John Holt 1642–1710', in: H.C.G. Matthew & B. Harrison (eds.), *Oxford Dictionary of National Biography,* Vol. 27 (Oxford: Oxford University Press, 2004), pp.830–2.

Hammond, J., 'Witchcraft in the West (Part One)', *What's On in the West* (May 1973), pp.4–5.

Handley, S., 'Sir Thomas Raymond, 1626/7–1683', in: H.C.G. Matthew & B. Harrison (eds.), *Oxford Dictionary of National Biography,* Vol. 46 (Oxford: Oxford University Press, 2004), p.192.

Hearn, M., *Frithelstock. Past and Present* (Frithelstock: Frithelstock Book Group, 2004).

Helm, P.J., *Jeffreys* (London: Robert Hale, 1966).

Hill, B., *Women Alone. Spinsters in England, 1660–1850* (New Haven & London: Yale University Press, 2001).

Hole, C., *Witchcraft in England* (London: B.T. Batsford Ltd., 1945).

Hole, C., *Witchcraft at Toner's Puddle, 19th C. From the Diary of the Rev. William Ettrick* (Dorchester: The Dorset Record Society, 1964).

Holmes, C., 'Women: Witnesses and Witches', *Past & Present*, No.140 (August 1993), pp.45–78.

Hunter, M., *The Decline of Magic. Britain in the Enlightenment* (New Haven & London: Yale University Press, 2020).

Hutton, R., *Charles the Second: King of England, Scotland and Ireland* (Oxford: Clarendon Press, 1989).

Hutton, R. (ed.), *Physical Evidence for Ritual Acts, Sorcery and Witchcraft in Christian Britain. A Feeling for Magic* (Houndmills, Basingstoke: Palgrave Macmillan, 2016).

Hutton, R., *The Witch. A History of Fear, from Ancient Times to the Present* (New Haven & London: Yale University Press, 2017).

Inderwick, F.A., *Side-Lights on the Stuarts* (London: Sampson Low, Marston, Searle & Rivington, 1888).

Jackson, P.W., *Nonconformists and Society in Devon, 1660–1689,* unpublished University of Exeter PhD thesis (July 1986).

Karkeek, P.Q., 'Devonshire Witches', *Report and Transactions of the Devonshire Association,* Vol.VI Part II (1874), pp.736–59.

Karlsen, C.F., *The Devil in the Shape of a Woman. Witchcraft in Colonial New England* (New York & London: W.W. Norton & Company, 1987 rpt. 1998).

Kermode, J., & Walker, G. (eds), *Women, Crime and the Courts in Early Modern England* (London: UCL Press, 1994).

Kittredge, G.L., *Witchcraft in Old and New England* (Cambridge, Massachusetts: Harvard University Press, 1929).

Knott, O., Legg, R., & Allsop, A., *Witches of Dorset* (Dorset Publishing Company: Milborne Port, Sherborne, Dorset, 1974).

Kounine, L., & Ostling, M. (eds.), *Emotions in the History of Witchcraft* (London: Palgrave Macmillan, 2016).

Larner, C., *Enemies of God. The Witch-Hunt in Scotland* (Oxford: Basil Blackwell, 1981 rpt. 1983).

Larner, C., *Witchcraft and Religion. The Politics of Popular Belief,* ed. and foreword A. Macfarlane (Oxford: Basil Blackwell, 1984).

L'Estrange Ewen, C., *Witchcraft and Demonianism. A Concise Account Derived from Sworn Depositions and Confessions Obtained in the Courts of England and Wales* (London: Heath Cranton Limited, 1933).

Lounsbury, R.G., *The British Fishery at Newfoundland, 1634–1763* (London: Archon Books, 1934 rpt. 1969).

Macfarlane, A., *Witchcraft in Tudor and Stuart England. A Regional and Comparative Study,* intro. J. Sharpe, Second Edition (London: Routledge, 1970 rpt. 1999).

MacInnes, C.M., *The Early English Tobacco Trade* (London: Kegan Paul, Trench, Trubner & Co. Ltd., 1926).

Macpherson, C.B., *The Political Theory of Possessive Individualism. Hobbes to Locke* (Oxford & New York: Oxford University Press, 1962 rpt. 1989).

Matar, N., *British Captives from the Mediterranean to the Atlantic, 1563–1760* (Leiden & Boston, USA: Brill, 2014).

Merrifield, R., *The Archaeology of Ritual and Magic* (London: Guild Publishing, 1987).

Middleton, A.P., *Tobacco Coast. A Maritime History of Chesapeake Bay in the Colonial Era* (Baltimore & London: John Hopkins University Press, 1953 rpt. 1984).

Miller, N.J., & Yavneh, N., *Maternal Measures. Figuring Caregiving in the Early Modern Period* (Ashgate: Aldershot, 2000).

Molland, J., 'Coming Home. Alice Molland was the Last Person to be Executed for Witchcraft in England, at Exeter, Devon in 1685', *Pagan Dawn*, no.117 (Samhain 1995), pp.12–14.

Molland, J., 'The Devon Witches', *Pagan Dawn*, no.124 (Lammas, 1997), pp.26–7.

Monod, P.K., *Solomon's Secret Arts. The Occult in the Age of the Enlightenment* (New Haven & London: Yale University Press, 2013).

Morgan, E., *Sir Bevill Grenville of Stowe* (Ilfracombe, Devon: Arthur H. Stockwell Ltd., 1969).

Morgan, L., 'Remembering the Essex Witches', *The Cauldron*, no. 153 (Summer 2014), pp. 12–14.

Morgan, L., *A Brief History of the Exeter Witches' Memorial in Rougemont Gardens* (No place: Devon & Cornwall Pagan Federation, August 1996).

Morison, S.E., *Builders of the Bay Colony* (London: Humphrey Milford / Oxford University Press, 1930).

Morley, I., *A Thousand Lives. An Account of the English Revolutionary Movement of 1660–1685* (London: Andre Deutsch, 1954).

Nash, B.C., *Temperance Lloyd. Hanged for Witchcraft in 1682* (Victoria, Canada: Friesen Press, 2012).

Neill, E.D., *Virginia Carolorum: The Colony under the Rule of Charles the First and Second, A.D. 1625 – A.D. 1685, Based upon Manuscripts and Documents of the Period* (Albany, New York: John Munsell's Sons, 1886).

Newall, V. (ed.), *The Witch Figure. Folklore Essays by a Group of Scholars in England Honouring the 75th Birthday of Katharine M. Briggs* (London & Boston: Routledge & Kegan Paul, 1973).

Norris, S., *Tales of Old Devon* (Newbury, Berkshire: Countryside Books, 1991).

Norway, A.H., *Highways and Byways in Devon and Cornwall* (London: Macmillan and Co., Ltd., 1919).

Notestein, W., *A History of Witchcraft in England from 1558 to 1718* (Washington, USA: The American Historical Association, 1911).

Oliver, B.W., 'The Early Seventeenth-Century Plaster Ceilings of Barnstaple', *Report & Transactions of the Devonshire Association*, Vol.LIX (1917), pp.190–9.

Parent, A.S., *Foul Means. The Formation of a Slave Society in Virginia, 1660–1740* (Chapel Hill & London: University of North Carolina Press, 2003).

Passmore, J., *Exeter's Almshouses* (Exeter: imprintdigital.net/self-published, 2010).

Patrides, C.A. (ed.), *Approaches to Sir Thomas Browne* (Columbia & London: University of Missouri Press, 1982).

Perrin, D., *Discovering Exeter 10: Public Inscriptions* (Exeter: Exeter Civic Society, 1999).

Phythian-Adams, C., 'Rural Culture', in: G.E. Mingay (ed.), *The Victorian Countryside*, Volume 2 (London, Boston & Henley: Routledge & Kegan Paul, 1981), pp.616–25.

Purcell, W., *Onward Christian Soldier. A Life of Sabine Baring-Gould, Parson, Squire, Novelist, Antiquary, 1834–1924* (London, New York, & Toronto: Longmans Green & Co., 1957).

Quaife, G.R., *Wanton Wenches and Wayward Wives. Peasants and Illicit Sex in Early Seventeenth Century England* (New Brunswick, New Jersey: Rutgers University Press, 1979).

Radford, R. & U., *West Country Witchcraft* (Peninsula Press: Newton Abbot, 1998).

Raines, R., *Marcellus Laroon* (London: Routledge & Kegan Paul, 1966).

Roberts, G., *The Life, Progresses, and Rebellion of James, Duke of Monmouth,* 2 vols. (London: Longman, Brown, Green and Longmans, 1844).

Roberts, S.K., *Recovery and Restoration in an English County. Devon Local Administration, 1646–1670* (University of Exeter: Exeter, 1985).

Rogers, I., *A Record of Wooden Sailing Sailing Ships and Warships built in the Port of Bideford from the years 1568 to 1938, with a brief account of the Shipbuilding Industry in the Town* (Bideford: Self-published, 1947).

Rogers, H.R. (ed.), *Report on Documents belonging to the Feoffees of the Long Bridge, Bideford* (Bideford: Bideford Library Sub-Committee, 1933).

Roots, I. (ed.), *The Monmouth Rising* (Exeter: Devon Books, 1986).

Roper, L., *Oedipus and the Devil. Witchcraft, Sexuality and Religion in Early Modern Europe* (London & New York: Routledge, 1994).

Rose, L., 'Stucley's Map of Bideford', *Devon and Cornwall Notes & Queries,* Vol.XXXVI Part VII (Spring 1990), pp.259–60.

Rowley, W., Dekker, T., & Ford, J., *The Witch of Edmonton,* eds. P. Corbin & D. Sedge (Manchester University Press, Manchester & New York, 1999).

Seaward, *The Cavalier Parliament and the Reconstruction of the Old Regime, 1661–1667* (Cambridge: Cambridge University Press, 1989).

Seth, R., *Stories of Great Witch Trials* (London: Arthur Baker Limited, 1967).

Sharpe, J., *Crime in Seventeenth-Century England. A County Study* (Cambridge: Cambridge University Press, 1983).

Sharpe, J., *Early Modern England. A Social History, 1550–1760* (London & New York: Edward Arnold, 1987 rpt. 1992).

Sharpe, J., *Instruments of Darkness. Witchcraft in England, 1550–1750* (London: Penguin Books, 1996 rpt. 1997).

Sharpe, J., *Witchcraft in Early Modern England* (Harlow & London: Longman, 2001).

Simmons, J., 'Some Letters from the Bishops of Exeter, 1668–1688', *Devon and Cornwall Notes & Queries,* Vol.XXII (January 1942 – October 1946), pp.143–4.

Sjoo, M., *New Age and Armageddon. The Goddess or the Gurus? Towards a Feminist Vision of the Future* (London: The Women's Press, 1992).

Slack, P., *Poverty and Policy in Tudor and Stuart England* (Longman: London & New York, 1988).

Spufford, M., *Contrasting Communities. English Villagers in the Sixteenth and Seventeenth Centuries* (Cambridge: Cambridge University Press, 1974).

Spurr, D., *Devon Churches. Vol.I Bideford, Barnstaple, and the Hartland Peninsula* (Braunton, Devon: Merlin Books Ltd., 1983).

Spurr, J., *The Restoration Church of England, 1646–1689* (New Haven & London: Yale University Press, 1991).

Stephens, W.B., *Seventeenth-Century Exeter. A Study of Industrial and Commercial Development, 1625–1688* (Exeter: The University of Exeter, 1958).

Stone, L., *The Family, Sex and Marriage in England, 1500–1800* (London: Penguin Books, 1977 rpt. 1988).

Stoyle, M., *Loyalty and Locality. Popular Allegiance in Devon During the English Civil War* (Exeter: University of Exeter Press, 1994).

Stoyle, M., *Exeter in the Civil War* (Exeter: Devon Archaeological Society Pamphlet No.6, 1995).

Stoyle, M., *Witchcraft in Exeter, 1558–1660* (Exeter: The Mint Press, 2017).

Thomas, K., *Religion and the Decline of Magic. Studies in Popular Beliefs in Sixteenth- and Seveteenth-Century England* (London: Penguin Books, 1971 rpt. 1991).

Thomas, K., *The Ends of Life. Roads to Fulfilment in Early Modern England* (Oxford: Oxford University Press, 2009).

Thompson, J.A., *Wives, Widows, Witches & Bitches. Women in Seventeenth-Century Devon* (New York: Peter Lang, 1993).

Thornton, W.H., 'The Plague at North Bovey', *Devon and Cornwall Notes & Queries,* Vol. VI (January 1910 – October 1911), pp.197–200.

Timbers, F., 'Witches' Sect or Prayer Meeting?: Matthew Hopkins revisited', *Women's History Review,* Vol.17 no.1 (February 2008), pp.21–37.

Timmons, S., 'Witchcraft and Rebellion in Late Seventeenth-Century Devon', *Journal of Early Modern History,* Vol. 10 no. 4 (2006), pp.297–330.

Valletta, F., *Witchcraft, Magic and Superstition in England, 1640–70* (Aldershot: Ashgate, 2000).

Vayne, J., *Magick Works. Stories of Occultism in Theory and Practice* (Oxford: Mandrake, 2008).

Walker, G., 'The Strangeness of the Familiar: Witchcraft and the Law in Early Modern England', in: McShane, A., & Walker, G. (eds.), *The Extraordinary and the Everyday in Early Modern England. Essays in Celebration of the Work of Bernard Capp* (Houndmills, Basingstoke: Palgrave Macmillan, 2010), pp.105–24.

Watkins, J., *An Essay Towards A History of Bideford in the County of Devon* (Bideford, Devon: The Lazarus Publishing Company, 1792 rpt. 1993).

Watson, J.N.P., *Captain-General and Rebel Chief. The Life of James, Duke of Monmouth* (London: George Allen & Unwin, 1979).

Weisman, R., *Witchcraft, Magic, and Religion in 17th – Century Massachusetts* (Amherst, USA: University of Massachusetts, 1984).

Whiting, F.E., & Christie, P., *The Long Bridge of Bideford,* fourth edition (Bideford: Lazarus Press, 1945 rpt. 2006).

Wigfield, W.M., *The Monmouth Rebels, 1685* (Gloucester: Alan Sutton / Somerset Record Society, 1985).

Williams, G.S., *Defining Dominion. The Discourses of Magic and Witchcraft in Early Modern France and Germany* (Michigan: University of Michigan Press / Ann Arbor, 1995 rpt. 1999).

Williams, S.F., *Damnable Practises. Witches, Dangerous Women and Music in Seventeenth-Century English Broadside Ballads* (Farnham, Surrey & Burlington, USA: Ashgate, 2015).

Willis, D., *Malevolent Nurture. Witch-Hunting and Maternal Power in Early Modern England* (Ithaca, USA, & London: Cornell University Press, 1995).

Wingfield, C., 'A Case Re-opened: the Science and Folklore of a "Witch's Ladder"', *Journal of Material Culture,* Vol.15 no.3 (2010), pp.302–22.

Winship, M.P., *Seers of God. Puritan Providentialism in the Restoration and Early Enlightenment* (Baltimore, Maryland: The John Hopkins University Press, 1996).

Worth, R.N., 'Notes from the Autobiography of Dr. James Yonge, FRS', *Report and Transactions of the Devonshire Association,* Vol.13 (1881), pp.335–43.

Index

Numbers in **bold** refer to Figures.

Abbott, John, 'the elder' 45, 62, 73–4
Abbott, John, 'the younger' 45, 74, 181, 243, **243**, 244
Ackland, Humphrey 99–101, 103
alehouses 53–9, 65
Andrew, John 63
Anglican Church 56, 58, 68–9, 72, 75, 78, 81, 84, 86–7, 111, 119, 143, 172, 181–2, 205, 242, 247

Bagelhose, Peter 57–8, 64, 227–8
Ball, Oliver 105, 108, 110, 117, 124, 153
Baring-Gould, Rev. Sabine 224, 250–7
Barnes, Grace 57, 116–17, 119–25, 128–9, 153–4, 156, 184, 186–8, 191, 207, 211
Barnes, John 116–17, 120–2, 188, 224, 227
Barry, Dr. Jonathan 176, 204, 217, 219
Bartlett, Rev. John 68–70, 72, 76, 78–80, 82, 84–7, 120, 205
Bartlett, Rev. William, 'the elder' 12, 16–17, 19, 67–9, 72, 78–80, 82, 84–7, 120
Bartlett, Rev. William, 'the younger' 242
Bath, John Grenville (later Granville), 1st Earl of 45, 49–51, 61–2, **62**, 72–5, 79–80, 86, 145, 225
Beale, Gabriel 67, 69, 77–9, 81, 84, 120, 181, 205, 225–8, 242
Beale, Thomas, 'the second' (Mayor of Bideford) 44, 46, 49, 67, 77, 79
Beare, Dr. George 117, 123–7, 153
Beare, Mary 189–90, 218, 230
Blackamoore, John 42, 227

Bodin, Jean 147, 161–2, 174, 177, 181
Boulton, Richard 69, 240–1, 257–8
Bovet, Sarah 234–5
Bradshaw, Ben, MP 272–3
Bremincombe, Thomas 123–4, 126–8, 192
Browne, Sir Thomas 169–71, 235, 238, 258
Bryant, Samuel 64–5
Budd, John 77–8
Burdon, Richard 46, 48–9
Burman, Lydia 99–101, 103–4, 106–7, 140, 191–2, 207, 211, 263

Caddy, Elizabeth 189–91, 218, 230
Camfield, Benjamin 182, 205
Catholicism 23, 80, 182
Charles II (King of England, Scotland and Ireland) 6, 38, 73, 75, 79–80, 88–9, 142, 157, 172, 182, 197–198, 200, 209, 224–5
Chope, Joseph 46, 51
Christie, Peter 271
Chuter Ede, James 261–3
Coleman, Dorcas, (nee Lidston) 72, 105–6, 108, 111, 123–8, 134, 154, 156, 170–1, 188, 191–3, 207, 211, 228
Coleman, Elizabeth 105–6, 108, 111
Coleman, John 111, 123, 126–8, 150, 171, 187, 192, 228
Collins, Freeman 193, 218
Conden, Joan 27, 31, 116
Conventicle Act (1670) 75, 79, 85
Conventicles 64, 68–71, **71**, 72, 75–7, 79–82, 84, 120, 189, 219, 224, 227–8

Cromwell, Oliver 68, 85, 176
Cullender, Rose 168–9, 171

Daemonologie 159–60, 162–7
Dallyn, Jane 140, 142–3, 148
Dallyn, Symon 142–3, 150
Darracott, John, (Mayor of Bideford) 59,
    72, 225, 228
Davie, Elizabeth 105–6, 108
Davie, John, (Mayor of Bideford) 43,
    48–50, 59, 64, 72, 101, 105, 113, 131,
    138–9, 141, 151, 154–5, 183, 185,
    188, 225, 227
Davy, Susan 69, 77, 181, 205
Defoe, Daniel 35–6, 43, 51, 181, 242
Dennis, Sarah 49, 69, 76–7
Dennis, Susanna 76, 181
Denny, Amy 168–9
Descartes, Rene, (and Cartesian thought)
    6, 86, 173
Dissent and Dissenters 39, 56–7, 64–5,
    67–9, 73, 75–82, 85–7, 89, 99, 111,
    120, 123, 131, 154, 172, 197, 200,
    204–5, 218, 225–6, 228, 242
Dunning, John 154–6, 167, 187–8
Dyre (or Dyer), 'the widow' 21, 29

Eastchurch, Elizabeth, (nee Thomas) 3,
    5–7, 11, 33, 72, 83–5, 88–9, 92, 98,
    112–13, 124, 131–2, 134, 136–8, 141,
    145–7, 155, 163, 171, 204–5
Eastchurch, Thomas 1–3, 5–7, 43, 83, 88–9,
    92–4, 98, 112–13, 124, 127, 131–2,
    135–8, 141–7, 150, 155, 163, 171,
    189, 202, 204–6, 213, 227–8
Eaton, Rev. Nathaniel 76, 86
Edwards, Katheryn 26, 29, 58
Edwards, Susanna, (nee Winslade) 9, 12,
    18, 30–3, 36, 38, 52–3, 57–9, 62–3,
    108, 115–17, 120–3, 128, 144, 150,
    154–6, 158, 163, 165, 168–72,
    182–93, 196, 217, 222, 228, 231,
    240–1, 247, 257, 269, 271–2, 274–5
    arrest of 129
    assault upon 126–7

early life 22, 25–9
    execution of 211–14
    possible pardon of 207–8
    posthumous reputation of 261, 263,
        267
    sentencing of 210
Edwards, William 25, 72, 122, 188, 190
Elizabeth I (Queen of England and
    Ireland) 60, 72, 166, 168
English Civil War 14, 33, 54, 61, 67, 73, 75,
    89, 101, 104, 168, 204

Faerie 220–1
Fellow, Anne, 'the elder' 105, 108–11, 117,
    124, 139
Fellow, Ann, 'the younger' 105–10, 124,
    139–40, 142, 149, 212
Fellow, Edward 105, 108, 110–11, 124, 139,
    150
Fortune My Foe 221–2
Frazer, Sir James 262–3

Galsworthy, Sisy 106–7, 110, 113
Gardner, Gerald 261
Gay, John 240, 244–5
Gearing, Thomas, (Mayor of Bideford) 39,
    59, 81, 224, 227
Gent, Frank 48, 266, 268
Germinn, 'the Widow' 31, 116
Gist, Thomas, (Mayor of Bideford) 51, 58,
    64–5, 72, 81, 113, 131–2, 138–9, 141,
    151, 154–155, 183, 185, 188–91,
    193–4, 218, 225, 227–8, 275
Glanvill, Joseph 157–9, 162–3, 172–7,
    181–2, 193, 204–5, 235, 240
Glorious Revolution (1688–9) 201, 242
Greenham Common 264–6
Grenville, John *see* Bath, Earl of

Hale, Sir Matthew 159, **159**, 163, 168–73,
    231, 233, 235, 241
Handford, Abigail 230–1
Hann, Rev. Francis 85–8, 101, 103, 108–9,
    137, 143–51, 153, 157, 162–3, 193–6,
    204–7, 209, 211–14, 218–20, 228, 258

Hathaway, Richard 236–9, 241
Heiman, Abraham, (Mayor of Bideford)
  41, 43, 78–9, **84**
Herbert, William, 'the elder' 33, 97–103,
  107, 139–40, 142, 145, 149, 188,
  191
Herbert, William, 'the younger' 97–100,
  102–4, 111, 139–40, 143, 191
Hill, John, (Bideford town clerk) 48, 58–9,
  65, 76, 81, 87–8, 111, 131, 134–6,
  183–6, 189–91, 193, 209, 218, 220,
  224–5, 227–8, 275
Hogarth, William 71–2
Holland, Henry 160–1
Holt, Sir John 209, 231, **232**, 233–41, 261
Hooper, Honor 2–6, 90, 92–4, 100, 107,
  112, 131–2
Hopkins, Matthew 133, 135, 147, 168
Horner, Elizabeth ('Bett') 231, 234–6
Huguenots 11, 32, 161
Hutchinson, Francis 236, 241

illegitimacy 22–7, 59, 107
Irish immigration 28, 30, 32–3

James I and VI (King of England, Scotland
  and Ireland) 147, 159–168, 176–7,
  181, 241
James II and VII (King of England,
  Scotland and Ireland) 73, 80, 88, 99,
  123, 143, 198–9, 224–229, 233
Jeffreys, Sir George, (Judge) 80, 225–6, 229
Jenkins, Sir Leoline 9, 197–8, 200, 202,
  207–9
John Andrew Charity and Dole 19–23,
  25–7, **28**, 28–31, 42, 63, 189, 249
Johns, Samuel 76–7, 79, 81, 205, 225–7
Johnson, Margaret 81, 224–5
Jones, Anthony 154, 156, 186–7, 189, 204
Jones, Joane 33, 154–6, 186–7, 189, 204,
  213
Jones, Johan (Joanna) 12, 17, 19
Jones, Phillemon 12, 17, 19
Jones, Temperance *see* Lloyd, Temperance
Jones, William, 'the elder' 12, 18

Jones, William, 'the younger' 12, 17, 19
Juno, Jackie 273–4

Keeling, Sir John 170–1
Kingsland, Jane 21–2, 27
Kingsland, Mary 21, 27

Labour Party 261, 272
Laity, Paul 267
Lamplugh, Thomas, Bishop of Exeter 81,
  85, 87–8
Lane, Sir Thomas 236–7
Laroon, Marcellus, 'the elder' 69–71,
  71, 72
Lee, Martha (or 'Matty') 248–51, 256
Lloyd, Cissily 12, 17
Lloyd, John, 'the elder' 12, 17, 44
Lloyd, Rhys 12, 19, 44, 103
Lloyd, Temperance, (nee Jones) **2**, 5–6,
  9–11, 27–33, 36–8, 43–4, 52–3,
  62–5, 84, 90, 93–8, 103–5, 111–12,
  115–16, 119, 121, 123, 128–129, 131,
  136–44, 146–7, 149–51, 154–5,
  157–8, 163, 165, 168–9, 172, 182–3,
  185–6, 188–92, 194–6, 201, 206–7,
  217–19, 222, 228, 231, 234, 240–1,
  247, 257–8, 269–72, 274–5
  arrest (1682) 113
  arrest and strip-search (1679) 106–10
  confession (1682) 135
  early life 12–13, 17–22
  execution of 211–15
  meets Grace Thomas 91–2
  possible pardon of 207–8
  posthumous reputation of 261, 263–7
  sentencing of 210
  strip-search (1682) 132–4
  tried for witchcraft (1671) 99–102
Lloyd, Thomas 17–18

Malleus Maleficarum 118, 160
Martin, Dr. 236–8, 240
Mather, Cotton 171, 205
Michelson, Thomas 64–5
Middleton, George 20, 30, 63

Molland, Alice (or Alicia) 229–30, 268–9, 271
Molland, Judy 268, 270–1
Monmouth, James Scott, Duke of **74**, 77, 80–1, 197, 200, 209, 225–6, 233
Montagu, Sir William 229–30
Moordike (or 'Moorduck'), Sarah 236–8, 240–1
More, Henry 159, 174, 176, 235
Morgan, Mary 19–20

Neuville, Claude de 52, **102**
New Poor Law (1834) 249–51, 255–7
Noble, Dr. Judith 266–7, 269, 271
North, Sir Francis 31, 80, 115, 196–7, **198**, 198–204, 206–10, 229, 235, 240, 267, 275
North, Roger 9, 29, 31, 193, 196–7, 199, 201–6, 209, 215, 230, 240, 263, 275
Norway, Arthur H. 257–9

Ogilby, Letitia 88, 111
Ogilby, Rev. Michael 41, 74–5, 86–8, 98, 104, 110–11, 141–5, 224, 227–8
Oxford Parliament 57, 80, 197

Pagan Federation 268–9, 274
Peacock, Elizabeth 191–2
plague 14–17, 26, 54, 80, 104, 125
Prance, Justinian 21, 30, 49
Puritanism 12, 15–17, 24, 36, 65, 75, 143, 180

Quakers 77–8

Ravening, Henry 14
Raymond, Sir Thomas, (Judge) 13, 80, 196–7, **199**, 199–200, 202–4, 206–7, 210, 229, 231, 235, 267
Remy, Nicolas 147, 174
Restoration of the Monarchy (1660) 19–20, 51, 54, 61, 67–8, 73, 75, 86, 168, 191, 227
Robin Goodfellow 220, **221**

Royal Society 6, 172
Russell, Lord William 46, 233
Rye House Plot (1683) 88, 224, 227

Saducismus Triumphatus 157, 159, 174, 182
Salem, witchcraft outbreak in 171, 241
Scot, Reginald 162, 164, 176, 203
Shaftesbury, Lord Anthony Ashley Cooper 57, 77, 80, 200, 233
Sharpe, Prof. Jim 167, 192
slave trade 41, 87, 226, 231, 233
smallpox 111, 125, 139, 242
Starhawk (aka Miriam Simos) 264–5
Stearne, John 133, 147, 168
Stoyle, Prof. Mark 192
Strange, John 11, 15–17, **36**, 36, 40, 45–6, **47**, 62, 243–4
Stuart, Annabel 157–8

Thomas, Grace 2–4, 6, 11, 33, 83–5, 88–94, 106–7, 112–13, 117, 119, 121, 123–6, 131–5, 137–9, 141–2, 145, 148–9, 153, 191, 193, 195, 206–7, 212–13, 215, 228, 263
Thompson, Dr. Janet A. 53–4
Tichborne Dole **23**
Tillinge, Anna 191–2
Timmons, Dr. Stephen 204–5, 217, 219
Titherley, William, (Mayor of Bideford) 40, 59, 227
Tory Party 46–9, 56–8, 64, 69, 72, 75, 79–81, 87–8, 99, 111, 123, 176, 193, 197–200, 204–5, 208–9, 218, 224–8, 231
Trembles, Honora 30
Trembles, Mary 9, 22, 27, 32–3, 36, 38, 52–3, 57, 62–4, 115–17, 120–1, 144, 150, 154–6, 158, 163, 165, 168–9, 172, 182–93, 196, 217, 222, 228, 231, 240–1, 247, 257, 271–2, 274–5
    arrest of 122–3
    early life of 29–31
    execution of 211–14
    possible pardon of 207–8

posthumous reputation 261, 263, 267, 269,
sentencing of 210
Trembles, Trojan (or 'Trudging') 30–1

Vagrancy Act (1824) 261–2
Voaden, Mary Ann (or 'Marianne') **250**, 250–6

Wadland, John 20, 30, 63
Wakely, Anne 2–7, 92–4, 100, 107, 112, 131–4, 137–8, 147
Wakely, William 138, 188
Watkins, John 247–8
Webb, Mary 64–5
Webber, 'Old' Robert 21, 30
Webster, John 173, 176–82, 203
Weld, John 148, 219
Welsh immigrant community 11–14, 18–20, 25, 32–3, 227
Weyer, Johann 162, 164, 203
Whig Party 46–7, 56–7, 64, 77, 87, 120, 172, 197–8, 200, 204–5, 208–9, 218, 224, 231, 233
Wicca 261, 264, 271, 274
Winslade, John 22–3, 25–6
Winslade, Rachel 22, 24–5, 29, 58
Winslade, Susan (or 'Susanna') 21, 25–9
Winslade, Susanna *see* Edwards, Susanna
Witchall, Judith 191–2
Witchcraft
    and charity 62–3, 90–2, 96–8, 109, 116, 120–1, 126, 155, 190, 254–5
    and counter-magic 104, 126–8, 147, 168–9, 222, 249, 259
    and curses 95–6, 109–10, 168, 186–7, 259
    and demonic magic 134–6, 139, 142, 145–6, 149–51, 153–4, 156, 163–4, 166, 169–70, 175–6, 183, 196, 206–8, 220, 235, 238
    and the demonic pact 136–7, 139–40, 142, 146–8, 150, 154–5, 157–8, 165, 174–5, 178, 180, 183–6, 188, 195, 212, 234

    and depression 164–5, 172, 174–5, 178, 202–3, 207
    and environmentalism 264, 266
    and familiar spirits 4, 6, 93–4, 100–1, 135–7, 139, 142, 146–7, 150–1, 157–8, 165–6, 168–9, 174–6, 184–6, 194, 196, 201–2, 208, 222–3, 234
    and Feminism 106, 117–18, 264–7, 271, 274–5
    and image magic 93–4, 132, 141–2, 146–8, 155, 157–8, 163, 178
    and maternity 107
    and the medical profession 2, 90, 97, 105, 108, 110, 117–19, 123–5, 145, 153, 157, 162, 169–71, 175–6, 179
    and midwives 118–19
    and misogyny 163, 178–9
    as a political crime 160, 205, 208
    and poverty 9, 19–23, 25–33, 38–9, 54, 60–2, 82, 90, 95, 107, 109, 116, 120, 142, 184, 190, 202–3, 205, 231, 248–9, 251–6
    as a religious crime 160, 217
    and scepticism 162, 173, 176–8, 231, 236
    and scratching a witch 104–5, 126–7, 134, 236, 238, 249
    and shape-shifting 100, 142, 146, 194, 234
    and spectral evidence 169–71, 188, 206–7, 235, 241
    and swimming a witch 167, 259
    and weather magic 163, 194
    and witch bottles 104
    and witch-hunters 153–5, 167, 172–4, 209, 222
    and witch's 'mark' 106–8, 110, 118, 132–4, 139, 150, 167, 169, 179, 222–3, 235–7, 241
Witchcraft Act (1563) 105, 166–8
Witchcraft Act (1604) 105, 166–8, 263
Witchcraft Act (1736) 261–4